History in the Plural

HISTORY IN THE PLURAL

An Introduction to the
Work of Reinhart Koselleck

Niklas Olsen

berghahn

NEW YORK · OXFORD
www.berghahnbooks.com

Published in 2012 by
Berghahn Books
www.berghahnbooks.com

Library of Congress Cataloging-in-Publication Data
Olsen, Niklas.
  History in the plural : an introduction to the work of Reinhart Koselleck / Niklas
Olsen.
      p. cm.
  Includes bibliographical references and index.
  ISBN 978-0-85745-295-5 (hardcover) -- ISBN 978-0-85745-296-2 (institutional eb-
ook) -- ISBN 978-1-78238-381-9 (paperback) -- ISBN 978-1-78238-382-6 (retail ebook)
  1. Koselleck, Reinhart. 2. History--Philosophy. 3. Historiography--Germany. 4. Ger-
many--Historiography. 5. Political science--History. 6. Geschichtliche Grundbegriffe 7.
Historians--Germany--Biography. I. Title.
  DD86.7.K65O57 2012
  943.0072'02--dc23

                                                                      2011037471

British Library Cataloguing in Publication Data

A catalogue record for this book is available from the British Library

Printed on acid-free paper

ISBN: 978-1-78238-381-9 paperback
ISBN: 978-1-78238-382-6 retail ebook

CONTENTS

ACKNOWLEDGMENTS

This book has its origins in September 2003, when Reinhart Koselleck invited me to his home in Bielefeld in the autumn of 2003 in order to discuss matters related to German historical writing during World War II. Leaving Bielefeld deeply fascinated and puzzled, not only by Koselleck's ideas about history and historical writing, but also by his exceptional willingness to listen to and discuss with young and inexperienced historians like myself, I soon after decided to write a dissertation about his work. After I began the project at the European University Institute in Florence, he kindly gave me permission to access his letters in Carl Schmitt's personal archives and granted me time for another informal interview specifically about his work. All of this has been vital for the writing of this book which would not exist without his remarkable openness. That he did not live to receive my gratitude for the attentive, critical, and illuminating support with which he accompanied my efforts remains a great regret to me.

I would like to record my warm appreciation to Felicitas Koselleck for her kind and very helpful support and advice. From Reinhart Koselleck we know that primary experiences never correspond to the later secondary memories, to which historical writing pertains. Still, I hope that the most important arguments in this book will be recognizable for those who were there.

My supervisor at the European University Institute in Florence, Bo Stråth, deserves special recognition for his tremendous support and advice in all phases of the project. Thanks moreover to Lucian Hölscher, Jörn Rüsen, Wolfgang Schieder, Willibald Steinmetz, and Hans-Ulrich Wehler for kindly agreeing to informal interviews at different stages of the project. I owe additional thanks to Rüsen for hosting me twice at Das Kulturwissenschaftliches Institut in Essen, where I (in the autumn of 2003) began preparing the project proposal and (in the winter of 2005) did important work in relation to the thesis. Thanks also to the excellent library staff at Das Kulturwissenschaftliches Institut in Essen and at the

European University Institute in Florence. I much appreciate the kind service and the enormous assistance that I received at both institutions.

Acknowledgements are due to Lars Erslev Andersen, Gisela Bock, Janet Coleman, Thomas Etzemüller, Martin van Gelderen, Heinz-Gerhard Haupt, Poul Fritz Kjaer, Jeppe Nevers, and Jens Troldborg. All of them provided me with useful criticism of various chapters and compelled me to write new and improved drafts. I would also like to thank Maurice Olender for taking time to discuss issues related to World War II, morality, and memory in the work of Reinhart Koselleck and Hans-Robert Jauss, in the course of an extensive exchange of emails in 2007 and 2008.

Three persons deserve special recognition. The first is Jens Busck, who commented on the first full draft of the text and in this process helped me frame the overall aim of my study. In addition, he generously provided detailed commentaries to all of my English translations of the German citations (needless to say, the responsibility for any errors is entirely my own).

The second is Reinhard Mehring. From 2001 onwards, when I was working on my MA thesis at the University of Copenhagen, I repeatedly benefited from his vast knowledge in the field of German intellectual history. Not only has he patiently answered all of my numerous questions about the works of Reinhart Koselleck, Karl Löwith, Martin Heidegger, Carl Schmitt, Hans-Georg Gadamer, Gerhard Ritter, and Friedrich Meinecke and the relations between them, but by reading and commenting on various chapters, he has moreover been an invaluable source of inspiration in developing several of the central lines of argument in this book.

The third is Henning Trüper, who from September 2004 and until the present day has been a very important sparring partner in framing this project and bringing it to completion. Henning has motivated me to constantly define and redefine the analytical frameworks that inform my thesis, and he again and again commented on questions of detail and lines of argument so that his enduring support resulted in a study that I would never have managed to pull off on my own.

Finally, and most importantly, I would like to thank Nina for the fantastic time we had together in Copenhagen, Seville, Beijing, Los Angeles, Brussels, Essen, Florence, and Frederiksberg, in the last decade, and for the extraordinary support she has given me in this period. In the most convincing of ways, she has at the same time managed to back up my academic projects and to remind me that the most important dimensions of the human *Miteinandersein* and *Miteinandersprechen* lie outside of academia.

Introduction

The second half of the twentieth century was a period marked by a tremendous multiplicity of discussions and innovations in historical writing and theory. A great number of fascinating authors and oeuvres, however, remain known only in the most selective fashion and are read primarily by specialists. The present study intends to examine, for the first time in its entirety, the work of one such author, the German historian Reinhart Koselleck (1923–2006).

Constantly probing and transgressing the boundaries of mainstream historical writing, he created numerous innovative approaches and exposed himself to a large range of impulses from other academic disciplines. His writings responded to the work of German philosophers such as Martin Heidegger and Hans Georg Gadamer and of political thinkers such as Carl Schmitt. Koselleck's thought also responded and added to the work of internationally renowned scholars such as Hayden White, Michel Foucault, and Quentin Skinner.

Reinhart Koselleck entered the academic scene in the 1950s with his dissertation "Kritik und Krise" in which he traced the birth of modern political thought to the Enlightenment. He achieved his *Habilitation* in 1965 with the social-historical work *Preußen zwischen Reform und Revolution.*[1] Three years later he became professor in Heidelberg, where, in the so-called Arbeitskreis für moderne Sozialgeschichte, he played a key role in the development of modern German conceptual history. Koselleck's achievement was to design the research framework of the monumental lexicon *Geschichtliche Grundbegriffe*, a work illuminating the transition to the modern world by means of analyzing changes taking place in social and political concepts during the period between 1750 and 1850.[2]

From the beginning of the 1970s, when he took up a chair in historical theory at the University of Bielefeld, Koselleck also wrote a great number of essays illuminating a range of different themes—the relation between language and social history, the rise of the modern world, and issues related to historical time, human historical consciousness, theoretical-methodological matters, and fundamental philosophical questions of what history is and how it can be studied. These essays, of which many have been republished in the collections *Vergangene Zukunft* (1979), *Zeitschichten* (2000), *Begriffsgeschichten* (2006), and *Vom Sinn und Unsinn der Geschichte* (2010), are characterized by the use of a wide range of source material, including paintings, recorded dreams, and war memorials, as well as theories and methods from several disciplines, including linguistics, sociology, and philosophy.[3] It is from this background that Koselleck continually reflected on the role of history in modern society and diagnosed the political conditions of his time, without committing himself to a fixed mode of historical writing or to a clearly defined ideological camp.

As a result of his inclination to constantly go beyond the boundaries of mainstream historical writing, Koselleck has been labeled an "outsider" and a "loner" vis-à-vis the profession.[4] Indeed, Koselleck was a thinker striving for individuality and originality, and if he won a degree of international fame unusual for a German historian after 1945, it is because he invented research projects and analytical vocabularies that were very original. *Sattelzeit, Erfahrungsraum und Erwartungshorizont* and *Zeitschichten* are among the notions from his writings that have inspired numerous research programs across disciplinary and national boundaries in the last thirty years. Koselleck has gained status not only as an important theorist of history and historiography, but also as an advocate of "grand theory," whose work scholars search for meta-theories of history and politics and of how such phenomena should be studied.

But what are, if any, the overarching themes, arguments and analytical features that hold together Koselleck's varied body of work? How and in which contexts did he develop his work? And what, more specifically, what was innovative about it?

Pursuing these questions, this book presents an intellectual biography of Reinhart Koselleck that examines his work and the intellectual and social contexts in which it emerged. The aim of the book is not only to contribute to our understanding of the life and work of a great thinker, but also to contribute to our understanding of complex theoretical and methodological issues in the cultural sciences, and to the history of political, historical, and cultural thought in Germany from the 1950s until the present. In the course of illuminating these matters, the book offers an overall interpretation of Koselleck's work.

The analytical framework behind this interpretation proceeds from the assumption that Koselleck's scholarly production cannot be understood from one single perspective. Instead of portraying method, theory, politics, personal experiences, institutional factors, questions of identity, or narrative arrangements as *the* epistemological center of his production of historical writing, this investigation addresses all of these perspectives and the relation among them. To do so, the analysis focuses on how Koselleck's historical writing was always made in *processes of reception*.[5] The analysis will show how, in these processes, Koselleck took up and transformed various discourses, and how his mode of reception was shaped by specific personal experiences, social constraints, and political factors.

To illuminate the processes of reception, the study will follow a methodological principle of continuously placing Koselleck's ideas in context.[6] It will, in other words, continuously sketch out his encounters with the discursive fields of scholarly and political language that he entered. The idea is not only to analyze how and why Koselleck drew on, reworked, or distanced himself in relation to the various discursive fields, but also to reveal the processes in question as mixing elements of deliberate appropriation and involuntary formation.

Koselleck's various texts are full of clues about his intellectual interaction with different discursive fields. These texts reveal the way in which he defined and positioned his work with reference to a wide range of different scholars, schools, and traditions in German and European history from Ancient Greece onwards. In addition, he often paid special recognition to his various teachers and sources of inspiration—both by referring to and using their notions and concepts and by describing a number of incidents relating to their intellectual and personal relationships, of which some unfolded and developed over long periods of time.

Against this background, the book demonstrates how Koselleck's appropriation of discourse was driven by individual expectations and aims, and how, in his work, he reworked and combined discursive elements that were often different in origin and meaning, in order to fit specific situations and problems. Hence the book shows that Koselleck's scholarly work constantly underwent a process of being shaped and reshaped. It consisted of many different discursive layers. Some layers appeared in the majority of his writings, whereas others were applied less frequently or gradually disappeared from his analytical vocabulary.

The analytical framework also involves a perspective on what has been referred to as the *making of the historian*.[7] This notion refers to how the construction of historical writing goes hand in hand with the construction of scholarly identities and positions. My analysis will approach this perspective from two angles. On the one hand, it will show how, by adapting to and challenging intellectual, institutional, and societal structures—and by positioning himself toward other actors in the field—Koselleck constructed a certain intellectual habitus and identity that shaped and gave meaning to his work. On the other hand, it will demonstrate how Koselleck was also made as a historian by means of being positioned by other actors in the field, through processes of reception, and in ways that eluded individual intention or control.

Pluralism against Utopianism and Relativism

The focus on the *processes of reception* and the *making of the historian* is crucial for the interpretation of Koselleck's work to be presented in this book. This interpretation takes its point of departure in the characterization of Koselleck as a "partisan" for "histories in plural" and against history in singular, which was put forward in a commentary by philosopher Jacob Taubes (1923–1987) in the early 1970s.[8] Taubes referred to the critique of modern philosophies of history that Koselleck began in *Kritik und Krise* and to his ambition of outlining an alternative concept of history: in opposition to historical-philosophic ideas of history as one, unified and progressive project, which human beings can program and direct toward a final aim, he wanted to thematize a mode of historical writing that view history as composed by a plurality of non-convergent histories that can never be shaped entirely according to human desire.

Taubes's partisan-metaphor has received little attention in the literature about Koselleck.[9] This book nevertheless maintains that the argument comprised in the metaphor is valid as a useful means of interpreting Koselleck's historical writing. I thus argue that his entire scholarly production can be interpreted as a series of attempts to undermine ideas of history in singular and as theorizing histories in plural, and it portrays in detail the scientific positions, political concerns, and theoretical-methodological components, as well as the changes and transformations, which were involved in these attempts from the 1950s to the 2000s.

The book also unfolds a more specific argument about Koselleck's work. It shows that his critique of historical philosophies also contained a critique of a certain type of historical relativism as a notion based on the very same conceptual assumption: history in the singular. Just as the utopian, teleological conception of history that he identified as underlying most historical writing from the eighteenth century onwards, this type of historical relativism presupposed the idea that one could formulate a coherent theoretical position on history as a totality. Koselleck believed that utopianism and relativism alike were based on theoretically-methodologically naïve and politically dangerous assumptions of history and politics that ignored or misunderstood the basic conditions of what is humanly possible. This is why he subjected both ideas of these ideas of history to ideological and epistemological critique.

This leads us to the key argument of this study: Koselleck's writings were always driven by the ambition to establish understandings of and approaches to science and politics that go beyond utopianism and relativism. The crucial point is that Koselleck insisted that history must be plural, and that it must be written from viewpoints that are also plural. From this perspective of pluralism and in contrast to relativism, he wanted to carve out a stable, non-relativistic common viewpoint from which historical change could be described and a parameter of judgment on the basis of which the past and the present could be discussed, without falling into the pitfalls of utopianism. This ambition and the related discursive features reveal a unifying pattern and a common objective in his varied body of work.

While illuminating Koselleck's search for plural viewpoints on history, this study does not argue that he devoted his career to writing a range of minor-scale and unrelated histories. The argument is rather that he wanted to integrate, theoretically as well as empirically, the plurality of histories into narrative forms of writing history that include generalizations, without relying on historical-philosophical notions of unity, progress, and meaning. The book emphasizes that Koselleck pursued this ambition with shifting degrees of clarity and coherence in his analytical framework. Perhaps more importantly still, the study emphasizes that this ambition was met with variable degrees of success. In addition, it shows that Koselleck's analytical categories and hypotheses were always in flux and aimed at conducting empirical research rather than at forming a definite analytical framework. In fact, as he rarely explained the more exact relation between his analytical features, Koselleck's method will be portrayed as somewhat unsystematic.

This lack of theoretical system will be explained with reference to Koselleck's intellectual temperament, but will also be related to his endorsement of theoretical-methodological plurality in historical writing. For Koselleck, historical writing was not about establishing one analytical model that leads to a state of certain knowledge about the human past, present, and future. To aim at such a model was to his eyes utopian and absurd. It was rather about developing a plurality of theories and methods with which historians can in the best possible way illuminate the specific themes and problems at stake. This plea for theoretical-methodological plurality and self-reflection is described as an integral part of his scholarly program.

Material and Structure

My investigation is primarily based on published texts: books, articles, reviews, interviews, research programs, newspaper articles, and memory pieces. A key source are the fifty-three letters dating from the period from 1952 until 1983 in which Koselleck wrote to the German jurist and political thinker Carl Schmitt, who from around 1950 until the early 1960s functioned as one of Koselleck's intellectual sparring partners with whom he discussed scientific questions and hypotheses and communicated political issues and personal experiences.[10]

About half of Koselleck's letters to Schmitt were written between 1952 and 1962. In these letters, we follow Koselleck through his exams in Heidelberg; his experiences at the University of Bristol in England, where he held a lectureship from 1953 to 1954; and his contemporary search for a more permanent position. We also read of how, in 1954, Koselleck became an assistant to the historian Johannes Kühn in Heidelberg, and how, in the 1950s, he attempted to conceptualize a project for his *Habilitation*, which ended with the social-historical work *Preußen zwischen Reform und Revolution*, written under the auspices of Werner Conze. After Koselleck secured himself a professorship, first at the department of political science in Bochum in 1966, then at the department of history in Heidelberg in 1968, and finally in Bielefeld in 1974, the frequency of his letter writing to Schmitt slowed down. There is thus relatively little about the processes in which he conceptualized his later writings on historical time, historical writing, and war experience.

While the described material offers insights that are useful in the drawing of Koselleck's intellectual profile, it should be emphasized that archival material and Koselleck's personal papers are not included in this investigation.[11] Consequently, there are many aspects of his scholarly production that the study cannot shed light on: first, the biographical dimensions of his work. The available material contains, for example, only very little information about the first twenty years of Koselleck's life. Here, the contextual part of the analysis has to rely on information found in memory pieces and interviews that were published during the last fifteen years of his life.

Hence, in many instances, in this study I describe the role of historical experience in his work by analyzing how he interpreted and wrote his experiences into a set of autobiographical and generational discourses which shaped his academic identity and his way of writing history. These discourses were deeply imbedded in what has been described as the *processes of reception* and the *making of the historian* and we will see them illuminated as vital dimensions of Koselleck's intellectual profile.

The book is made up of seven chapters. It opens with a background chapter that includes a biographical view of the first three decades of Koselleck's life and broadly illuminates the intellectual, cultural, and political contexts in which his dissertation "Kritik und Krise" originated. The background chapter is followed by six chapters that highlight various dimensions of Koselleck's intellectual profile. These chapters are organized and ordered pragmatically in a compromise between chronology and themes. This is the most cogent way to pursue the main discursive features of Koselleck's work, the unifying patterns as well as the diverging aspects, through different texts and periods of his long career.

Notes

1. Reinhart Koselleck, "Kritik und Krise: Eine Untersuchung der politischen Funktion des dualistischen Weltbildes im 18. Jahrhundert", unpublished dissertation (University of Heidelberg, 1954). The dissertation was published with a new subtitle as *Kritik und Krise: Eine Studie zur Pathogenese der bürgerlichen Welt* (Freiburg, 1959). Reinhart Koselleck, *Preußen zwischen Reform und Revolution: Allgemeines Landrecht, Verwaltung und soziale Bewegung von 1791 bis 1848* (Stuttgart, 1967).
2. Otto Brunner, Werner Conze, Reinhart Koselleck, ed., *Geschichtliche Grundbegriffe: Historisches Lexikon zur politisch-sozialen Sprache in Deutschland*, Bd. I–VIII, (Stuttgart, 1972–1997).
3. Reinhart Koselleck, *Vergangene Zukunft: Zur Semantik geschichtlicher Zeiten* (Frankfurt am Main, 1979); *Zeitschichten: Studien zur Historik* (Frankfurt am Main, 2000); Begriffsgeschichten: *Studien zur Semantik und Pragmatik der politischen und sozialen Sprache* (Frankfurt am Main, 2006); *Vom Sinn und Unsinn der Geschichte: Aufsätze und Vorträge aus vier Jahrzehnten* (Frankfurt am Main, 2010).
4. See Rudolf Vierhaus, "Laudatio auf Reinhart Koselleck," *Historische Zeitschrift*, Bd. 251 (1989): 529.
5. Reception theory is commonly associated with the work conducted by literary scholars such as Hans Robert Jauss and Wolfgang Iser at the University of Konstanz from the 1960s onwards. See Paul de Man's introduction to Hans Robert Jauss, *Toward an Aesthetic of Reception* (Minneapolis, 1982). Processes of reception have also received much attention in the work by scholars such as Carlo Ginzburg, Roger Chartier, and

Kevin Sharpe on the dynamics of reading and writing at play in the construction of texts. For an overview of the field, see Kevin Sharpe, *Reading Revolutions: The Politics of Reading in Early Modern England* (London, 2001), 3–62.

6. Quentin Skinner, "Meaning and Understanding in the History of Ideas," *History and Theory* 8, (1969): 3–53.

7. Thomas Etzemüller, "How to Make a Historian: Problems in Writing Biographies of Historians," *Storia della Storiografia* 53 (2008): 46–57.

8. Jacob Taubes, "Geschichtsphilosophie und Historik: Bemerkungen zu Kosellecks Programm einer neuen Historik," in *Poetik und Hermeneutik V. Geschichte—Ereignis und Erzählung*, ed. Reinhart Koselleck and Wolf-Dieter Stempel (München, 1973), 493 [above and elsewhere, translations of German texts have been provided by the author unless noted otherwise].

9. It was, however, brought up in an interview conducted by Carsten Dutt, in which Koselleck was asked to reflect on his critique of modern historical philosophy and the categories with which he had theorized history in the plural. Carsten Dutt, "Geschichte(n) und Historik: Reinhart Koselleck im Gespräch mit Carsten Dutt," *Internationale Zeitschrift für Philosophie* 2 (2001): 257–71. The most comprehensive interpretation of Koselleck's work is found in Kari Palonen, *Die Entzauberung der Begriffe: Das Umschreiben der politischen Begriffe bei Quentin Skinner und Reinhart Koselleck* (Münster, 2004). This study draws considerably on interpretations from Palonen's book but leaves aside one of its key arguments: namely that Koselleck's and Skinner's way of studying politics and language can be traced back to Max Weber. Even if Skinner in various writings has referred to Weber, it is difficult to connect his work to a Weberian point of departure or standpoint, and Koselleck never mentioned Weber among his sources of inspiration. See Bo Stråth, Review of *Die Entzauberung der Begriffe*, by Kari Palonen, *European Journal of Social Theory* 8 (2005): 530–32. For the latest contributions to the literature about Koselleck, see Hans Joas and Peter Vogt, eds., *Begriffene Geschichte: Beiträge zum Werk Reinhart Kosellecks* (Frankfurt am Main, 2010); Carsten Dutt and Reinhart Laube, eds., *Reinhart Koselleck: Sprache und Geschichte* (Göttingen, 2013).

10. The letters are located in Schmitt's archive in Hauptstaatsarchiv Düsseldorf (registration number: RW265). So far, only Reinhard Mehring has used this correspondence in his biography *Carl Schmitt: Aufstieg und Fall* (München, 2009), and in his article "Begriffsgeschichte mit Carl Schmitt," in *Begriffene Geschichte: Beiträge zum Werk Reinhart Kosellecks*, ed. Hans Joas and Peter Vogt, 138-168 (Frankfurt am Main, 2010).

11. Koselleck's archive is now accessible at Das Deutsche Literaturarchiv Marbach and at Das Bildarchiv Foto Marburg.

1

FAMILY—WAR—UNIVERSITY
The Various Educations of Reinhart Koselleck

The present chapter describes Koselleck's intellectual formation in a broad sense: a process of the formation of a scholarly individual, defined in part by habitus and in part by a specific set of intellectual aims, in his interrelations with a given variety of historical contexts. Attention is paid to background and to a perspective on Koselleck as an agent of his own formation, by means of the interpretations through which he attempted to grasp what was happening to himself. While Koselleck's academic identity was being shaped, he was also shaping himself. The concept of "generation" is of particular importance in this respect, as it expresses this negotiation between the inexorable forces of context and the agency of the scholar in the making.

The organizing themes of the chapter are: Koselleck's family background in the German *Bildungsbürgertum*; his experiences during World War II and captivity, and the way in which he used these experiences as an instrument for constructing a generational as much as a personal identity; and postwar academic life and the discipline of history as the prime environments in which his education was completed and his identity staged with the monumental characters of Koselleck's teachers as temporary protagonists. The contexts covered in this chapter, then, are somewhat diverse; yet in the case of Koselleck they were bound together by temporal coherence and by their function as stages in a unified process.

What emerged as the result of this process were the contours of a peculiar scholarly persona and his intellectual program.

Family Background

Reinhart Koselleck was born on 23 April 1923 in Görlitz, then in the Prussian province of Lower Silesia (now located in Saxony, on the border to Poland), one of three sons of Arno Koselleck and his wife Elisabeth. Embodying a typical blend of Prussian patriotism, liberal Republicanism and Protestantism,[1] his family formed part of that influential section of German society, the *Bildungsbürgertum* (roughly, a segment of the middle class distinguished by its devotion to education), which emerged from the middle of the eighteenth century onwards and became the primary carrier of scientific and humanistic scholarship, cultural life, and some parts of state service.[2]

Most of his immediate forebears were academics, primarily university professors, doctors and lawyers with careers in state administration.[3] His father was a historian and a professor of a teacher training college; his mother had studied French, geography and history, and had, moreover, studied the violin. Koselleck grew up—as he has vividly described it—in the famous *Bildungsbürgerliche* traditions of "house music, reading and more reading, visits to concerts and museums, pride in the family history and in letter writing."[4] Goethe, Schiller and Kleist were read, both alone and aloud; poems, drawings and melodies were composed for individual and common pleasure.

Koselleck in many ways identified himself with, took pride in and attempted to maintain certain of the social practices, values and norms of his family background.[5] To a large extent focused on the literary canon, art and aesthetics, and of course the *Bildungsbürgertum*, Koselleck's choice of academic topics testifies to this view.[6] The same can be said of his *habitus* as a historian. Koselleck was never a scholar who carried out his research in isolation from his colleagues. On the contrary, his was an academic persona, who deeply appreciated intellectual exchange, and he was known for his ability to listen to and discuss with his colleagues and students in a liberal and open-minded fashion. "He was a *Bildungsbürger* and a learned man," a former colleague said of Koselleck, "but he also had bohemian traits. He enthused and influenced students. He loved conversation, discussion, dispute, even polemic, but he never intended to hurt anyone."[7]

Similar to other (but certainly not all) members of the *Bildungsbürgertum*, he made himself known as a teacher committed to educational ideals

(*Bildung*) and a politically engaged citizen, who continually commented on the times in which he lived. His social-political engagement was first of all expressed in historical writing and in public debates, but he also habitually captured his impressions of the world around him in carica-ture-drawing.[8]

In fact, as a young man, Koselleck wanted to pursue his talent for draw-ing by attending the academy of arts, but his father wanted him to study something "reasonable" and pushed him into a scientific career.[9] Arno Koselleck had been active in the movement of educational reformers of the 1920s. Starting out as a history teacher, in 1928 he became director of the Heilig-Geist-Gymnasium zu Breslau, and two years later, in 1930, he founded the Pädagogische Akademie in Kassel. The academy was closed shortly after the Nazis came to power in January 1933. According to his son, Arno Koselleck was dismissed at the same time owing to his republi-can views, and he remained unemployed for three years, before finding a provisional job as a professor in historical didactics in Saarbrücken.

Arno Koselleck's dismissal was one of many effects that the rise of National Socialism had on Koselleck's family—and for the *bürgerliche* (bourgeois) layer of German society more generally.[10] Already in a pro-cess of disintegrating, the social-cultural status and traditions of the Ger-man bourgeoisie were facing serious challenges during the Weimar Re-public, characterized as it was by political instability and cultural crisis. Many members of the bourgeoisie reacted to the societal developments by adopting National Socialism as a political solution. This solution—it has been said—"seemed on the one hand to promise the continuity of certain elements (for example private property), but on the other hand it included the individual in a larger collective and thus reinstated a van-ished orientation, though the price was a loss of individual independence and bourgeois freedom."[11]

Still according to his son, Arno Koselleck was "republican and liber-ally minded," and although his unemployment led to a lower standard of living for his family, he was not among those who were attracted to Nazism. He did, however, with certain reservations, sympathize with the contemporary "Pan German-national and anti-semitic" (*großdeutsch-na-tional-antisemitisch*) ideas, and during the late 1930s he adapted to the re-gime, among other things, by joining the Reiter-SA.[12] More enthusiastic about National Socialism was Koselleck's older brother. Initially unhappy with the compulsory transfer from one of the German youth movements to the Hitlerjugend, within a period of three months he was promoted to the rank of Hitlerjugendführer in Dortmund, where Koselleck and his family were living at the time.[13] Reinhart Koselleck entered the Hitler-jugend in 1934, when he was eleven years of age, and, when the family eventually moved from Dortmund to Saarbrücken, he joined the equestrian Hitlerjugend.[14]

Due to the geographical moves necessitated by his father's career and the unstable societal-political situation in Germany in general, over the course of his childhood Koselleck lived in five different cities and went to eight different schools. The last of these was the Ludwigsgymnasium in Saarbrücken.[15] While at the gymnasium in Saarbrücken, at the age of nineteen, Koselleck volunteered along with his entire class for duty in the German army, and soon after—in May 1941—he was drafted.[16]

It is difficult to provide a more detailed description of Koselleck's reasons for going to war and his reactions to growing up during National Socialism—to its ideology, organizations, foreign policy achievements, and to its impact on his family—as he never commented directly on these issues in his published writings, memory pieces or interviews.[17] In these texts, however, next to growing up in the enjoyable family traditions of the *Bildungsbürgertum*, Koselleck described societal disintegration, conflict, and uncertainty as some of the key experiences of his childhood. As such, he linked this period of his life to the key theme of his autobiographical texts: his experiences of World War II and his attempts to deal with these experiences in his historical writing. One example of how Koselleck linked the two periods appears in a 2004 speech: "In my childhood, I experienced—very closely in the brawls in elementary school—the breakdown of the Weimar Republic. The liberals were gone. What followed, in my youth, was the rise of the National Socialistic movement . . . ; and then, while I was a soldier, war, total bombing, multiple death; then intensification and at the same time a dissolving of the totalitarian system; finally, breakdown and Russian captivity."[18]

But what, more exactly, did Koselleck experience in the war—and how did he relate these experiences to his historical writing?

War and Captivity

Koselleck first served in the German artillery in the Soviet Union in 1941–42. After an accident in which he hurt his foot as the army advanced toward Stalingrad, he was transferred to service in Germany and France. As part of a radar company, he became responsible for the electronic instruments which supplied the German anti-aircraft and aircraft with information. His military participation in World War II ended when, as an infantry soldier on 1 May 1945 at Oderberg in Mähren, he was captured by the Soviet Army.[19]

On 8 May, under Soviet command, Koselleck and his fellow German soldiers started on a long walk that ended in Auschwitz, where for some weeks he carried out working duties,[20] before being transported to a Soviet prisoner camp in Karaganda (Kazakhstan) in central Asia.[21] Koselleck spend fifteen months there. He was released with the help of a friend of his family, a German doctor, who cited Koselleck's foot injury to diagnose him unable to do any more work, but able to survive the four weeks of transportation via train to Germany. At the end of 1946, Koselleck arrived in Germany and returned to the family's apartment in Saarbrücken, where his mother lived.[22]

In many later interviews and writings, Koselleck described his experiences as well as his reactions and emotions during and especially after the war. Among the central elements in these accounts is the immense fear that he and his fellow German soldiers felt during and after their capture by the Soviets in May 1945; the state of existential insecurity during the demanding walk to Auschwitz; the shocking confrontation with the—at first unbelievable—information about the German mass killings that had taken place there; the renewed fear when transported to the Soviet Union; and the conditions of hunger and suffering in the camp in Karaganda. Koselleck's accounts of these experiences are narrated as a long series of extreme experiences, which made a deep and permanent impression on his mind. "There are experiences"—he once said of his war experiences—"that flow into the body like red-hot lava and petrify there. Irremovable, they can be retrieved at any time without changing."[23]

In line with this, Koselleck often emphasized how his decision to study history, as well as his scientific interests and beliefs, were deeply influenced by what he experienced in World War II and in Russian captivity between 1941 and 1946.[24] That is to say, he presented his work as personally motivated attempts to grasp the historical background of the modern world, in particular World War II, including how it was experienced, and how it could be understood and coped with. With reference to these experiences, he also explained his fixation on topics such as "crisis," "conflict" and "death," as well as his aversion to pathos-ridden notions such as "nation," "fatherland," and "heroism," as well as his skepticism regarding all talk of progress in modern society, its politics, and its science.

One of many examples of this is found in a 2005 interview, where, faced with the question of how his experiences of the war had influenced his historical writing, Koselleck replied: "Anyone who has been deluded in his expectation of victory must search for reasons, he or she did not have before, to explain the defeat. And the achievement of significant historians is to have transferred these reasons into methodological approaches . . . . A minimum of skepticism is so to say the professional disease from which a historian has to suffer. Taking into account that condition, I would say that my experience of war determined my entire course of study. My stance was that of skepticism as a minimal condition to deconstruct utopian surplus."[25]

With statements as these, Koselleck positioned himself within a larger generational discourse that was articulated by a group of German academics and intellectuals, who in the post-World War II years to various degrees and in various ways defined their identities, interests, and beliefs with reference to their experiences of National Socialism, war, and captivity. Like many of his contemporaries, Koselleck conceived of himself as a member of what the sociologist Helmut Schelsky once labeled the "skeptical generation."[26] According to Schelsky, the "skeptical generation" included all young German men who grew up in postwar Germany, after the experiences of National Socialism, Hitlerjugend, war, captivity, assisting in the defense against the allied bombings, or of the total breakdown in May 1945.[27] Due to their experiences—Schelsky argued—members of the "skeptical generation" were characterized by a critical, skeptical, and distrustful attitude toward political ideology and long-term societal planning, yet they gradually developed a more pragmatic, functional, and largely democratic attitude toward politics and life.

In broad terms Schelsky's label of a "skeptical generation" fits Koselleck's generational self-conception. Using the concept of generation as a *Selbstthematisierungsformel*,[28] Koselleck often stated that his age-related experiences led him to conceive of the world in different terms than members of other generations—including those who were too young to experience World War II and captivity, and those who perhaps experienced World War II and captivity, but for whom World War I, the upheavals in the Weimar Republic, and the National Socialist takeover in 1933 were their formative experiences. Habitually, he viewed himself as more skeptical and disillusioned than the younger generation and less skeptical and more pragmatic than the older generation.[29]

At the same time, the generational identity and the interest and beliefs that Koselleck articulated with reference to his war experiences differed distinctly from certain other generational discourses that have been constructed by members of the "skeptical generation" in the Federal Republic. Most importantly, his generational discourse diverged on crucial points from the one found in the work of a group of historians born around or after 1930, including Hans Ulrich Wehler, Gerhard A. Ritter, Hans and Wolfgang Mommsen, and Helmut Berding.[30] Some of these figures belong to the generation of the so-called *Flakhelfer*, who were too young to participate in the war outside of Germany but assisted in the defense of Germany at the end of the war and experienced the total breakdown, while others were too young to be *Flakhelfer* and emphasize instead the Allied bombings or the confusion in the immediate postwar years as the formative experiences of their childhood.[31]

What unites these historians is a common generational discourse that viewed German cultural and political traditions as totally discredited after National Socialism and wanted to implement fundamental political and also scientific changes using measures from outside Germany, especially from the United States. Scientifically, these historians developed their approach in opposition to what they understood as a theoretically weak, anti-normative, and power-glorifying tradition of German historical writing that was referred to as "historicism."[32] More concretely, as a reaction to the way in which a line of mostly conservative historians from Leopold von Ranke to Gerhard Ritter (1888–1967) had connected the strong German State and its success in foreign policy, especially during the reign of Bismarck, to a distinct German spirit and development, or *Sonderweg*, the historians born around or after 1930 criticized what they described as a negative German *Sonderweg* into modernity in theoretically informed analyses of the authoritarian societal structures during the Empire and the Weimar Republic.

This shift of focus from *Außenpolitik* to *Innenpolitik* was explained with reference to the experience of National Socialism, that is, to the need to illuminate and warn against the specifically German elements that led to Hitler's rise to power. From a political position that has become known as left-liberal, this is how the generation of historians born around or after 1930 has energetically tried to defend and improve the democratic structures underpinning the German Federal Republic since the 1960s.

One of the significant common features of the two "skeptical generation" discourses as articulated by Koselleck and the left-liberals has been described by A. D. Moses in his recent study *German Intellectuals and the Nazi Past*. Renaming the "skeptical generation" the generation of "forty-fivers," that is, the generation of German intellectuals born between 1922 and 1933, for whom the collapse of the Nazi regime was the turning point of their lives, Moses writes: "The generational question of the forty-fivers was how and why National Socialism could come to power; its mission was to ensure that the Federal Republic would succeed." To this, Moses adds: "The task was to identify and root out those intellectual traditions, discourses, ideologies, and political languages that had led to the German catastrophe" in order to keep the Federal Republic on the right track in the present and the future.[33]

While these features indeed fit both generational discourses at issue, there are—as mentioned—also crucial differences between these discourses. Nowhere are these differences more evident than in the comparison between Koselleck and Hans-Ulrich Wehler, the prototype of the *Flakhelfer*. Where, with reference to his generational experiences, Wehler has emphasized "moral against distance, Enlightenment against skepticism, linearity and progress against pluralism and decentralization,"[34] Koselleck focused on the possibility of crisis, conflict, and war, on change and contingency, and he nurtured a much deeper skepticism toward every kind of long-term planning, morality, and belief in societal progress.

Against this background, the generational identity, concern, and aim informing Koselleck's work and scholarly activities is much closer to the so-called liberal conservatives. The liberal conservatives have been described as yet another subgroup within the "skeptical generation."[35] It encompasses a group of scholars, including the philosophers Odo Marquard, Hermann Lübbe, and Robert Spaemann, and the jurists Ernst Wolfgang Böckenförde and Martin Kriele, who in the 1950s and 1960s all gathered around the philosopher Joachim Ritter in Münster.[36]

Driven by a profound skepticism toward utopian ideology, the liberal conservatives have not followed a plan of realizing a certain societal vision. As *Verfassungspatrioten* (constitutional patriots) they have instead attempted to defend and improve the liberal-democratic pillars of the German Federal Republic by emphasizing "responsibility against attitude, institutionalized decision against ideas of a discourse free of domination, tradition and ethics [*Sittlichkeit*] against idealized reason and morality."[37] In addition, they have tried to compensate for the consequences of the accelerated processes of modernization by referring to lessons of historical experience and by arguing for a critical preservation of tradition, focusing especially on certain bourgeois values and practices.

The liberal conservatives are known to primarily move within a nationally defined intellectual context that comprises a variety of scholars including Kant, Hegel, Martin Heidegger, and Carl Schmitt. And while liberal conservatism has nothing to do with the conservative-antidemocratic ideas that were articulated in the interwar writings of figures such as Heidegger and Schmitt, with the aim of discussing problems and possibilities in the social-political areas of the German Federal Republic, the liberal conservatives are moreover known for their attempts to formalize and liberalize theories from these intellectually-politically compromised figures.[38]

Arguments for a critical reuse of certain German traditions is one of the many liberal conservative features that can be found in the writings of Koselleck, whose work to a large degree must be understood within the framework of his generational discourse and identity. It must also be understood against the background of the intellectual inspiration that he gleaned from various teachers and intellectual sparring partners during his time as a student in Heidelberg at the end of the 1940s and in the beginning of the 1950s.

As Moses has pointed out, generations always depend on preexisting political (and scientific) languages in coming to terms with their circumstances.[39] Hence, what the "forty-fivers" who began their studies after experiences of National Socialism, war and captivity would make of their experiences and which lessons they would draw from the past was greatly influenced by the concepts and categories they learned at university, most often from charismatic teachers. These teachers offered the intellectual tools with which the forty-fivers interpreted and freed themselves from the National Socialist past and made their own way by means of continuing and developing the political (and scientific) languages at their disposal.

University Studies

When Koselleck returned to Germany in the autumn of 1946, it was to a country that had been badly destroyed by the war. The vast majority of the Germans were deeply affected and disoriented by the events of the recent past, and, while living in material hardship, they felt confused, uncertain, and pessimistic about what the future might bring.[40]

The occupying powers soon set out their own plans concerning German politics, economy, culture—and de-nazification. One of Koselleck's encounters with these plans took place at a castle near Dannenberg in Lower Saxony, where he participated in a re-education course arranged by the British. Here he met (and drew a caricature of) the later famous English historian Eric Hobsbawm, to whom Koselleck must have appeared a peculiar young man: extraordinarily cultivated, intelligent and open-minded, but at the same time deeply affected and disillusioned by his experiences in the war and in Russian captivity and skeptical of the prospects of once again having to be subjected to political-ideological education.[41]

Parallel to the political measures taken by the occupying powers to re-educate the Germans, German intellectual life underwent a process of reconstruction in the immediate postwar years.[42] Old discussion groups were resumed, new ones were established, and the various universities were one by one reopened—including the University of Heidelberg.

Unlike most other German cities, Heidelberg, which did not hold major bombing targets and never became a battleground, was largely intact after the war. Its university had been closed on 1 April 1945, and because its professorate had been extensively involved with National Socialism, the American occupying power subjected the institution to a process of de-nazification, before it was reopened in January 1946. However, the American initiatives were met with strong resistance by most of the faculty, and they were consequently limited in scope and severity. Not only were most of the compromised professors allowed to teach again; no organized efforts were made to bring about the return of Jewish scholars who had been dismissed.[43]

Soon the University of Heidelberg gained the status of one of the most important universities in the western zone of Germany, by, among other things, hosting a great number of respected and established scholars who were active and influential in the political and intellectual debate of postwar Germany.

On the one hand, the university also hosted figures such as the sociologist Alfred Weber and Max Webers's widow Marianne, the jurist Gustav Radbruch, the political scientist Dolf Sternberger, the philosopher Karl Jaspers and the psychoanalyst Alexander Mitscherlich. Each of these figures was known for having been critical of National Socialism, and some of them had been persecuted by the regime.[44] They were known for their liberal-democratic attitudes and were on the Americans' so-called "white list." On the other hand, the university also employed scholars, who had been close to, if not directly involved with National Socialism, such as the jurists Hans Schneider and Ernst Forsthoff, who was ousted from his chair in Heidelberg in 1945 but allowed to return in 1950.[45]

Koselleck entered the university in the summer of 1947 through some influential friends of his mother's who had stayed in his family's apartment in the months after the war.[46] Once accepted at the university, Koselleck did not have to pay study fees, due to his father's status as a professor, which, in addition, earned him 110 Marks each month.[47]

Koselleck has retrospectively described how his privileged position as a student made him feel obliged to pass all the second semester tests which were necessary to receive the normal scholarship. However, as reported by his contemporary fellow students Nicolaus Sombart and Ivan Nagel, Koselleck enjoyed his reunion with and felt at home in the world of culture and books. Working his way through huge piles of books, he was "the most solid, untiring and thorough worker"[48]—"his brain was reflecting, critical, penetrating, and always at work."[49]

The reason for Koselleck's energetic program of study undoubtedly also had a generational dimension to it. For many students, the university offered itself as a sanctuary from the upheavals and the violence that they had experienced in the preceding years of National Socialism, war, and captivity. Studying was often perceived of as a kind of self-protection from and reworking of these experiences—it was a way of regaining a normal existence. Moreover, it provided an opportunity for the students to investigate why the world had collapsed before their eyes.[50] This was undoubtedly also Koselleck's aim as he entered the University of Heidelberg.

Studying not only history, but also philosophy, *Staatslehre* (political science), and sociology, Koselleck enjoyed the liberal academic atmosphere and the relatively free curriculum at the university.[51] In his curriculum vitae, which he submitted along with his dissertation in 1954, he reported that he had especially followed seminars and lectures with thirteen professors, who represented a mix of people from the compromised and the formerly persecuted side: the jurists Walter Jellinek, Ernst Forsthoff, and Alfred Vogt; the philosophers Hans-Georg Gadamer, Karl Löwith, and Franz-Josef Brecht; the historians Johannes Kühn, Fritz Ernst, Hans Schäfer, Walther Peter Fuchs, and Hans Rothfels; the pre-historian Ernst Wahle; and the sociologist Alfred Weber.[52] These experiences helped Koselleck to develop his remarkably broad intellectual horizon in which insights from philosophy, sociology, anthropology, law, and history were to be combined.

Five scholars seem to have made an extraordinary impression on Koselleck during his time as a student in Heidelberg and must be regarded as highly important to the way in which he developed his academic work and habitus, especially during the early years of his career. These five scholars—whom Koselleck referred to and/or honored in various texts and interviews—were the historian Johannes Kühn, the jurist Carl Schmitt, and the philosophers Karl Löwith, Hans-Georg Gadamer, and Martin Heidegger.[53] Formed by different personal experiences and characterized by different personalities and political convictions, he shared with them a deep and personal engagement with their academic projects; an interest in fundamental and existential questions of life and science; and an interest in world historical perspectives, characterized by a skeptical and critical attitude toward aspects of the modern world. In the work of Schmitt and Heidegger, this attitude was distinctly antimodernist.

Below follow five sketches that describe the careers and the work of these scholars and outline perspectives on the inspiration Koselleck drew from them. These sketches are not exhaustive. Rather, the aim is to introduce information on persons, writings, and themes that are central to an understanding of the different parts of Koselleck's intellectual work and profile, on which I elaborate in the later chapters.

Johannes Kühn and Historical Method

Johannes Kühn (1887–1973) grew up in a Protestant vicarage and went to high school in Silesia, before he carried out his university studies in Breslau, Munich and Leipzig. He was known as an extremely learned man, who investigated all fields within the discipline of history—including the history of ideas, history of religion, historical theory, social history, and political history—with the aim of merging these into a larger structural history.[54] His most famous work was his 1923 *Habilitation, Toleranz und Offenbarung,* in which he investigated the various forms of tolerance and intolerance in Protestant churches and sects between the Reformation and the Enlightenment with a conceptual approach.[55]

In 1945, due to his involvement with National Socialism, Kühn was suspended from his professorial chair at the University of Dresden,[56] but soon after he acquired a position at the University of Leipzig. Once he had left Leipzig in 1949, at the age of sixty-two, to take up the professorial chair in modern history in Heidelberg,[57] Kühn added little to his scholarly production. According to the sympathetic obituary that Koselleck wrote on the occasion of Kühn's death in 1973, his authority as a historian during his time in Heidelberg was built upon his ethos of embodying "a life of intensive work and the highest intellectual concentration *(Sammlung).*" Kühn's work was—still in the words of Koselleck—devoted to reflections on nothing less than "the being *(das Sein)* and the enigma *(die Rätsel)* of history,"[58] and he allegedly possessed the special gift of reducing worldviews, historical philosophies, and utopias to their political core.

First his doctoral student and later his assistant, Koselleck worked beside Kühn (who was in fact also his godfather) at very close range at the University of Heidelberg over a period of about ten years. How deeply he sympathized with Kühn's academic work and *habitus* is indicated in the obituary. With a few changes, it might be read as Koselleck's scholarly manifesto.

One of the more direct ways in which Koselleck acknowledged the inspiration that he found in Kühn's work was by describing him as one of the "fathers" of his approach to conceptual history on account of the methodological insights that emerged from Kühn's method of reading texts.[59] In line with this, Koselleck's fellow student in Heidelberg, Nicolaus Sombart, recalls in his vivid memoirs that it was from Kühn that Koselleck learned the "serious trade of the historian"—a method of source criticism, which, according to Sombart, informed Koselleck's way of working with texts. "He was," Sombart writes, "not a paranoid hermeneutic, but had, as a historian, learned to approach historical sources in a critical manner.

He did not hesitate to accept texts in their literal meaning, as plain text, but he required that they be scrutinized regarding their authenticity."[60]

It was from this belief in historical method—Sombart continues—that Koselleck became

> the ideological-critical historian for whom the reality of life has not dissolved into signs and interpretations, but for whom facts and persons still exist, and who eased out his dissatisfaction with the possibilities of knowledge by saying: 'What you have on black and white, you can confidently take home with you.[61]

Sombart's description of Koselleck's convictions and working habits is apt in many ways: He was an ideological-critical historian who constantly reflected the limits of his field, without taking a relativistic position. And Sombart is undoubtedly right that Kühn was a key inspiration for Koselleck in forming his approach and identity as a scholar, although Koselleck was never so elaborate concerning the inspiration he found in Kühn.

When Koselleck described Kühn as one of the "fathers" of conceptual history, it was with reference to the conceptual approach that Kühn had practiced in *Toleranz und Offenbarung*. Koselleck also turned the central theme of this book—the "historical problem of tolerance"—into a key theme of his own work. He first dealt with the theme in his dissertation, which he wrote under Kühn's supervision, and which was partly motivated by Kühn's suggestion, in relation to a course the latter gave in the winter semester of 1949–50, on *Geschichte der Geschichtsphilosophie*, to investigate the history and the characteristics of modern utopias.[62] Like Kühn, Koselleck was of the opinion that the meaning of tolerance is never pregiven, but always the result of concrete social-historical constellations. In addition, he made it one of his scientific ambitions to show that the modern world's demands for tolerance have recurrently developed into new and more radical forms of intolerance and to provide the foundations for what he understood as more realistic and less dangerous forms of tolerance.

Karl Löwith and *Meaning in History*

Another central feature in Koselleck's work is a focus on the rise of the modern world and on its relations to the rise of modern historical philosophy, which he interpreted as so-called *secularized eschatology*. Koselleck developed this conception during his time as a student in Heidelberg through readings of the renowned expert in historical philosophy, German-Jewish philosopher Karl Löwith (1897–1973).

A volunteer in World War I, Löwith was badly wounded and spent time in Italian captivity, before he returned in 1917 to Munich, where he began his university studies in biology and philosophy. During his studies at the University of Freiburg, Löwith met Martin Heidegger, afterwards following him to the University of Marburg, where he earned his *Habilitation* under Heidegger's supervision in 1928. In the 1930s, Löwith was about to begin a promising academic career in Germany, when, because of his Jewish origins, he was forced to emigrate after the National Socialists' rise to power. He therefore immigrated—first to Italy, later to Japan, and finally to the United States.[63] Once the war was over, in 1952, with the help of Hans-Georg Gadamer, he returned to Germany to take up a chair in philosophy at the University of Heidelberg, where he became Koselleck's second examiner on "Kritik und Krise".

At this time, Koselleck had already acted as co-translator of what is often regarded as Löwith's most important work, his 1949 *Meaning in History*.[64] In the book, Löwith tried to explain the rise of modern historical philosophy. By the term historical philosophy, Löwith meant "a systematic interpretation of universal history in accordance with a principle by which historical events and successions are unified and directed toward an ultimate meaning,"[65] and he further contended that all modern philosophies of history are merely forms of secularized eschatology.

More concretely, tracing the theological implications of modern historical philosophy from the writings of Jacob Burckhardt back to the Bible, Löwith explained how the rise of modern historical philosophy had to do with a change in historical awareness, and especially in the perception of time, which took place from the period of the Ancient Greeks to the nineteenth century. Whereas, according to the Greek view of life and the world everything moves in recurrent and eternal life-cycles, the Christian conception about the world was based on teachings about the coming of the end of world. Yet the Christian belief in the Kingdom of God also involved an expectation of salvation in history: the expectation of an eschatological future. Hereby a new temporal horizon was opened.

According to Löwith, modern historical philosophy was created in the moment where the eschatological idea was secularized—as man placed himself in the position of God and started to believe that he was capable of and responsible for creating and directing history toward a future and ultimate goal within this world. In this process, as modern people sought to remove themselves from all ontological constraints, including the finitude of human temporal existence, they projected their demand for meaning onto history and conceived of all of their own actions as mere preparations for the historical final aim: a new and better world.

Detecting in writings of Hegel and Marx the first full-blown and all-encompassing philosophies of history, Löwith's view on modern historical consciousness was characterized by a profound skepticism. While refuting the idea that history has any inherent meaning or direction, in the preface to *Meaning in History*, he announced that his analysis did not offer any constructive results. In a tone of resignation, he added that "[man's] planning and guessing, his designs and decisions, far-reaching as they may be, have only a partial function in the wasteful economy of history which engulfs them, tosses them, and swallows them."[66]

Meaning in History continues to stand as a masterpiece in the studies of philosophies of history. The book also made a deep impression on Koselleck, who retrospectively described how, over the course of his life, he rarely learned so much as during the quarter of a year when he translated the last three chapters and the annotations in Löwith's book.[67]

The result is evident in most of Koselleck's writings from *Kritik und Krise* onwards. Not only did Koselleck make use of the idea of modern historical philosophy as secularized eschatology in his analysis of the roots of modern political thought; in addition, he repeatedly criticized and warned against ideas in which history is viewed as one progressive project, which human beings can program and direct toward a final aim, because such ideas—as Koselleck saw it—had proved to have disastrous consequences for societal-political planning and decision-making ever since the French Revolution. But, in contrast to Löwith, Koselleck attempted to develop an antidote and an alternative to the historical philosophies—an alternative that aimed at a more realistic and responsible way of conceptualizing history.

Carl Schmitt and his "Students": Modernity, Revolution, and Civil War

Carl Schmitt (1888–1985) was educated as a jurist and taught at several universities, and he worked as juridical advisor first for the Weimar governments and after 1933 for the Nazis.[68] In the 1920s and 1930s, Schmitt rose to fame as he formulated a series of critiques of the liberal incapacity to respond to the crisis that had emerged in the classical sovereign state and interstate system. His critique of liberalism stemmed from the fact that in his view, it avoided the very essence of politics: taking responsibility and making decisions. His major concern, in his contributions to legal and political theory, was to provide theories capable of upholding law and order in national as well as international affairs, and, in order to avoid the false universalism and political anarchy that liberalism supposedly brings with it, he continually argued for a strong state and for an international political system consisting of classically sovereign states.

It was consequently with the aim of establishing clear criteria for political decisions that Schmitt developed his controversial definition of "the political" in his most famous work, *Der Begriff des Politischen*, from 1932.[69] With the concept of "the political," he introduced a criterion for making decisions by reducing all political actions and motives to a distinction between "friend" and "enemy."

Schmitt also wrote a variety of essays and books on different topics including the history of ideas, geopolitics, and the relation between church and state. Common to all his writings is a focus on concepts. Schmitt conceived politics as a battle between worldviews as embodied in concepts, and he pursued a method of uncovering how liberal key concepts had allegedly attained certain insufficient and dangerous qualities when they were coined in the transition to the modern world. He contrasted the liberal concepts with concepts that he argued would guarantee more clarity, order, and permanence. The aim of his conceptual investigations was unequivocal: to establish and fight contemporary intellectual and political positions.[70]

During the 1920s and 1930s, Schmitt was a controversial, but also a widely read and respected, scholar. He influenced not only numerous legal theorists, but also a variety of other scholars all along the political spectrum. However, on account of his energetic attempt to become the "Crown Jurist" of the Third Reich, after the war he was banned from teaching and denounced in public debates. At the same time, however, he became a celebrated figure in academic and political discussion groups at universities and in more private settings.[71]

Heidelberg was one of the places were some academic circles kept in touch with Carl Schmitt. Koselleck came into contact with Schmitt as a consequence of attending seminars given by the sociologist Alfred Weber. Weber attracted a circle of students, who, like Koselleck, had returned from the war and captivity, and who then developed a special interest in the conflicts of modernity. Among these students, of whom many found an intellectual sparring partner in Schmitt, were Hanno Kesting and Nicolaus Sombart.[72] In the eyes of Kesting, Sombart, and Koselleck, Schmitt appeared as a fascinating personality who possessed not only admirable intellectual capacities, but also a firm conception of the world and an insight into some of the realities of the past and the present that were allegedly about to be forgotten at the postwar German universities, with their focus on re-education and American social science.[73]

Due to Koselleck's immediate intellectual fascination with Schmitt, the latter soon became his informal mentor while he was working on his dissertation "Kritik und Krise". Koselleck later recalled his encounter with Schmitt in the following way:

> I have rarely been asked so clever questions; I have rarely had as inspiring conversations as back then. I had just translated Hobbes for my dissertation. Schmitt asked, what I wanted to do with Hobbes, and then I spelled out my thesis: the rise of the utopia from the imbalanced relation to political responsibility in the absolutist system. He then asked me questions systematically and repeatedly encouraged me to stick to the structure of my thesis, which I presented in three chapters in my dissertation; I should not let myself be influenced by professors, who might be of the opinion that one should write more or different things.[74]

The meeting between Koselleck and Schmitt also resulted in a personal acquaintance that lasted until Schmitt's death. The reason for Koselleck's interest in Schmitt in the 1950s is probably not only to be found in his intellectual fascination with the older scholar but also in their shared tendency to embrace a *habitus* of defeat after the war. In this period, Schmitt reflected in a strongly apologetic fashion on the war, its causes, and not least his own role in it. This he did, among other places, in the book *Ex Captivitate Salus* in which he suggested that extraordinary history is written not by the "winners" but by the "vanquished."[75]

Koselleck never shared Schmitt's self-pity, his apologetic attitude, or his political positions. However, his self-understanding was in this period influenced by Schmitt's aphorism—he too felt like one of the "vanquished" in history.[76] In fact, as is discussed in more detail further on, Koselleck later developed Schmitt's reflections into a theory of how the vanquished, in their attempt to rework and understand their negative experiences, are those who develop new methodological tools and thereby reveal new insights into history.[77]

For German students in the postwar period, it was not unusual to look for a teacher or a mentor who was interested in discussing with the students, and who might serve as a point of orientation or a source of inspiration.[78] What made Schmitt's status among the Heidelberg trio of Koselleck, Kesting, and Sombart a somewhat unusual case was that, according to Sombart's memoirs, the three friends planned to found a journal devoted to studies in topics that originated from Schmitt's writings: *Das Archiv für Weltbürgerkrieg und Raumordnung.*[79]

The title embodied central lines of a worldview that centered around a theory of modernity, which Schmitt developed in his postwar writings, and which the three students picked up on and refined to their own uses. According to this view, as outlined by Sombart, the modern world was born in a moment of crisis, during the civil wars of the French Revolution, and the condition of crisis, revolution, and civil war had never come to an end: It constituted in fact the very characteristic of the modern world. Hence the contemporary Cold War between USSR and the United States was nothing but a civil war on a worldwide level—a *Weltbürgerkrieg*—in which the historical philosophies of liberalism and communism provided the central and legitimizing weapons.[80]

In order to end the crisis-condition, Sombart, Kesting, and Koselleck defined it as their task to study the laws, dynamics, and immanent structure of history. Sombart writes: "In the forefront of these future solutions, we experienced our present, which did not begin in 1945, but in 1789, as *Époque de transition*—as crisis. Sociology as a crisis-science should help us to understand and end the crisis."[81]

All three dissertations were inspired by this worldview—Koselleck and Kesting's more than Sombart's—although Koselleck was the only one to openly acknowledge this inspiration in the introduction by thanking Schmitt "who in conversations helped me to ask questions and find answers."[82] Also in many of Koselleck's subsequent writings, there are several references to Schmitt's work. Koselleck's reception of Schmitt was, as we will see, always double-sided: In framing his work, he on the one hand drew on discursive features from Schmitt's work, while, on the other, he distanced himself from and tried to counter its political implications.

Hans-Georg Gadamer and Martin Heidegger: Hermeneutics, Time, and Finality

The philosopher Hans-Georg Gadamer (1900–2002) grew up and studied in Breslau under Richard Hönigswald, but soon moved to Marburg to study with Paul Natorp and Nicolai Hartmann. After defending his dissertation in 1922, he went to Freiburg to study with Martin Heidegger with whom he earned his *Habilitation* in 1929. He spent most of the early 1930s lecturing in Marburg, before he acquired a professorial chair in Leipzig in 1939, where he became rector in 1945. In 1948, he moved to the University of Frankfurt, and in 1949 he arrived at the University of Heidelberg, where he took over the chair of Karl Jaspers.[83]

Koselleck has explained how, when Gadamer arrived at Heidelberg, he was largely unknown to the students due to the fact that he had published very little. However, because of the personal and intellectual qualities that Gadamer displayed in the seminars, he was at once deeply respected and appreciated.[84]

It was partly through these seminars that Gadamer finished his famous main work: the widely acclaimed *Wahrheit und Methode* from 1960.[85] Gadamer's project in the book was to uncover the nature of human understanding and awareness through a concept of philosophical hermeneutics, which Martin Heidegger had initiated but never dealt with in depth, and which was based on notions of language and of human temporal consciousness. Gadamer argued in *Wahrheit und Methode* that "truth" and "method" were at odds with one another, and he took issue with two approaches within the *Geisteswissenschaften*. On the one hand, he criticized the modern approaches to humanities that are modeled on the natural sciences and their rigorous methods. On the other hand, he criticized the traditional German approach to the humanities, represented for example by Friedrich Schleiermacher and Wilhelm Dilthey, for believing that correctly interpreting a text meant recovering the original intention of the author who wrote it.

In contrast to these positions, Gadamer stated that all human understanding and interpretation takes place through language and that people have a *wirkungsgeschichtliches Bewusstsein* (effective-historical consciousness), meaning that they are always embedded in the particular history and culture that shape them and their understanding of the world. To interpret a text or work of art thus involves a *Horizontverschmelzung* (fusion of horizons) between the horizon of the text and that of its interpreter. With these and other reflections, in *Wahrheit und Methode*, Gadamer did not intend to launch a programmatic statement about a new method of interpreting text. Rather he sought to describe what we always do, and what happens, when we interpret things.

That the role of language and processes of reception became revolving points in Koselleck's analysis of how human beings understand and act in the world clearly owed much to his encounters with Gadamer in Heidelberg. From the beginning, Koselleck's approach to history was deeply hermeneutical, and his entire oeuvre displays a profound interest in classical aesthetic topics in the hermeneutic tradition. In addition, as we will see, from the 1960s onwards Koselleck attempted to turn the Gadamerian hermeneutics in the direction of analyzing collective experience and larger social-historical dynamics and processes, and, on his way to developing his analytical assumptions and framework, he tried to outline a concept of history that is less bound to language than Gadamer's.

Gadamer was unquestionably among Koselleck's academic role models. Koselleck admired not only his teacher's intellectual capabilities, but also his tolerant and undogmatic attitude and his readiness to always engage in a dialogue with colleagues and students.[86] In Koselleck's eyes, these were qualities that distinguished Gadamer from two other famous philosophers that formed part of the intellectual milieu in postwar Heidelberg: Karl Jaspers (1883–1969) and Martin Heidegger (1889–1976).

Already appointed as a professor in philosophy in Heidelberg in 1916, Jaspers was a widely read and respected scholar before he was dismissed as a university teacher in 1933 and later prohibited from publishing because his wife was Jewish.[87] When Jaspers reassumed his position as a prominent figure in the German intellectual and cultural debate in the postwar period, it was largely due to his speeches—published in 1946 as *Die Schuldfrage*—in which he made one of the most famous attempts in Germany to master the National Socialist past.[88] Jasper's reflections dealt with questions of personal, collective, and national responsibility in relation to National Socialism. In summary, he argued that the Germans should not only discuss, but also accept responsibility for the crimes committed during National Socialism, and he called for a German renewal along democratic lines. The negative reactions to these pleas in the German public—as well as among some of his colleagues in Heidelberg, who allegedly neglected his personal experiences and problems—led Jaspers to accept a call to the University of Basel in 1948.[89]

Jaspers is mentioned here not because Koselleck found in him an important source of intellectual inspiration or an academic role model, but rather because he represented features that Koselleck sought to avoid in shaping his academic work and *habitus*. Whilst Koselleck attended Jaspers's seminars in Heidelberg, neither Jasper's personality nor his philosophy appealed to the younger man. As a person, Koselleck found Jaspers morally stiff, too self-confident, and vain. As a philosopher, he thought him too aloof and in a certain sense also dangerous, as he viewed Jasper's philosophy as impregnated with historical-philosophical traits. More precisely, Koselleck believed it to be encumbered with "the classical tradition of liberal historical philosophy, which sees freedom as a future goal that can be achieved through practical reason."[90]

Koselleck was no less critical toward Martin Heidegger.[91] Like Schmitt, due to his affiliations with National Socialism, Heidegger was banned from teaching in the immediate postwar years. However, his work remained widely read and discussed. This was also the case at the University of Heidelberg, where Heidegger's famous 1927 book *Sein und Zeit*—according to Koselleck—assumed status of a "book of initiation" among the students. Koselleck first encountered the central categories of the book in seminars given by Franz-Josef Brecht and in Gadamer's seminar, where Heidegger occasionally appeared as a guest.[92]

Heidegger's work made a deep impression on Koselleck. On the one hand, Koselleck held strong reservations toward a certain normative pathos and a historical-philosophical notion of history as unfolding in the eschatological sense with movements of descent and decay that he detected in *Sein und Zeit*. On the other hand, the same book provided inspiration for two of his most important scholarly projects that were both aimed at criticizing history in the singular and thematizing history in the plural. The first project concerned an anthropologically based assumption of how history is created and can be understood; the other concerned a theory of historical time in which individual and collective self-understanding and action is analyzed through the historical actor's conceptions about time and finality. This accounts for Koselleck's statement in an interview that central aspects of his work should be understood within the dynamics of the Heidegger-reception that he entered during his studies in Heidelberg.[93]

In the following chapters, we will see in more detail how Koselleck referred to the work of his teachers as he shaped his scholarly projects and presented himself to the disciplinary field. What is worth noticing is that, during his time as a student in Heidelberg, Koselleck primarily found intellectual inspiration in scholars who were either on the fringes of or outside of the historical discipline, and not by any of its prominent and celebrated figures. This does not mean that Koselleck was unfamiliar with the work of these figures; rather that he was deeply skeptical toward and sought to break with the discursive features they in his eyes represented. We shall end the chapter with a brief description of these discursive fields and Koselleck's attitude toward them.

The Historical Profession in the Postwar Years

Two of the most famous historians of modern German and European history (the field Koselleck was entering) in the immediate postwar period were Gerhard Ritter and Friedrich Meinecke (1862–1954). For decades both had put their distinct fingerprints on the profession through occupying important scholarly and administrative positions and through extensive publications. While Meinecke was famous for his work on the history of ideas, and Ritter for his work on political, diplomatic, and military history, both were interested in issues related to the German state and its great personalities.

When World War II ended, Meinecke was more than eighty years old, and while he enjoyed the status of a widely read and respected living classic in the discipline, he did not participate in the practical reorganization of the German historical profession in the postwar years.[94] Ritter, on the other hand, as a result not only of his academic merit, but also of his reputation of having been critical toward and also involved in active resistance against the Nazis, came to play an important role in the reorganization of the profession.[95]

In spite of widespread adaptation to and cooperation with National Socialism among the German historians, Ritter used his authority to secure a strong continuation in the profession—both in terms of approaches, persons, and institutions.[96] This continuation was effected smoothly. Around 1950, the institutions of the historical profession were practically recovered; the departments at the universities had started teaching, and the Historikerverband had been reestablished; important research-institutions such as the Historische Kommission at the Bayerischen Akademie der Wissenschaften and the Monumenta Germaniae Historica were continuing their activities; and the historical journals were again being published. The processes of de-nazification had little impact on the personnel at these institutions, and there were few examples of internal sanctions against compromised scholars. Hence, the profession continued to be dominated by a group of national-conservative and nationalistic historians, who, spearheaded by Ritter, attempted to marginalize the few Catholic, liberal, or Marxist scholars in the profession, and to maintain the traditional (non-theoretical) approach of the discipline with its focus on a political and diplomatic history of events.

It was not until the late 1950s, after the rise of a number of new research-institutions (including the Institut für Zeitgeschichte in Munich and the Arbeitskreis für moderne Sozialgeschichte in Heidelberg) that various alternatives to historical writing gradually gained influence. During the 1960s, a period discussed in more detail in chapter 5, the profile of the discipline was challenged in a considerably more direct fashion as the generation of younger and so-called left-liberal scholars combined a critique of the values informing the traditional approach to historical writing with an attempt to redefine the theoretical-methodological fundament of the discipline. More concretely, the left-liberals launched a model of historical writing that was not only supposed to be more theoretically nuanced, but also more politically responsible than the approach to history in the work of Ritter and Meinecke, which they labeled as "historicism." While, in the opinion of this generation, Meinecke had taken refuge from the rise of Nazism in idealistic and naïve ideas of eternal progress in history, and Ritter had done little to counter the fascination with political power and pathos that had led to and characterized National Socialism, the left-liberals aimed at an approach that would relate history to social reality and be unambiguously committed to political democracy.

Also Koselleck expressed from the very beginning of his career a deep skepticism toward Meinecke's work. Similar to the left-liberals, he detected in it a theoretically weak and politically dangerous variant of "historicism." More concretely, according to Koselleck, Meinecke's analytical framework was both relativistic and utopian, as it combined a supposedly anti-normative position vis-à-vis history with an overtly positive belief in its progressive course and development, which altogether prevented Meinecke from interpreting history in a realistic and responsible way. Against this background, Koselleck made it one of his fundamental scholarly ambitions to construct an approach to history that would account for the flaws that he saw in Meinecke's work.

This ambition was already present in the dissertation "Kritik und Krise," in which Koselleck interpreted the rise of the modern world with reference to the various contexts that he came from: the bourgeois society and the literary classics; the conflict, crisis, and wars of the twentieth century; and the work of his teachers at the University of Heidelberg.

Notes

1. The phrase is borrowed from Stefan-Ludwig Hoffmann, "Reinhart Koselleck (1923–2006): The Conceptual Historian," *German History* 24 (2006): 477.
2. Koselleck has described his family background and upbringing in "Formen der Bürgerlichkeit: Reinhart Koselleck im Gespräch mit Manfred Hettling und Bernd Ulrich," *Mittelweg 36: Zeitschrift des Hamburger Instituts für Sozialforschung*, 12. Jg (2003): 63–82. For the history and the characteristics of the *Bildungsbürgertum*, see Werner Conze et al., eds., *Bildungsbürgertum im 19. Jahrhundert*, 4 Bd. (Stuttgart, 1985–1992). See also Manfred Hettling and Bernd Ulrich, eds., *Bürgertum nach 1945* (Hamburg, 2005); M. Rainer Lepsius, "Bürgertum und Bildungsbürgertum," in *Demokratie in Deutschland*, 289–34 (Göttingen, 1993); Hans-Jürgen Puhle, ed., *Bürger in der Gesellschaft der Neuzeit: Wirtschaft, Politik, Kultur* (Göttingen, 1991); and Lutz Niethammer, ed., *Bürgerliche Gesellschaft in Deutschland: Historische Einblicke, Fragen, Perspektive* (Frankfurt am Main, 1990).
3. His parents, however, came from different societal backgrounds: "My family is a fusion of a well-established academic *bürgerlich* (bourgeois) family of Huegenot origin on my mother's side and my father's social climbing family. He was a third generation social climber—following the stages of craftsman, merchant and academic. My family thus has its background in the *Bürgertum* (bourgeoisie)." Koselleck, "Formen der Bürgerlichkeit," 68.
4. Ibid., 68.
5. See Koselleck, "Formen der Bürgerlichkeit," in which Koselleck portrayed the cultural self-understanding of his family between the two world wars and in the early Federal Republic. He moreover listed a number of occurrences and decisions in his life and academic career, which he ascribed to the norms, structures, and networks of

the *Bildungsbürgertum*. Among these are his release from captivity in Russia; his admission to study at the University of Heidelberg; and the lectureship he subsequently earned at the University of Bristol. We shall later return to all of these issues.

6. Reinhart Koselleck, ed., *Bildungsbürgertum im 19. Jahrhundert*, Bd.2, *Bildungsgüter und Bildungswissen* (Stuttgart, 1990); Reinhart Koselleck and Klaus Schreiner, eds., *Bürgerschaft: Rezeption und Innovation der Begrifflichkeit vom Hohen Mittelalter bis ins 19. Jahrhundert* (Stuttgart, 1994).

7. Jürgen Kocka, "Die Zukunft der Vergangenheit," *Der Tagesspiegel*, 6/2 (2006). For descriptions of Koselleck's *habitus*, see also Lucian Hölscher, "Abschied von Koselleck," in *Begriffene Geschichte: Beiträge zum Werk Reinhart Kosellecks*, ed. Hans Joas and Peter Vogt, 84-93 (Frankfurt am Main, 2010); Willibald Steinmetz, "Nachruf auf Reinhart Koselleck (1923–2006)," *Geschichte und Gesellschaft*, Bd. 32 (2006): 414; Jörg Fisch, "Die Suggestivkraft der Begriffe," *Tagesanzeiger* 6,bno. 2 (2006); Michael Jeismann, "Geschichte und Eigensinn. Zum siebzigsten Geburtstag des Historikers Reinhart Koselleck," *Frankfurter Allgemeine Zeitung* 23, no. 4 (1994).

8. See Vierhaus, "Laudatio auf Reinhart Koselleck," 530. Some of Koselleck's drawings are published in Reinhart Koselleck, *Vorbilder—Bilder, Gezeichnet von Reinhart Koselleck: Eingeleitet von Max Imdahl* (Bielefeld, 1983). The drawings depict teachers and friends from the University of Heidelberg, scenes and impressions from the processes of re-education and from German and international politics from 1947 until 1980.

9. Koselleck, "Formen der Bürgerlichkeit," 69–73. See also Eric A. Johnson and Reinhart Koselleck, "Recollections of the Third Reich," *NIAS Newsletter* 22 (1999): 14, where Koselleck mentioned that he also considered becoming a medical doctor.

10. In the following, *bürgerlich* and *bürgerliche* will be translated as bourgeois and *Bürgertum* with bourgeoisie.

11. Manfred Hettling, "Bürgerlichkeit in Nachkriegsdeutschland," in *Bürgertum nach 1945*, ed. Manfred Hettling and Bernd Ulrich (Hamburg, 2005), 15. This was of course not the case for the many Jewish members of the *Bildungsbürgertum*. Generally, it is difficult to find evidence in the literature as to how the *Bildungsbürgertum* reacted to the social-political challenges in the Weimar-Republic and to the rise of National Socialism.

12. Koselleck, "Formen der Bürgerlichkeit," 70. According to Koselleck, his father, who served as a lieutenant in World War I, did this primarily to protect his students. In the same interview, Koselleck mentioned that his father made other "concessions" around 1937–38 without specifying what they were.

13. According to Koselleck, his brother's enthusiasm for National Socialism caused tension with his father. Koselleck, "Formen der Bürgerlichkeit," 71.

14. Koselleck never joined the Nazi party. When asked in a 1999 interview whether he thought about joining, he answered: "It was beyond my imagination, because I was eighteen years old and had become a soldier by then." Johnson, "Recollections of the Third Reich," 9.

15. Vierhaus, "Laudatio auf Reinhart Koselleck," 530. See also the *Lebenslauf* (curriculum vitae) in Koselleck, "Kritik und Krise: Eine Untersuchung."

16. According to Koselleck, the decision to volunteer for duty did not necessarily imply that they were all National Socialists but rather "that you wanted to mobilize for your fatherland" (*daß man sich für seine Vaterland einsetzen wollte*). Only one Catholic in the class did not volunteer. When joining the army, Koselleck and his classmates were awarded the baccalaureate. Koselleck, "Formen der Bürgerlichkeit," 71–73.

17. As witnessed in the following example, Koselleck's few direct accounts of his experiences of the political turmoil in Germany as a child were recalled with the retrospection of the historian: "My first political experience was what followed the disaster of the parliamentary system in 1930. I grew up with all this, also with the brawls in elementary school over the presidential election for the German Reich. Communists and conservatives fought each other, while I was watching from the sideline. I was so to speak already then a historian." Koselleck, "Formen der Bürgerlichkeit," 82. Somewhat more explicit about why young German men like Koselleck joined the German army in the early 1940s was Hans Robert Jauss (1921–1997), a famous literary scholar, who, in 1996, gave a full-page interview with Le Monde after it became public that he had joined the Waffen-SS in October 1939 at the age of seventeen. Downplaying the role of political ideology, Jauss, whom Koselleck befriended in Heidelberg, said: "What persuaded me to enter the Waffen-SS was not really an adherence to Nazi ideology. As a son of a teacher, member of the petty bourgeoisie, I was a young man who wanted to conform with the atmosphere of the time. That said, I had read Spengler's Das Untergang des Abendlandes, written by an author banned by the Nazis, and it had made me sceptical of the Hitlerian Empire. But along with other future historians—I am thinking of my friends Reinhart Koselleck and Arno Borst—what we had in common was the desire not to stand apart from current events. One had to be present in the field, where history was made, by participating in the war. In our view, to do otherwise would have been to flee, to confine ourselves within an aesthetic attitude, while our comrades of the same age were risking their lives." Maurice Olender, "'The Radical Strangeness of Nazi Barbarism Has Paralyzed a Generation of Intellectuals': Dialogue with H. R. Jauss" [1996]; Maurice Olender, Race and Erudition, (Cambridge, 2009), 139–40. For the life and work of Arno Borst (1925–2007), see the autobiography by Arno Borst, Meine Geschichte (Lengwil, 2009).

18. Reinhart Koselleck, "Dankrede am 23 November 2004," in Reinhart Koselleck (1923-2006). Reden zum 50. Jahrestag seiner Promotion in Heidelberg, ed. Stefan Weinfurter (Heidelberg, 2006), 58.

19. Basic facts about Koselleck's whereabouts before and during the war are found in the Lebenslauf in Koselleck, "Kritik und Krise: Eine Untersuchung." For more detailed and vivid accounts of his experiences, see Koselleck, "Ich war weder Opfer noch befreit. Der Historiker Reinhart Koselleck über die Erinnerung an den Krieg, sein Ende und seine Toten," Berliner Zeitung, 7/5 (2005); Johnson, "Recollections of the Third Reich"; Reinhart Koselleck: "Die Diskontinuität der Erinnerung," Deutsche Zeitschrift für Philosophie 47, no. 2 (1999): 213–14; Koselleck, "Glühende Lava, zur Erinnerung geronnen"; and Koselleck, "Vielerlei Abschied vom Krieg," in Vom Vergessen vom Gedenken. Erinnerungen und Erwartungen in Europa zum 8. Mai 1945, ed. Birgitte Sausay, Heinz Ludwig Arnold, and Rudolf von Thadden, 19–25 (Göttingen, 1995).

20. Koselleck worked on disassembling the IG-Farben industrial complexes.

21. The camp was a part of the GUPVI system of camps for prisoners of war which had been established in 1939 and functioned until 1960. Andreas Hilger, Deutsche Kriegsgefangene in der Sowjetunionen, 1941–1956. Kriegsgefangenenpolitik, Lageralltag und Erinnerung (Essen, 2000); Stefan Karner, Im Archipel GUPVI. Kriegsgefangenschaft und Internierung in der Sowjetunion 1941–1956 (München, 1995).

22. His father was at that time in Hannover. On their reunion, he allegedly failed to recognize his son, who had been away for more than five years. While Koselleck had been away, his older brother had died as a soldier in the war, his younger brother had died during the Allied bombings, and his aunt on his mother's side had been mur-

dered by the Nazis in the "euthanasia-action." Koselleck, "Formen der Bürgerlichkeit," 73.

23. Koselleck, "Glühende Lava, zur Erinnerung geronnen."

24. For two examples of how Koselleck's friends, colleagues, and students have also related his war experiences to his historical writing, see Vierhaus, "Laudatio auf Reinhart Koselleck," 530: "These events, the military service and the Russian captivity—experienced history, that is—caused him . . . to turn to history as the subject for his reflections and activities as a scholar, academic teacher, university-politician and author." And according to Christian Meier, "It is a consequence of personal experiences of war, captivity, the euthanasia-murder of his aunt, the death of his brother during the bombardments, that memory and coping with memory came to interest him. The same can be said about his interest in war memorials . . . ." "In den Schichten der Zeit," *Die Zeit*, 10/2 (2006). For a comprehensive analysis of the relations between Koselleck's experiences of war and his historical writing, see Michael Jeismann, "Wer bleibt, der schreibt. Reinhart Koselleck, das Überleben und die Ethik der Historikers," *Zeitschrift für Ideengeschichte*, Hf. III/4 (2009): 69–81.

25. Koselleck, "Ich war weder Opfer noch befreit."

26. Helmut Schelsky, *Die skeptische Generation: Eine Soziologie der deutschen Jugend* (Düsseldorf-Köln, 1957).

27. In fact, Schelsky included all those who were between fourteen and twenty-five years old in the years between 1945 and 1955, that is, all who were born between 1920 and 1941. For a historicization of Schelsky's book, see Franz-Werner Kersting, "Helmut Schelsky's 'Skeptische Generation' von 1957. Zur Publikations- und Wirkungsgeschichte eines Standardwerkes," *Vierteljahresheft für Zeitgeschichte*, Jg. 50 (2002): 465–95. For various perspectives on generational research, see Ulrike Jureit, *Generationenforschung* (Göttingen, 2006); and Ulrike Jureit and Michael Wildt, "Generationen," in *Generationen: Zur Relevanz eines wissenschaftlichen Grundbegriffs*, ed. Ulrike Jureit and Michael Wildt, 7–26 (Hamburg, 2005).

28. That is, he used it as a notion to describe himself. See Jureit, *Generationenforschung*, 7–19. Koselleck also used the concept of generation as an analytical category in his writings, a point to which we return below.

29. Examples will be given in chapter 6 within the context of his reactions to the student revolt in the late 1960s.

30. The following draws on Paul Nolte, "Der Historiker der Bundesrepublik. Rückblick auf eine 'lange Generation,'" *Merkur*, no. 53 (1999): 413–32.

31. For biographical information on Wehler, Ritter, and Hans and Wolfgang Mommsen, see Rüdiger Hohls and Konrad H. Jarausch, eds., *Versäumte Fragen: Deutsche Historiker im Schatten des Nationalsozialismus* (Stuttgart, 2000). For how generational identities are a product not of common experiences but of common discourse, see Jureit, *Generationenforschung*. Against this background it makes sense that Nolte, in "Der Historiker der Bundesrepublik," includes Heinrich August Winkler and Jürgen Kocka in describing the above-mentioned generation, even though they were born in 1938 and 1941, respectively.

32. In chapter 2, I discuss the many different meanings that have been attached to the term "historicism."

33. A. D. Moses, *German Intellectuals and the Nazi Past* (Cambridge, 2007), 66.

34. The citation is taken from Nolte, "Der Historiker der Bundesrepublik," 427, who uses it to contrast Wehler to the historian Thomas Nipperdey (1927–1992), to whom we will return to in chapter 6.

35. The following is based on Jens Hacke, *Philosophie der Bürgerlichkeit: Die liberalkonservative Begründung der Bundesrepublik* (Göttingen, 2006), 11–34.
36. Koselleck knew and cooperated on several occasions with Marquard, Lübbe, and Böckenförde.
37. Hacke, *Philosophie der Bürgerlichkeit*, 14. The concept of *Verfassungspatriotismus* describes the identification of a citizen with the political culture of a democratic constitution. It was originally coined by the political scientist Dolf Sternberger and is often associated with the famous left-liberal philosopher Jürgen Habermas, who in many ways can be viewed as an intellectual antithesis to the liberal conservatives. When Hacke appropriates the concept in his description of the liberal conservatives, it is to emphasize that the "liberalization" of the Federal Republic is not primarily a leftist project, but a result of the activities of many different intellectual orientations and practices, including those of the liberal conservatives. Hacke, *Philosophie der Bürgerlichkeit*, 11–16.
38. It is on account of their different attitudes toward the German past that A. D. Moses places scholars belonging to the left-liberals and the liberal conservatives in two different camps of "forty-fivers": the "Non-German Germans" and "German Germans" (to be sure, Moses does not use the categories of left-liberals and liberal conservatives in his work). According to Moses, these camps are proponents of two different languages of republicanism: respectively, "redemptive" and "integrative," with "the former expressing the Non German German wish for a republic divorced from corrupted national traditions, and the latter articulating the German German imperative for positive, national continuity." Moses also places Koselleck in the camp of "German Germans." Moses, *German Intellectuals*, 9–10, 109.
39. Moses, *German Intellectuals*, 53, 57, 72.
40. See, for example, Sven Reichardt and Malte Zierenberg, *Damals nach dem Krieg: Eine Geschichte Deutschlands 1945 bis 1949* (München, 2008). For broader overviews, see Eckart Conze, *Die Suche nach Sicherheit: Eine Geschichte der Bundesrepublik Deutschland von 1949 bis in die Gegenwart* (München, 2009), 21–34; Konrad Jarausch, *After Hitler: Recivilizing Germans, 1945–1995* (New York, 2006), 3–71; Edgar Wolfrum, *Die geglückte Demokratie: Geschichte der Bundesrepublik Deutschland von ihren Anfängen bis zur Gegenwart* (Stuttgart, 2006), 20–41; and Manfred Görtemaker, *Geschichte der Bundesrepublik Deutschland: Von der Gründung bis zur Gegenwart* (Frankfurt am Main, 2004), 24–43.
41. Eric Hobsbawm, *Interesting Times: A Twentieth-Century Life* (London, 2002), 179.
42. See, first of all, Reinhard Mehring, *Carl Schmitt zur Einführung* (Hamburg, 2001), 463–548; and Dirk van Laak, *Gespräche in der Sicherheit des Schweigens: Carl Schmitt in der politischen Geschichte der frühen Bundesrepublik* (Berlin, 1993).
43. Steven P. Remy, *The Heidelberg Myth: The Nazification and Denazification of a German University* (Cambridge, 2002). For broader historical perspectives on the University of Heidelberg, see Eike Wolgast, *Die Universität Heidelberg 1386-1986* (Berlin, 1986); Karin Buselmeier, Dietrich Harth, and Christian Jansen, eds., *Auch eine Geschichte der Universität Heidelberg* (Mannheim, 1985).
44. For an account of how Mitscherlich's political attitudes in the 1930s were different than many presumed in the postwar period, see Martin Dehli, *Leben als Konflikt. Zur Biographie Alexanders Mitscherlichs* (Göttingen, 2007).
45. Remy, *The Heidelberg Myth*; Laak, *Gespräche in der Sicherheit*, 86–191, 240–45. We shall later return to Forsthoff with whom Koselleck took exams and later collaborated on various occasions.
46. Koselleck, "Formen der Bürgerlichkeit" 73–74.

47. In this respect, Koselleck was very privileged. First of all, it was difficult to be accepted at university in the immediate postwar years (in the autumn of 1945, between 25,000 and 45,000 applicants for university places were turned down). Secondly, the students who had taken their baccalaureate after 1942 were usually obliged to retake this or pass other forms of exams before entering university. Thirdly, many of the postwar students, of whom presumably more than ninety percent had served in the army during the war, were financially dependent on their parents or had to work in order to raise the 100 Marks, which was the minimum sum required to live as a student. See Valdemar Krönig and Klaus Dieter Müller, *Nachkriegs-Semester: Studierende und Studienbedingungen nach Kriegsende* (Stuttgart, 1990).

48. Nicolaus Sombart, "Rendezvous mit dem Weltgeist": *Heidelberger Reminiszenzen 1945–1951* (Frankfurt am Main, 2000), 265–66. We shall return to Sombart below.

49. Ivan Nagel, "Der Kritiker der Krise," in *Reinhart Koselleck (1923–2006): Reden zum 50. Jahrestag seiner Promotion in Heidelberg*, ed. Stefan Weinfurter (Heidelberg, 2006), 27. Nagel and Koselleck befriended each other in the summer of 1951, when Nagel was almost twenty and Koselleck twenty-eight years old. Shortly before, Nagel had left his native Hungary (Budapest) to study in Heidelberg. Later, he became a critic and dramatic advisor, occupying posts at several famous cultural institutions around the world.

50. See, for example, Borst, *Meine Geschichte*, 17; and Krönig, *Nachkriegs-Semester*, 63–119.

51. For a description of the liberal milieu at the University of Heidelberg in this period, see also Hans Robert Jauss, "Antrittsrede vor der Heidelberger Akademie der Wissenschaften," *Jahrbuch der Heidelberger Akademie der Wissenschaften* (1982): 71–75.

52. Koselleck, "Kritik und Krise: Eine Untersuchung", 1. In the summer semester of 1950, Koselleck studied at the University of Bristol. In 1952, he terminated his registration as a student in Heidelberg in order to finish his dissertation. Autobiographical accounts of Koselleck's experiences during his time as a student in Heidelberg are found in "Formen der Bürgerlichkeit" and "Dankrede am 23 November 2004."

53. Heidegger was the only one of the five scholars whom Koselleck never formally honored. On the contrary, as we shall see, Koselleck kept a distinct intellectual distance from Heidegger. Werner Conze is not mentioned above because Koselleck first met him in the late 1950s. Conze will be introduced in chapter 3.

54. Eike Wolgast, "Die neuzeitliche Geschichte im 20. Jahrhundert," in *Geschichte im Heidelberg: 100 Jahre Historisches Seminar, 50 Jahre Institut für Fränkisch-Pfälzische Geschichte und Landeskunde*, ed. Jürgen Miethke (Berlin, 1992), 147–49; Detlef Junker, "Theorie der Geschichtswissenschaft am Historischen Seminar der Universität Heidelberg im 19. und 20 Jahrhundert," in Miethke, *Geschichte im Heidelberg*, 171; and Reinhart Koselleck, "Zum Tode von Johannes Kühn," *Ruperto Carola*, Bd. 51 (1973): 143–44.

55. Johannes Kühn, *Toleranz und Offenbarung* (Leipzig 1923).

56. For a description of how Kühn after 1933 propagated anti-semitic theory and supported Hitler's wars, see Eberhard Demm, "Alfred Weber und die Nationalsozialisten," *Zeitschrift für Geschichtswissenschaft*, Nr. 47 (1999): 232. See also Remy, *The Heidelberg Myth*, 228. Kühn's political past seemingly never became a public issue in his lifetime. However, in his memoirs Nicolaus Sombart attacked Kühn for having been a radical anti-semite who had participated in projects related to the Nazis' population policies in the east and thus helped to prepare and justify the extermination policies. Sombart's attack prompted Koselleck to defend Kühn in a 2006 speech, where he stated that Sombart's account of Kühn's past was blatantly wrong. See re-

spectively Sombart, "Rendezvous mit dem Weltgeist," 265; and Koselleck, "Dankrede am 23 November 2004," 50–51. In his review of Sombart's book, Eberhard Demm writes that Sombart probably confused Kühn with the economist Helmut Meinhold, who taught in Heidelberg between 1952 and 1962. Demm, "'Student Prince' der Nachkriegszeit: Nicolaus Sombarts dritter Memoirenband über seine Studienzeit in Heidelberg," *Rhein-Neckar-Zeitung*, 7/11 (2000).

57. Kühn took over the chair from Willy Andreas (1884–1967), who was discharged from his chair by the military government in February 1946 because of his affiliation with National Socialism. Andreas was in 1947 exonerated by the de-nazification trial court, but was later the same year awarded the status of emeritus upon his own proposal. See Wolgast, "Die neuzeitliche Geschichte," 146–47, and "Geschichtswissenschaft in Heidelberg 1933-45," in *Nationalsozialismus in den Kulturwissenschaften. Bd. 1. Fächer—Milieus—Karrieren*, ed. Hartmut Lehmann and Otto Gerhard Oexle), 166–68 (Göttingen, 2004). For details of the department of history in Heidelberger in the twentieth century, see also Werner Conze and Dorothee Mussnug, "Das historische Seminar," *Heidelberger Jahrbücher*, Bd. 57 (1979): 133–52.

58. Koselleck, "Zum Tode von Johannes Kühn," 143.

59. Reinhart Koselleck and Christof Dipper, "Begriffsgeschichte, Sozialgeschichte, Begriffene Geschichte: Reinhart Koselleck im Gespräch mit Christof Dipper," *Neue politische Literatur*, Nr. 2 (1998): 187.

60. Sombart, *Rendezvous mit dem Weltgeist*, 265.

61. Ibid.

62. "In response to my seminar work, on the foundation of Communism in the Communist Manifesto or on the foundation of eternal peace in Kant's text of the same name, Kühn encouraged me to follow the traces of the modern utopias: the main question and theme of my dissertation, in which I went on a search for the utopian charges also in Kant's three Critiques." Koselleck, "Dankrede am 23 November 2004," 51. For Kühn's interest in historical philosophy, see Reinhard Laube, "Zur Bibliotek Reinhart Koselleck," *Zeitschrift für Ideengeschichte*, Hf. III/4 (2009): 106–08; and Brigitte Altemos: "Lehrende und Lehrprogramm. Kontinuität und Wandel der Heidelberger Historie unter personellen Geschichtspunkten," in *Eine Studie zum Alltagsleben der Historie. Zeitgeschichte des Faches Geschichte an der Heidelberger Universität 1945–1978*, ed. Robert Deutsch, Heilwig Schomerus, and Christian Peters, 71 (Heidelberg, 1978).

63. See Löwith's memoirs from 1940, which were published posthumously in 1986, with a foreword by Reinhart Koselleck—Karl Löwith, *Mein Leben in Deutschland vor und nach 1933, Ein Bericht mit einem Vorwort von Reinhart Koselleck und einer Nachbemerkung von Ada Löwith* (Stuttgart 1986). For introductions to Löwith, see Richard Wolin, "Karl Löwith: The Stoic Response to Modern Nihilism," in *Heidegger's Children: Hannah Arendt, Karl Löwith, Hans Jonas, and Herbert Marcuse*, 71–100 (Oxford, 2001); *Burckhard Liebsch, Verzeitlichte Welt. Variationen über die Philosophie Karl Löwiths* (Würzburg, 1995); *Wiebrecht Ries, Karl Löwith* (Stuttgart 1992); Jürgen Habermas, "Karl Löwiths stoischer Rückzug vom historischen Bewußtsein," in *Philosophisch-politische Profile*, 195–216 (Frankfurt am Main, 1987; Manfred Riedel, "Karl Löwiths philosophischer Weg," *Heidelberger Jahrbücher*, Nr. 14 (1970): 120–33. For focused perspectives on Löwith's *Meaning in History*, see Jeffrey Andrew Barsch, "The Sense of History: On the Political Implications of Karl Löwith's Concept of Secularization," *History and Theory* 37, no. 1 (1998): 69–82; and W. Emmerich, "Heilsgeschehen und Geschichte," *Sinn und Form*, Bd. 46 (1994): 894–915.

64. Löwith, *Meaning in History: The Theological Implications of the Philosophy of History* (Chicago, 1949).

65. Ibid., 1.
66. Ibid., vi.
67. Koselleck, "Formen der Bürgerlichkeit," 77. The main translator was Koselleck's friend Hanno Kesting, who had been recommended for the job by Carl Schmitt. Laak, *Gespräche in der Sicherheit*, 272; and Jan-Werner Müller, *A Dangerous Mind: Carl Schmitt in Postwar European Thought* (New Haven, 2003), 109 and n. 26. Schmitt's interest in *Meaning in History* also appears from his review of the book in "Drei Stufen historischer Sinngebung," *Universitas* 5 (1950): 927–31. See also Mehring, *Carl Schmitt*, 475; and Reinhard Mehring, "Karl Löwith, Carl Schmitt, Jacob Taubes und das 'Ende der Geschichte,'" *Zeitschrift für Religions- und Geistesgeschichte* 48, no. 3 (1996): 234–38.
68. Mehring, *Carl Schmitt*; and Reinhart Mehring, *Carl Schmitt zur Einführung* (Hamburg 2001).
69. Carl Schmitt, *Der Begriff des Politischen* (München, 1932). The book was an elaborate version of a text that Schmitt had first published in 1927 in the journal *Archiv für Sozialwissenschaften und Sozialpolitik*.
70. Thus the title of a collection of Schmitt's essays: See *Carl Schmitt: Positionen und Begriffe im Kampf mit Weimar-Genf-Versailles 1923–1939* (Berlin, 1940).
71. Mehring, *Carl Schmitt*, 463–504; Müller, *A Dangerous Mind*; Laak, *Gespräche in der Sicherheit*.
72. For Kesting, born in 1925 and a member of the Hitlerjugend in the 1930s, the experience of the violent battle of Normandy, followed by four years of imprisonment, led to a very pessimistic view of life. After finishing his dissertation in Heidelberg, he began an academic career that started at the Sozialforschungsstelle in Dortmund and ended with a position as a professor at the department of political science at the University of Bochum. He died in 1975 following an operation. For Sombart, the son of the famous economic historian Werner Sombart, the transition from the safe surroundings of his childhood to being a corporal in the German army, later in British imprisonment, resulted in a feeling of existential despair, although seemingly not for long. Soon after finishing his dissertation, Sombart went to Strasbourg to pursue a long career in the European Council. See Laak, *Gespräche in der Sicherheit*, 266–76; and Sombart, *Rendezvous mit dem Weltgeist*, 268–76.
73. See also Mehring, *Carl Schmitt*, 510–70. Sombart, who knew Schmitt from his youth in Berlin in the 1940s, introduced Koselleck to Schmitt.
74. Koselleck, "Formen der Bürgerlichkeit," 76.
75. Carl Schmitt, *Ex Captivitate Salus* (Köln 1950), 25.
76. Nagel, "Der Kritiker der Krise," 26.
77. Reinhart Koselleck, "Erfahrungswandel und Methodenwechsel. Eine historisch-anthropologische Skizze," in *Historische Methode*, ed. Christian Meier and Jörn Rüsen, 27–57 (München, 1988).
78. Krönig, 1990, 67–80. In Göttingen, for example, a group of students, who had returned from war and captivity and spent time in German working and concentration camps found in the philosopher Helmut Plessner (1892–1985) a teacher in whom they sought inspiration to come to terms with the disasters of the immediate past with the aim of preventing similar disasters in the future. Helmut Plessner had as "half-Jew" been forced to emigrate to Holland in 1933 and returned to take up a position as a professor in sociology in Göttingen in 1933. Carola Dietze, *Nachgeholtes Leben. Helmut Plessner: 1892–1985* (Göttingen, 2006), 376–78.
79. Sombart, *Rendezvous mit dem Weltgeist*, 268–76. Labelling the three friends the "the mythical German troika of Faust, Mephisto und Wagner," Sombart portrayed himself

as a happy and liberal "Weltkind"; Kesting as the pessimist, who represented the "cult of the negative"; and Koselleck as the "somewhat grey" figure, who stood in the shadows of the other two.

80. Sombart, *Rendezvous mit dem Weltgeist*, 268–76.
81. Ibid., 271–72. Whereas Sombart and Kesting submitted their dissertations at the department of sociology, Koselleck submitted his at the department of history, but—as we shall discuss later—viewed his study as a sociologically framed analysis of history.
82. Koselleck, "Vorwort," *Kritik und Krise: Eine Studie*, Koselleck also thanked Johannes Kühn, his father, and his friends Gerhard Hegt, Hanno Kesting, and Nicolaus Sombart.
83. For Gadamer's life and work, see Jean Grondin, *Hans-Georg Gadamer: A Biography* (New Haven, 2004).
84. Reinhart Koselleck, "Er konnte sich verschenken—Hans-Georg Gadamer gedenkend, des Lehrers und Freundes, der vor einem Jahr Starb," *Süddeutsche Zeitung*, (14/3-2003).
85. Hans-Georg Gadamer, *Wahrheit und Methode: Grundzüge einer philosophischen Hermeneutik* (Tübingen, 1960).
86. See Koselleck, "Er konnte sich verschenken."
87. For Jasper's life and work, see Werner Schüssler, *Jaspers zur Einführung* (Hamburg, 1995); Jeanne Hersch, ed., *Karl Jaspers: Philosoph, Arzt, politischer Denker. Symposium zum 100. Geburtstag in Basel und Heidelberg* (München, 1986).
88. Karl Jaspers, *Die Schuldfrage: ein Beitrag zur deutsche Frage* (Zürich 1946).
89. Thus Jasper's recollections in Karl Jaspers, "Von Heidelberg nach Basel," in *1945: Befreiung und Zusammenbruch. Erinnerungen aus sechs Jahrzehnten*, ed. Peter Süss, 60–69 (München, 2005).
90. Reinhart Koselleck, "Jaspers die Geschichte und die Überpolitische," in Hersch, *Karl Jaspers*, 298. See also Koselleck, "Er konnte sich verschenken," and "Formen der Bürgerlichkeit," 2003, 77–78, in which Koselleck expressed reservations toward about Jasper's reflections in *Die Schuldfrage*, especially against the way in which Jasper differentiated among guilt, responsibility, and metaphysical guilt.
91. Tellingly, Koselleck drew ridiculing caricatures of both. See Koselleck, *Vorbilder—Bilder*, 31 and 101 (ridiculing respectively Jasper's vanity and work), and 105 (ridiculing Heidegger's jargon of Eigentlichkeit).
92. Martin Heidegger, *Sein und Zeit* (Halle 1927). Concerning the seminars given by Brecht, see Koselleck, "Dankrede am 23 November 2004," 44; concerning *Sein und Zeit* as a "book of initiation," see Koselleck, "Formen der Bürgerlichkeit," 77. In a letter to Schmitt written in 1977, Koselleck mentioned that he had read Heidegger's book already in the third semester. RW265-8172: 3/1 (1977).
93. Reinhart Koselleck, Jussi Kurunmäki, and Kari Palonen, "Zeit, Zeitlichkeit und Geschichte—Sperrige Reflexionen: Reinhart Koselleck im Gespräch mit Wolf-Dieter Narr und Kari Palonen," in *Zeit, Geschichte und Politik: zum achtzigsten Geburtstag von Reinhart Koselleck*, ed. Jussi Kurunmäki and Kari Palonen, 9 (Jyväskylä, 2003).
94. Meinecke will be introduced in more detail in chapter 3.
95. Christoph Cornelissen, Gerhard Ritter: *Geschichtswissenschaft und Politik im 20. Sahrhundert* (Düsseldorf 2001).
96. For lines of continuation in the profession, see Jan Eckel, *Hans Rothfels: Eine intellektuelle Biographie im 20. Jahrhundert* (Göttingen, 2005), 269–72; Winfried Schulze, *Deutsche Geschichtswissenschaft nach 1945* (München, 1989); and Ernst Schulin, ed., *Deutsche Geschichtswissenschaft nach dem Zweiten Weltkrieg: 1945–1965* (München, 1989).

2

EXPLAINING, CRITICIZING, AND REVISING MODERN POLICITAL THOUGHT

The initial objective of Koselleck's dissertation was to investigate the origins of modern utopian thought via readings of Kant's three critiques.[1] Soon, however, the project developed into a broader analysis of the birth of modern political thought in the Enlightenment. Koselleck just managed to submit the dissertation in October 1953, as was the precondition for taking up the position he had accepted as a lecturer at the University of Bristol from the beginning of 1954. According to Koselleck, the pressure of time forced him to submit the text without its notes. Moreover, it was this pressure which caused what he later called "the slightly mannered strictness in the line of argumentation."[2]

In the dissertation, Koselleck nevertheless presented several thematic, argumentative, and theoretical-methodological features that reappear in many of his subsequent writings. Since the study was originally published in 1959,[3] it has been republished several times in a paperback version. It has also been translated into Spanish, Italian, French, and English. And after achieving status as an international classic in the discussions of the Enlightenment and the rise of the public sphere, and in the field of political theory, it has been referred to as the most successful dissertation of the twentieth century by a German academic in the humanities.[4]

However, right from the 1950s up until today, "Kritik und Krise" has also been subjected to severe criticism. While many have criticized the book for being highly biased in its treatment of the Enlightenment, some have in addition argued that it should in fact be read as a conservative contribution to the postwar German political debate.

This chapter is an analysis of "Kritik und Krise"; the intellectual processes in which the dissertation was constructed; and the later reception of the book. After placing "Kritik und Krise" in the context of the academic debates of the postwar period concerning the relations between the extreme political events of the twentieth century and Enlightenment thought, I will approach the text from three different contextual angles.

The first angle will present the basic plot and argumentation with which Koselleck in "Kritik und Krise" constructed what amounted to a profoundly critical historical interpretation of modern political thought. More concretely, we will see how he described modern political thought as being born around the French Revolution and as characterized by dangerous, irresponsible, and utopian features that generated a modern world dominated by permanent crisis, revolution, and civil war. This is followed by a discussion about the normative agenda of Koselleck's interpretation and the extent to which his accounts of the processes of secularization and of the relations between morality and politics in the study converged with, and diverged from, the work of his teachers.

This discussion leads to the second contextual angle, from which I focus on the deeper normative and theoretical-methodological foundations of "Kritik und Krise" and the intellectual processes in which these foundations emerged. These issues are approached by analyzing a dense five-page letter that Koselleck wrote to Carl Schmitt on 21 January 1953. The letter presents a microperspective on reception processes that illuminates Koselleck's thinking at work. The aim is to disclose a constructive dimension of the dissertation that has never previously been discussed in relation to Kritik and Krise—namely, Koselleck's attempt to revise modern political thought by outlining a new concept of history. This concept was to depart from all utopian notions of history as a singular, unified, and goal-directed process. It embodied, as will be shown, an anthropological understanding of history, premised on the idea that history is composed of a plurality of histories. This section of the chapter will moreover show that Koselleck's aim with this concept of history was to provide a formalistic way of understanding and containing the potential for conflict in human societies and that the discursive features embodied in the concept came to provide his work with a certain analytical, thematic, and argumentative unity.

The illumination of Koselleck's concept of history opens up the third contextual angle of the book. In this angle, I examine "Kritik und Krise" in terms of the "making" of Koselleck; that is, it reads the dissertation as a text with which, by positioning himself toward various discourses articulated by other scholars, Koselleck sought to construct an identity and a position as an innovator and an outsider to the academic field. The analysis then uses the reception of the book to illustrate how Koselleck's eventual reputation as an outsider was shaped in ways that he neither controlled nor desired. Here the analysis first turns to a very critical review authored by the philosopher Jürgen Habermas as a way to discuss certain problematic aspects of Koselleck's dissertation. The book ends with a summing up of the entire analysis of the study.

What Went Wrong?
The Twentieth Century and the Enlightenment

What are the historical preconditions of German National Socialism and of modern totalitarianism? What went so wrong as to allow Nazism and totalitarianism to take over large areas of Europe in the 1930s and 1940s? And what lessons are there to be drawn from the past in discussions of the present and the future? These were questions that many scholars, informed by different academic backgrounds, political beliefs, and personal experiences, attempted to answer in the years during and after World War II.

A number of contributions to the debate focused on the relations between the extreme political events of the twentieth century and Enlightenment thought. Among these were *Dialektik der Aufklärung* (1944) written by the two leading proponents of the Frankfurt School, Max Horkheimer and Theodor Adorno; *The Open Society and its Enemies* (1945) by the Austrian-British philosopher Karl Popper; the German philosopher Hannah Arendt's *The Origins of Totalitarianism* (1951); *Die deutsche Katastrophe* (1946) and *Europa und die deutsche Frage* (1948) by the historians Friedrich Meinecke and Gerhard Ritter, respectively; and *The Origins of Totalitarian Democracy* (1960) written by the Israeli historian J. L. Talmon.[5] This was the body of literature to which Koselleck's dissertation "Kritik und Krise" (1954) belonged. Although it was not written in direct response to any of the books mentioned above, its agendas overlapped with and diverged from each of these works in crucial ways.[6]

To begin with, as Koselleck himself noted on several occasions, there are striking similarities between *Dialektik der Aufklärung* and "Kritik und Krise".[7] Hence, similar to Adorno and Horkheimer, Koselleck argued that National Socialism was not an aberration of modern history, but instead rooted deeply in Western civilization in a fateful and self-destructive dialectic inherent in the birth of the Enlightenment. But where Adorno and Horkheimer sought to explain the problems of the modern world by illuminating how the Enlightenment's rational and instrumental logic had wiped out its mythical and emancipatory potential and caused a lack of freedom in modern society, Koselleck located the problems in the subordination of politics to morality in Enlightenment thought. More concretely, like Popper, Koselleck found the roots of totalitarianism in philosophical patterns of thought that culminated in the Enlightenment and claimed the existence of an inevitable and deterministic pattern to history, but where Popper's book expressed a vigorous defense of liberal democracy, Koselleck's analysis was rather designed as a historical diagnosis of the contemporary political situation.

Similar to Arendt, Koselleck interpreted both Nazism and communism as totalitarian movements and traced the antecedents of totalitarianism to Enlightenment thought.[8] However, like Meinecke and Ritter, he limited the analytical focus to the Enlightenment. In line with these two older historians, Koselleck thought Nazism was not a German but a broader European phenomenon, having its roots in the birth of modern European civilization, beginning with the French Revolution. However, "Kritik und Krise" was not—like *Die deutsche Katastrophe* and *Europa und die deutsche Frage*—an attempt to rehabilitate German idealism and the national political tradition.[9] Rather, like Talmon's *The Origins of Totalitarian Democracy*, it was an attempt to illuminate what Koselleck in a review of the book labeled the dangerous relation between "terror and unquestioned political confession (*Glaubensgewißheit*), between dictatorship and the total claim to salvation (*Erlösungsanspruch*)."[10] This was a relation, Koselleck agreed with Talmon, which had permeated *all* political thought since the French Revolution.

In line with this, Koselleck was undoubtedly deeply skeptical toward Meinecke's idealistic suggestion that the "German catastrophe" should be overcome by re-establishing the best of the bourgeois traditions in the form of congregations devoted to Goethe. When Koselleck provided the published version of his dissertation with the subtitle *Eine Studie zur Pathogenese der bürgerlichen Welt* ("A Study of the Pathogenesis of the Bourgeois World"), it was in fact because he believed that the bourgeois world was born with a disease that caused its own destruction. Koselleck later stated that the notion of pathogenesis was inspired by the medical-anthropologist Viktor von Weizsäcker (1886–1957), whose seminars Koselleck followed in Heidelberg,[11] but the idea that the modern world was born with self-destructive elements can be found in writings of several anti-historicist thinkers from Jakob Burckhardt to Max Weber and Carl Schmitt.[12]

The original subtitle of "Kritik und Krise—Eine Untersuchung der politischen Funktion des dualistischen Weltbildes im 18. Jahrhundert" ("An investigation of the political function of the dual worldviews in the eighteenth century")—aimed to describe the nature of the modern world's disease. This disease was, according to Koselleck, to be found in a dual worldview that had its roots in the eighteenth century, and which saw in politics and morality an irreconcilable dualism. Since Koselleck's portrayal of the dual worldview can hardly be understood without taking into account developments in the understanding of and attitude toward politics in Germany in the decade after World War II, a brief contextual perspective is needed before we begin the textual analysis.[13]

In the immediate postwar period, when most Germans were primarily occupied with their own experiences, losses, and needs during and after the war, there was a general disinterest, bordering to apathy, when it came to a personal involvement in politics.[14] This pattern of reaction was presumably also caused by the fact that there were few political options in the years following the war. Those which existed had been decided by the occupying powers, whose plans for reordering and restructuring Germany were awaited with uncertainty, distrust, and fear by many Germans.

In line with this, there was at that time in Germany a prevalent, deeply skeptical attitude toward American liberalism and Soviet communism, the two central political ideologies behind the founding of the two German states, West Germany and East Germany in 1949. In West Germany, the political alliance with the United States and the Western powers in terms of foreign and domestic politics was in many circles conceived as the necessary political protection against what many Germans spoke of as the "evils of communism"—drawing on a discourse, which had its roots in the Empire era and had been influenced by National Socialist propaganda, by recent German experiences of the Eastern front, Russian captivity, and the Russian march toward Berlin, and by interpretations of the contemporary political developments in Eastern Germany. In fact, during the process of the "westernization" of West Germany, a strong discourse of anti-communism served as an effective integrative ideology, especially in conservative circles.[15]

At the same time, until the mid 1950s, there was a prevalent skepticism among many Germans toward the ideology of American liberalism and its pillars of technology, mass culture, and political democracy. The skepticism stemmed from, among other things, an anti-liberal discourse going (at least) back to the Weimar Republic, the measures taken by the Americans in the process of de-nazification, and an extensive fear of the

contemporary American military mobilization against the Union of Soviet Socialist Republics.[16]

The Cold War mobilization made a deep impression on many Germans, whose World War trauma was merged with a nuclear fear, as they
found themselves in the center of a political confrontation that had divided the world and Germany into a bipolar order, and threatened to
escalate into armed conflict. Around 1950, the year in which the Korean
War broke out, about half of the German population was living in latent
fear of the outbreak of a third world war between the United States and
the Soviet Union.[17]

The period was dominated by a profound feeling of uncertainty, and
the concept of "crisis" was one of the most frequently used catchwords in
interpretations and discussions of the social-political situation.[18] In this
respect, there were strong lines of continuation going back to the first
decades of the twentieth century, where the seemingly unstoppable processes of modernization, the collapse of the German Empire, the defeat
in World War I and the social-political problems of the Weimar Republic
had resulted in a sweeping crisis-consciousness.[19]

It is evident even in the opening lines of "Kritik und Krise" that the
political concerns and the crisis-consciousness of the 1950s also informed
this study. There Koselleck sketched out its central question and main
argument by effectively coupling Schmitt's ideal-type framework for the
development of world history from the French Revolution to the present—including Schmitt's existential understanding of politics as an eternal fight for influence, power, and domination—to Löwith's interpretation of modern historical consciousness:

> From a historical point of view, the contemporary crisis in World History,
> which is politically defined through the tensions between the two world
> powers, America and Russia, is a result of the European expansion over the
> globe. As it is the case with the global spread of bourgeois society, the pres-
> ent crisis is related to a historical-philosophical and largely utopian self-
> conception of modern man. Both phenomena, the political crisis, which,
> if it really is a crisis, presses for a decision, and the historical philosophies
> that correspond to the crisis, and in whose name we seek to anticipate the
> decision to, or to prevent it if it seems disastrous, is a historically unified
> phenomena. Their common historical root lies in the eighteenth century,
> and this outlines the questions we may ask from our present situation.[20]

According to Koselleck, as he specified in his introduction, the reason
for the world historical crisis between the United States and the Soviet
Union was that communism and liberalism refused to acknowledge the

rule of "the political": that politics is always an arcane area of conflicts and interests in which all participants strive for influence and power. Instead, guided by their moral and utopian ideologies, shaped as historical philosophies and involving a future-oriented pursuit of better worlds, the United States and the Soviet Union were headed for mutual destruction, as there was simply no room for the opponent in these worlds.

The historical explanation for this development was, Koselleck specified, to be found in the Enlightenment. More specifically, it was to be found in certain changes in the relations between politics and morality that took place between the civil wars in the sixteenth and the seventeenth century and the French Revolution. Employing a rigorously dialectical mode of analysis, Koselleck set out to explain these changes in three chapters. First, he described the rise of the absolutist state as a political answer to the situation of the religious civil wars.[21] Secondly, he described the moral critique of the Enlightenment thinkers as an answer to the situation of the absolutist state. And finally, he described how the critique created a political crisis and consequently led the way to a new civil war, in the form of the French Revolution, which was legitimized via historical philosophy and which continued to haunt the world.

The Rise and the Fall of the Absolutist State

Koselleck's chapter on the rise and the fall of the absolutist state drew on a sociopolitical argument that he drew from Schmitt's *Der Leviathan in der Staatslehre des Thomas Hobbes* from 1938. In line with Schmitt, he described the origins of the absolutist state as a reaction to the violent religious civil wars and its function as a protecting, neutral, and peacekeeping power that mediated between the combatting parts by monopolizing physical violence.[22]

It was—Koselleck wrote—the particular achievement of Thomas Hobbes to have formulated the principle on which the absolutist state was constructed: the principle of separating politics from morality. Hobbes found this separation necessary: Because of their passions, moral convictions, and will to power, human beings are always bound to conflict with each other. The inevitable result, if sufficient boundaries are not set for these inclinations, is strife, war, and civil war, to which only violent death puts an end, as had been demonstrated in murderous religious civil wars.

It was as an answer to this condition, with the aim of securing peace, that Hobbes confined politics to the domain of the state and morality to the private sphere of its subjects. He did so by demanding the "outer" obedience of its subjects in return for the protection of the state, while allowing the subjects their "inner" freedom: a free consciousness regarding issues of religion and morality. According to Koselleck, this conceptual distinction at once successfully created the absolutist state and planted the seeds of its brutal destruction.

Koselleck explained the initial success of the absolutist state with reference to a process of secularization in which theological forms of representing and symbolizing power were made political: "Within the frames of the national church, theology was subordinated the state," he wrote, again following Schmitt, "and the absolute ruler recognized no other authority over himself than God, whose attributes he appropriated in the political and historical field he appropriated."[23] As a secularized god, at the same time standing above the law and being its fundament, by following a formal principle of decision-making, the sovereign decided what was right and wrong. He did not, Koselleck specified, pay attention to social interests or religious beliefs, but only to the principle of protecting his subjects: His political function was solely to provide and keep order. And as soon as the subjects decided to pledge their "outer" obedience to the sovereign, the state—as the highest symbol of power, authority and sovereignty—immediately fulfilled its purpose: "The finality, which in civil war is felt by every man due to the deadly threat from others, becomes a responsibility of the state. The saving of the mortal individual is no longer effected in the afterlife through an immortal God but in this world through the protection of the state, the mortal god."[24]

However, according to Koselleck, the man-made, secularized, and mortal god of the absolutist state was eventually killed by the same individuals whose lives it was created to protect and prolong. Pushed out of the outer sphere of politics, the subjects reacted to their situation by channeling the utopian surplus of their inner freedom into a rising public sphere, where they as individuals secretly began to discuss increasingly controversial topics, including the politics of the state, on the basis of individual moral values. The result was a division between politics and morality that proved fateful for the absolutist state.

The Emergence of the Public Sphere—and of the Bourgeoisie

In the second chapter, Koselleck's analysis went beyond that of Schmitt by demonstrating how the public sphere emerged in the clubs, salons, and societies of the Enlightenment and how its emergence took place in convergence with the rise of the bourgeoisie. As a new social group, manifesting itself in the "turn to modernity," it brought with it a new social consciousness in which the concepts of morality and politics and their mutual relation were viewed in a new light.[25] According to Koselleck, the members of the bourgeoisie saw morality not only as different, but also as better as and superior to politics. Hence, in the public sphere, they began to subject the politics of the absolutist state to a fierce moral criticism.

It was John Locke, Koselleck stated, who first detected the rise of a new set of moral laws among the members of the new bourgeois society, who—as individuals—began to judge what was "good" or "bad," "true" or "false," "reasonable" or unreasonable." As these judgments were applied alongside the politics of the absolutist state, the established order of protection and obedience between the state and its subjects was suddenly threatened, and the known criteria for political decision-making became unclear. "Which authority decides?" Koselleck wrote. "The moral authority of the citizen or the political authority of the state? Or both of them jointly? And if both jointly, how do they interrelate?"[26]

According to Koselleck, these questions were left unanswered by Locke, but on the continent they found clear answers in the rising public sphere, where a strong critique of the absolutist state was articulated first of all among the Enlightenment philosophers. As exponents of the pervasive changes taking place in European thought, the latter began to reject the authority of the state on behalf of the authority of morality and gradually began to conceive of morality as something "true," "authentic" and "natural," while they considered politics as "evil," because it prevented morality from unfolding. Hence, instead of seeking protection by the state, its subjects now sought protection from the state in the institutions of the public sphere, where the moral criticism had to be carried out in secrecy—and with the claim of being unpolitical—as it conflicted with the statutes of the absolutist state.

Koselleck explained that the system of secrecy was most radically expressed in the mysterious lodges of the freemasons in which the rule of politics was substituted with the rule of reason, taste, and fashion and by demands for total equality and tolerance. However, pursuing themes from Kühn's *Toleranz und Offenbarung*, Koselleck argued that the lodges were characterized by intolerance rather than by tolerance and that their members were far from equal.[27] The lodges were thus organized along a hierarchy of knowledge and insight in which the system of secrecy became an instrument of power. Because certain members shared a greater knowledge of good taste, moral judgment, and criticism than others, they saw it as their responsibility to educate their fellow members. It was in these secret societies that Koselleck recognized the chime of modern tyranny and dictatorship. "The lodges," he wrote, "became the strongest social institution of the moral world in the eighteenth century,"[28] thus arguing that the utopian rejection of political authority instead led to an authority based on ideology, where supposedly anti-authoritarian Enlightenment concepts such as "reason," "equality," and "morality" were used as weapons of power and control.

The new society, Koselleck explained, became embedded in a fundamentally dual worldview that contrasted the absolutist state to the new society, and politics to morality; a world of total evil to a world of total equality, humanity, and righteousness—and its totalitarian potential truly manifested when it made a move from "protection to attack."[29] The new society thus began to question the legitimacy of the absolutist state and its politics more directly. Moreover, it developed indirect, but strong political visions of how to govern according to moral principles. The result of the critique was, according to Koselleck, a crisis-situation, which demanded a decision between the two alternatives.

However, the new society still insisted on being unpolitical, and, blindfolded with what Koselleck portrayed as a deeply hypocritical and self-deceptive belief in the neutral nature of its criticism, its adherents attempted to conceal the political nature of the criticism. According to Koselleck, the hypocritical criticism launched by the bourgeoisie was based on a misunderstanding of the nature of its own role in politics, and it did nothing but reinforce the crisis. It was in fact precisely the claim of being unpolitical that made the moral critique political: "The political anonymity of reason, morality, nature, and so on, defined their political character and effectiveness. Their political essence lay in being un-political."[30] It was thus also with a refusal to govern directly from their morality principles that the bourgeoisie soon took specific measures in an attempt to plan and create a world of total morality, equality, and happiness in its own image.

The Historical-Philosophical Component and the Worldwide Crisis

In the third chapter, Koselleck went on to explain the source of the confidence of the bourgeoisie that a new world was about to be born. He wrote: "It was the *philosophy of history*. This was the power that the Illuminati possessed, a power they shared with the Enlightenment in general."[31] According to Koselleck, modern historical philosophy not only guaranteed the bourgeoisie that it was capable of creating a new world; it also offered a political line of action, which was projected forwards in time and seemingly needed only to be programmed according to mathematical models in order to accelerate and anticipate the future world.

Following Karl Löwith, Koselleck defined historical philosophy as a form of Christian eschatology which had been secularized through Enlightenment thought and transferred to the human historical consciousness during the course of the eighteenth century.[32] Koselleck, however, elaborated significantly on *Meaning in History* by arguing that modern historical philosophy originated in a specific social-historical situation: in connection with the rise of the public sphere in the Enlightenment. It was in this process, he stated, that the theological idea of salvation was transformed into a rational plan for history, and man into the "'earthly god,' claiming the command of history."[33] Relying on the contemporary mechanical worldview, and convinced about the idea of progress, modern man now thought it possible "to identify history as a totality and determine its entire future."[34]

It was thus from a historical-philosophical consciousness, Koselleck further stated, that Enlightenment thinkers such as Turgot, Rousseau, and Raynal at first indirectly began to predict and then legitimize civil war and revolution as a way to overthrow the state and its immoral politics on behalf of a world based on humanity, reason, and truth. According to Koselleck, historical philosophy proved extremely effective as a political weapon. On the one hand, by promising a progressive design of movement, purpose, and finality in history, leading to an ideal world in which politics, power, and domination are abolished on behalf of absolute freedom and equality, it legitimized and even demanded the eradication of everything and everyone that might question or in other ways slow down the realization of the new world. On the other hand, historical philosophy made it possible for individuals to evade political responsibility for their actions, because these actions could be attributed to the idea that human beings were merely serving and obeying history's inherent movements and demands. Koselleck wrote: "The necessity of planning posited by the philosophy of history relieved the planners of political responsibility. The Illuminatus is a philosopher of history to the extent that he remains politically not responsible. Thus the revolution was papered over by the structure of historical progress, but this same structure mandated the factually revolutionary aspect: the plan to occupy the state and do away with it."[35]

As the historical-philosophical beliefs spread throughout bourgeois society and grew into visions of a worldwide moral voiced by a so-called *Weltbürgertum* (cosmopolitism), the utopian expectations of change, action and progress could no longer be held back. The situation simply demanded a decision. "The French Revolution," Koselleck wrote, "was the first instance of that loan being called in."[36]

This ending emphasized that "Kritik und Krise" should be read as a critique of the historical-philosophical justification of the French Revolution and of the role that historical philosophy had come to play in the allegedly deeply self-deceptive and hypocritical processes of modern political decision-making. Since 1789, men and societies had according to Koselleck been unable to resolve the contradiction between morality and politics in their conduct of politics. Hence they had failed to transform the Enlightenment crisis-consciousness into rational and responsible political action, where the existence of enemies is recognized and problems are dealt with in a peaceful manner. Instead of accepting past experience and present reality, they sought refuge in historical-philosophical ideas of future worlds with reference to which they sought to carry out their utopian political plans and moreover acquitted themselves from the responsibility of their actions. In Koselleck's eyes, historical philosophy had accordingly not only accelerated the French Revolution, but also, as he stated in the cited opening lines of the study, paved the way to the later ideologically-based civil and World Wars, including the contemporary Cold War, a war that threatened to wipe out the entire planet.

Koselleck's perspective on the contemporary situation was in this respect similar to those found in contemporary writings of Carl Schmitt, who interpreted the Cold War as a *Weltbürgerkrieg* that was fought with historical philosophies as the key weapons. Like Schmitt, Koselleck painted a picture of a modern world in which totalitarianism, revolution, and war potentially belong to the daily order, and where the conditions for a durable political order are absent as long as historical-philosophical worldviews prevent the recognition of political opponents and of political responsibility.

Koselleck in Relation to Löwith's Secularization and Schmitt's Modern World

Koselleck's use of phrases like "world historical crisis" and his unconditional desire to address what he perceived as the burning problems of the modern world raises the question of the normative agenda pursued in "Kritik und Krise". It further raises the question of the extent to which the book follows the scheme provided by the works of Carl Schmitt. Previous interpretations have often been reduced to a matter of whether, in his interpretation of the modern world, Koselleck merely employed a rigidly Schmittian mode of analysis and shared Schmitt's antimodernism and political conservatism, or whether he only used selected aspects of Schmitt to present a critique of the Enlightenment that solely served to criticize the aporias of modern political thought. The present study holds the second line of interpretation to be more correct than the first. However, it shifts the issue of discussion by showing that some of the most important discursive features that Koselleck found in Schmitt were of a different and more constructive kind than hitherto presumed. It also shows how, in combination with discursive features from other scholars, the latter were utilized in the creation of an intellectual project and a normative agenda that ultimately had little to do with Schmitt's writings.

It is indisputable that Koselleck's profoundly skeptical interpretation of the modern world in "Kritik und Krise" was to a considerable extent constructed through concepts and categories from the works of Löwith and Schmitt. Arguments about the processes of secularization played an important role in this respect. Most importantly, Koselleck followed Löwith's argument concerning modern historical philosophy as secularized eschatology and echoed his critique of modern man for taking upon him the authority of powers he does not posses. He also used Schmitt's argument concerning the secularization of theological forms of power to contrast the clear criterions of the absolutist state to the supposedly unclear criterions of the modern world. In line with this, judging the protagonists on their ability to respect politics as an eternal fight for power in which clear principles of sovereignty and decision-making must be followed if plain disaster is to be avoided,[37] Koselleck portrayed the absolutist state as a victim of its critics and dealt with the latter's way of conducting politics in an indicting and condemning tone.[38] This biased scheme of interpretation amounted to a pessimistic *Verfallsgeschichte* that has parallels in the work of Löwith and Schmitt, but which is still more closely related to the self-destructive dialectic of the Enlightenment described in Adorno and Horkheimer's *Dialektik der Aufklärung*.

Unlike Löwith and Schmitt, Koselleck did not portray the modern world as "inferior," "illegitimate" or "criminal," nor did he in any way criticize or reject Enlightenment thought *per se*.[39] Instead, he talked (in the published version) about the modern world's pathogenesis: of how it was born with certain problems that caused serious disease. He located the causes of this disease in an exaggerated focus on the future, overstated claims of rationality, equality, and freedom, and a lack of political responsibility that was allegedly bound to have disastrous consequences for political planning and decision-making.

Moreover, in his attempt to provide a cure to these ailments of the modern world, Koselleck did not follow Löwith's or Schmitt's backward-looking perspectives concerning a return to earlier conditions. Thus he did not idealize the Greek idea of the cosmos, like Löwith. Nor did he like Schmitt argue for a return to a political system similar to the absolutist state by calling upon counter-revolutionary thinkers such as Joseph de Maistre and Juan Donoso Cortés.[40] While Koselleck criticized the utopian, hypocritical, and irresponsible features of modern politics, he also criticized the system of absolutism for being incapable of turning its subjects into citizens by allowing them to participate in politics. To illuminate this problem, Koselleck wrote:

> The absolute ruler kept his hand on each and every access to the state's machinery of command—on legislation, police and military, and he was further embroiled in a bitter struggle with the remnants of the old estate organizations in which the new elite was represented, at least, in part and could protect some of its interests. Completely closed to it, though, was the field of foreign policy, with its decisions of war and peace. These men, who determined the cultural physiognomy or bore the burdens of the state, were not allowed to decide its fate, for it was intrinsic to the system, to the absolutist order, that there was nothing at all for them to decide; they were all subjects. The tension between their increasing social weight, on the one hand, and the impossibility of lending political expression to that weight, on the other, was defining the historical situation in which the new society constituted itself. This characteristic was to be crucial to its nature and evolution. The critical split between morality and politics, noted by the bourgeois intelligentsia, resulted from this difference and exacerbated it at the same time.[41]

One of the implicit normative agendas in "Kritik und Krise" was therefore the necessity of striking a proper relation between morality and politics. In a speech given at the celebration of the fiftieth year of his *Promotion* in Heidelberg, Koselleck elaborated on this issue:

> The normative implication of my line of argumentation concerned precisely the mutual dependency of moral and politics. My critique of the utopia was based on the identified antagonism between those two fields, behind which the mauvaise foi or the hypocrisy lurked: The utopian visions for the future, with the realization of which the sovereign as tyrant should disappear, as there would be no more tyranny, which would also bring the wars to a permanent end—and, finally, even the state itself would be done away with by peaceful citizens (as seen in the Illuminati, in Mercier, then in Fichte, and finally in Marx and Engels): All these, which we know now, dangerous and blood-stained illusions followed the imbalances in the attempts to think and enforce morality without politics or politics without morality. Only by participation in the political power could the subjects become citizens. Only at that point could they take on political responsibility.[42]

Moreover, in a key chapter of the dissertation, Koselleck described how one of the Enlightenment thinkers had in fact outlined a scenario in which the politics of the state and societal morality (in the form of the critical voice of the bourgeoisie) coexist in such a way that politics might be conducted in a responsible manner. This thinker was John Locke. In his description of bourgeois public opinion, Locke had not, Koselleck argued, defined the moral content of the bourgeois critique, but concentrated instead upon identifying the origins and the form of the laws prevailing in the social life.[43] From this basis, Koselleck reasoned:

> … it remained entirely possible for their [the moral laws'] essential concretions to coincide with the laws of God or the state. Locke could simply allow the different powers to coexist without delimiting them one against another. His choice not to perceive them as antithetical is one of the particularities of his political theory.[44]

With this descriptive outline, Koselleck stated, Locke had provided the justification of the English form of government that had been founded in 1688 with the rising profile of the economically defined Whig aristocrats. The parliamentary interplay between leading representatives of society and the royal executive had, Koselleck added, served to prevent intensification in the opposition between morality and politics into a domestic political clash.

This was possible, as Koselleck saw it, because Locke made a distinction between morality and political law. On the one hand, the law of the state is affected directly and on the basis of the monopoly on the legitimate use of physical power. The moral law, on the other hand, is enforced indirectly, through the pressure of public opinion. Nonetheless, the moral law does have an effect within the state, because it is carried out by citizens (and not subjects), who are responsible for validating the laws of the state by openly voicing acceptance or disapproval of these laws as well as supplementing the authority of the state by subjecting public action to its moral authority.[45] As such, Locke had, in the eyes of Koselleck, outlined a new path to the partitioning of morality and politics; a political system in which stately politics and bourgeois morality as unfolding in the public sphere (and in the parliament) might coexist, not in an unnecessary competition that would ultimately lead to mutual exclusion, but in a responsible and sound system of checks and balances.[46]

However, according to Koselleck, the subjects of the absolutist states on the continent had been unable to make use of the possibilities outlined by Locke: "Unlike Locke, those citizens did not turn the subordination of politics into a coordinated, co-subordinated or correlated relation.

Instead, they radicalized the antithesis, accomplishing a polarization that was to become the symptom as well as the instigator of the looming political crisis."[47]

Describing the subsequent "inability of men to resolve the contradiction between morality and politics and the inability of people to transform their crisis-consciousness into rational and responsible political action," Koselleck's message in "Kritik und Krise" was—it has been said—that "those [utopian politicians] speaking in the name of humanity and morality should examine their real motives" and construct some sort of political system in which morality and politics is balanced in a more appropriate manner.[48]

But how was this to be done? According to which standards and rules were rational and responsible politics to be conducted in the modern world? While "Kritik und Krise" has been interpreted as devoid of constructive answers to these questions, its entire analysis was in fact informed by a set of more concrete political reflections that were closely related to its theoretical-methodological framework.

In the book, however, this framework was only referred to in a few unelaborated sentences in the introduction. Here Koselleck explained how the methodological approach was double-sided: "Depending on the focal point, the analysis will sometimes concentrate on textual interpretation and will in other passages deal with the social context." But, he added, "all the analyses begin nevertheless with the given, concrete situation . . . ."[49] The specific analytical aim of the method was, as stated elsewhere, to investigate "the function of the bourgeois thought and action within the setting of the absolutist system."[50] For this reason, the method renounced what Koselleck labeled *geistesgeschichtliche* abstractions."

The methodological ambition to combine interpretations of texts with social-historical context was pursued via a conceptual approach that unfolded in long passages and notes in which Koselleck explored the history of concepts such as "critique," "crisis," "revolution," and "politics" in writings of authors from Ancient Greece to the Enlightenment. This conceptual analysis was based on the theoretical premise that historical agents use language and concepts to create history. In the introduction, Koselleck wrote: "Historical philosophy provided the concepts to justify the rise of the bourgeoisie."[51] And in the analysis he provided several examples of how the Enlightenment thinkers used their action- and future-oriented concepts to single out the absolutist state as their enemy as a way of accelerating its destruction. Their strategy was to delegitimize the state by attributing to it a series of negatively loaded concepts and contrasting these to a series of positive counter-concepts. To explain how the Enlightenment thus unfolded as a battle between worldviews and concepts,

Koselleck wrote: "The series of concepts and counter-concepts that are dominant in the writings of the Enlightenment philosophers and their enemies, such as reason and revelation, freedom and despotism, nature and civilization, trade and war, morality and politics, light and darkness can easily be extended, without damaging the ability of those concepts to include and exclude their counter-concepts simultaneously."[52]

In "Kritik und Krise", the theoretical premise that historical agents use language and concepts to create history was related to the assumption that the main political and societal experiences of an epoch can be deciphered through its key concepts. Central in the study is first of all the concepts of "critique" and "crisis." On the one hand, the concept of critique, which Koselleck labeled a "*Schlagwort*" (slogan) of the eighteenth century,[53] layered the epochal experience of the need to judge everything in dualistic terms of right or wrong, moral or immoral, real or unreal, friend or enemy.[54] On the other, the concept of crisis embodied the perceived need of taking vital decisions for the future, which was connected to the epochal expectation of change and disintegration of the known social and political orders.[55] While emphasizing that the concept of crisis was in fact rarely used by the contemporaries and never in combination with the concept of critique,[56] Koselleck described how the practice of critique created an experience of crisis that again reinforced the critique. As such, in "Kritik und Krise" the two concepts assumed status of what Koselleck would later in *Geschichtliche Grundbegriffe* term leading concepts of the historical movement.

In later writings and interviews, Koselleck explained how, when he wrote his dissertation, he was encouraged by Schmitt to use dictionaries and encyclopedias as a way to investigate how different historical meanings have been attached to concepts and how conceptual meanings have changed.[57] However, Koselleck neither clarified in detail what it was that he found so useful in Schmitt's conceptual approach in the early 1950s nor explained how it was in fact related to a specific understanding of history and politics that offered a solution to the "world historical crisis" and a proposal as to how similar political conflicts might be avoided in the future. In order to illuminate these issues, what follows extends the contextualizing interpretation by examining the letter that Koselleck wrote to Schmitt on 21 January 1953, a few months before he finished his dissertation.[58]

Scientific Crisis: "Historicism" and the Relativity of Values

The letter stands out from the others in the collection because of its highly engaged tone, very clearly illustrative of Koselleck's intellectual concerns at the beginning of the 1950s. It is also distinguished by the detailed, chaotic, and determined way in which he explained the assumptions behind the analytical approach in the dissertation and unfolded certain other theoretical-methodological features that came to play important roles in his historical thinking. As is discussed in more detail later, it seems as if Koselleck, at the time of writing the letter, had only very recently developed these features. The letter thus reveals insights into a process of innovation in his historical thinking and gives us certain clues as to how this innovation came about.

Focusing on the letter, the chapter shows how many of Koselleck's renowned thoughts on history originated as solutions to the scientific and political crises that in his eyes marked the early 1950s. More precisely, it demonstrates how, in an attempt to solve these crises, Koselleck—with inspiration from Schmitt—deconstructed the theoretical-methodological fundaments of what he labeled "historicism," and—by reworking ideas from Heidegger—outlined a new anthropologically based concept of history, a concept that was supposed to describe the basic dynamics that create and structure all human history. This concept of history originated as an answer to a specific situation and as a highly philosophical enterprise, but it came to assume great importance in Koselleck's theoretical framework and empirical analysis.[59]

Koselleck began his letter by thanking Schmitt for his hospitality during a recent visit to Plettenberg and for Schmitt's continuous engagement in his work. He then explained precisely what he found so useful in Schmitt's thinking: "The difficulties of combining 'systematic' and 'historical' approaches from which present historical writing suffers—one only has to think of the separation between sociology and history!—have become increasingly clear to me, and I am thankful for your strict appeal always to trace the concepts back to their specific situation in order to clarify their meaning. There can be no doubt that this approach offers the only way out of historicism for the science of history, if it will persist at all, in so far as one understands historicism as the science of the 'relativization of values'."

With these lines, Koselleck initiated a devastating critique of what he referred to as "historicism" in several instances in the letter. Since its coinage at the end of the eighteenth century, this term has been assigned many different meanings in the German cultural science disciplines.[60] The roots of the way in which Koselleck and many of his contemporaries understood it are to be found in a complex history of reception of the term after Friedrich Nietzsche's famous 1874 essay "Vom Nutzen und Nachteil der Historie für das Leben."[61] Here Nietzsche attacked the widespread tendency in the nineteenth century, when history became a science, to historicize all aspects of life. The problem with this tendency was, Nietzsche argued, that the focus on the past was unrelated to, and thus constrained, people's ability to act and live in the present. In his view, the preoccupation with history invalidated all values by making them merely historical and relative to a situation given in time and space, thus undermining all foundations for judgment and action.

When, in the 1920s, the Protestant theologian Ernst Troeltsch followed up on Nietzsche's critique and called attention to the fundamental historicization of knowledge and thought, he labeled this phenomenon "historicism."[62] Similar to Nietzsche, Troeltsch believed that it had become impossible to think of an event from the past without subjecting it to the mechanism of historicism: to the idea that it could only be considered historically on its own terms and according to its own unique development. According to this idea, which had a certain influence on how historians in the Wilhelmine Era thought of the past and the present, all events had their individual characteristics, and, instead of being part of a larger, coherent plan or system, they floated around in an aimless and uncoordinated fashion in the flow of history.

What Troeltsch detected in his observations was the problem of relativism—that is, the absence of any parameter of judgment of the past and the present—as a threatening theoretical position. The pervasiveness of historical relativism came with Troeltsch to be known as the "crisis of historicism" and developed in the interwar years into a subject of complex debate in various disciplines and contexts. Troeltsch's solution to the problem of relativism was to connect historicism to a system of cultural values that was to be related to a scientific approach to history and a so-called philosophy of history. However, Troeltsch died in 1923, and he never articulated the specific content of his system of cultural values, which he had constructed with the intention of linking history to life by providing certain objective standards of orientation in the atmosphere of cultural crisis in the wake of World War I.

In the 1930s, Friedrich Meinecke, one of Germany's most prominent historians, gave the term historicism yet another meaning in his book *Die Entstehung des Historismus*.[63] Meinecke disconnected the problems of relativism from the term and constructed a definition of historicism as a way of thinking of history as composed of singular events and as a matter of individualities undergoing a process of unfolding and developing in a constant interplay with the world. More specifically, identifying the tradition of historicism with a movement of primarily German authors culminating with Goethe and Herder, Meinecke presented historicism as a positive and, in a Hegelian sense, historically progressive phenomenon corresponding to the logic of the historical philosophy that Troeltsch had sketched out in the previous decade. Meinecke's interpretation of historicism had a considerable impact on the understanding of it within the German historical profession. When the term was again debated (and criticized) in the late 1960s and early 1970s, it was often his interpretation of historicism as a progressive and positive German cultural phenomenon that was discussed.

Following up on the problems raised by Nietzsche and Troeltsch, and with Meinecke as his main target of critique, Koselleck's attempt to deconstruct historicism once and for all was inspired by the connection of history and a very specific type of sociology via the conceptual approach, described in the passage cited above.[64] To be sure, Koselleck did not disagree with the hermeneutical claim that true historical thinking must take account of its own historicity. But—he explained to Schmitt, fusing the meanings of historicism articulated by Troeltsch and Meinecke—the "relativity of values" in historicism becomes a problem when the role of the historian in the process of historical writing is ignored. It was, he wrote, exactly this isolation that caused Friedrich Meinecke, among others, to view "the values" as something that exists "in themselves." Koselleck thus drew attention to what he saw as a fatal theoretically methodological flaw in historicism. In their radical claim to historicize all values, historicists forgot to historicize themselves and thus, more or less unconsciously, carried certain time-bound values into their analyses. It was this self-contradiction and the values connected with it that Koselleck elaborated on in the following page and a half in his letter to Schmitt from January 1953.

The elaboration centered around two specific issues between which Koselleck ventured back and forth. First of all, he pointed to the fact that most modern values, including those of historicism, were products of history, and that their origins were rooted in the historical philosophies of the eighteenth century (Koselleck's object of study in "Kritik und Krise"). Hence he criticized what he believed to be a disregard among historians of the historical character and status of the modern historical philosophies. He wrote: "To relate the values to history and to view them as a part of a changing process, as the historians have done . . . , remains an insufficient approach as long as the tacit presuppositions of historical philosophy remain unquestioned. The so-called relativization of values through inserting them into the historical process is historical-philosophically biased and specifically unhistorical, since it is only made possible through a blurred vanishing point in the past."

Secondly, parallel to his historicization of historicism, Koselleck elaborated on the specific characteristics of the historically-philosophically charged values that historicists carried with them from the eighteenth century into twentieth century historical analysis. He wrote: "These tendencies and their connection to the historical 'process' . . . always remain tied to the linear temporal construction of history, whose evidence is mathematical and historical-philosophical." In other words, historicism's adoption of historical philosophy revealed a linear, unified and progressive view of history that is focused on the future.

The attempt to plan and accelerate history was exactly what Koselleck's analysis had focused on in "Kritik und Krise". As he was undoubtedly aware, Schmitt had criticized historicism on this point, too. This was, for example, the case in *Die Buribunken* from 1918, which was essentially a mocking critique of the, according to Schmitt, exaggerated belief in societal and scientific progress in nineteenth century historicism—a critique that Koselleck wrote about in the article *Die Verzeitlichung der Utopie* thirty years later.[65]

In Koselleck's view, as stated in the letter, it was the ever-present possibility of conflict, crisis, and war rather than steady, overarching progress that characterized modernity, and his verdict on historicism was unequivocal: "It is a residual product, that manifests the power and endurance of the bourgeois way of thinking, and not as Meinecke thinks, a genuine achievement. It is less an answer to our situation, as it is a part of the situation, since it can not conceptualize it, which would in fact be its purpose."

It was exactly this answer that Koselleck was looking for in his letter to Schmitt. He did not, however, find the full answer in Schmitt's work. Instead, he found a sociological, systematic, and supposedly more realistic way of thinking, based on analysis of concepts, with which he wanted to blow away the smoke that seemingly prevented him from finding the answer. This smoke was caused by what Schmitt and Koselleck understood as a theoretically, but also politically naïve and dangerous, legacy of German historicism, represented by Friedrich Meinecke and his famous book *Die Idee der Staatsräson* from 1924.[66]

To understand Koselleck's attitude toward the book, a brief introduction to Meinecke is needed.[67] Meinecke was born in 1862, the son of a civil servant. After studies in German language and literature, history, and philosophy in Berlin under famous figures such as Johann Gustav Droysen, Heinrich von Sybel, and Heinrich von Treitschke, he earned his dissertation in 1886 under Reinhold Koser. In 1887, he started working in the Prussian archives, and he achieved his *habilitation* in 1896 under Sybel in Berlin. From 1893 he was one of the editors, and since

1896, the main editor of the *Historische Zeitschrift*. He became professor in Strasbourg in 1901; in Freiburg from 1906, at the Berliner Friedrich Wilhelm-University (which in 1949 was renamed the Humboldt University of Berlin) in 1914; and in 1948 he became the first *Rektor* at the Free University of Berlin, where the department of history in 1951 was named after him. He died in 1954—the same year Koselleck finished his studies in Heidelberg.

With his first famous book *Weltbürgertum und Nationalstaat* from 1907,[68] Meinecke, together with Wilhelm Dilthey und Ernst Troeltsch, had become widely respected and recognized as one of the paragons of the history of ideas. In the book, he portrayed the history of the German national state from the Prussian reforms to Bismarck as a harmonic and progressive development, and he sought to demonstrate how the thought of poets, writers, and philosophers contributed to the development of nationalism and was reflected in the minds of the political leaders who achieved German unification. In his next great work, *Die Idee der Staatsräson*, Meinecke turned to investigate the interests and tendencies of the great powers since the sixteenth century. He came to the conclusion that statesmen always have to strike a balance between dual concepts of politics—such as Ethos and Kratos, morality and power, spirit and nature—to find the right *Staatsräson* (reason of state).

Meinecke's view of history and politics in *Die Idee der Staatsräson* was intensely debated among its contemporary readers, and, in a 1926 review, Carl Schmitt subjected it to a devastating criticism.[69] Schmitt was especially critical of what he believed was a poor conceptuality and primitive opposition between power politics and morality in the book: an opposition, which in his eyes, depended on and justified a kind of superiority deriving from a constant change of standpoint, an eternal movement backwards and forwards, that legitimized the refusal among German historicists to take any political responsibility in the present.

Whereas Schmitt's critique of Meinecke's idealism was focused on the political question of *who decides?*, Koselleck was, in his letter to Schmitt, attempting to dismantle what he conceived of as an erroneous approach to the study of history: he wanted to radicalize the project of historicism. In fact, this aim also informed "Kritik und Krise", as witnessed in a long note in the original version of the dissertation that illuminates more closely how Koselleck drew on Schmitt's writings and the method of conceptual history in this endeavor. In the note, with the following words, he outlined precisely how he viewed the differences between Schmitt and Meinecke:

Unlike C. Schmitt, who always elucidates the historical connection between intellectually convincing evidence and the related political and sociological structures, [Meinecke's] historical magnum opus on the question of "morality and politics," "Die Idee der Staatsräson," is entirely a-historical in its approach. The basic concepts Meinecke deploys: "power and justice," "nature and spirit," etc., are conceived of as invariable for the whole period from Machiavelli to Treitschke. On the one hand, Meinecke uses the polemical terms of the eighteenth century in a historical fashion, that is to say: reconciling them by means of their mutual relativization. In this way, all findings are equivocal; unequivocal is only Meinecke's personal notion of the "reason of state," which is for him an extra-historical magnitude.[70]

With this theoretical-methodological justification of his extensive use of conceptual history in "Kritik und Krise", Koselleck left no doubt that, similar to Schmitt, he found Meinecke's approach in *Die Idee der Staatsräson* theoretically-methodologically naïve. Because it portrayed concepts as timeless and unchangeable—and not as having been created in historically concrete situations by specific actors with shifting and conflicting motives and aims—Meinecke's historicism was allegedly utterly incapable of explaining how concepts are created and how they function and change.

However, in the cited note, Koselleck not only portrayed Meinecke's approach as theoretically naïve due to its ignorance of the social-historical context and significance of language. He also portrayed the approach as politically dangerous, by indicating that Meinecke's "unhistorical" interpretation of the past made him blind to how ideas are used for specific political purposes in the present. Koselleck thus concluded his note with an indirect criticism of how, in an attempt to fit the turbulent political events of the Weimar Republic into an allegedly idealistic and optimistic understanding of history as an ongoing clash of higher moral principles and energies, Meinecke had purportedly removed himself from reality and thus the possibility of taking a responsible standpoint toward contemporary events.[71]

In contrast to Meinecke, as he saw him, Koselleck wanted to position himself toward the contemporary situation, and in conceptual history he had seemingly found a method that would enable him to do so. However, Koselleck aimed at more than unearthing a method.

The Limit of Relativism: Heidegger's Notion of "Finality"

Koselleck continued his reflections on historicism in the letter by making a radical proposal:

Historicism has reached the resigned conclusion that the relativity of all historical events and values must be subjected to total 'relativity.' As far as I see, this is the starting point for every analysis of historicity. One should—through this still very historiographical insight—once and for all break through to a historical ontology, which is not merely the latest methodological approach, but the beginning of a conceptualization, which makes it possible to cut the historical philosophy off from its water supply and consequently give an answer to our concrete situation.

It was the lack of this kind of "ontology"—and, consequently, the lack of stable concepts—that prevented Koselleck from attaining a better grip on his analyses. Though he praised the sociologist Hans Freyer's *Weltgeschichte Europas* (1948) for having achieved a great deal in this direction, it is evident that Koselleck found the basis for his ontology elsewhere.[72] He wrote: "The reduction of all intellectual expressions to the historical situation puts an end to all further relativization forwards and backwards, up and down. The finality (*Endlichkeit*) of the historical human beings should thus be the centre of attention, not in regard to individual existence . . . , but with respect to history's eternal coming into being: that is, with respect to the structures of a 'situation' without which such a thing as history would not exist."

What Koselleck did in these passages was to present the foundation of what he called an "ontology of history" by which he meant certain fundamental existential structures of the human condition—or "situation"—that supposedly create and structure all human history. As revealed by the discursive features in the citation, he located this foundation in Heidegger's *Sein und Zeit*. Leaving to one side the first part of *Sein und Zeit*, which examined the philosophical tradition of asking about the meaning of Being (*Sein*), Koselleck focused on the analysis of the historicity of Being that is found in the second part of Heidegger's book. Here, in an attempt to uncover the ontological conditions of human existence, Heidegger argued that, unfolding between birth and death, Being is an essentially temporal and historical phenomenon—that for humans, *to be is to be in time*—and that any analysis of human awareness, behavior, and possibilities should begin from the fact that we are thrown into and must act in the world, which includes the possibility and the inevitability of one's own mortality or "finality."

Koselleck evidently agreed with Heidegger's belief that human existence is conditioned by the limitations and possibilities given by its temporal-existential condition, and not by any metaphysical power in history.[73] But Koselleck's project was different than Heidegger's. What he did in the cited passage was to present Heidegger's notion of finality as a (brutal) fact of human existence, which no relativity can permeate and no human life can escape. It was from this notion that he wanted to develop an ontological outline of what creates and shapes all human history. Koselleck continued: "History is not transcendent for human beings, even though people die, but because it encompasses a finality of human things, which permanently questions the historical space that every human being is assigned to. The teaching of this finality is as eschatology also to be given ontological primacy in all historical sciences."

However, to outline this "historical space" within which all human beings move, and which delineates the basic conditions of the humanly possible, Koselleck found it necessary to go beyond Heidegger's notion of finality.[74] More concretely, he found it necessary to add a number of further existential features, or facts about the human existence to the one of finality. He wrote: "Master and slave, friend and enemy, gender (*Geschlechtlichkeit*) and generation and all geopolitical questions belong to here. Heidegger has passed by all these phenomena in the course of his existential analysis in *Sein und Zeit*, and the result shows in his history of Being as an all encompassing construction, which is often made fun of due to the idea of an intellectual fall from grace after the pre-socratic philosophers—in a way similar to Jaspers's *Ziele und Ursprünge* (....)."

With these sentences, Koselleck completed his project of, first, deconstructing the approach of historicism, and subsequently—revising Heidegger's notion of finality and adding to it four other conceptual pairs—laying out an assumption of what creates and limits all human history, and of the conditions, or the situation, which human beings are always thrown into and in which they must act. These four conceptual pairs comprised those of friend/enemy, taken from Schmitt; master/slave, taken from Hegel; man/woman, and parents/children (which belong to the concept of generativity, and which Koselleck later integrated with Arendt's concept of nativity), and the geopolitical concepts (that he in later writings specified as "inner" and "outer," taken from Hobbes).[75]

Koselleck's stance on Heidegger's notion of finality was distanced, as is demonstrated by the subtly mocking critique of Heidegger's attitude in *Sein und Zeit* toward the history of philosophical thought—a history he (in Koselleck's eyes) conceived in terms of a teleological total construction following an eschatological scheme with Heidegger himself in the role of the savior.[76] According to Koselleck, the critical deficiency in Heidegger's analysis of Being, which opened the door to such historical-philosophical traits, was to be found in its reliance on a monolithic notion of human existence, according to which human beings are born and die on their own, a notion leading to an impoverished and ultimately equally monolithic notion of human history. It was to make up for this deficiency that Koselleck added the four conceptual pairs to the one of finality. With the categories, he wanted to rework Heidegger's analysis of Being into a larger anthropological system of human existence that emphasizes the importance of interpersonal and social relations in human life—or, in other words, he wanted to outline a historical space in which humans are open to co-exist and conflict with their fellow beings. What the study of history is left with, according to Koselleck, is the ontology of Being, but Heidegger's finality must be supplemented with counter-concepts that Koselleck takes up from other authors, including Schmitt.

By means of these concepts, Koselleck could integrate a variety of ever-contested social relations into the foundations of historical writing. Thus he was able to accommodate a Schmittian conception of an essentially political society in permanent conflict, and a normative notion of how such conflicts were to be contained, in his ideas for an ontology of history. In this way, the latter became inseparably connected with the domain of political thought. This anthropological way of bringing in social considerations with the counter-concepts aimed to criticize and undermine the very foundation of the historical philosophies, the idea of a unified and universal history, and to replace them with a framework that thematized how human history unfolds in different ways, as histories, within the described historical space.

That the categories are supposed to emphasize the importance of social relations and conflict in human life and thus thematize plurality is not stated explicitly in the letter from 1953. However, from the speech titled "Historik und Hermeneutik" that Koselleck gave on the occasion of Hans-Georg Gadamer's eighty-fifth birthday in 1985, we can conclude that this was the general intention.[77] With the aim of outlining what he called a Historik,[78] the doctrines of the conditions of possible history, Koselleck here echoed and elaborated on the basic argumentative line from the letter. This included a presentation of his conceptual pairs (which he no longer called ontological, but anthropological) and an account of how these formed part of a project of elaborating Heidegger's notion of finality away from a monolithic idea of history and into an idea of histories that are created in a given historical space in which human beings interact and conflict with each other.

Summing up his arguments as to how Sein und Zeit with its singular notion of history fail to take account of the many conflicts and contingencies that supposedly characterize the human interaction and, so, the conditions of possible history, Koselleck wrote:

> There is therefore a need for oppositional definitions that push forward this temporal finality, in which tensions, conflicts, ruptures, inconsisten-

cies appear, which can never be given an immediate solution, but a dia-chronic one, in which all units of political-social action must partake, whether it leads to survival or death. Friend and enemy, parents-children, generational successions, sooner or later, the tensions between high and low, as well as the tensions between inside and outside as well as between secret and public—they are all constitutive for the rise, the course and the effectiveness of histories. We have so far aimed at a theoretical outline, which is aimed at developing Heidegger's existential analysis in a direction that Heidegger did not envision, that is, to understand what makes histo-ries possible, where Heidegger was content with the category of historicity. This category gave the experience of relativity within historicism a durable positive interpretation, without contributing to a transcendental substan-tiation of the pluralities of the actual histories.[79]

Aiming at an analytical framework in which relativism and utopia-nism would be replaced by the perspective of pluralism, Koselleck drew attention to how, in his reworking of Heidegger's analysis of Being into a larger anthropological system of possible human history, he picked up on a theme that Karl Löwith had presented in his 1928 *Habilitation Das Individuum in der Rolle des Mitmenschen*.[80] Löwith had written his study under the supervision of Heidegger, but with the latter's *Sein und Zeit* as his main target of critique. Where Heidegger focused on the individual being, Löwith emphasized that human beings must always reflect on their social relations to other beings: A human being is always a person that ex-ists through his or her social roles and is as such defined as a fellow human being and through his or her fellow human beings.[81]

Löwith understood his analysis of the human *Miteinandersein* and *Mit-einandersprechen* as a contribution to the field of philosophical anthropol-ogy, a subfield that was expanding rapidly in the years after World War I.[82] In this period, due to an increasing doubt in societal progress and in human capabilities, which converged with the changing status of philoso-phy vis-à-vis the sciences, attempts were made to develop a new funda-ment for human self-understanding, among other things with references to biology and through comparisons of humans and animals. The works of Max Scheler (1874–1928), Helmut Plessner (1892–1985), and Arnold Gehlen (1904–1976) stood at the center of philosophical anthropology. In spite of many differences, each of these figures was trying to rethink philosophy, in the hope that a natural science approach to philosophical anthropology would lead to a more secure knowledge about what defines the human condition, character, and possibilities.

After 1945, features from this tradition of philosophical anthropology influenced many disciplines in German academia, including psychology, pedagogic, psychiatry, philosophy, and sociology, the discipline in which both Plessner and Gehlen acquired professorial chairs in the postwar years.[83] Koselleck was familiar with the tradition of philosophical anthropology through reading Gehlen during his years in Heidelberg,[84] and although his project differed from and was apparently not directly inspired by the works of Scheler, Plessner or Gehlen, he evidently shared their ambition to define the human condition and capabilities with anthropological categories based on concrete and empirical observations.

What the letter thus illustrates is how Koselleck developed his anthropologically based categories as a scientific answer and political cure to what he conceived as the demands and dangers of historicism and modern historical philosophy. This was an answer that aimed to take account of the social relations existing among human beings, and which set pluralism against utopianism and relativism in order to understand (historically) and contain (politically) the potential conflict in human societies.

As for the political dimension, the strict formalism of the categories was supposed to bypass all forms of (utopian) meaning, unity or direction in history. The categories were exclusively intended to sketch out the limits of what is humanly possible and to point out the dangers in ignoring these limits. On the one hand, they represented the idea that history can unfold in different ways, depending on how the categories are filled out by human agents; on the other hand, they were meant to point to the eternal potential for conflict, which is embedded in human nature and must be considered and contained in every planning of the present and the future if the aim is a responsible and durable political order. In other words, the categories were supposed to comprise the *conditio humana* that can never be done away with, nor shaped entirely according to human desire and ideology. As for their scientific dimension, Koselleck considered the categories compatible with a notion of radical historicity (the idea that all things are subject to change in time and space), but because their conceptual distinctions in a formalistic sense transcend history, he saw also in them a timeless and hence analytically stable viewpoint from which historical change could be described, explained, and evaluated. With his categories, Koselleck thus tried to answer the famous request made by Friedrich Meinecke after his reading in 1923 of Ernst Troeltsch's book on the "crisis of historicism": "Everything flows, show me a place where I can stand."[85]

Koselleck, it should be added, was far from the only scholar to criticize historical philosophy and historicism in the postwar period. Confrontations with moral, political, and idealistic universalism, as embodied in all-encompassing ideas about the progressive course of history, were frequently articulated in writings of the older generations of scholars—including Löwith, Adorno, and Schmitt. Then, from the late 1940s onwards, such confrontations developed into something like an intellectual fashion among members of the generation of younger scholars, who began their studies in the first decade after the war and established their positions in German academia through a critique of traditions.

What is important to understand about Koselleck's theoretical-methodological efforts at the beginning of the 1950s is that they were not only directed toward solving a crisis within the historical discipline. They were also directed toward solving a specific political crisis.

Political Crisis and the *Weltbürgerkrieg*

Directly after having presented the ontology, Koselleck explained to Schmitt how its purpose was determined by the contemporary political situation. He wrote: "The starting point of a historical-ontological analysis must . . . be the contemporary civil war." And he added that by means of the categories in Schmitt's 1950 book *Nomos der Erde* it would be possible to disprove and counter the American and Soviet understandings of the civil war.[86] Hence, the letter not only shows how, in line with Schmitt, Koselleck conceived the confrontation between the United States and the Soviet Union as a *Weltbürgerkrieg*. It also shows how he believed that the prospect of the *Weltbürgerkrieg* in the 1950s could be understood as well as countered through a disclosing of its historical roots. In other words, for Koselleck, it was possible to find an answer to the situation. This is clear from the subsequent lines in his letter to Schmitt from January 1953: "The truth of such a historical ontology should be demonstrable by means of every correct prognosis, and it must also have a prognostic character itself, inasmuch as it can devalue the historical-philosophical prophesies (Whether or not it has power to do so is another question, but that is all the 'science of history' can achieve as a science)."

Koselleck evidently thought of historical writing in practical terms. Like Nietzsche, he wanted to make history useful for life. Put simply, his aim of analyzing the past was to criticize the present as a way to influence the direction of the future. He sought not to formulate specific social-political visions, programs, or plans for the future, but to point to the anthropological conditions for history and politics as well as to the dangers in ignoring these conditions. More specifically, Koselleck was hoping for a mode of political order that respects human finality—and in which categories such as friend and enemy, and master and slave are filled out not in excessively asymmetrical fashions that generate exclusion, aggression, and conflict, but in ways that aim at political recognition and plurality.

Only by these measures, according to Koselleck, could the modern world be saved from self-destruction.

Viewed against the background of the letter, Koselleck's diagnosis of the political situation in the early 1950s involved evidently not only a critical historical deconstruction of the modern world, but also a set of constructive ideas about how a more responsible and durable political order might be created, though he did not recommend a concrete model or ideology on which this order should be based. When some readers nevertheless interpreted "Kritik und Krise" as a politically conservative manifesto, it was partially due to a combination of two dimensions of the book. First, the normative implications were not explicitly spelled out in the analysis: It was simply left to the reader to decipher Koselleck's perspective on how secular justifications for individual freedom might be handled successfully in modern politics, that is, how the entry of morality into politics can be solved in a peaceful and pragmatic manner by striking a proper balance between the two opposites and by acknowledging the *conditio humana*. Hence, center stage in the study is given neither to the Locke interpretation, the critique of absolutism, nor to the scientific-political project, but to the pessimistic critique of the aporias and dead-ends of the modern world and to the profound doubt in the capability and durability of political democracy.[87]

Secondly, this critique was to a certain degree constructed through interpretative themes and notions that were at the time associated with the work of conservative thinkers. To be sure, in the 1950s, political pessimism, critique of the Enlightenment, and a vision of progressive ideas of history as the vehicle of the contemporary crisis were voiced by thinkers from various political camps, however these topoi held a particular stronghold among conservative scholars and debaters, many of whom had voiced their dissatisfaction with liberal democratic forms of government and argued for the necessity for a strong state by criticizing the Weimar *Öffentlichkeit* (public sphere) in the 1920s and 1930s.[88]

Among the topoi in "Kritik und Krise" that were associated with conservative thinkers were Koselleck's interpretation of the contemporary confrontation between the United States and the Soviet Union as a "world historical crises" that had its roots in and was structured similarly to previous civil wars. The idea of interpreting the political events of the twentieth century as an ongoing *Weltbürgerkrieg der Ideologien* (World Civil War of Ideologies) had been used with distinct political intentions by conservative thinkers such as Ernst Jünger and Carl Schmitt from the 1930s onwards.[89] While, in the late 1930s, Schmitt had legitimized the Nazi wars in Europe by portraying them as a defense against the universalistic historical philosophies of liberalism and communism, in the postwar era his references to the *Weltbürgerkrieg der Ideologien* served to downplay German guilt in World War II (as it reduced National Socialism to a minor event in the age of historical philosophies) and to position postwar Germany as a victim in the ongoing ideological battle for world power between the United States and the Soviet Union that was culminating in the Cold War. In this scenario, a vision of a de-radicalized or technocratic conservatism, which was to revolve not around a charismatic leader, but around institutions and structures, appeared as a bulwark and an alternative to the destructive ideologies of communism and liberalism.[90] Schmitt's reference to the *Weltbürgerkrieg der Ideologien* went hand in hand with private writings in which he downplayed the German war crimes and his own activities during National Socialism by labeling the trials in Nüremberg a product of the moral discrimination of the victorious powers.[91]

Like many other German historians at the time, Koselleck focused in "Kritik und Krise" on liberalism and communism in explaining the conflicts and the wars of the twentieth century and in constructing a theory of modern totalitarianism that did not deal directly with the role of National Socialism. However, he did not attempt to exonerate certain German traditions from the past, nor did he portray a vision of German conservatism as an alternative "third way" between liberalism and communism on the contemporary political scene. He referred instead to the "world historical crises" with a distinctively different agenda than Schmitt.

This agenda connected analytically to Schmitt's ideas of a *Weltbürgerkrieg* via the interpretation of how an apolitical bourgeois morality originated in the Enlightenment that had visions of spreading its moral authority all over the world, that is, of manifesting as a *Weltbürgertum* (cosmopolitanism).[92] When, to follow Nicolaus Sombart, "*Weltbürgerkrieg* [in "Kritik und Krise"] refers to *Weltbürgertum*,"[93] it is because, in line with Schmitt, Koselleck argued that the traditional laws of international conflict were being effectively reshaped with the diffusion of a revolutionary and aggressive universalistic spirit.

The core of this argument is found in Koselleck's Hobbes chapter on the rise of the absolute state.[94] With references to Schmitt's *Nomos der Erde*, Koselleck here described the rise of the traditional system of international law as a system—the Jus Publicum Europaeum—which was based on a strict separation of a state's interior from the mutual external and political relations among states.[95] In this system, Koselleck explained, states possessed the same right to wage war against other states, and as free agents in the system, the sovereigns of the states were subject to their conscience alone and not to a common and institutionalized authority. According to Koselleck, the problem that in the field of morality only one side in the quarrel can be right was neutralized by a reality-oriented political reason. And while the system allowed sovereign rulers to turn the inner tensions out and thus avoid civil war, the mutual recognition of states and of transparent rules of international warfare created, Koselleck argued, an *europäisches Gleichgewicht* (European equilibrium), in which each one understood each other as *justus hostis*, a rightful enemy.

Koselleck's interpretation of the transformation of this system was not as explicitly outlined as its origins. However, it can be deduced from the way in which he connected the moral laws of the *Weltbürgertum* to the "world historical crises." What replaced the allegedly reality-oriented, responsible, and transparent Jus Publicum Europaeum was thus a non-defined, irresponsible and non-transparent system of international law, where with reference to abstract notions of moral and ideological justice, states can randomly break the traditional principle of non-intervention among states, and where ideas of absolute enmity opened the way to a permanent, unbound, and worldwide use of violence. It was this condition that Koselleck appealed political leaders to put an end to by reinserting a more responsible basis for political decision-making in international law—a basis that was founded on a pluralistic instead of an antagonistic understanding of politics. Hence, while taking over elements from Schmitt's historical interpretation of the *Weltbürgerkrieg*, which relied on the idealized model of the Jus Publicum Europaeum and on a specific set of polemical anti-British (and eventually anti-American) topoi that were born in the period around World War I, Koselleck's political agenda thus diverged crucially from Schmitt's.[96]

Seen retrospectively, the allusions to the "world historical crisis" in "Kritik und Krise" stand in Koselleck's work as a symbol of the analytical language that Kesting, Sombart, and he developed as students in Heidelberg during their intellectual exchanges with each other and with Schmitt.[97] "You have so far grasped our time in concepts with which we from the younger generation have conceptualized this epoch," Koselleck symptomatically wrote to Schmitt not long before submitting his dissertation.[98] On his way into the disciplinary field, as he refined and expanded his analytical language, Koselleck left behind many of the notions that he had picked up from Schmitt—including the one of *Weltbürgerkrieg*. In fact, after "Kritik und Krise", he never again alluded to it.

In contrast to the notion of *Weltbürgerkrieg*, the anthropological pairs that Koselleck presented in his letter to Schmitt from January 1953 became a central discursive feature in his work. They came first of all to provide a basic theoretical fundament and starting point for his attempts to thematize history in the plural. This is clear from several published writings, where, to counter notions of relativism and in discussion of the relation between time, language, and history, Koselleck referred to the conceptual pairs as features capable of stabilizing and structuring investigations into human history.[99] Most famous in this respect is the mentioned speech "Historik und Hermeneutik."[100]

In addition, the anthropological categories came to provide a certain thematic and argumentative unity to Koselleck's work, as he managed to connect his theoretical assumptions to his practical research by analyzing the themes comprised by the categories in empirical analyses and to use them as a reference point from which to assess human history and politics. These connections are in fact already made in the dissertation: Although the categories are not presented as part of a larger theoretical arrangement, the analysis aims to investigate and evaluate how different units of political action have dealt with the anthropologically given limits and possibilities as found in the human "finality: and in the friend/enemy, master/slave, and inner/outer relations.[101]

But—we might ask, to illuminate this issue in more depth—to what extent was the concept of history in Koselleck's letter to Schmitt a result of only very recent reflections? On the one hand, the intense tone and the chaotic structure of the letter suggest that the concept was in a process of development. It should also be stressed that Koselleck presented his ideas after thanking Schmitt for taking an interest in his work once again during his recent visit to Plettenberg. This might indicate that he was trying to present a comprehensive plan of his new project, perhaps encouraged by his conversations with Schmitt.

In line with this, it is worth noting that Koselleck made only one reference to Heidegger's notion of "finality" in the dissertation, and that this itself was relatively undeveloped. This is in a note in which he states that, in his Hobbes interpretation, the political scientist Leo Strauss has shown that "the fear of (in particular the violent) death is for Hobbes the first quality of conscience (*Gewissensqualität*) and the most important expression of a sensible consciousness." Koselleck continues: "If one ignores that the sharp opposition between the fear of death and the vanity that Strauss has shown in Hobbes was worked out with an eye on Heidegger's categories in *Sein und Zeit*: *Eigentlichkeit* and *Verfallenheit*, there still remains a factual inner relation. Both thinkers, Hobbes and Heidegger in *Sein und Zeit*, proceed from *Sorge* (anxiety) to death—without stating anything about the afterlife—to develop categories that in their apparent formality could not avoid the accusation of being immoral."[102]

Regardless of whether Koselleck's interpretation does justice to Strauss's analysis, the cited passage indicates that in the early 1950s, his investigation into the political roots of the modern world convinced him of the need to outline a new fundament for the study of history, which he did not have time to develop sufficiently to integrate into his dissertation, and that the anthropological concept of history was completed after he finished "Kritik und Krise". Perhaps it was in this period that Koselleck pursued his idea of reading Heidegger anthropologically, with Löwith and alongside Hobbes, thus expanding Schmitt's interpretation of *Leviathan* in a philosophical direction. Seen from this perspective, Koselleck's letter to Schmitt suggests that a breakthrough in his historical thinking took place in the period of its writing.

However, in creating the concept, Koselleck obviously drew on notions and ideas that had been familiar to him for some time, and which he to a certain extent had already applied in the dissertation. This raises the question of whether Koselleck had in fact developed an elaborate version of the concept but chose not to include it in the study. Further investigations into unpublished material are needed to answer this question. However, there can be no doubt that the concept and "Kritik und Krise" was created in processes in which Koselleck had to balance scientific theory, political concerns and social-institutional factors, and in which he could not openly announce the sum of his aims and intentions.

Here we touch upon issues related to the impact of the social situation on the content of a book that was obviously meant as a statement in the field; a statement with which Koselleck sought to establish himself as an innovative scholar within the scholarly community. But, to speak with Löwith's analysis of the human *Miteinandersein* and *Miteinandersprechen* in *Das Individuum in der Rolle des Mitmenschen*, Koselleck was navigating among fellow scholars in the disciplinary field. In order to acquire a position within that field, he had to balance his individualism with a certain conformity to the given standards, norms, and hierarchies.

In the following, we take a closer look at the processes through which Koselleck created and positioned his project (and himself) within the scholarly community. We begin with a more detailed analysis of the ways in which he drew on and deviated from the intellectual discourses that he found in Martin Heidegger and Carl Schmitt, respectively, and in the historical profession. Koselleck's dialogue with these discourses provides clues not only to how he constructed and gave meaning to his intellectual project in the 1940s, but also to an understanding of his intellectual profile more generally.

The Scholar as a Fellow Scholar

One of the striking aspects about the origins of "Kritik und Krise" and the related concept of history is the degree to which Koselleck constructed his understanding of the political and scientific constellations of the early 1950s through revisiting academic writings and debates from decades earlier, especially from the 1920s and the 1930s. It was also the period during which discussions of historicism and philosophical anthropology had peaked, and Friedrich Meinecke, Carl Schmitt, and Martin Heidegger wrote their principle works. Whereas Schmitt and Heidegger had attempted to define the essential problems and tasks in the spheres of politics and philosophy, respectively, in the 1920s, Koselleck used their works to conceptualize and resolve what he experienced as scientific and political crises in the 1950s.

While drawing inspiration from Schmitt and Heidegger, Koselleck was obviously very conscious about the difference between his and their projects. In outlining his concept of history, he picked out specific assumptions and concepts from their writings and substantially reworked these to fit his own purposes. A common feature of his reception of notions from works such as *Der Begriff des Politischen* and *Sein und Zeit* is that he substantially formalized and depoliticized their analytical potential before he applied them to a historical analysis.

At the same time, Koselleck encountered and dealt with these two sources of inspiration in very different ways. It is worth noting that, for analytical purposes, Koselleck only used Heidegger's early work *Sein und Zeit*. The same was true of Löwith and with Gadamer, who remodelled Heidegger's temporal and hermeneutic investigations into the question of Being toward a history of human self-understanding and awareness. Koselleck was later to follow in Gadamer's footsteps.[103] However, with its focus on death, his first intellectual encounter with Heidegger, that is, his reworking of the notion of finality, had a more existential twist to it than Gadamer's. This difference is presumably attributable to their different generational and personal experiences: unlike Gadamer, Koselleck had experienced human finality at close range during and after World War II and subsequently constructed his scholarly identity and work around this experience.

On several occasions Koselleck described his personal relations with Heidegger as having been very formal. One example is found in a letter to Schmitt from January 1977, where, whilst evidently deeply impressed by the intellectual capabilities that Heidegger displayed in Gadamer's colloquiums, Koselleck talked of "the schoolmasterly manner of Heidegger": "I have never really blamed the old man from the mountain," Koselleck added, "since it was after all very instructive."[104]

In the letter to Schmitt from January 1977, the same ironic tone is present when Koselleck explained how, in the postwar years, *Sein und Zeit* presented a normative program and a pathos toward which he was deeply skeptical.[105] Looking back at his meeting with Heidegger in Gadamer's colloquiums in Heidelberg, Koselleck recalled how he back then had labeled *Sein und Zeit* a *Koppelschlossphilosophie* (buckle-belt philosophy): "As I returned from captivity, still marked by it, and read Heidegger, I conceived *Sein und Zeit* as a kind of *Koppelschlossphilosophie*, which is certainly not justified, when one looks at its long-term impact. I have learned as much from this book as I have learned from your *Begriff des Politischen*."[106]

Koppelschloss is the German word for the belt buckles of German soldiers, which during World War II had been inscribed with the religious slogan *Gott mit uns* (God with us).[107] The imagery of these passages therefore served to mark an affinity between the ethos of militarism and what Koselleck interpreted as the existential, heroic, and quasi-religious pathos of *Sein und Zeit*.[108] Returning from war and captivity, he seems to have been of the opinion that Heidegger's philosophical program, which drew on notions such as authenticity, destiny, and death—and urged a *Freisein zum Tode*—had launched a book that from the 1920s onwards could function as some sort of quasi-militaristic and quasi-religious soldier's vademecum.[109] Therefore, Koselleck aimed at a more concrete and formalistic way of thinking than he detected in *Sein und Zeit*. This included both getting rid of what he referred to as historical-philosophical traits and normative dimensions in the book.

One of the fundamental differences between the projects of Koselleck and Heidegger can be described using an observation made by Jacob Taubes on Koselleck's reception of *Sein und Zeit*: "[Koselleck's] historical writing will not describe a Being toward death (*Sein zum Tode*), but instead take the sting of death away."[110] This observation might be qualified with the perspective that Koselleck drew on the notion of finality to draw attention to the fragile existential condition of human beings, which—in his eyes—was constantly put at risk in the age of modernity, where the humanly possible was either misunderstood or ignored. Instead of acknowledging the anthropologically given human limits and possibilities as encompassed in the human finality and in the friend/enemy and master/slave relations, modern man envisioned worlds in which these distinctions were either done away with or defined in excessively asymmetrical fashions. The aim to counter these visions is the crux of Koselleck's work, and his reinterpretation of the notion of finality is essential to this aim.

Whereas Koselleck's reception of Heidegger derived largely from his study of *Sein und Zeit*, his entire oeuvre can be read as a constant dialogue with a whole range of Schmitt's texts. Koselleck always remained more subtle in expressing his intellectual-political deviations from Schmitt than from Heidegger. The reason was undoubtedly that Koselleck was personally closer to Schmitt. This does not mean, however, that he refrained from expressing their differences. The most direct examples of this are found in texts written after "Kritik und Krise", where Koselleck toned down his reception of Schmitt significantly. But he also diverged from and went beyond Schmitt's work in the dissertation, even if he tended not to emphasise this.

To begin with, the fact that Koselleck's deconstructive approach to politics connected the study of history to politics in a way that diverged from Schmitt's work is of key importance. Instead of placing his historical analysis in the service of political ideology, Koselleck sought to counter the ideologization of politics. It is also significant that the concept of history described in the 1953 letter goes beyond Schmitt's writings both theoretically and politically.

That Koselleck in the letter nevertheless presented the concept as inspired by his recent conversations with Schmitt, and as to a considerable extent constructed with the use of Schmitt's categories, might indicate that he attempted to downplay the extent to which he in fact went beyond Schmitt. If so, this was, as we shall later see, not the last time that Koselleck was to brush over his analytical distance from or elaborations on Schmitt's work, presumably to avoid confrontations. When, in this particular instance, Koselleck presented a way of thinking of history and politics, which, while he expressed admiration for and affiliation to Schmitt's work, embodied a highly independent project, it was perhaps to give the impression that he was not departing too radically from his teacher. Interpreted along these lines, the letter functioned not only as a way of sharing his ideas with and expressing his gratitude to Schmitt, but also as a respectful way of communicating that he was pursuing his own plans.

Koselleck was somewhat clearer as to how the ideas of history and the role of the historian in modern society that he presented in relation to his dissertation was meant to diverge from the predominant ideas in the German historical profession at the time. Still, the way in which Koselleck portrayed this divergence was the result of a very biased and often only indirectly described conception of norms, positions, and identities. In the dissertation and in the letter, Koselleck created this conception by presenting himself as an outsider to the historical profession: as someone who was closer to a group of more pessimistic and supposedly more realistic thinkers who were in the 1950s positioned outside or on the margins of the disciplinary discourse—such as Karl Löwith, Johannes Kühn and Carl Schmitt—than he was to the established trends and scholars in the historical discipline. In respect to describing this discipline, alongside a very biased reading of only one scholar, Friedrich Meinecke, Koselleck referred only to a generalized idea of the discipline as being deeply embedded in historicism. Hence, it was seemingly as an indirect way to express his understanding of the difference between the outsiders and the representatives of the historical discipline, in terms of duties and abilities, that, at the very end of his letter to Schmitt, he quoted Kant's interpretation of Job:

> For, God honors Job, in that he shows him the wisdom of his creation predominantly with respect to its inscrutability. He lets him cast his looks on the beautiful side of the creation . . . ; but also on the terrifying one, in that he specifies for him the products of his power, among which also damaging and dreadful things.

To this quotation, Koselleck added: "Hiob's friends, who strive more for the grace of the mighty than for truth, are not initiated." The quotation shows in exemplary fashion that Koselleck's construction of historical writing went hand in hand with the making of a position and an identity within the disciplinary field, as a way of becoming a historian. This construction was attempted through playing around with the issues related to religion and authenticity informing Kant's interpretation of Job.[111] Interpreted in a straightforward manner, Koselleck depicted the situation as if his determination to face realities, as unpleasant as they may be, and to follow his own convictions, would bring him closer to the truth than thinkers who predominantly strove for the favor of the mighty. Whereas the latter were bound to fail, Koselleck's analytical quest would be vindicated in the future, even if was depreciated in the present. This was an ironic self-portrait, with the application of theological language and philosophy of religion out of context. Still, the quotation overlapped with the issues at stake in the letter in one respect: It thematized an appropriate relation to a "source."[112] In this respect, historical writing seemed to demand a commitment to "truth" that permitted and even called for the moral and religious pathos of Kant's remarks on Job.

More concretely, with analytical framework, Koselleck believed he had found a more appropriate relation to and understanding of historical writing than Meinecke, and the quote thus formed part of the argument and the act of a self-fashioning that he made explicit in the letter and stated implicitly in the dissertation. In Koselleck's opinion, there was an urgent need to substitute Meinecke's approach to history, with its allegedly naïve notions of meaning, unity and progress, with his own conceptually framed approach, which emphasized crisis and rupture in history, envisioned a close relation between the past and the present, and from a purportedly firmer analytical standpoint proposed a more direct and responsible role for the historian and to historical writing in debates about the present and the future. This need was seemingly not only scientific, but also political and in fact, existential.

However, it is worth noting that, when in the 1950s Koselleck attempted to straighten out the crooked paths that history and its study had allegedly entered in the modern world, he refrained from announcing many of his arguments in public. First of all, in the published version of "Kritik und Krise", the severe criticism of Meinecke was deleted, along with the reference to Schmitt's review of *Die Idee der Staatsräson* in the bibliography. In this version, Koselleck merely provided a considerably shorter and less controversial explanation of the theoretical-methodological framework underpinning the approach: "The applied method combines thus *geistesgeschichtliche* analyses with analyses of sociological conditions."[113]

The reason that Koselleck decided to first hide and then delete the note is presumably to be found in considerations regarding his future in the historical profession. To be sure, in the early 1950s, to venture into a direct confrontation with the Nestor of the discipline, Friedrich Meinecke, might have been interpreted as an inappropriate challenge of the prevailing social structures and cultural norms of the profession. Students were supposed to treat older members of the profession with respect, if they wanted to make a career, since their prospects were largely dependent on the goodwill and decisions of established professors.[114] It should be added that Meinecke died in the period before the dissertation appeared as a book, and that it was perhaps even more inappropriate for Koselleck to criticize a recently deceased scholar, who was greatly missed by his colleagues and unable to defend himself.

When, along with deleting the criticism of Meinecke in "Kritik und Krise", Koselleck refrained from introducing his social-historical and conceptually framed approach and concept of history until the late 1960s and early 1970s respectively, this was presumably also a choice that considered the disciplinary situation.[115] Not only was Koselleck undoubtedly aware that his ambitions exceeded the disciplinary expectations of a dissertation. He also knew that, at the time, historical theory and social history were placed at the boundaries of the discipline, and that anyone aspiring to renew the field of historical writing with a focus on these issues would have been viewed with suspicion. It is thus no coincidence that the first time Koselleck reflected on the need for a new *Historik* in a published writing, it was ten years later and only indirectly in a review article dealing with publications of other historians,[116] and that his first public pleas for the necessity of analyzing the social dimensions of history via a conceptual approach were made within the secure auspices of Werner Conze's Arbeitskreis für moderne Sozialgeschichte. It was, in line with this, and as we shall later return to, only after acquiring a professorship and thus becoming a full member of the profession in the late 1960s that he proposed reworking the approach of historicism with discursive features that included a conceptual approach and anthropological assumptions of human history.

The described disciplinary norms and Koselleck's choices of how to negotiate them in order to position his project had consequences for how it eventually was received and the identity he was given by other scholars in the field, as we will see in final part of this chapter.

The Reception of "Kritik und Krise"

According to Koselleck, what delayed the publication of "Kritik und Krise" for five years was a lack of money. After submitting his dissertation, he received an offer from Gadamer to publish it in the series of *Heidelberger Forschungen*, but he did not have the 1,000 DM required for the publication. The text finally went to press when Conze arrived in Heidelberg in 1957 and arranged a publication at the Alber Verlag to which Koselleck was not required to contribute financially.[117]

While Koselleck did not subject the plot line or the line of argumentation in the dissertation to major revisions between 1954 and 1959,[118] the intellectual-political climate in Germany underwent considerable changes in this period. Most importantly, processes of economic progress, societal stability and political democratization converged with a change in mentality that brought an end to the long period from around 1900 to the 1950s, in which notions of uncertainty, change, and crisis had dominated social-political thought among Germans.[119] Now, due to a stronger faith in the capability and durability of political democracy, they were increasingly oriented toward concepts such as stability, welfare, and progress. The easing of tensions in the Cold War likewise resulted in a different way of talking of international politics. "Today, the word crisis has almost disappeared from daily language," a German publicist thus observed in 1959. "[I]t has been replaced by the magic word détente (*Entspannung*)."[120] More generally, the 1950s was a period in which the political language of the Federal Republic changed drastically.[121]

In combination with Koselleck's choice to hide and leave important issues of the book open to the reader's interpretation, and his use of categories that were typically regarded as politically conservative, the social-political developments during the 1950s undoubtedly had an impact on the reception of "Kritik und Krise". While many reviewers found that Koselleck's analysis was characterized by a remarkable intelligence and erudition, others saw serious problems in his pessimistic conception of the modern world, and some found the analytical language and the world-view in "Kritik und Krise" reactionary and conservative and criticized Koselleck's intellectual affinities to Carl Schmitt in the book. This was the stance, for example, of Jürgen Habermas, Germany's most famous postwar philosopher, who is known to have participated in the great majority of debates about Germany's past and political self-understanding since the 1960s, and who interpreted "Kritik und Krise" as a politically conservative manifesto.

Born in 1929, Habermas served at the end of World War II as a *Flakhelfer*. In the 1950s, he went to study with Theodor Adorno at the refounded Institut für Sozialforschung in Frankfurt, and from a left-liberal ideological position similar to Hans-Ulrich Wehler's, he argued for a democratic society, based on a public sphere, and for a critical attitude toward Germany's past—in particular toward National Socialism.[122]

In his fight against the more politically conservative forces in German intellectual and political life that Habermas believed did not confront Germany's past to a sufficient degree, he chose first Martin Heidegger and then Carl Schmitt—including the latter's associates—as his primary opponents.[123] One of Habermas's early attempts to draw the boundaries of his ideological frontline appears in a 1960 double review of "Kritik und Krise" and Kesting's dissertation *Geschichtsphilosophie und Weltbürgerkrieg* in which Kesting analyzed the role of historical philosophy in modern politics from the French Revolution until the Cold War.[124]

When Habermas reviewed the two books, he was in the process of conceptualizing his famous 1962 *Habilitation Strukturwandel der Öffentlichkeit*.[125] Of all the books in which young German academics from the mid 1950s onwards attempted to rethink the idea of the public sphere, *Strukturwandel der Öffentlichkeit* was to become the most influential.[126] In it Habermas presented an interpretation of the Enlightenment and the rise of the modern European public sphere that simultaneously overlapped and conflicted with the interpretation in "Kritik und Krise". Habermas's theory of the public sphere, it has been said:

> reworks Koselleck's narrative, using most of its building blocks: the concept of the absolutist state, the idea of the absolutist state, the idea of moral criticism as the primary weapon against the state, the dichotomy of private and public, and the understanding of the Enlightenment project as a fundamental critique of authoritarian structures. Habermas, however, coming from the Hegelian-Marxist tradition, reversed the trajectory of the narrative. Where Koselleck perceived decline (already during the eighteenth century), Habermas saw the beginning of modernity, containing the very project that was supposed to shape postwar Germany. This project he

defined as the development of a postauthoritarian civil society, based on democratic political structures.[127]

According to Habermas, based on a bourgeois culture of coffeehouses, literary salons, and the print media, it was the rise of a such a civil society, or public sphere of rational debate on matters of political importance that had facilitated parliamentary democracy and Enlightenment ideals of equality, reason, and justice in social-political debates. The public sphere was, he argued, guided by a norm of rational argumentation and critical discussion in which the strength of one's argument was more important than one's social belonging. Unfortunately, a variety of factors resulted in the eventual decay of the bourgeois public sphere. Most importantly, structural forces, especially the growth of commercial mass media, turned media into more of a consumer commodity rather than a tool for public discourse, and the merging of mass media into mass party politics proved to have seriously damaging effects for deliberative parliamentarian politics and for rational-critical public debate. In line with this, for Habermas, "the ideal public sphere during the nineteenth century functions as an engine for progressive political development; during the twentieth century, on the other hand, this ideal serves as a reminder of what should take place."[128]

Although Habermas also outlined a critical account of the decay of the public sphere, *Strukturwandel der Öffentlichkeit* and "Kritik und Krise" obviously represented two distinctly different models and appraisals of the public sphere. Whereas Habermas constructed an Enlightenment public opinion model around Kantian concepts such as rationality, morality, and equality, Koselleck focused rather on how these concepts were exploited as weapons of dictatorship, and his public opinion model was more in line with Rousseau's expression of the general will. Where Habermas emphasized the possibilities of openness, dialogue, and consensus in processes of decision-making in the public sphere, Koselleck emphasized the existence of secrecy, domination, and conflict. And where Habermas optimistically interpreted the Enlightenment public sphere as an unfulfilled promise of how a new kind of human communication can break down hierarchical power relationships, Koselleck pessimistically spoke of the pathogenesis of the Enlightenment and highlighted the destructive potential of Enlightenment thought and the public sphere in modern politics.[129] As such, Habermas's and Koselleck's accounts of the rise of the public sphere and of the possibilities of human communication fundamentally conflicted. In fact, Habermas's account of these issues should be read as a direct response to Koselleck's.

The intellectual-political fundament of Habermas's response was unfolded already in his review of "Kritik und Krise" and *Geschichtsphilosophie und Weltbürgerkrieg* in which he took issue with the ideological presuppositions and aims that he believed informed Koselleck's and Kesting's dissertations. He began his evaluation by placing these within a wave of so-called "new conservatism" emerging in the postwar era in West Germany, thus positioning himself as Koselleck and Kesting's antipode. In "Kritik und Krise", Habermas detected a dubious tradition of conservative counter-Enlightenment thought according to which individual thinking and criticism of the political order necessarily lead to the terror and civil war unless controlled by authoritarian political institutions; in *Geschichtsphilosophie und Weltbürgerkrieg*, Habermas further detected an attempt to redeem German political conservatism into a positive power that might tame the destructive forces in the ongoing *Weltbürgerkrieg*.

In line with this, Habermas attempted to undermine what he read as a political conservatism in the two books by highlighting their intellectual debt to Carl Schmitt. Not only did he attack the references to the notion of civil war by stating that, according to the logic of Schmitt's writings, in modern societies such a civil war can only be overcome "in the form of the totalitarian state."[130] In the very last passage of the review, he in addition reduced the two authors to mere mouthpieces of Carl Schmitt. He wrote: "After all, we appreciate to learn—from such competent authors—how Carl Schmitt, a specialist in this field, views the world today."[131]

In later reprints of the review, Habermas decided to delete the last passage, presumably to reduce the polemical acerbity or because he had begun to have a different opinion of Koselleck's writings.[132] In any event, to accuse Koselleck of being a conservative Schmittian does not do justice to Koselleck's analysis. As we have seen, his theoretical and normative project was distinctively different to Schmitt's, and he provided historical perspectives on the Enlightenment and on the origins of modern political thought that are found neither in the work of Schmitt nor in Löwith's *Meaning in History*.

However, if Habermas exaggerated the affinities to Schmitt, he was more to the point in his critique of the features with which Koselleck created his dialectical account of the modern world as a phenomenon characterized by a permanent crisis, conflict, and war and embedded in historical philosophies. According to Habermas, this account was made possible only by a scheme of interpretation, which was itself characterized by historical-philosophical traits.

This scheme of interpretation was also observed and described in more detail in a review by the philosopher Helmut Kuhn. In Kuhn's eyes, Koselleck's dialectical and pessimistic analysis was so one-dimensional that it came close to annulling itself, because it merely substituted one historical philosophy with another. He wrote: "The chimerical expectation (*phantastische Hoffnung*) is replaced by implausible despair (*unwahrscheinliche Hoffnungslosigkeit*), the utopia as historical-philosophical point de repère is replaced by the absolute crisis, the futurism by existentialism. But this redrawing does not change the schematizing effect: the alienation is not reduced."[133]

Habermas found Koselleck's dialectical and pessimistic interpretation problematic because its scenario disregarded a human need of some belief in the feasibility of history as a means of survival, but also because the interpretation neglected the complexity and diversity of the Enlightenment. This neglect was elaborated upon in a review by the historian Heinz Gollwitzer, who wrote, "Koselleck's book shows what the dialectical method can achieve in historical writing and what it cannot achieve."[134] It can, Gollwitzer argued, illuminate a certain problem in an acute and penetrating way, but will always evade the complexity and the diversity in history. He thus pointed to how, in constructing his interpretation of the Enlightenment, Koselleck had given primacy to the old conception of France and the violent dynamics of the French Revolution as the ideal-type model nation for the European Enlightenment in favor of alternative developments (not least the English), and neglected many different variants of Enlightenment thought, including the enlightened conservatives, the Christians, and the patriots; and, how, via a severely biased reading, Koselleck reduced many of the philosophers to nothing but radical revolutionaries.[135]

It is tempting to relate the historical-philosophical traits in "Kritik und Krise" to Koselleck's reception of Löwith's *Meaning in History*. In relation to Löwith's discussion of eschatology, teleology, and universal vis-à-vis cyclical, repetitive history embedded in an unchanging cosmic order, Koselleck tended in his early work to employ a scheme in history with quasi-Hegelian traits that in some respects resembled the one he was criticizing. That is, he employed a notion of history in the singular, in which the historical process is conceived as unified, one-directional, and broad enough to verge on the universal.

As "Kritik und Krise" gradually assumed status of a classic in the field of Enlightenment studies, the critique of its too narrow line of interpretation was frequently repeated and elaborated upon.[136] On later occasions, Koselleck acknowledged this critique,[137] and in his subsequent writings he worked hard to modify the dialectical, schematic, and pessimistic interpretation of the modern world that characterizes "Kritik und Krise".

However, this does not mean that Koselleck ever theorized the ideal of a rational and consensus-based practice of public politics that Habermas's sketched out in *Strukturwandel der Öffentlichkeit* and which he has elaborated in many of his later works. In his assessments on the Enlightenment, the public sphere, and the dynamics of human communication, Koselleck continued to focus on secrecy instead of openness, conflict instead of consensus and on the existence of friends and enemies rather than on equal opportunities between discussion partners, and he would often point to how his views on these issues differed from those of Habermas as a way to delineate his viewpoints and positions.[138]

"Kritik und Krise" was relatively soon taken up and recognized as a classic in the field of Enlightenment studies, where it has been particularly praised for illuminating the social and radical dimensions of the Enlightenment.[139] In recent years, however, political theorists have paid increasing attention to its perspective on how the meaning of politics is always defined in an ongoing conflict and contestation between political actors. What they draw from "Kritik und Krise" is inspiration for how to study the form of such contestation, the ways it changes over time, and the role of linguistic expressions in political conflict. And due to its emphasis on the historical character of politics, and the close connection between social settings and political language, they deduce from "Kritik und Krise" (and from Koselleck's later work) an understanding of politics that is different than the interpretations found in Habermas as well as in Schmitt.[140]

In the 1960s, however, it was *Strukturwandel der Öffentlichkeit* and not "Kritik und Krise" that became the most influential theory on the public sphere in Germany, where it reflected the contemporary political atmosphere, characterized by attempts to reform practically every societal sphere in a more democratic direction. Whereas Habermas was undoubtedly satisfied with his reputation of being a democratizer, Koselleck felt misrepresented as a conservative and Schmittian pessimist in Habermas's review.[141] Yet, because other commentators similar to Habermas connected Koselleck with a circle of people that were affiliated with Schmitt in the 1950s, he acquired a difficult to escape reputation of being a Schmittian.[142] In fact, according to a 2003 interview with Koselleck, in which he described how his acknowledgement to Schmitt in "Kritik und Krise" was met with widespread distrust in German academia, his reputation as a Schmittian even caused him to be omitted from the list of applicants to a position in Konstanz.[143]

At the same time, the reviews of "Kritik und Krise" portrayed Koselleck as an outsider to the historical profession. Not because his project aimed to renew the theoretical-methodological fundament of the discipline, but because his narrow approach to the past, together with his strong focus on the present and his use of analytical features from scholars outside the profession, did not match the standards of mainstream historical writing. In the opening sentence of his review, Helmut Kuhn thus wrote: "The book in front of us is not a piece of historical writing. One might define it as a historical-philosophical situational analysis that is based on historical erudition."[144] Estimating the book to be greatly inspired Schmitt, but also by Adorno, Kuhn concluded: "We might judge it as the work of a promising beginner, who is still on the path to finding his own approach."[145]

The only entirely enthusiastic review of "Kritik und Krise" appeared in the journal *Das Historisch-Politische Buch*. This text was authored by none other than Carl Schmitt, somewhat remarkably, considering his role in the conceptualization of "Kritik und Krise".[146] In one remarkable passage in the review, Schmitt described how, in contrast to the other reviewers, he saw in Koselleck's study an innovation in the study of history and in the understanding of politics: "The book is, in spite of its excellent conceptual- and word-historical analyses, not a history of ideas in the style of Meinecke's Idee der Staatsräson; nor is it a materialist historical dialectic in the manner of Mehrings Lessing-legend. It is much more the thoroughly concrete enforcement of the historical insight that every period, with the questions and answers of the historical situation, makes its own concept of the political, which must be understood in order to grasp or handle that period."[147]

With these sentences, Schmitt pointed to some of the central analytical aspects that Koselleck introduced in "Kritik und Krise" and reused and refined in his later work. The most important of these aspects can be divided into three features that are outlined below.

The first feature concerns an ideal-type for the development of the modern world from the French Revolution onwards that portrayed modernity as characterized by a dangerous, irresponsible, and utopian mode of political thought. This ideal-type involved a critique of the modern world, that is, a critique of what Koselleck described as its exaggerated focus on the future, its exaggerated and destructive claims of rationality, equality, and freedom, and its inability to establish a political system in which politics and morality coexist in a balanced and responsible way.

The second theme concerns the theoretical-methodological approach with which Koselleck described and deconstructed this ideal-type of the modern world. This approach combined interpretations of texts with analysis of social-historical contexts, and it was practiced in the form of a conceptual approach that was based on two theoretical assumptions. The first is that central political and societal experiences of an epoch can be deciphered through an analysis of its key concepts; the second is that concepts are created in historically concrete situations by different historical actors to meet the ends of political actors using them.

The third theme is the deeper theoretical framework on which Koselleck's conceptual approach is based, that is, his concept of what creates and structures all human history. This concept was developed as an antidote to the utopian and relativistic ideas that Koselleck argued characterized historical philosophy and historicism. Combining a theory of knowledge and a political dimension, it aimed to provide a purely formalistic way of understanding and containing the potential conflict in human societies. The categories encompassed in the outline became important in Koselleck's subsequent work, as they came to provide his writings with a certain analytical, thematic, and argumentative unity.

However, this is not to say that the categories became *the* key feature in Koselleck's work. First of all, they certainly do not appear in all his texts; and, secondly, they are rarely introduced alone, but most often alongside a variety of other theoretical-methodological frameworks and anthropological categories that Koselleck presented in his later work.[148]

As we will see in chapter 5, it is difficult to estimate the precise epistemological status of the categories and their relation to other epistemologies. This difficulty also pertains to Koselleck's letter to Schmitt from the early 1950s. The letter is characterized by a very imaginative, but also a somewhat chaotic and unelaborated way of connecting assumptions and interpretations, which were deduced from the writings of only a few scholars that were well known to the receiver of the letter and therefore not described in depth. However, the overall intention of the letter is clear: to establish an antidote to ideas of history in the singular and create a notion of history in the plural.

Still, Koselleck's break with the historical-philosophical ideas of unity, linearity, and progression in history in relation to "Kritik und Krise" was less clear than he thought. In spite of his attempt to thematize the possibilities of writing history in the plural, his interpretation of the modern world in the dissertation relied on the same conception of world history as one progressive movement that he attempted to do away with. There was here an unresolved tension in Koselleck's thought (and reception processes) between a choice for the universal narrative or the pluralist narrative. This tension was presumably caused by his reception of Löwith—and perhaps also of Schmitt. Regardless of their specific origins, certain universalistic and historical-philosophical traits continued to inform many of Koselleck's writings in the 1950s and 1960s, where he refined, developed and added to the discursive features that he took with him from "Kritik und Krise".

Notes

1. See Koselleck, "Dankrede am 23 November 2004," 51; and Reinhart Koselleck, *Critique and Crisis: Enlightenment and the Pathogenesis of Modern Society* (Oxford, 1988), 1.

2. Koselleck, "Dankrede am 23 November 2004," 52. The time pressure is also documented by a sheet later accompanying the dissertation on which Koselleck corrected several typos and errors in the manuscript.

3. We will later return to the reasons for the delayed publication.

4. See for example Friedrich Wilhelm Graf, "Die Macht des Schicksals entschuldigt gar nichts," *Frankfurter Allgemeine Zeitung*, 1/11 (1999).

5. Max Horkheimer and Theodor W. Adorno, *Dialektik der Aufklärung: Philosophische Fragmente* (Amsterdam, 1947) (first published as *Philosophische Fragmente*, New York, 1944); Karl Popper, *The Open Society and Its Enemies* (London, 1945); Hannah Arendt, *The Origins of Totalitarianism* (New York, 1951); Friedrich Meinecke, *Die deutsche Katastrophe: Betrachtungen und Erinnerungen* (Zürich, 1946); Gerhard Ritter, *Europa und die deutsche Frage: Betrachtungen über die geschichtliche Eigenart des deutschen Staatsdenkens* (München, 1948); and J. L. Talmon, *The Origins of Totalitarian Democracy* (New York, 1960).

6. Perspectives on how "Kritik und Krise" related to this body of literature and an excellent introduction to the published version of the study are found in Jason Edwards, "*Critique and Crisis* Today: Koselleck, Enlightenment and the Concept of Politics," *Contemporary Political Theory* 5 (2006): 428–46. For another excellent introduction, which—as the only existing introduction to "Kritik und Krise"—takes into account the unpublished version, see Palonen, *Die Entzauberung der Begriffe*, 182–89.

7. He also stated that he intended to give his dissertation the title *Dialektik der Aufklärung* until he discovered the 1947 edition of Adorno and Horkheimer's book (which is listed in the bibliography of the 1954 edition of "Kritik und Krise"). See Koselleck, "Dankrede am 23 November 2004," 34.

8. Koselleck later reported how *The Origins of Totalitarianism* belonged to the books one had to read in Heidelberg in the 1950s (since the original English edition is not listed in the 1954 edition of "Kritik und Krise", he was presumably referring to the German translation *Elemente und Ursprünge totaler Herrschaft* from 1956). Koselleck, "Formen der Bürgerlichkeit," 77. On another occasion, Koselleck stated that his argumentation in the 1959 edition of "Kritik und Krise" was influenced by Arendt's book. Koselleck, "Dankrede am 23 November 2004," 53. The only direct trace of this in the 1959 edition is found in a note in which Koselleck both highly praised and criticized aspects of Arendt's Hobbes-interpretation. Koselleck, "Kritik und Krise": *Eine Studie*, 161 n. 32. In addition, Koselleck has described how, in 1956, he invited Arendt to Heidelberg to discuss her book. See Reinhart Koselleck, "Laudatio auf François Furet," *Sinn und Form*, Hf. 2 (1997): 297–300. For a comparison of Koselleck's and Arendt's work, in particular of their critiques of historical philosophy and their use of anthropological categories in this endeavor, see Stefan-Ludwig Hoffmann, "Zur Anthropologie geschichtlicher Erfahrungen bei Reinhart Koselleck und Hannah Arendt," in *Begriffene Geschichte: Beiträge zum Werk Reinhart Kosellecks*, ed. Hans Joas and Peter Vogt, 171-204 (Frankfurt am Main, 2010).

9. For a portrayal of Meinecke and Ritter as *Nationalapologeten*, see Nicolas Berg, *Der Holocaust und die westdeutschen Historikern: Erforschung und Erinnerung* (Göttingen, 2002), 64–142. For a different reading of Meinecke, see Gisela Bock, "Meinecke, Machiavelli und der Nationalsozialismus," in *Friedrich Meinecke in seiner Zeit: Stu-*

dien zu Leben und Werk, ed. Gisela Bock and Daniel Schönpflug, 145–75 (Stuttgart, 2006).

10. Reinhart Koselleck, Review of *Ursprünge des modernen Krisenbewußtseins*, by Ehrenfried Muthesius, and of *Die Ursprünge der totalitären Demokratie*, by J. L. Talmon, *Neue politische Literatur*, Hf. 11/12 (1963): 866.

11. Koselleck, "Formen der Bürgerlichkeit," 78; and Koselleck, "Dankrede am 23 November 2004," 35. Known as one of the founders of medical anthropology, Weizsäcker came to Heidelberg in 1945 and retired in 1952. For introductions to Weizsäcker's work, see Dehli, *Leben als Konflikt*, 87–100; Sven Olaf Hoffmann, "Viktor von Weizsäcker: Art und Denker gegen den Strom," *Deutsches Ärzteblatt*, PP. 5 (April 2006): 161.

12. Concerning Burckhardt and Weber, see Wolfgang Hardtwig, "Jacob Burckhardt und Max Weber: Zur Genese und Pathologie der modernen Welt," *Geschichtskultur und Wissenschaft* (München, 1990), 189–223. Concerning Schmitt, see the entry in his diary notes on 23 September 1947: "I hear 'critique' and 'critical' and know and hear: 'critique, critique': I hear primordial ooze (*Urschleim*) and see the entire nineteenth century from 1848 to 1948." Carl Schmitt, *Glossarium: Aufzeichnungen der Jahre 1947–1951* (Berlin, 1991), 17.

13. Concerning these developments, see Conze, *Die Suche nach Sicherheit*, 21–154; Jarausch, *After Hitler*, 19–147; Wolfrum, *Die geglückte Demokratie*, 181–86; Edgar Wolfrum, *Die Bundesrepublik Deutschland 1949–1990* (Stuttgart 2005), 231–42; Görtemaker, *Geschichte der Bundesrepublik Deutschland*; Ulrich Herbert, "Liberalisierung als Lernprozeß: Die Bundesrepublik in der deutschen Geschichte—eine Skizze," in *Wandlungsprozesse in Deutschland: Belastung, Integration, Liberalisierung 1948–1980*, ed. Ulrich Herbert, 7-47 (Göttingen, 2002); Anselm Doering-Manteuffel, *Wie westlich sind eigentlich die Deutschen? Amerikanisierung und Westernizierung im 20. Jahrhundert* (Göttingen, 1999); and Axel Schildt, *Moderne Zeiten. Freizeit, Massenmedien und "Zeitgeist" in der Bundesrepublik der 50er Jahre* (Hamburg, 1995).

14. Jarausch, *After Hitler*, 111–20; Wolfrum, *Die geglückte Demokratie*, 183–84; Schildt, *Moderne Zeiten*, 314.

15. Jarausch, *After Hitler*, 103–27; Wolfrum, *Die geglückte Demokratie*, 182–83; Wolfrum, *Die Bundesrepublik*, 233–34; Görtemaker, *Geschichte der Bundesrepublik Deutschland*, 250–60; Schildt, *Moderne Zeiten*, 333.

16. For the skepticism against American liberalism and how it gradually diminished, see Jarausch, *After Hitler*, 112–13; Wolfrum, *Die geglückte Demokratie*, 183; Wolfrum, *Die Bundesrepublik*, 35; Görtemaker, *Geschichte der Bundesrepublik Deutschland*, 253–60; Doering-Manteuffel, *Wie westlich sind eigentlich die Deutschen?*, 20–71; and Schildt, *Moderne Zeiten*, 333.

17. Jarausch, *After Hitler*, 142; Wolfrum, *Die geglückte Demokratie*, 88; Wolfrum, *Die Bundesrepublik*, 232; Schildt, *Moderne Zeiten*, 308–09.

18. Hugo Steger, "Sprache im Wandel," in *Die Geschichte der Bundesrepublik Deutschland. Band 4: Kultur*, ed. Wolfgang Benz, 14–52 (Frankfurt am Main, 1989).

19. Wolfgang Hardtwig, "Die Krise des Geschichtsbewusstseins in Kaiserreich und Weimarer Republik und der Aufstieg der Nationalsozialismus," *Hochkultur des bürgerlichen Zeitalters* (Göttingen, 2005), 77–102; Wolfgang Küttler, Jörn Rüsen, and Ernst Schulin, eds., *Geschichtsdiskurs 4. Krisenbewusstsein, Katastrophenerfahrungen und Innovationen 1880–1945* (Frankfurt am Main, 2001).

20. Koselleck, "Kritik und Krise: Eine Untersuchung," i.

21. The very first chapter, a prelude, titled *Politische Kritik und moralischer Dualismus*, describes the role of the theater stage in the emergence of moral critique and the history of the concept of "critique" from Ancient Greece to the Enlightenment.

22. Carl Schmitt, *Der Leviathan in der Staatslehre des Thomas Hobbes: Sinn und Fehlschlag eines politischen Symbols* (Hamburg, 1938). In his chapter on Hobbes, Koselleck made thirteen references to Schmitt, out of a total of fifteen references to Schmitt in the dissertation. Koselleck referred altogether to six of Schmitt's writings: *Politische Theologie: Vier Kapitel zur Lehre von der Souveränität* (Berlin, 1922); *Der Nomos der Erde im Völkerrecht des Jus Publicum Europaeum* (Köln 1950); *Die Diktatur*, 2 Aufl. (München, 1928); *Der Leviathan in der Staatslehre des Thomas Hobbes* (Hamburg, 1938); "Der Staat als Mechanismus bei Hobbes and Descartes," *Archiv für Rechtsphilosophie und Staatsphilosophie*, Bd. XXX, Hf. 4 (1937): 622–32; and "Zu Friedrich Meineckes 'Idee der Staatsräson,'" *Archiv für Sozialwissenschaften und Sozialpolitik*, Bd. 56 (1926): 226–34. Koselleck's use of Schmitt's writings in the published version of "Kritik und Krise" has been discussed in a number of articles. See first of all Timo Pankakoski, "Conflict, Context, Concreteness: Koselleck and Schmitt on Concepts," *Political Theory*, no. 20 (2010): 1–31; Edwards, *"Critique and Crisis Today,"* 432–34; Jan-Friedrich Missfelder, "Die Gegenkraft und ihre Geschichte: Carl Schmitt, Reinhart Koselleck und der Bürgerkrieg," *Zeitschrift für Religions- und Geistesgeschichte* 58, no. 4 (2006): 310–36; Müller, *A Dangerous Mind*, 104–15; William E. Scheuerman, "Unsolved Paradoxes: Conservative Political Thought in Adenauer's Germany," in *Confronting Mass Democracy and Industrial Technology: Political and Social Theory from Nietzsche to Habermas*, ed. John P. McCormick, 221–42 (Durham, 2002); Reinhard Mehring, "Carl Schmitt and His influence on Historians," *Cardozo Law Review* 21 (2000): 1653–64; Michael Schwartz, "Leviathan oder Lucifer: Reinhart Koselleck's 'Kritik und Krise' Revisited," *Zeitschrift für Religions- und Geistesgeschichte*, Jg. 45 (1993): 33–57; Anthony J. La Vopa, "Conceiving a Public: Ideas and Society in Eighteenth-Century Europe," *The Journal of Modern History* 64, no. 1 (1992): 79–116; and Jeremy Pompkin, "The Concept of Public Opinion in the Historiography of the French Revolution," *Storia della Storiografia*, 20 (1991): 77–92.

23. Koselleck, "Kritik und Krise: Eine Untersuchung," 23. The quoted sentence was followed by a reference to Schmitt, 1922, which contains the following sentence on the relation between the processes of secularization and the concepts of modern politics: "All significant concepts on the theory of the modern state are secularized theological concepts" (43). On several other occasions in his analysis of Hobbes, Koselleck referred to *Politische Theologie* and *Die Diktatur* in building his argument about the relations between the process of secularization and the rise of modern politics. Koselleck's reception of Schmitt's work on this issue is mentioned in Edwards, *"Critique and Crisis Today,"* 432 and in Friedrich Wilhelm Graf, "Ein Theoretiker unaufhebbarer Differenzerfahrungen: Laudatio auf Reinhart Koselleck," *Das Jahrbuch der deutschen Akademie für Sprache und Dichtung* (2000): 139–45.

24. Koselleck, "Kritik und Krise: Eine Untersuchung," 31–32.

25. Ibid., 46.

26. Ibid., 52–53.

27. Koselleck, however, made only three references to Kühn. "Kritik und Krise: Eine Untersuchung," 7 n. 25, 21 n. 64, and 27 n. 90. Three writings of the French historian Bernard Faÿ were also important for Koselleck's investigation of the rise of public opinion in the lodges of the freemasons. These books, to which Koselleck referred seven times in the chapter on the rise of the public sphere, were *La Franc-Maconnerie et la Révolution intellectuelle du XVIIIe siècle* (Paris, 1925); *Benjamin Franklin* (Paris,

1929); and *L'esprit révolutionnaire en France du XVIIIe siècle* (Paris, 1925). A professor at the College de France and director of the National Library, Faÿ was after World War II sentenced to forced labor for life for having collaborated with the Germans during the German occupation of France. Having released card indexes with lists of names of freemasons to the Vichy Government, which was convinced that freemasons were at the heart of France's problems, Faÿ was deemed responsible for the death of many freemasons. Faÿ only served four years before escaping to Switzerland, where he was appointed to an instructorship at the Institut de la Language Francaise. He was forced to resign during the student protest in the 1960s. While drawing on Faÿ's writings, Koselleck evidently did not take over Faÿ's conspiracy theory concerning the role of freemasons in French history.

28. Koselleck, "Kritik und Krise: Eine Untersuchung," 73.
29. Ibid., 84.
30. Ibid., 114. As pointed out by Palonen, *Die Entzauberung der Begriffe*, 188, this notion of how every unpolitical critique is deeply political follows the formula in Schmitt, *Der Begriff des Politischen*, according to which labeling the enemy political and oneself as unpolitical is a typical and particular intensive practice in conceptualizing politics.
31. Koselleck, "Kritik und Krise: Eine Untersuchung," 96.
32. In crucial places, when thematizing modern historical philosophy, Koselleck referred to the German edition of *Meaning in History*, *Weltgeschichte and Heilsgeschehen*, from 1953. Koselleck, "Kritik und Krise: Eine Untersuchung", 9 n. 31, 20 n. 65, 46 n. 158, 97 n. 10, and 97 n. 12. Moreover, several implicit references to Löwith's work are found throughout the analysis—especially in the nine-page introduction, in which Koselleck referred to "historical philosophy" more than thirty times.
33. Koselleck, "Kritik und Krise: Eine Untersuchung," 98.
34. Ibid.
35. Ibid., 101.
36. Ibid., 145.
37. See Edwards, "*Critique and Crisis* Today," 432:
    [Koselleck] was clearly influenced by [Schmitt's] arguments about the concepts of politics, the state and sovereignty. In particular, it was Schmitt's view of politics as centered on the friend-enemy distinction . . . , and of sovereignty as the power to decide the exception . . . , that informed Koselleck's view of the emerging Enlightenment public.
38. See Steinmetz, "Nachruf auf Reinhart Koselleck," 417.
39. See Hans Blumenberg's critique of Löwith's and Schmitt's secularization arguments in *Die Legitimität der Neuzeit* (Frankfurt am Main, 1966). For a broad account of the historical-philosophical interpretations of modernity in the 1950s and 1960s, and the role of the notion of secularization in these debates, see Wilhelm Schmidt-Biggemann, "Säkularisierung und Theodizee: Anmerkungen zu geschichtstheologischen Interpretationen der Neuzeit in den fünfziger und sechziger Jahre," in *Religion und Vernunft: Philosophischen Analysen*, ed. Helmut Holzhey and Jean-Pierre Leyvraz, 51–67 (Stuttgart, 1986).
40. This is the point where Nagel, in "Der Kritiker der Krise," detects the key analytical divergence between Schmitt and Koselleck in "Kritik und Krise": "[Koselleck] reflects the state starting out from Hobbes, but not towards Donoso Cortés", 27.
41. Koselleck, "Kritik und Krise: Eine Untersuchung," 60–61.
42. Koselleck, "Dankrede am 23 November 2004," 56.
43. Koselleck, "Kritik und Krise: Eine Untersuchung," 51.
44. Ibid., 53.

45. Ibid., 51, 52, 54.
46. For a perspective on Koselleck's Locke chapter along similar lines, see Missfelder, "Die Gegenkraft und ihre Geschichte," 335–36.
47. Koselleck, "Kritik und Krise: Eine Untersuchung," 55.
48. Quoted in Sisko Haikala, "Criticism in the Enlightenment: Perspectives on Koselleck's Kritik und Krise Study," *Finnish Yearbook of Political Thought* 1 (1997): 70. See also Müller, *A Dangerous Mind*, 107.
49. Koselleck, "Kritik und Krise: Eine Untersuchung," vi.
50. Ibid., ii.
51. Ibid., ii.
52. Ibid., 2.
53. Ibid., 15.
54. Ibid., 4–19, including n. 15–57. Koselleck explained here how the concept of "critique" had acquired this meaning in stages from Simon to Kant and moreover provided perspectives on the histories of the word in Greek, Latin, French, English, and German.
55. Ibid., 91–94, 124–127, including n. 101.
56. Ibid., 124 and 5 n. 15. The two concepts originated from and had been used together in the Greek medical vocabulary.
57. Koselleck, "Begriffsgeschichte, Sozialgeschichte, Begriffene Geschichte, " 188; Koselleck, "Dankrede am 23 November 2004," 34. The only study that examines Koselleck's use of Schmitt's conceptual approach in "Kritik und Krise" is found in Palonen, *Die Entzauberung der Begriffe*, 183–84.
58. In a letter dated 8 July 1953, Koselleck informed Schmitt that the dissertation was finished. RW265-8132: 8/7 (1953).
59. Koselleck's attempt to provide a new concept of history has been analyzed in two excellent articles by Stefan-Ludwig Hoffmann: "Zur Anthropologie geschichtlicher Erfahrungen"; and "Was die Zukunft Birgt: Über Reinhart Kosellecks Historik," *Merkur: Deutsche Zeitschrift für europäisches Denken*, Jg. 63 (2009): 546–50. See also Palonen, *Die Entzauberung der Begriffe*, 297–304.
60. The first reference to "historicism" was made by Friedrich Schlegel in 1797. The following account, which highlights certain texts and themes in the reception of the term, draws on Annette Wittkau, *Historismus: zur Geschichte des Begriffs und des Problems* (Göttingen, 1992); Otto Gerhard Oexle, *Geschichtswissenschaft im Zeichen des Historismus* (Göttingen, 1996); Wolfgang Hardtwig, *Geschichtskultur und Wissenschaft* (München, 1990); and Georg G. Iggers, *The German Conception of History: The National Tradition of Historical Thought from Herder to the Present* (Middletown, 1968).
61. Friedrich Nietzsche, *Werke*, Bd. 1 (Berlin, 1972–1997).
62. Ernst Troeltsch, *Der Historismus und seine Probleme* [1922], *Gesammelte Schriften*, Bd. 3 (Tübingen, 1961), 9.
63. Friedrich Meinecke, *Die Entstehung des Historismus* (München, 1936).
64. Koselleck did not refer explicitly to Meinecke's *Historismus* book. However, the cited passage suggests that this book served as the starting point for Koselleck's discussion.
65. Reinhart Koselleck, "Die Verzeitlichung der Utopie," in *Utopieforschung*, ed. Wilhelm Vosskamp, 1–14 (Stuttgart, 1982).
66. Friedrich Meinecke, *Die Idee der Staatsräson in der neueren Geschichte* (München, 1924).
67. Ernst Schulin, "Friedrich Meinecke und seine Stellung in der deutschen Geschichtswissenschaft," in *Friedrich Meinecke Heute: Bericht über ein Gedenk-Colloquium zu seinem 25. Todestag am 5. und 6. April 1979*, ed. Michael Erbe, 50-75 (Berlin, 1981);

Ernst Schulin, "Friedrich Meinecke," in *Deutsche Historiker*, ed. Hans-Ulrich Wehler, 39–57 (Göttingen, 1973); and Gisela Bock and Daniel Schönpflug, eds., *Friedrich Meinecke in seiner Zeit: Studien zu Leben und Werk* (Stuttgart, 2006).

68. Friedrich Meinecke, *Weltbürgertum und Nationalstaat: Studie zur Genesis des Deutschen Nationalstaats* (München, 1907).

69. Schmitt, "Zu Friedrich Meineckes 'Idee der Staatsräson'". See also Reinhard Mehring, "Begriffssoziologie, Begriffsgeschichte, Begriffspolitik. Zur Form der Ideengeschichtsschreibung nach Carl Schmitt und Reinhart Koselleck," in *Politische Ideengeschichte im 20. Jahrhundert. Konzepte und Kritik*, ed. Harald Bluhm and Jürgen Gebhardt, 33–35 (Baden-Baden, 2006); and Gopal Balakrishnan, *The Enemy: An Intellectual Portrait of Carl Schmitt* (New York, 2000), 79–81.

70. Koselleck, "Kritik und Krise: Eine Untersuchung," 24 n. 72. Following an explanation in the main text of the historical reasons why absolutist states separated politics from morality, in the note, Koselleck first referred to Schmitt's *Die Diktatur* to support his argument and then ventured to compare Meinecke's approach to Schmitt's. Koselleck's estimation of the differences between the approaches of Meinecke and Schmitt was seemingly not only based on a comparison of *Die Idee der Staatsräson* to *Die Diktatur*, but also deduced from Schmitt's review of *Die Idee der Staatsräson* that is listed the bibliography of the unpublished version of Koselleck's dissertation.

71. Koselleck wrote: "Since Meinecke sees the reason of state as bound up with the 'historical forces' of the time, the state itself transmutes into an 'amphibian' between ethics and nature . . . . Meinecke himself, who continues to employ the anti-state, dualist concepts of the eighteenth century, remains so convinced by the moral self-understanding of the modern state, that he only finds reason to draw a distinction between morality and politics in the field of foreign politics. In domestic politics—as he believes in 1924 and still today—the 'more refined moral sentiment' will counteract and prevent a bloody revolution, and otherwise, in case of need, state of emergency legislation will carry a moral character since the necessary concentration of power will be capable of being 'legalized.' The twofold possibilities of the 'amphibian' state, and at the same time the sociological function of the attempt to ease out the oppositions, become manifest here." "Kritik und Krise: Eine Untersuchung," 24 n. 72.

72. Hans Freyer, *Weltgeschichte Europas*. 2 Bd. (Wiesbaden, 1948), signaled the "radical conservative" sociologist Hans Freyer's politically de-radicalized return to postwar German intellectual life. Describing the becoming of Europe from an epochal-geographical narrative, the book contains short sections on the nature of historiography and the role of the historian, and it was presumably to these sections that Koselleck referred in his letter to Schmitt (Koselleck also referred to them in "Kritik und Krise"). Freyer's reflections unfold as a critique of idealism and of notions of objectivity in historical writing and are based on keywords such as "crisis," "existentialism" and "decision." His argument is that historical writing can never be separated from existential questions. According to Freyer, the present is not merely to be conceived as a viewpoint from which we can look back on a distant past and measure how far we have progressed in history. Instead, the past is present as a "heritage"—it is part of us. Hence, writing critical history entails awareness of the existential element in historical writing and of the close relation holding between the past and the present. Moreover, since it is constantly confronted with decision-making in the present, critical historical writing is concerned with the third temporal dimension—the future. It is on this particular point, Freyer explained, that critical history differs from idealistic historical philosophy: It sees the present not as an end, but ". . . also as a critique of the contemporary crisis" (159). This does not imply, Freyer added, that critical his-

torical writing should predict fixed schemes of actions for the future. Instead, it must establish a "self-aware historical reality, which, to the very same extent to which it is in the debt of the past, recognizes its responsibility for the future" (160). As we shall see, the "ontology" that Koselleck outlined had many similarities to Freyer's vision of historical writing. For excellent comments on Freyer's book, see Thomas Etzemüller, *Sozialgeschichte als politische Geschichte: Werner Conze und die Neuorientierung der westdeutschen Geschichtswissenschaft nach 1945* (München, 2001), 282.

73. On how Heidegger developed aspects of his work through critiques of historicism, see Charles R. Bambach, *Heidegger, Dilthey and the Crisis of Historicism* (Ithaca 1995); Günther Scholz, "Zum Historismusstreit in der Hermeneutik," in *Historismus am Ende des 20. Jahrhundert: eine Internationale Diskussion*, ed. Günther Scholz, 198–202 (Berlin, 1997).

74. When Koselleck in the cited passage spoke of "finality" as "eschatology," it was seemingly to state that the only "coming" that human beings are to expect from their future is their own death.

75. See Reinhart Koselleck, "Historik und Hermeneutik," in *Sitzungsberichte der Heidelberger Akademie der Wissenschaften*, 1 (1987): 9–28, to which we will return below.

76. As witnessed in the passage quoted above, in Koselleck's opinion, this was an interpretive scheme that is replicated in Karl Jaspers, *Vom Ursprung und Ziel der Geschichte* (Zürich, 1959), a book in which, against the background of a vision of history as universal history divided into four epochs, Jaspers discussed the issue of the origin and the meaning of history.

77. Koselleck, "Historik und Hermeneutik."

78. In the German historical profession, the notion of *Historik* is often used to refer to the tradition beginning with Johann Gustav Droysen (1808–1884) that aims to define the topics, methods, and aims of historical writing.

79. Koselleck, "Historik und Hermeneutik," 21. At least two features diverged from the categorical outline in the speech vis-à-vis the letter from 1953. The first is that he reworked the notion of finality into a conceptual pair by extending the notion *Vorlauf zum Tode* (being toward death) to *Totschlagenkönnen* (the ability to kill) and *Sterbenmüssens* (having to die). The second is that Koselleck, as witnessed in the above citation, elaborated the content of the conceptual pairs: the pair of master and slave, for instance, is in the speech included in the relation of "above and below."

80. Karl Löwith, *Das Individuum in der Rolle des Mitmenschen. Ein Beitrag zur anthropologischen Grundlegung der ethischen Probleme* (München, 1928). "Man as Being is never independent of his fellow man [(a theme from Löwith) and not open to conflicts with others. The historical times are not identical to or even deducible from the existential modalities, which are developed around the concept of man as Being. The historical times are from the outset interpersonally constituted. It is always about the *Gleichzeitigkeit des Ungleichzeitigen*, about asserting differences that contain their own finalities and cannot be reduced to any form of 'existence'." Koselleck, "Historik und Hermeneutik," 12.

81. Löwith's analysis also encompassed an ethical ideal that emphasized the need for dialogue and responsibility in human relations. Helmut Fahrenbach, "Karl Löwith in der Weimarer Zeit (1928-1933): Philosophie—nach dem 'revolutionären Bruch im Denken des 19. Jahrhunderts,'" *Deutsche Zeitschrift für Philosophie* 53 (2005): 851–69; and Reinhard Mehring, "Heidegger und Karl Löwith: Destruktion einer Überlieferungskritik," in *Heidegger-Handbuch: Leben-Werk-Wirkung*, ed. Dieter Thomä, 373–75 (Stuttgart, 2003).

82. For a historical perspective on various traditions of philosophical anthropology, see Odo Marquard: "Anthropologie," in *Historisches Wörterbuch der Philosophie*, Bd. 1, ed. Joachim Ritter, 362–74 (Basel, 1971).

83. Joachim Fischer, "Philosophischer Anthropologie: Ein wirkungsvoller Denkansatz in der deutschen Soziologie nach 1945," *Zeitschrift für Soziologie*, Jg. 35, Bd. 5 (2006): 322–447. The philosopher Helmut Plessner was as "Halbjude" dismissed from the University of Cologne in 1933. He then immigrated to the Netherlands, where he taught at the University of Groningen until 1943, when he went underground, facing the threat of being deported by the Nazis. After the war, he regained his position in Groningen, and in 1951 he accepted a professorship in Göttingen. He became emeritus in 1962, but remained academically active until his death in 1985. Arnold Gehlen made a successful career in Nazi Germany, not least due to his cooperation with the regime. In 1947, he obtained a professorial chair at the Verwaltungshochschule in Speyer, and in 1962 he acquired a chair in sociology in Aachen. He retired in 1969 and died in 1976. See Carola Dietze, *Nachgeholtes Leben: Helmut Plessner: 1892–1985* (Göttingen, 2006); and Christian Thies, *Arnold Gehlen zur Einführung* (Hamburg, 2000).

84. Koselleck, "Formen der Bürgerlichkeit," 77.

85. Friedrich Meinecke, "Ernst Troeltsch und das Problem des Historismus" [1923], *Zur Theorie und Philosophie der Geschichte* (Stuttgart 1959), 369.

86. Koselleck wrote: "With the categories that lie at the basis of your 'Nomos der Erde,' dear professor, it is certainly possible to show that the current *Weltbürgerkrieg* is not an ontic or contingent event that actually should not be taking place (for the Americans), but an event deeply rooted in the ontological structures of our historicity, yet something that—given these structures—does not have to be the way it is (for the Russians)." This interpretation contrasted, in Koselleck's opinion, as stated in the citation, with the American and the Soviet ways of understanding of the Cold War: The American attitude to the Cold War was allegedly that it should not be taking place and that the world should be a liberal-democratic utopia instead; for the Soviets, with their ideology of class struggle, the Cold War was class struggle and therefore part of the very historical condition of mankind. While acknowledging the point about the historical condition, by use of the anthropological analytical framework, Koselleck would in turn argue that history does not have to manifest itself in such a class struggle.

87. When Koselleck later remarked that the "missing" chapter on the English constitution that was supposed to follow the section on Locke "fed" certain "wrong" interpretations of the book, he undoubtedly first of all referred to the review by Jürgen Habermas to which we shall return. Koselleck, "Dankrede am 23 November 2004," 56.

88. For the topoi used to describe modernity by German conservatives in the postwar period, see Jin-Sung Chun, *Das Bild der Moderne in der Nachkriegszeit. Die westdeutsche 'Strukturgeschichte' im Spannungsfeld von Modernitätskritik und wissenschaftlicher Innovation 1948–1962* (München, 2000). Among the most famous critics of the Weimar *Öffentlichkeit* were Schmitt and Heidegger. For a history of the concept of *Öffentlichkeit* in the nineteenth and twentieth century, see Peter Uwe Hohendahl, ed. *Öffentlichkeit: Geschichte eines kritischen Begriffs* (Stuttgart, 2000). For a broader history of the concept, see Lucian Hölscher, "Öffentlichkeit," in *Geschichtliche Grundbegriffe. Historisches Lexikon zur politisch-sozialen Sprache in Deutschland*, Bd. 4, ed. Otto Brunner, Werner Conze, and Reinhart Koselleck, 413–67 (Stuttgart, 1978).

89. Missfelder, "Die Gegenkraft und ihre Geschichte," 325–34.

90. For such interpretations of World History among German conservatives in the 1940s and 1950s, see for example Dirk van Laak, "'Nach dem Sturm schlägt man auf die Barometer ein . . .' Rechtsintellektuelle Reaktionen auf das Ende des 'Dritten Reiches,'" *Werkstatt Geschichte*, Bd. 17 (1997): 25–44; Dirk van Laak, "Trotz und Nachurteil. Rechtsintellektuelle im Anschluß an das 'Dritte Reich,'" in *Verwandlungspolitik. NS-Eliten in der Westdeutschen Nachkriegsgesellschaft*, ed. Wilfried Loth and Bernd-A. Rusenik, 55–77 (Frankfurt am Main, 1998); Jean Solchany, "Vom Antimodernismus zum Antitotalitarismus. Konservative Interpretationen des Nationalsozialismus in Deutschland 1945–1949," *Vierteljahreshefte für Zeitgeschichte*, Jg. 44, Hf. 3 (1996): 373–94; Axel Schildt, "Ende der Ideologien. Politisch-ideologische Strömungen in der 50er Jahren," in *Modernisierung im Wiederaufbau: die Westdeutsche Gesellschaft in der 50er Jahre*, ed. Axel Schildt and Arnold Sywottek, 627–35 (Bonn, 1993); and Chun, *Das Bild der Moderne in der Nachkriegszeit*. The notion of *Weltbürgerkrieg* was given a special niche in German historical writing in the 1970s and in the so-called *Historikerstreit* of the 1980s, as Ernst Nolte referred to it in his attempt to explain the rise of National Socialism and its radicalization as a reaction to and shelter against communism.

91. Schmitt, *Glossarium*. See also Reinhard Mehring, "Zu Schmitts Dämonologie—nach seinem Glossarium," *Rechtstheorie. Zeitschrift für Logik, Methodenlehre, Kybernetik und Soziologie des Rechts*, 23 Bd., Hf. 1 (1992): 258–71.

92. Koselleck, "Kritik und Krise: Eine Untersuchung," 134–35. See also Missfelder, "Die Gegenkraft und ihre Geschichte," 332; and Louiza Odysseos, "Violence after the State? A Preliminary Examination of the Concept of 'Global Civil War,'" *http://www.louizaodysseos.org.uk/resources/OdysseosSGIR2007.pdf*, 2007 (accessed 24/7-2011).

93. Thus, Sombart, "*Rendezvous mit dem Weltgeist*", 273. Ernst Jünger was among the first to use the term *Weltbürgerkrieg*. Schmitt began to use the term after a conversation with Jünger—the first time in Carl Schmitt, "Die letzte Globale Linie" [1943], *Carl Schmitt: Staat, Grossraum, Nomos: Arbeiten aus den Jahren 1916–1969* (Berlin, 1995), 441–52. See Odysseos, *Violence after the State?*; Missfelder, "Die Gegenkraft und ihre Geschichte," 328–30.

94. Koselleck, "Kritik und Krise: Eine Untersuchung," 39–45.

95. The following chapter analyses this book in more detail.

96. For the historical background of these topoi, see Kurt Flasch, *Die geistige Mobilmachung: Die deutschen Intellektuellen und der Erste Weltkrieg* (Berlin, 2000); and Wolfgang J. Mommsen, *Kultur und Krieg: Die Rolle der Intellektuellen, Künstler und Schriftsteller im Ersten Weltkrieg* (München, 1996).

97. For how their uses of the notion of *Weltbürgerkrieg* related to the social-political conditions in which Schmitt communicated with his "associates," see Missfelder, "Die Gegenkraft und ihre Geschichte," 332–34.

98. RW265-8132: 8/7 (1953).

99. See also Steinmetz, "Nachruf auf Reinhart Koselleck," 427: "As always when Koselleck approached new themes, he did not stick to empirical observations. Already in his early works, he tried to fixate his theoretical perspective on general 'anthropological categories' that should allow comparisons from Antiquity to the present."

100. However, the critique of historicism, the reworking of Heidegger and the conceptual pairs already feature in Koselleck's texts in the beginning of the 1970s, as we will see in chapter 5.

101. Hence the analytical vocabulary in the study frequently refers to the anthropological categories, first of all those of death, inner/outer, friend/enemy, up/down, and master/slave.

102. Koselleck, "Kritik und Krise: Eine Untersuchung," 31 n. 108.
103. For an account of Gadamer's reception of Heidegger, see Jean Grondin, "Heidegger und Hans-Georg Gadamer: Zur Phänomenologie des Verstehens-Geschehens," in *Heidegger-Handbuch: Leben-Werk-Wirkung*, ed. Diether Thomä, 384–90 (Stuttgart, 2003).
104. RW265-8172: 3/1 (1977).
105. See also the later interview—Koselleck, "Formen der Bürgerlichkeit," 76.
106. RW265-8172: 3/1 (1977). See also Koselleck, "Formen der Bürgerlichkeit," 76.
107. *Gott mit uns* was the slogan of the Prussian royal house (from 1701) and the German emperor and a part of the Prussian (and later German) military emblem. Later, it was also used by the German army (and the German armed forces (*Reichswehr*) between 1921 and 1935). During World War II, the German soldiers carried the slogan on their buckle-belts, while the members of the SS carried the slogan *Meine Ehre heißt Treue* (My honour is called loyalty). For the history of the slogan, see Gerd Krumreich, "'Gott mit uns'? Der Erste Weltkrieg als Religionskrieg," in *"Gott mit uns": Nation, Religion und Gewalt im 19. und frühen 20. Jahrhundert*, ed. Gerd Krumreich and Hartmut Lehmann, 273–83 (Göttingen, 2000); and Peter Franz, "Gott mit uns," in *Kleines Lexikon historisches Schlagwörter*, ed. Kurt Pätzold and Manfred Weißbecker, 136–38 (Köln, 2005).
108. For comments on Heidegger's heroic and militaristic language, see Thomas Rentsch, *Das Sein und der Tod. Eine kritische Einführung* (München, 1989), 158–74. For an account of Heidegger's fascination with death, see Hans-Ulrich Gumbrecht, "Stichwort: Tod im Kontext. Heideggers Umgang mit einer Faszination der 1920er Jahre," in *Heidegger-Handbuch. Leben-Werk-Wirkung*, ed. Dieter Thomä, 98–103 (Stuttgart, 2003).
109. See also the comments in the interview in Koselleck, "Formen der Bürgerlichkeit," 76.
110. Taubes, "Geschichtsphilosophie und Historik," 497.
111. Immanuel Kant, "Über das Mißlingen aller philosophischen Versuche in der Theodicee," *Kants Werke, Akademie-Ausgabe*, vol. VIII (Berlin, 1902), 253–71. The passage in the letter is a quotation from page 266.
112. For the implications of Kant's interpretation of Job, see Rudolf A. Makkreel, "The Confluence of Aesthetics and Hermeneutics on Baumgarten, Meier, and Kant," *The Journal of Aesthetics and Art Criticism* 54, no. 1 (1996): 69–70.
113. Koselleck, "Kritik und Krise": *Eine Studie*, 4.
114. For a historical perspective on the traditions in the German academic community, see Fritz K. Ringer, *The Decline of the German Mandarins: the German Academic Community, 1890–1933* (Cambridge, 1969).
115. In the published version of "Kritik und Krise", Koselleck had also deleted the note that compared Hobbes's and Heidegger's categories of death.
116. Reinhart Koselleck, "Im Vorfeld einer neuen Historik," *Neue Politische Literatur*, Hf. 7 (1961): 577–87. See also Reinhart Koselleck, "Review of Theodor Schieder: *Begegnungen mit der Geschichte* (Göttingen, 1962)," *Das historisch-politische Buch*, Jg. XI (1963): 295.
117. Koselleck, "Dankrede am 23 November 2004," 53. In 1955, in relation to reading Koselleck's manuscript, Schmitt tried to arrange a publication at the Diederichs-Verlag. Mehring, "Begriffsgeschichte mit Carl Schmitt," 140.
118. The most substantial changes were made in the introduction and in the chapter on the absolutist state. In the speech given in the occasion of the fiftieth year of his

Promotion, Koselleck stated that he only slightly reworked the original version of the dissertation for the publication. Koselleck, "Dankrede am 23 November 2004," 53.
119. Herbert, "Liberalisierung als Lernprozeß," 35. For broad overviews of the period, see also Conze, *Die Suche nach Sicherheit*, 45–330; Jarausch, *After Hitler*, 1–155; Wolfrum, *Die geglückte Demokratie*, 43–187; Wolfrum, *Die Bundesrepublik Deutschland 1949–1990*, 78–239; Görtemaker, *Geschichte der Bundesrepublik Deutschland*, 119–328; Schildt, *Moderne Zeiten*.
120. The observation made by the publicist Fritz René Allemann is quoted from Steger, "Sprache im Wandel," 23.
121. See Paul Nolte, *Die Ordnung der deutschen Gesellschaft. Selbstentwurf und Selbstbeschreibung im 20. Jahrhundert* (München, 2000), 20, 231–35.
122. For an account of how Habermas along with other intellectuals such as Ralf Dahrendorf argued for a further democratization of the society outside of the political institutions in the 1950s and 1960s, see Moritz Scheibe, "Auf der Suche nach der demokratischen Gesellschaft," in *Wandlungsprozesse in Deutschland: Belastung, Integration, Liberalisierung 1948–1980*, ed. Ulrich Herbert, 245–77 (Göttingen, 2002).
123. See Jan-Werner Müller, *German Intellectuals, Unification and National Identity* (London, 2000), 90–120.
124. Jürgen Habermas, "Verrufener Fortschritt—Verkanntes Jahrhundert: Zur Kritik an der Geschichtsphilosophie," *Merkur*, Jg. XIV (1960): 468–77; and Hanno Kesting, *Geschichtsphilosophie und Weltbürgerkrieg: Deutungen der Geschichte von der Französischen Revolution bis zum Ost-West-Konflikt* (Heidelberg, 1959).
125. Jürgen Habermas, *Strukturwandel der Öffentlichkeit* (Berlin, 1962). For the origins and aims of the book, see Peter Uwe Hohendahl, "Recasting the Public Sphere," *October* 73 (1995): 27–54.
126. For an account of how *Öffentlichkeit* in the mid-1950s became "Das akademische Thema der Stunde," see Stephan Schlak, *Wilhelm Hennis: Szenen einer Ideengeschichte der Bundesrepublik* (München, 2008).
127. Hohendahl, "Recasting the Public Sphere," 31.
128. Ibid., 32.
129. The described differences between *Strukturwandel der Öffentlichkeit* and "Kritik und Krise" draw on passages from Vopa, "Conceiving a Public," and Pompkin, "The Concept of Public Opinion."
130. Habermas, "Verrufener Fortschritt—Verkanntes Jahrhundert," 474.
131. Ibid., 477.
132. It has been suggested that Habermas deleted the sentence, because his analysis in *Strukturwandel der Öffentlichkeit* in fact drew on both Koselleck and Schmitt. Hence, in his chapter on the public sphere, Habermas stated that he owed many references to Koselleck's "excellent investigation," and in his analyses of models of ideal public discussion and of the underlying presuppositions of parliamentary government, he referred frequently to Schmitt's writings. Habermas, *Strukturwandel der Öffentlichkeit*, 161 n. 2. In the estimation of Pompkin, "The Concept of Public Opinion," 82: "Habermas's whole ideal of ideal public discussion parallels Schmitt's analysis of the underlying presuppositions of parliamentary government." For the intellectual relations between Schmitt and Habermas, see also Ellen Kennedy, "Carl Schmitt und die 'Frankfurter Schule': Deutsche Liberalismuskritik im 20. Jahrhundert," *Geschichte und Gesellschaft*, 12 Jg. (1986): 380–419.
133. Helmut Kuhn, Review of "Kritik und Krise", by Reinhart Koselleck, *Historische Zeitschrift*, Bd. 192 (1961): 668. Kuhn was from 1948 a professor in Erlangen. In 1953 he transferred to Munich. As a *Privatdozent* in Berlin in the 1930s, he had been the

director of the Kant-Gesellschaft and with Arthur Liebert the editor of *Kant-Studien*. Because of his Jewish origins, he was forced to give up his posts in 1935 and emigrated in 1937, settling in the United States. Before emigrating, he wrote a very critical review of Carl Schmitt's *Der Begriff des Politischen* in *Kant-Studien*, Bd. XXXVIII, Hf. 1/2 (1933): 191–96. See also Mehring, *Carl Schmitt*, 278–79.

134. Heinz Gollwitzer, Review of "Kritik und Krise", by Reinhart Koselleck, *Geschichte in Wissenschaft und Unterricht*, 11 Jg. (1960): 304. Gollwitzer held the chair of modern political and social history at the University of Münster from 1957 until he retired in 1982. Gollwitzer grew up in Munich. After being severely wounded in World War II, he began studying history and German literature at the University of Munich, where he achieved his *habilitation* in 1950 with a study titled *Europabild und Europagedanke*. For other contemporary critiques of the narrow analytical focus in "Kritik und Krise", see Kurt Schilling, Review of "Kritik und Krise", by Reinhart Koselleck, *Archiv für Rechts- und Sozialphilosophie*, Bd. XLVI (1960): 147–53 and Leo Franke, Review of "Kritik und Krise", by Reinhart Koselleck, *Philosophische Literaturanzeiger*, Nr. 14 (1961): 275–77. See also Christian Meier, Review of "Kritik und Krise", by Reinhart Koselleck, Ruperto Carola, Nr. 29 (1961): 258–64.

135. On account of its biased and pessimistic analysis, "Kritik und Krise" has also been criticized outside of Germany. In his review of the second edition, the Czech historian Bedrich Loewenstein called the analysis "a highly one-sided interpretation" that is "not fair to the Enlightenment." Review of *Critique and Crisis*, by Reinhart Koselleck, *Journal of Modern History* 48, no. 1 (1976): 122–24. The English historian T.C.W. Blanning found the English translation "elusive and insubstantial" and compared the analysis with "a minuet, in which the dancer displays much skill and grace but ends up exactly where he started." Review of *Critique and Crisis*, by Reinhart Koselleck, *German History* 7 (1989): 265–66. Impressed by Koselleck's analytical skill, John Mackrell thought only "Spengleareans . . . likely to swallow the author's thesis whole . . . ." John Mackrell, Review of *Critique and Crisis*, by Reinhart Koselleck, *History* 74 (1989): 93–94.

136. An excellent appraisal of the strengths and the biases in Koselleck's dissertation is found in Haikala, "Criticism in the Enlightenment." See also Edwards, *"Critique and Crisis* Today"; Vopa, "Conceiving a Public"; and Pompkin, "The Concept of Public Opinion."

137. Koselleck, *Critique and Crisis*, 1–4; Koselleck, "Dankrede am 23 November 2004," 57.

138. One example of this is found in Koselleck, "Historik und Hermeneutik," 17, where he challenges Habermas's ideal of *herrschaftsfreier Diskurs*, that is, the contention that we can critically evaluate political life from the perspective of a rational consensus that is attained in a *herrschaftsfrei* (domination-free) practical discourse. What Koselleck challenged in this ideal is its reliance on a suspension of time. According to Koselleck, temporal scarcity is always a constitutive element of the political situation and in many instances decisions must be taken within an infinite temporal horizon: Due to the lack of time to reach a broad consensus, some decisions must be taken by a limited number of people and often against the desires and aspirations of others. From this basis, Koselleck sees in the ideal of *herrschaftsfreier Diskurs* a disregard of the role of power struggles in politics and of what conditions the humanly possible (see the excellent comments in Kari Palonen, "The History of Concepts as a Style of Political Theorizing: Quentin Skinner's and Reinhart Koselleck's Subversion of Normative Political Theory," *European Journal of Political Theory* 1, no. 1 (2000): 100). Much of Koselleck's historical writing was directed against such ideals, and his challenge of the ideal of *herrschaftsfreier Diskurs* is one of many examples of how he came

to conceive of Habermas as an intellectual counterpart against whom he defined his positions and concepts after "Kritik und Krise".

139. The list of studies taking up themes from "Kritik und Krise" is too long to be mentioned here.

140. For some of the latest examples in the Anglophone literature, see Edwards, "Critique and Crisis Today"; Jason Edwards, "The Ideological Interpellation of Individuals as Combatants: An Encounter between Reinhart Koselleck and Michel Foucault," *Journal of Political Ideologies*, 12 (2007): 49–66. The most comprehensive attempt to apply and further develop Koselleck's writings in the field of political theory has been made by Kari Palonen, to whom we return in chapter 5.

141. See for example Koselleck, "Dankrede am 23 November 2004," 56.

142. We shall return to the circle around Schmitt in chapter 3.

143. Koselleck, "Formen der Bürgerlichkeit," 75. As late as 1965, Koselleck is mentioned in an article by the political scientist Christian Graf von Krockow who warned against the authoritarian alternative to the German democracy that Ernst Forsthoff and other associates of Schmitt allegedly argued for in the journal *Der Staat*. Christian Graf von Krockow, "Staatsideologie oder demokratisches Bewußtsein: Die deutsche Alternative," *Politische Vierteljahresschrift*, Jg. VI. (1965): 118–31. For recent readings of "Kritik und Krise" as a conservative book, see Schwartz, "Leviathan oder Lucifer" and Hohendahl, "Recasting the Public Sphere." See also Franz Leander Fillafer, "The Enlightenment on Trial: Reinhart Koselleck's Interpretation of *Aufklärung*," in *The Many Faces of Clio: Cross-Cultural Approaches to Historiography*, ed. Franz Leander Fillafer and Edward Q. Wang, 322–45 (Oxford, 2007).

144. Kuhn, Review of "Kritik und Krise", by Reinhart Koselleck, 666.

145. Ibid., 668.

146. Carl Schmitt, Review of "Kritik und Krise", by Reinhart Koselleck, *Das Historisch-Politische Buch*, Jg. VII (1959): 301–02. Schmitt read the manuscript before the publication and Koselleck asked him for a review. See Mehring, "Begriffsgeschichte mit Carl Schmitt," 140. Schmitt's reflections on the applied method in the review were prompted by a request made by Koselleck. See his letter to Schmitt, RW265-8151: 18/6 (1959).

147. Schmitt, "Review", 302. An excerpt of Schmitt's review was printed on the back page of the later editions of "Kritik und Krise". In the cited passage, Schmitt referred to the book *Die Lessing-Legende* (1882), written by the German publicist, politician, and Marxist historian Franz Mehring (1846–1919). The book was directed against the patriotic school of German literary historians who tried to prove that the renaissance of German literature in the eighteenth century was due to the rise of Prussia as a European power, and that there was a close connection between the despotism of Prussian King Frederick II and the birth of classical German literature.

148. In addition, some of the anthropological categories that Koselleck presented in the 1950s never came to play central roles in his writings. This is for example the case with the category of *Geschlechtlichkeit* (gender). For comments on the lack of focus on gender in Koselleck's conceptual history, see Ute Frevert, *"Mann und Weib, und Weib und Mann": Geschlechter-Differenzen in der Moderne* (München, 1995), 14–15.

3

SOCIAL HISTORY BETWEEN REFORM AND REVOLUTION

After submitting his dissertation at the end of 1953, Koselleck moved to Bristol, England, where he worked as a lecturer from 1954 until the autumn of 1955. Following some administrative delays, Koselleck returned to finish his oral exams in Heidelberg in January 1954. According to a letter he afterwards wrote to Schmitt, the exams took place in a very peaceful atmosphere.[1] Ernst Forsthoff, whom Koselleck had met only briefly twice before, was his examiner for *Staatsrecht* (constitutional law). The historical questions he posed on this subject resulted in "a conversation that always ended up in the contemporary situation," Koselleck further reported to Schmitt. In philosophy, Hans-Georg Gadamer examined Koselleck on Descartes, Leibniz, and Heidegger. The majority of his questions, however, were focused on Kant, and here he let Koselleck talk freely on "the historical-philosophical chord that runs through Kant's work." Finally, in history Koselleck "took a walk" with Johannes Kühn "through World History focusing on the example of Germany and its historical motto 'always too late'." The two magna and one summa that Koselleck received in history meant that in February 1954 he could look back on the oral exams with a "certain contentment."

Koselleck had been somewhat more worried about how Johannes Kühn and the second reader Karl Löwith would react to the dissertation itself. He feared first of all possible criticisms of the applied method, for its not being neutral.[2] "Professor Kühn is so tolerant a person that he acknowledges my question of interest (*Fragestellung*), but I fear that with the present work I have already reached the limits of his tolerance," Koselleck wrote to Schmitt in November 1953. However, Koselleck added, he knew that Kühn was in agreement with his verdict on Meinecke, and as for the report from his second examinor, Karl Löwith, Koselleck did not see an inevitable opposition between his work and Löwith's "historical-philosophical scepticism."[3]

Eventually, Koselleck received the second best grade, magna cum laude, for his dissertation; his worries turned out to be unfounded.[4] The most important criticism made by Kühn and Löwith was, as Koselleck expected, directed against the method he had employed in his study, which oscillated among three academic fields: history, philosophy, and sociology.[5]

In this chapter, we will see how, in his next major work after "Kritik und Krise", the *Habilitation Preußen zwischen Reform und Revolution*, Koselleck once again applied an interdisciplinary approach, but in a way that was less controversial vis-à-vis the standards of the discipline. In fact, one of the aims of this chapter is to demonstrate how, in the years between his dissertation and *Habilitation* Koselleck reshaped and repositioned himself into a more conventional and broadly respected scholar in the field.

The chapter proceeds in three sections. Each maintains a perspective both on Koselleck's intellectual production and on his attempt to navigate in the discipline. It begins by illuminating Koselleck's intellectual activities from 1953 to 1957, the period during which he first worked as a lecturer at the University of Bristol and then as an assistant to Johannes Kühn in Heidelberg. With a focus on the processes of reception, we will see how Koselleck developed a theory of the historical dynamics of political geography with which he substantiated his arguments concerning the need to respect the anthropological condition of human beings, and moreover developed an analytical framework that became an integral part of his historical thought more generally. With a focus on the course of Koselleck's career in the 1950s, we will in addition see how the processes in which he was "made" as a historian were to a certain extent a result of coincidences, unforeseen events, and unexpected choices that he was facing and had to deal with at the time.

The second part of the chapter deals with how, under the supervision of Werner Conze in Heidelberg, Koselleck conceptualized *Preußen zwischen Reform und Revolution*. On the one hand, we will see how, in his work on the Prussian *Vormärz*, Koselleck complied with the standards and norms of Conze's social-historical program, even if this program did not entirely fit his analytical tastes. On the other hand, we will see how Koselleck not only learned and adapted to, but also refined Conze's program, by outlining a temporal-historical framework that was related to and became crucial for his attempts at thematizing history in the plural.

Finally, via an analysis of his contribution to the 1969 book *Das Zeitalter der europäischen Revolution 1740–1848*, the chapter sums up the pragmatism, innovation, and ambiguity that characterized Koselleck's work in the first twenty years of his academic career.

From Heidelberg to Bristol: From Land to Sea

Throughout his stay in England, besides teaching, Koselleck attempted to find a new academic topic for his *Habilitation* and to find the proper academic setting in which to carry out the work. "The question of what I should focus on now depends very much on my current position," he wrote to Schmitt in February 1954.[6]

Koselleck had, he added, recently been offered a second year of lecturing in Bristol. Although the position did not offer the most promising perspectives for the future, he was tempted to accept, because with a good salary, paid holidays and a reasonable amount of free time, he would be well set to work on an English theme and—possibly—be able to finish his studies in the United States by means of a scholarship.

In Koselleck's opinion, one of the advantages of staying in Bristol would be that he could continue on the path of his earlier work: "to investigate the philosophy of progress (and of circularity) of the eighteenth century with its political and historical implications." However, Koselleck also described a range of other academic topics to Schmitt, which he had recently started to look into, and which he hoped to pursue along the lines of, or rather to combine with his earlier work. "I do not know," he wrote, "if there is anything new to be said about this range of questions: England-Continent, Europe, America, world-unity and revolution—that goes beyond your ascertainments (*Feststellungen*)." He therefore listed three further topics that he considered less researched and on which he could work from England: the "democratization" of England; the role of the British Empire in this process; and finally, Marx and Disraeli.

Although Koselleck was to pursue some of these topics later, in February 1954, when he wrote the cited letter to Schmitt, he was uncertain about his future academic plans. His uncertainty was further deepened by an offer he had received from the sociologist Heinrich Popitz during the Christmas break, to possibly become an assistant at the newly founded Dortmunder Institut für Sozialforschung. Focusing on sociological analysis of the technical-industrial age, the institute in Dortmund was to become one of the most important centers for social research in the early Federal

Republic. At the time, it already had numerous prominent sociologists connected to it, such as Hans Freyer, Günther Ipsen, and the younger Helmut Schelsky.[7] From what Koselleck knew about the institute, first of all from Hanno Kesting, who was already employed there, it was an interesting place, and as he told Schmitt, he was tempted to join it.

Koselleck's first publication after he submitted his dissertation "Kritik und Krise" reflects some of both his academic interests and dilemmas in the mid 1950s. It was a rather remarkable fourteen-page article called "Bristol, die 'zweite Stadt' Englands. Eine sozialgeschichtliche Skizze," which was published in 1955 in the journal *Soziale Welt*, that emanated from the Dortmunder Institut für Sozialforschung.[8] In the article, Koselleck gave the impression of wanting to simultaneously fulfil the demands of the journal (of illuminating the processes of industrialization); continue developing his earlier work (on the origins of modern political thought); as well as include his newly acquired interest in certain Anglo-Saxon and global themes (with a focus on the democratization of England).

He did this, in a narrow sense, by focusing on the reasons for and consequences of the industrial revolution, through describing the role of a group of merchants in the city of Bristol so as to illuminate its social-historical significance as the second-most important city in England from around 1200 until 1900. In addition, from a broader perspective, focusing on the origins of liberalism and the special relation between state and society that it allegedly embraces, he described England's move into political modernity and her role in modern world history. In order to connect these topics, Koselleck used a narrative structure rather than making a strict analysis, and he merged a social-historical approach with a somewhat peculiar geographical perspective. He argued that England's historical-political development was most heavily influenced by the specific element surrounding the country: the sea. Since this interpretation rested on several discursive features that were to dominate his historical thinking in the 1950s, the text is examined in detail below.

At the beginning of the article, Koselleck introduced a group of Bristol merchants. He noted that these figures had from an early stage held important wealth privileges, such as the monopoly on tax and trade, "and as such the de facto monopoly of power" in the city, and he moreover described the merchants using many of the same terms that he had used to describe Enlightenment thinkers in "Kritik und Krise".[9] They were "modern," "individual," and "independent," and they secured their interests and privileges through principles of exclusivity in their fellowships, which manifested themselves as independent societies, and by holding municipal posts.[10]

However, the "turn to modernity" took place in a very different way in England than on the continent. In England, Koselleck argued, the absolutely crucial event in this respect was what he labeled the "turn to the ocean": the decision, taken already in the sixteenth century, to turn to the sea and to conquer the great oceans.[11] This move had enormous consequences not only for the merchants in Bristol, but also for the city itself and for England—and even for the course of world history.

In their attempt to set out to explore "the mysteries of the Atlantic Ocean" and "the secrets of the open West" in the sixteenth century, the adventurous merchants used Bristol's "advantageous geographical location" and allied themselves with experts who were trained in the new geographical sciences.[12] As such, they came to play an important role in the battle of the world seas—a conflict over the space, resources, and domination of the world. According to Koselleck, this fight soon acquired its own particular characteristics: "The battle of the world seas was a battle of secrets: the secrets of nature and the secrets of the others."[13]

In the battle for the new world, he added, victory became more important than a clean conscience, as in their conquering of the oceans, the merchants did not refrain from solving the lack of capital in the eighteenth century through piracy—a venture that was supported financially by the English Queen in the fight between Protestantism and Catholicism for the spaces and the treasures of the world. Moreover, already after the English civil war, from which they emerged relatively unscathed, the merchants allied themselves with the English government, whose aim was to turn England into the leading sea power. This was achieved via industrial-technological developments, expansion overseas, and increasing trade, the convergence of which turned England into a world power and brought profit to the Bristol merchants, who, among other things, secured themselves a leading position in the lucrative trade of gold, ivory, and slaves in Africa by defending their monopolies from other interest groups.

The African trade, and the general behaviour of the colonizing British Empire, was, Koselleck stated, characterized by exploitation, robbery, and humiliation: "It is not the place," he wrote, "to go into all the atrocities committed by the brutal captains or the arguments with which the Bristol merchants tried to justify them: the well-being of the colonies, the economic existence of the city, and even the trade and the income of the country depended on this."[14] According to Koselleck, the merchant's political power was thus not only based on secrecy and exclusion, but also on self-justified crime and violence.[15]

Before the nineteenth century, when the city of Bristol had, as a result of developments connected to the industrial revolution and the "epoch of technology," lost its widely recognized significance, the merchants began to use the "outer" power to direct their "inner" activities into public religious, philanthropic, and pedagogical undertakings. By changing their "open political power" into "a quiet societal power," operating as a "political club" within the state, the merchants were able to maintain their leading position in English society.[16]

Affirming that in spite of certain changes, the merchant society had kept its political function and significance, Koselleck finished his article by subtly linking the historical rise of liberalism and the formation of the English state to the present social-political situation in England. "Hence, as long as England maintains that tradition," he wrote in the very last sentence, "the state does not break away from society."[17]

Obviously, the article on Bristol evidenced a clear continuation in Koselleck's work on the origins of political modernity, with its focus on the relation between state and society, and on the emergence of international law as seen from a global perspective. However, the article also highlights two new dimensions in Koselleck's historical writing as he moved from Heidelberg to Bristol—from the land to the sea. The first is the attention that he devoted to the origins of English political modernity, including the important events of the industrial-technological revolution, overseas expansion, and the unusual relationship between state and society, to which he attributed the rise of the British Empire. The second change is the way that he used the explanatory framework to elevate geography into the vital factor for state formation and political organization—and thereby into the central vehicle of world history as such. This explanatory framework was to become central in Koselleck's work in the mid 1950s. But where did Koselleck find the inspiration for this? And what role did it play in his contemporary writings—and in his historical thinking more generally?

In answer to the first question, it seems clear that Koselleck again drew extensively upon the writings of Carl Schmitt. More concretely, Koselleck drew on a discourse, including a variety of themes and arguments, which since the mid 1930s Schmitt had presented in his work on international law and synthesized in *Der Nomos der Erde*—the book that Koselleck made use of in "Kritik und Krise" to conceptualize his idea of the "world historical crisis."

In Schmitt's *Der Nomos der Erde*, the word *nomos* (law) is used to refer to an eternal division and order of political space. All political organization, national as well as international—so goes the basic argument of the book—must be understood as a continuous battle between political powers for the earth's spaces and resources, a constant *Nehmen-Teilen-Weiden* (meaning a constant taking, distributing, and producing). Moreover, starting from the belief that nation states developed their ideals of state formation, political ethics, and international warfare relating to the element surrounding them, Schmitt further argued that land and sea had long designated two distinctively different political modes of organization.

Specifically, along the same lines as Koselleck, Schmitt described how through its discovery and increasing domination of the sea in the seventeenth century, England had created an open world of colonization, slavery, and piracy, which was fundamentally opposed to the absolutist continental states that based their political organization on war, diplomacy, and taxation. Without the strongly centralized kind of state that existed on the continent, England instead nurtured the dynamic activity of privateers, merchants, and pirates, and through this was able to manifest a unique position as a power both inside and outside the European interstate system. Furthermore, Schmitt argued, the English maritime empire had initiated and contributed to the breakdown of the traditional European power-state and the traditional system of international law, thus paving the way for the blurry, self-justifying, and discriminating concept of war promoted by liberalism.[18]

Written as a comment on the contemporary political situation in which the United States and the Soviet Union were manifesting themselves as superpowers, Schmitt ended his book by reflecting on the consequences that the exploration of a new element, air, and the new technologies of warfare and communication would have for future international law, and modes of political power and organization. In other words, Schmitt attempted to interpret the new *Nomos der Erde.*

Geography, Technology, and Politics

Together with his correspondence with Schmitt, Koselleck's first writings after "Kritik und Krise" show that his thoughts in the mid 1950s drew on the political-geographical discourse that he to a considerable degree derived from Schmitt's work on international law. Through their correspondence, we can follow how Koselleck continued to discuss such matters with Schmitt while he was in Bristol.[19] At discussion was the historical dynamics of political geography: the new world order that would arise from these dynamics, the relations among politics, power, and technology in this order; and the consequences of these new relations. Having direct access to English and American books in Bristol, Koselleck kept Schmitt up to date on the latest relevant literature—either by sending books directly to Plettenberg or by providing Schmitt with lengthy abstracts in his letters. Schmitt often replied by sending Koselleck his latest publications. As we will see, in the comments on Schmitt's publications that he provided in these letters, Koselleck outlined a set of interpretations of interests that were inspired by Schmitt, but framed according to individual aims and concerns.

One of the books Schmitt sent to Koselleck was *Gespräche über die Macht und den Zugang zum Machthaber* from 1954.[20] Dealing with questions of the nature of and access to power, one of its central arguments is that the early modern concepts of autonomy and sovereignty had been dissolved in the transition to the modern world and that political power had been removed from the hands of human beings. More concretely, while humans were officially still in power and considered themselves powerful, they were in reality dependent on invisible and indirect forces of authority operating behind the political scene as well as on technological means of power that were beyond their control. In line with this, Schmitt argued that technology had developed into the *sine qua non* in all human affairs, including politics, and he argued that it was only possible to understand this development and to interpret the future Nomos der Erde by scrutinizing the dynamics of political geography.[21]

In a letter to Schmitt written in November 1954, Koselleck told him that *Gespräche über die Macht und den Zugang zum Machthaber* had made him realize the "qualitative changes of politics that have taken place via the expansion of technique."[22] For Koselleck, the invention of the atomic bomb represented the completion of a long technological-political process in which the conditions for exercising power, most notably between a state and its people, had been fundamentally altered. He wrote:

> The relation analyzed by Hobbes between the danger of death and the nature of politics has not only been forgotten, but has consequently been abstractly detached from the people living in a given age. In Hegel, I once read that the invention of gun powder and consequently the indirect methods of killing is the precondition for the individual's partake in the modern state as a supra-individual unity. One can say that nuclear weapons are the "completion" of this technical-political process. Power is no longer a relation between men, or a "force," as it was still possible for Burckhardt to say; it is itself a potential condition of death, whose bearers are anonymous crowds. The difficulties of ending the state of things seem according to your analysis to be located in a specifically modern dialectic in which all relations of power are embedded today: power is removed from concrete human beings through the entelechy of technique, though it still is in human hands.

The solution to the "problem of power" was, according to Koselleck, to be located in the right relation that must exist "between a responsible partake in the power and its representation . . . ." When this relation had been achieved, he added, the potential dangers inherent in the dialectic between direct and indirect power would be contained as far as it was humanly possible.

Directing the issue of political power to that of the "the stage of world politics of today," Koselleck argued that the two world powers had gained their supremacy through technical development, but without having exercised actual political work. For this reason, he did not view their supremacy as a political achievement, comparable to that of the British Empire, but merely as a byproduct of their power. And, he added, for as long as the United States and the Soviet Union did not acknowledge the helplessness of being only the abstract executors of their apparati of power, their "highflying consciousness" (*hochgeschossenes Bewusstsein*) represented merely a "false consciousness." Koselleck continued: "This raises the 'old' question: is it still possible to make hidden power on the European continent apparent and visible in such a way, that the indirect impact of the world powers are reduced to their proper frames?"

The letters suggest that neither Koselleck nor Schmitt harbored any expectations that a power on the continent would come to play an important political role in the contemporary political scene. Their attention seemed in the mid 1950s instead to be directed toward Asia, Russia, and the Anglo-Saxon spaces, and to the historical dynamics of political geography and political power more generally.

As a way to understand Koselleck's take on the issue of political power, we might note that he and Schmitt were far from unique in approaching the nature of history and politics and the condition of the modern world through probing the relation among geography, space, and technology. During the 1950s, technology had an increasingly pervasive impact on all levels of Western society. New weapons and communication systems transformed the modes of warfare and politics while industrial and cultural innovations altered people's working conditions and their social relations, as well their everyday lives. Human existence, it seemed, was being fundamentally revolutionized, and, whatever the attitude toward the technological development, the "age of technology" was seen as unstoppable and inevitable. This belief was also held among German intellectuals, who were busy analyzing the question of technology and its influence on modern existence. The question had already dominated many philosophical schools and debates of the interwar period. It had been especially virulent in the politically right-wing intellectual milieu of those whom Jeffrey Herf labeled "reactionary modernists," most prominently Ernst Jünger, Freyer, Schmitt, and Heidegger.[23]

Some of the "reactionary modernists" also belonged to the most widely read authors on the issue in the 1950s, who adapted their argumentative lines to suit post-World War II politics and society. This was the case with Schmitt, Freyer, and Heidegger, who expressed serious concern over the consequences of the development of technology for "the political" (Schmitt), the sphere of social relations (Freyer), and the question of Being (Heidegger). While the majority of the scholars discussing the technological developments came from the conservative camp, the issue also caught the attention of many liberal and left-wing intellectuals. Common for the debaters, regardless of their political and generational affiliation, was a considerable skepticism toward the increasing technological impact on human existence and a wish to contain its potentially negative consequences.[24]

Another widespread feature in the attempts made by philosophers, sociologists, and political scientists to analyze the origins, character, and consequences of technological developments, which were conceived of as a key characteristic of modernity, was the replacement of the traditional focus on national history with a global-historical perspective. This trend was also widespread among historians.[25] Some historians, such as Gerhard Ritter, had long portrayed the contemporary world as a direct result of an ongoing fight between geographically opposed empires, civilizations, and countries.[26] Others, such as Werner Conze, argued that the revolutionary processes of the eighteenth century, including technological developments, had resulted in a historically new dimension of space and time. More concretely, as they saw it, the process triggered by the spatial discoveries and challenges in relation to overseas expansions and technological developments had resulted in a constant acceleration of time and transgression of spatial boundaries: The result was a much smaller and increasingly unified world.[27] In this world, they argued, states and societies were subjected not only to permanent and interrelated changes, but also to a new global order that was based on mass politics and modern political ideology, and, in the twentieth century, marked by the confrontation between the geographically opposed East and West.

These global-historical perspectives were applied for a variety of reasons and purposes by German scholars. For some, an emphasis on Germany's "Western" nature helped ease German postwar integration into the Atlantic Federation. For others, recourse to geopolitical determinants served to relieve Germany from guilt in relation to World War II and thus to portray German history in a more favorable light. Indeed, this was the case in the writings of many conservative scholars, including Carl Schmitt.

What in analytical terms distinguished Schmitt's work in this field was its particular focus on the dynamics between geography and technology in the age of modernity and the consequences of this for the nature of "the political." This was an issue that Schmitt investigated from the perspective of international law and approached through a particular type of analytical realism, as unfolded in *Nomos der Erde*, which emerged as one of the important German and European contributions to the contemporary discussion about the end of territoriality and visions of global order.[28]

Several analytical features from Schmitt's work on political geography appear in Koselleck's writings in the mid 1950s. However, Koselleck's position on the age of technology, and on questions of political power in the modern world, had a distinctively different political concern than had Schmitt's. In general, Koselleck's geopolitical texts from the mid 1950s follow the anthropological and political concerns laid out in the letter to Schmitt, as discussed in chapter 2, such as the insistence on finality and the preoccupation with the current world historical crises. The cautious dissociation from Schmittian notions also prevailed.

All these notions are spelled out in more detail in a series of reviews published in various German journals from the mid 1950s onwards. For Koselleck, who was still a young scholar in the process of finding an institution that could fund and support his work, the review articles functioned as a medium through which he used the work of other scholars to voice his own interests and views in an indirect fashion.

This was the case, for example, in a 1956 review article dealing with writings of and about the second president of the United States, John Adams, which was published in the journal *Neue politische Literatur*.[29] In the course of his introduction to Adams's writings, Koselleck not only presented a set of geopolitical perspectives on the political making and dynamics of the modern world, but also expressed a plea for a mode of political order that respected the human finality, in which power is shared between different political bodies representing both state and society. Koselleck's broader motivation for occupying himself with Adams's political thought was twofold: to formulate a (critical) account of the origins and premises of American foreign and domestic politics, and thus to bring into focus what he perceived as fundamental differences between the European and American political *Erfahrungshorizont* ("horizon of experience").[30]

According to Koselleck, despite being one of the most important political philosophers in the US War of Independence, Adams did not create a philosophical system. In fact, he practiced only a method—that of the polemical discussion. With great self-confidence, Adams had according to Koselleck conceptualized his entire philosophy as a series of responses to the position of his opponent, be it the democrats, merchants, the Brits, Europeans, or the French philosophers.

Conscious of being American, Koselleck added, Adams first of all realized that Natural Law, like any other law, can be used as an instrument of power, and, in spite of strong objections, Adams managed to include a reference to Natural Law in the Declaration of Rights (1774), claiming that American settlers could evade the European rules of sovereignty and the colonies could achieve independence and create a new concept of sovereignty. Not long after, Adams's son, John Quincy utilized this insight to pave the way for the famous Monroe Doctrine to gain political independence on behalf of the Americans. The basic premise of the Monroe Doctrine (one of the central themes in Schmitt's work on international law), Koselleck explained, is the drawing of a line of American political sovereignty along the Atlantic Ocean. Quite simply, it declares that the American territory is free from the jurisdiction of all European law, and that European law is thus inapplicable on American soil.

Koselleck described the part of Adams's writings that focused on "the principal difference between American and Europe" (a result of the different geographical locations) as full of "aggression," "ideologization," and "propaganda." Always locating the aggressor on the other side of the ocean, Adams, Koselleck wrote, showed himself cognizant of the "weapons of ideologization" and of the means through which to deploy them outwards.[31]

At the same time, according to Koselleck, Adams was characterized by stoic confidence and humility, which especially dominates the second phase of his writings. Here, Koselleck stated, Adams provided a historical-sociological foundation for the liberal constitutional law, by reflecting on a constant set of political alternatives that were first discussed by Thucydides, but which are found throughout history: the alternative between civil war and order.

To avoid a civil war, Adams proposed two things, said Koselleck: a strong executive and an equal partake of all social forces in the legislature. While aiming at a system in which the executive could not be paralyzed by the participating forces, he also proposed a system of an upper and a lower house, where all interests could be represented. Distinguishing between two forms of state, one in which this aim was reached, and one in which all power was one-sidedly accumulated, be it with the people, the aristocracy, or the Monarch, Adams ultimately aimed to avoid a tyranny either from above or from below.

Since this was the background against which Koselleck praised Adams's "incorruptible and down-to earth sense of historical realities and actions,"[32] he had, it seems, begun to use Adams to voice his own historical-political interests and beliefs. Koselleck continued: Adam's' idea of power was related to religion, the meaning and necessity of which he never ignored, because he believed politics to be a godly science with historical experience as its guiding principle. All the same, Koselleck added, qualifying the religious attitude in Adams: "Adams uses the afterlife as a kind of heuristic grasp to make visible the finality of everything historical. The weakness of the human race . . . prevents a constant progress. All progress is rather a temporary result of stately order."[33]

By reading Adams's text against the background of the concept of finality, Koselleck clearly appropriated the text into his own line of anthropologically based historical-political thought. This centered around a formalistic conception of the human being as a vulnerable creature, whose existence is not naturally progressing toward a better and more advanced stage in the age of modernity, in which the possibility of human conflict and sudden death had on the contrary been radically increased. Like Adams, Koselleck viewed politics from the alternative between civil war and order, and, in line with the protagonist of his review, he believed in progress within the domain of politics as something that can only unfold on the basis of a responsible order that respects the anthropological human condition and includes the interests of both state and society. In spite of his new thematic interests, these convictions continued to be central to Koselleck's ideas about history and politics in the mid 1950s.

The continuation of Koselleck's pattern of thought was expressed even more forcefully, and in more detail, in a 1955 review of *Christianity, Diplomacy and War*, written by the English historian Herbert Butterfield.[34] In Koselleck's words, Butterfield's book addressed a new phenomenon in history caused by the unity of the bipolar earth—a world in which the recognized boundaries between war and peace, and between war and civil war had allegedly been replaced by the notion of a "war of righteousness." The main objective of Butterfield's investigation was thus to answer the key question of the contemporary political situation: "Is a war for justice, 'the war for righteousness,' justifiable or not?"[35]

Butterfield, Koselleck explained, did not deliver a material Christian historical philosophy like Arnold Toynbee. He was more of a *Fachhistoriker*, who approached the problem from the perspective of a Christian vision of history, or, as Koselleck phrased it, of a Christian historical ontology. According to Koselleck, the double approach (of deciphering history from the perspective of its fundamental condition, understood from a Christian viewpoint, and the historical-scientific method) led to striking insights, but also, because of the lack of conceptual distinctions, to a certain distortions.

Since, from the Christian perspective, all wars originate from sin, and because sin can by nature never be righteous or monopolized, Butterfield conceived of the notion of a war of righteousness as a fundamental contradiction. The result was a moral simplification of historical reality—in Koselleck's words: "The enemy becomes a criminal, while the self-righteous becomes a party-member as well as a judge."[36] In line with this, Koselleck explained, Butterfield pointed to another violation of theological reality that he argued has grave consequences when applied to politics: the belief that war and evil can somehow be overcome. Butterfield's stance on this issue was clear: The world will not be made righteous by politics—the war to end all wars does not lead to a more righteous world, only to more intensive wars. The only consequences that emanate from war, Koselleck added to Butterfield's perspective, are the new distributions of land and of power. For Butterfield, the crucial question deduced from this perspective was simple: "In a world where we cannot eliminate war, how can we control it, and how can we maintain an international order still?"[37]

According to Butterfield, Koselleck added, the problem was that ideologies had obscured the notions of friend and enemy as well as of winner and vanquished, thus paving the way for a criminalization of the enemy, which in turn led to the total wars of the twentieth century. Here Butterfield referred to National Socialism and World War II as consequences of World War I by means of questioning whether the crimes of National Socialism would have been committed, had Germany not been labeled the exclusive criminal after World War I. This criminalization had resulted in a fixation on questions of guilt and complexes of inferiority which influenced the rise of National Socialism in the 1920s and 1930s. In Butterfield's perspective, there would, Koselleck explained, always be enemies: "The problem is not to have an enemy; it is rather how one sees, identifies and understands the enemy."[38]

Butterfield's solution to this problem was allegedly to transfer the Christian duty of learning to understand and to evaluate one's enemy to the field of politics. In order to apply this principle to politics, and to control the forces of power, he recommended recourse to the sphere of diplomacy. His specific model was the European interstate system of the eighteenth century in which there was room for neutrality and total wars were never waged. "War was not abolished," Koselleck explained, "and peace was not merely a slogan; rather a political achievement."[39]

Although he approached the issues of human nature, war and diplomacy, the past and the present from a Christian perspective, Butterfield's stance was in many respects close to Schmitt's and Koselleck's lines of interpretation. At least it was read as such by Koselleck, who, in his enthusiastic review, eventually ventured to compare *Christianity, Diplomacy and War* to Schmitt's *Der Nomos der Erde*. In this comparison, Koselleck praised Butterfield for presenting "many and subtle analyses that are worth paying attention to and which aim at making visible a political space for tolerance."[40] Yet he detected a crucial difference between the two works. Although Koselleck was of the opinion that Butterfield's Christian ontology was not tainted by eschatological and intolerant features, he saw a dangerous potential in his appeal to Christianity in that utopian Christian demands for equality would have grave revolutionary consequences if they were applied to real history.

Consequently, the work of Schmitt was given the last word in the article. "Carl Schmitt," Koselleck wrote, "has in his work shown a decisive condition for the past ordering of the earth: the relative stability in Europe could only be maintained due to the engagements overseas and across the Urals, where the bulk of its accumulated energies could be displaced."[41] Affirming that a new world was in the making (in which the role played by England would be decisive), the implicit assumption underlying Koselleck's review of Butterfield—and the bulk of his other texts from the mid 1950s—was that this world order could only be interpreted with the use of Schmitt's analytical categories and conceptions.[42]

It was also from this perspective, in a letter to Schmitt from February 1954, that Koselleck criticized the work of his teacher Johannes Kühn on "the historical problem of tolerance."[43] According to Koselleck, Kühn was right to observe that there exists no "tolerance as such"—"it is rather so that power, society and religion always tend to drift into intolerance, that is, tolerance is as such only possible due to historical constellations . . . which leave open a space for tolerance." However, Kühn also pointed to two other possibilities of tolerance of which Koselleck was deeply skeptical. The first concerned a "religious-universal outlook (with mythical roots)"; and the second an idea of "a mutual consideration and recognition of the rules of the game for which he uses the subordinate concept of apparatus and machinery." In spite of their qualities and intentions, according to Koselleck, Kühn's reflections were simply unfit for the challenges of modernity. Koselleck wrote: "As today, in the age of technique, he uses this concept of machinery in the sense of a political balance he does not find a way out of the liberal way of thinking, in spite of his fight against all utopias. Even if he sees and thinks further, he cannot avoid the destiny that his words will trail off, as they are used up and will no more be heard."

Koselleck's comments on Butterfield and Kühn testify to his view on history and politics—and to his habit of positioning himself using the work of other scholars. He drew to a certain extent on and shared their ideas, but modified or added to these in order to articulate his own (and supposedly superior) understanding of the issue at stake. To be sure, Koselleck agreed with the basic line of thought outlined by Butterfield and Kühn, but, as was the case in his critique of Meinecke, he did not find their ideas sufficiently radical. In his eyes, a realistic and responsible framework for politics in the age of technology could not be established simply through applying ideas from the sphere of religion to politics or through a quasi-liberal conception of politics as a game organized around mutually recognized rules. Criticizing their interpretations, he instead argued that the only way to master, or to provide some sort of damage control for the massive destructive potential inherent in the age of technology was to systematically undermine all notions of history in the singular by means of disclosing the eternal conditions of human nature, as originating from its finality.

However, there was still an unresolved tension in Koselleck's thought, as he to some extent continued to replicate the account of history as one progressive movement that he so heavily criticized. It was this schematic interpretation of the modern world and not a focus on pluralism that informed Koselleck's work in the mid 1950s, even after he finally found an institution at which he could pursue his interests, as we will see in the following section.

Heidelberg, Vienna, Prussia

As well as his correspondence with Schmitt, Koselleck's published writings suggest that at the beginning of 1955 he was hoping to write a *Habilitation* with a political-geographical perspective on Anglo-Saxon political modernity. However, since he had not yet found an institution in which to carry out his work, his future plans were still uncertain.

In the summer of 1955, Koselleck was once again contacted by Heinrich Popitz, who was still trying to find a position for him in Dortmund. This time around the plans were more concrete, as Koselleck told Schmitt in a letter from early July 1955.[44] First of all, Koselleck already had an appointment for an interview with Günther Ipsen, who was head of department at the institute. Moreover, Popitz had already suggested a concrete topic for Koselleck to work on: Rationalisierung und Arbeitsersparnis als soziologisches Problem (Rationalization and Labour Saving as a Sociological Problem). Although Koselleck was interested in the topic, he found it difficult to evaluate how far a career move to the institute in Dortmund would take him from the discipline of history. For the moment, Koselleck added, as if to emphasize that his primary interest lay in the study of history, his readings were concentrated on two themes: "Prognosis and historical philosophy (as counter-concepts), and the role of America in the English nineteenth century."

Koselleck's worries about his academic future finally came to an end in the following month. When he returned to Bristol in August 1955 from his interview in Dortmund, he found a letter from Johannes Kühn, who asked Koselleck to become his assistant in Heidelberg.[45] This was both unexpected and surprising for Koselleck, who, in his own words, was "forced to commit a least one error."[46] Eventually, however, he opted for the position in Heidelberg. Although he missed out on the chance "to become acquainted with the current developments in the very concrete context of the large scale industry," Heidelberg was, Koselleck told Schmitt, the best move as long as he aimed at a *Habilitation* in history.

Back in Heidelberg, Koselleck became busy teaching "pro-seminars" and assisting Kühn in his more specialized seminars. His enthusiastic tone in his letters suggests that he much enjoyed teaching and took great interest in the topics, the applied methods, and the students.[47] It was also through one of these seminars that Koselleck came across the topic that he initially wanted to turn into the subject of his *Habilitation*: the Congress of Vienna.

Koselleck's decision to work on this topic appears to have been a conscious choice to use the political-geographical discourse on modernity largely inspired by Schmitt, with which he had acquainted himself in England. It was consequently with some enthusiasm that Koselleck told Schmitt about the seminar and his reflections on the topic in a letter from July 1956.[48] He informed Schmitt that he had begun with the geopolitical preconditions, and he then drew attention to the exchange of notes between the two negotiators, the English Foreign Secretary Viscount Castlereigh and the Russian Emperor Alexander I—an exchange which he found to be of remarkable topicality. The entire train of thought as well as the vocabulary found there was—he stated—echoed in the contemporary discourses of the United States and the Soviet Union. "The theme of land and sea has not yet faded away," he further observed. "Likewise, the concept of Nehmen-Teilen-Weiden remains unexcelled for the political questions of the congress."

In addition, Koselleck intended to use the concept of "legitimacy" (a concept that Schmitt had analyzed in several studies) in order to demonstrate the political changes that took place around the Congress of Vienna.[49] According to Koselleck, the men of the *ancien régime*—Talleyrand as much as Metternich—had realized early on that legitimacy was no longer related to the *ancien régime*. Koselleck interpreted Talleyrand's definition as follows: "In the end it all comes to this: Legitimate is what I [Talleyrand] find right." Koselleck added: "The concept of legitimacy changed with the changing circumstances, revolution was incorporated into the concept, and one might even say: the concept is located at the dividing line between historical philosophy and historicism."[50]

In other words, according to Koselleck, from being a concept with a stable and shared meaning at the onset of modernity, legitimacy was now linked to the concept of "revolution" and in this process used functionally to fit the shifting interests of various political powers, thus constantly undergoing a change of meaning. Pursuing an idea which originated during his conceptualization of "Kritik und Krise", and which he would further refine in the *Geschichtliche Grundbegriffe*, he proposed to analyze the changes that took place in the epochal transition to modernity through a focus on one concept: that of legitimacy.

Elaborating on his conceptual reflections by linking the past to the present, Koselleck found the Congress of Vienna "as 'modern' much more topical than the French Revolution." The catastrophe (i.e., the Revolution) had occurred, Koselleck explained, and the aim was now to control its further consequences. In this situation, he noted, "the confusion at the fronts were astonishing" and even seemingly clear and commonly used concepts such as "legitimacy" and "revolution" had turned into "interchangeable, empty phrases that had a pragmatic and effective rather than a clarifying function."

By approaching the Congress of Vienna through a focus on the concept of legitimacy, Koselleck seemed to have found an excellent topic through which he could use his newly acquired geo-political terminology and arguments on the origins of European political modernity and—with it—the power structures of the contemporary world. The outcome might have been a highly interesting account of world history as an attempt to explain the conditions and the characteristics of the Cold War.

However, in spite of his initial enthusiasm, Koselleck decided to stop working on the topic not long after he wrote the above-cited letter to Schmitt. This decision was the result of the arrival of Werner Conze at the University of Heidelberg, who succeeded Kühn as a professor there in 1957. Conze was simply not interested in the topic.[51] Instead, he convinced Koselleck that he should work on a social-historical theme (and one for which actual archival studies and the application of the techniques of historical research were necessary) with a focus on the Prussian *Vormärz* (denoting in a broad sense Prussian history from 1815 to 1848). In July 1958, Koselleck thus informed Carl Schmitt that he was working in the West German archives, "to investigate the tension between state and society in the Prussian *Vormärz* by looking at the Prussian constitutional records." Koselleck added: "The entire theme comes from Professor Conze, who strongly emphasizes the social-historical direction in the seminar. He wants me to write a *Habilitation* . . . about the topic."[52]

Conze's intervention in respect to the topic of Koselleck's *Habilitation* evidences a continuation of longstanding cultural norms and social structures in German academia as a system in which younger colleagues and students were largely dependent on the goodwill and decisions of their professors.[53] These norms had important consequences on the future course of Koselleck's scholarly work. Having pursued geopolitical and global-historical themes that related to Schmitt's idea of the *Nomos der Erde*, as a student of Conze, Koselleck now shifted his focus to a local and detailed investigation of Prussian social history, and the geopolitical and Anglo-Saxon themes that had occupied him in the mid 1950s were thus overshadowed in his publications and letters in the following years.[54] The outcome was a range of new discursive features, themes and approaches that involved a shift of focus from criticizing history in the singular to how histories in the plural can be analyzed and written in practice, which he referred to and further developed for the rest of his career. This is not to say that Koselleck's reflections on the relations between space, time, and politics disappeared from his analytical framework. Even if only few aspects of the geopolitical discourse can be found in his work on Prussia, it was layered in and became central for his historical thought, as we will later return to. First, we will illuminate how, during his work on the Prussian *Vormärz* and in a process that lasted almost ten years, Koselleck both learned and refined the methods of structural history.

Werner Conze and Structural History

It is well-known that Conze played an important role in shaping Koselleck's work on Prussia. In fact, neither Koselleck's conceptualization of *Preußen zwischen Reform und Revolution* nor his work on the *Geschichtliche Grundbegriffe* can be understood without paying close attention to Conze, who was first the supervisor of Koselleck's *Habilitation* and subsequently became a close collaborator on *Geschichtliche Grundbegriffe*.

Werner Conze was born in 1910 into a family belonging to the North German Protestant *Bildungsbürgertum*.[55] He belonged to a generation whose primary political experiences were the social-political upheavals in the Weimar Republic, Hitler's rise to power in the early 1930s and the later war. In this turmoil, Conze sided early on with national-conservative forces.

As for his academic career, Conze initially studied briefly with the sociologist Hans Freyer in Leipzig, and from 1934 with the ethnologist

Günther Ipsen and the historian Hans Rothfels in Königsberg. He wrote his dissertation in Königsberg and earned his *Habilitation* with Ipsen in Vienna in 1940. In Königsberg, Conze teamed up with Theodor Schieder and other researchers, who were all deeply disappointed with the liberal *Rechtsstaat* as well as with modern industrial society, and who doubted the capability of the traditional approaches in the German sciences to respond adequately to the interests and the fate of the German *Volk* in the age of modernity.

In Königsberg, where he worked on a project that was paid for by the Nazis and closely related to the German *Volkstums- und Bevölkerungspolitik* (politics of people and population) in the East, Conze was trained in the tradition of the so-called *Volksgeschichte*.[56] This tradition concerned itself with the history of ethnically defined groups of people and drew on different academic disciplines such as ethnography, statistics and sociology, and regional, social, and economic history. The proponents of *Volksgeschichte* included a variety of scholars, such as Ipsen and Freyer and the historians Hans Rothfels, Hermann Aubin, and Otto Brunner. These scholars were all radical nationalists, who in the 1930s pursued revanchist and annexationist objectives and explicitly conceived of their scientific activities in terms of political strife. They became pillars of academic Nazism from 1933 at the latest.[57]

During the war, Conze obtained a position at the *Reichsuniversität* in Posen, a newly-founded university in the annexed westernmost part of Poland staffed with ideologically reliable faculty.[58] Due to continuous assignments as an officer on the Eastern front, however, he never taught there. Similar to Koselleck, he ended the war badly wounded and in Russian captivity. Conze entered the postwar German historical profession in 1946, working six years in a fairly unremarkable (and for a period unpaid) post as an external lecturer in Göttingen. In 1952, he achieved the position of an associate professor at the University of Münster, where he was soon after given a full professorship in social and economic history. Finally, in 1957, he took over Kühn's chair of modern history in Heidelberg, where he remained for the rest of his career.[59]

In addition, it was in 1957 that Conze published what is regarded as his most detailed piece on the program of the socalled *Strukturgeschichte* (structural history): the article "Die Strukturgeschichte des technisch-industriellen Zeitalters als Aufgabe für Forschung und Unterricht."[60] The text was motivated by a plea to adapt historical research to historical reality. More concretely, Conze argued that historical writing should be adjusted to the separation between state and society and to the breakthrough of the technological-industrial age that took place in the eighteenth century. In terms of themes and style, recent history should not be written in the form of heroic epics describing the dramas of great individuals and states. It was instead to be analyzed through the larger societal processes, movements, and tendencies, including the technological and economical developments that had taken place in the period under discussion.

In addition, in order to relate historical method to the historical reality of the modern epoch, Conze wanted to combine history and sociology, and to employ the methods of political science and economics. Through this interdisciplinary approach, Conze aimed at substituting the topical and methodological specialization current in the historical discipline with a wider and more encompassing historical synthesis—a structural history.[61]

In his conceptualization of structural history, Conze was heavily influenced by Hans Freyer, especially by the latter's *Theorie des gegenwärtigen Zeitalters* from 1955, which was one of the most influential interpretations of the technological impact on modern society in postwar Germany.[62] In his book, Freyer continued his reflections from his 1948 *Weltgeschichte Europas* on the problems caused by the industrial, political, and social revolutionary processes taking place at the end of the eighteenth century. Freyer now argued that the social and technological processes, which he believed permeated human life, had become ever more autonomous and difficult to control. Because these processes did not arise from an organic order, he labeled them *sekundäre Systeme* (secondary systems).

Freyer perceived many dangers as inherent to these systems, including the increasing human dependence on incomprehensible technology, as well as on the social state, leading to a loss of responsibility, duties, and freedom and increased demands for social unity, leading again to a loss of individuality and to personal alienation. More generally, Freyer argued that the secondary systems divided man's life into various mechanical functions, while at the same time reducing him to merely a part of a huge and only functionally differentiated mass. This development signalled the definitive end of man's natural life as part of an organic entity, according to Freyer.

However, Freyer had not given up all hope for a meaningful modern existence. He put his faith in what he called *haltende Mächte* (restraining powers)—such as history, family, authority, friendship—to stabilize the *sekundäre Systeme*. More concretely, Freyer hoped that these "restraining powers" would provide what was missing in the *sekundäre Systeme*: meaning, human depth, and richness. Since its systems were designed in such a way that it was possible to resist their supposed totality, he thought of the early Federal Republic as the healthier alternative in comparison to other political and societal forms such as socialism.[63]

This latter dimension of Freyer's analysis was typical among former radical conservatives at the time. While calling for powers to restrain, or counter the negative aspects of modernity, by emphasizing the origins, characteristics, and dangers of communism, they partly attempted to divert attention away from National Socialism, including their own intellectual-political activities in the 1930s and 1940s. This argumentative strategy to some extent explains why Freyer's diagnosis of modernity was received positively and shared widely in German intellectual life, not least among his former students, colleagues, and associates, many of whom regrouped in various academic settings in the Federal Republic.[64]

While Freyer's activities were especially important in relation to the reestablishment of sociology as a discipline in the 1950s,[65] he also played an important role in gradually changing the track of German historical writing in the direction of structural and social history in the same period. At the time, neither structural history nor social history were precisely defined terms. In fact, ever since the historian Karl Lamprecht had at the end of the nineteenth century lost the so-called *Methodenstreit* (in which he had challenged the primacy of political history and argued for a more encompassing social-historical approach), the label of social history had by and large been confined to the fringes of the historical discipline.[66]

It was not least through the initiatives and networks of Werner Conze and Theodor Schieder that structural history, with its distinct social-historical dimension, was established as a separate and increasingly popular field in the historical profession during the 1950s. In this process, Conze and Schieder frequently cited and in other ways drew attention to the work of Freyer and the other fathers of *Volksgeschichte*. Among other things, on the initiative of Schieder, Freyer gave a successful talk at the historian's conference in Marburg in 1951 on the need to combine "Soziologie und Geschichtswissenschaft" (Sociology and History). And two years later, in 1953 in Bremen, Otto Brunner gave a talk on "Das Problem einer europäischen Sozialgeschichte," (The Problem of a European Social History) on which Conze was given the responsibility to comment, and which the latter would later refer to as a huge benefit for the conference.[67]

Werner Conze was also among the enthusiastic audience, who, in Marburg in 1952, heard Freyer announce the main focus of historical sociology to be the bourgeois society of the nineteenth century.[68] At one of the first meetings in the Arbeitskreis für moderne Sozialgeschichte, which was founded in 1957 with the University of Heidelberg as its base, Conze pointed to the inspiration that he found in Freyer, as he announced that it was the task of historians "to historically-critically substantiate or test a 'theory of the contemporary age,' as it has been outlined by for example

Hans Freyer; in other words to investigate the structure of the modern world in its historical depths since the emancipations and the revolutions, both in respect to the specifically new in the modern world-epoch and the continuity of endurable, pre-revolutionary traditions."[69]

Why was Koselleck attracted to the structural-historical program of Werner Conze, who was after all some thirteen years older than he? And how did he position himself within this program? To answer these questions, we must start by highlighting certain similarities between the two scholars in terms of historical experience and historical thinking. Due to experiences of upheaval, war, and captivity—and intellectual exchange with different scholars, who developed their main ideas in the crisis-ridden 1920s and 1930s—both men had developed a crisis-consciousness when it came to evaluating the condition of the modern world. Indeed, their historical thinking centered to a large extent on a mode of thinking that aimed at bringing social-political order into what they perceived as the chaos of modernity.[70]

Central for Conze and Koselleck was an understanding of the processes of modernity taking place at the end of the eighteenth century as a crucial rupture separating the old, stable world from the new epoch in which conceptions of space, time, and politics were fundamentally altered; both were interested in analyzing the consequences of these processes, not least the tensions between state and society; and while sharing a skeptical and critical view of modernity, they both hoped to find means to counter or balance certain allegedly negative and potentially dangerous aspects of the modern world, especially those of technological developments, in order to create a more stable social-political order.

Moreover, as for their theoretical-methodological vision, both were critical of traditional historicism and sought to go beyond this approach by combining history and sociology (although they undoubtedly had two different conceptions of sociology), and they both saw in conceptual history an important instrument in this endeavor, as we will see below.

However, Koselleck's interest in and approach to studying modernity was also very different from Conze's. Koselleck came from a more philosophical and philological background, and his main interests were first of all in political modernity: in questions related to political power, its forms of representation, and its semantic and temporal configurations. Conze, on the other hand, came from a background in *Volksgeschichte*, and inspired by his sociological training, he was more interested in societal structures and in studying these with methods from disciplines such as demography, ethnology, and economics.

While he was in Heidelberg, Conze became known as a dynamic initiator of new experiments, constantly attracting a wide range of both established and promising new scholars.[71] Rather than pursuing theoretical questions, he was primarily interested in integrating themes, methods, and interests through practical work. Hence, whereas when he met Conze, Koselleck had long attempted to theorize history, Conze never developed a theory of structural history.[72] This is probably the reason why Koselleck later stated that meeting Conze was not an "eye-opening experience" (*Erweckungserlebnis*) and that he did not find an intellectual source of inspiration in him.[73] What Koselleck mainly learned from Conze, then, was to view the historical processes leading to modernity from the more comprehensive perspective of structural and social history and to apply the methods required to do so. However, Koselleck did not put his theoretical reflections on hold when he entered Conze's program. On the contrary, the field of social history provided him with a number of discursive features with which he found new ways to deconstruct history in the singular and write history in the plural.

State and Society in Germany, 1815–1848

One of the first projects that Conze initiated in his working group was a larger investigation of the theme of state and society in the Prussian reform period. It was within this project that Koselleck developed his approach to social history, and some of his early reflections on the topic appeared already in a 1962 volume edited by Conze and titled *Staat und Gesellschaft im deutschen Vormärz, 1815–1848*.[74] The volume contained contributions to the investigation of the German *Vormärz* by seven members of the Arbeitskreis—three established scholars (Werner Conze, Theodor Schieder, and Otto Brunner) and four somewhat younger scholars (Reinhart Koselleck, Wolfgang Zorn, Wolfram Fischer, and Erich Angermann).[75]

Conze's long essay "Das Spannungsfeld von Staat und Gesellschaft im Vormärz" ended the volume and presented a general presentation and summary of the entire study.[76] Conze thus sketched out the main political, social, and economic problems of the period—focusing on the many tensions between state and society, new social groups and older powers, liberal constitutional ideas and authoritarian forces, tradition and emancipation, and among reform, restoration, and revolution.

The themes of Conze's essay, I might add, were not merely things of the past, but also issues that were being heavily discussed in contemporary political debates. Observing how a process that had taken more than two hundred years had slowly seen the state lose its status as the sole fundament of political authority and order to societal powers, German politicians and intellectuals were discussing intensively how the state should react to the ongoing societal changes and claims, not least to the increasing influence of economic groups and political parties, including how state and society should ideally relate to each other. Should societal issues and the social order be given primacy on behalf of the political organization? And, if so, how were the conflicts between the state and society to be solved? And which symbol, if not the state, should provide the Germans with a social-political identity?

Conze gave no specific answer to these questions, but focused strictly on a historical analysis of the relation between state and society, with a special focus on Prussia, set within what he portrayed as larger European processes of modernity. His verdict on these processes was not simply one of blunt rejection. Stating that the structural changes that occurred on the verge of modernity were not all of a very radical kind, Conze argued that the political and social problems of the epoch could not be solved merely through a fundamental restoration. Acknowledging the need for social-political reform, he praised the leading role of the absolutist state in the early reform phase, highlighting not least the fact that it had warded off the revolution, while he criticized Friedrich Wilhelm IV's "conservative-romantic retreat" in the 1840s for eventually having rendered the state incapable of dealing with the forces of emancipation, revolution, and counter-revolution.[77]

However, Conze also drew attention to certain uncontrollable negative consequences of social-political modernity, in particular the sudden emancipation, social upheaval and disintegration of the traditional social groups. These changes, which had been caused by social emancipation and had led to a greater social-economic inequality between societal groups, gave rise to a form of structural asymmetry in terms of various social groups and trades, leading to a permanent social insecurity and unrest, as well as the loss of traditions, norms, and manners that eventually paved the way for the *Zeitalter der Ideologien* (age of ideologies, an expression coined by Brunner). According to Conze, these problems, symbolized by the tension between state and society, remained unsolved during the reform period and triggered eventually the revolution of 1848 in the German states.

Koselleck's article "Staat und Gesellschaft in Preußen 1815-1848" was designed within Conze's framework.[78] The focus of the article was on constitutional history, a dimension of history which Conze, with reference to Hans Freyer and inspired also by Otto Brunner, spoke of as "constituted power" (*gesetzte Herrschaft*) and incorporated as an integral part of structural-history.[79] More concretely, Koselleck's article focused on what he described as the "the polemical antithesis of state and society: the interrelation between administration and revolution" in Prussia between 1815 and 1848.[80] Although revolution and administration appear to be contradictory terms, they turned out, he stated, to be closely related in the case of Prussia, as the state bureaucracy promoted certain trends of the revolution, and the revolution in turn provoked a continual growth of power within the bureaucracy.

At the beginning of the article, Koselleck described how, at the end of the eighteenth century, in reaction to the French Revolution, and as an attempt to secure its existence, the Prussian bureaucracy initiated a series of reforms. While avoiding the violent and radical aspects that had been generated during the French Revolution, the bureaucracy worked toward implementing some of the more moderate and beneficial political and social dynamics toward change caused by this event. The desired model was the so-called *Mittelweg* (middle-way), which involved political, economic, and social reforms but mediated between two extremes of fundamental revolution and total restoration.

Aimed at creating a "synthesis between an enlightened absolutism and a society that is still to be liberalized," the first phase of reforms resulted in the so-called *Allgemeines Landrecht* (Prussian Law Code) of 1794.[81] However, Koselleck explained, this set of reforms was not very successful, and after the economically disastrous military defeats of Prussian by Napoleon's forces in 1806–07, a new phase of reform was initiated by officials who wanted to pursue further reform. This second phase of reform was not only more far-reaching but also more radical: Its aim was to create a growth-oriented capitalist economy, more liberal social institutions, and a more democratic and open social structure.

Crucial to the planning and implementation of the reform was the socially and intellectually homogenous Prussian bureaucracy—the so-called *Beamtentum*, which was constituted by professionals from the rising bourgeoisie. In the period after 1815, at a time of confessional, linguistic, and juridical pluralism, according to Koselleck, it was the bureaucracy that constituted the continuity, unity, and spirit of the Prussian state. Yet, the purpose of the bureaucracy was not only to serve the state, but also to mediate between state and society, that is, to be "the body of the state—and of the society."[82]

Koselleck's somewhat idealized concept of the state as a neutral and dignified entity bore similarities to his description of the state in "Kritik und Krise". In fact, with its focus on the relations between state and society, questions of political order and the rise of the bourgeoisie, Koselleck's article on the Prussian reforms appear in many ways as both a thematic and chronological continuation of his dissertation. However, the article on Prussia was in reality different in several aspects. To begin with, the article was not an investigation into the origins of political ideology—it was a study of how a concrete social-political order was constructed through juridical measures by the principally apolitical Prussian bureaucracy. In addition, Koselleck did not ground his study upon a reading of the literary classics, but upon an empirical analysis of law and administration texts, and he now included economic and demographic aspects in such a way as to analyze the composition of and interaction among various social groups in the Prussian *Vormärz*. It was through this approach, and within Conze's framework, that Koselleck entered a new phase of his scholarly production.

However, one of the most important dimensions of Koselleck's approach went beyond Conze's framework: the use of the concept of time as a guiding and organizing analytical tool. More concretely, in the article, Koselleck analyzed the temporal conceptions among the contemporary agents (the bureaucracy, the various social groups, and individuals) as a way to understand the expectations that sparked the reforms and the direction they took. Elaborating on the conception in "Kritik und Krise" of modernity as characterized by a focus on the future, an experience of temporal acceleration, and an expectation of change, he wrote: "The temporal experience of the epoch was the 'movement'."[83]

Koselleck consequently argued that it was the experience and the expectation of immediate change and progress that made it inconceivable for the agents in the Prussian *Vormärz* to draw back from the demands for political and social reforms that were manifested in the period. The only possibility was to catch the dynamics of modernity and to direct them toward the specific and planned goals that the Prussian bureaucracy set for itself: "Within this temporal horizon, the administration understood itself as the only institution that mediated between the extremes as to balance between the powers of the 'reaction' and the 'progress'."[84]

Koselleck was, we should remember, not unique among German academics in the 1950s and 1960s in claiming that the nineteenth century bourgeois society (and modernity as such) was characterized by a temporal focus on the future and by an expectation of rapid change. One of the most famous examples, as we have seen, appears in Löwith's *Meaning in History*, which was influential in shaping Koselleck's view on these issues. Another example is *Theorie des gegenwärtigen Zeitalters* in which Freyer presented an idea similar to Löwith's concerning expectations of future progress and change as a characteristic for modern societies.[85] Echoes of Freyer can be found in Conze's writings from the 1950s,[86] but Conze never organized his analysis according to a temporal aspect. Neither did he produce a theory of historical time, as Koselleck eventually did. In these respects, Koselleck was original within the German historical profession, a fact to which we return below.

The way Koselleck described the temporally-motivated political project of the Prussian bureaucrats was similar to his portrayal in "Kritik und Krise" of the project pursued by the Enlightenment thinkers. The Prussian project was similarly suffused with historical philosophy: "All laws of the reform-machinery were aimed at movement; a movement that was understood in line with the idealistic historical-philosophies ideas of the fulfilling of a world-plan encompassing universal freedom and morality."[87] In the view of the reformers, the Prussian state was involved in "a progressive world-plan"—the aim was to defeat the existing order "to release the potential powers of a future in freedom."[88]

However, in spite of the initial optimism, in the end, the Prussian reforms turned out to be a failure, symbolized in the revolution of 1848. To use one of Koselleck's temporal-analytical terms, the period in which successful reforms might have been implemented eventually "passed." But exactly why did the Prussian reforms fail?

The Failure of the Prussian Reforms:
Economic vs. Political reforms

According to Koselleck, the roots of the failure were to be found in some of the very basic tensions that occurred while implementing the reforms. While the reformers were relatively successful at creating a liberal economic society, based on a growth-oriented capitalist economy, they were much less successful at creating parallel political and social reforms, because such reforms were strongly resisted by the existing *Stände* (social bodies), especially by the nobility.

In reaction to the reaction of the nobility, instead of creating a constitution or parliamentary institutions, the bureaucracy chose to step in as a mediator between the various social groups to solve the social-political problems created by the reforms. However, the decisions taken by the bureaucracy were not always satisfactory or fair to all parts of society. This was, for example, the case with the implementation of the massive reform of the rural agrarian constitution; ultimately it was the peasants who paid the price for the transition from natural-economy to money-economy with the *Gutsherren* (lairds) benefiting all down the line. The administration thus gradually lost its moral credit with the various social groups as the process of reform went forward, leaving the traditional status layers and the rising capitalist bourgeoisie as the most privileged groups in its wake.

Eventually, however, *Verwaltung als Verfassung* (administration as con-stitution) proved insufficient. According to Koselleck, once it began to initiate its reforms, the Prussian bureaucracy released forces hostile to its own interest and became entangled in a process over which it no longer had control—neither in temporal nor in political terms. In other words, it was constantly trying to adapt the reforms to the dynamics and de-velopments it had unleashed, and as it lost its initiative and goodwill, it also lost its mediating position between the state and society. In addition, not only the traditional status layers, but also two newborn social groups put the bureaucracy under pressure. The first of these two groups was the capitalist bourgeoisie, which was economically extremely influential and pushed for further political influence and freedom. The second group was the proletariat, which was sheltered neither by the old status layers nor by the state and demanded further social and political reforms. Observ-ing these less successful dimensions of the economic reforms, Koselleck defined liberal progress as progress of ambivalence, symbolized by the si-multaneous increase of prosperity and poverty. Among other things, he noted how the rise of the proletariat witnessed the "social downside" of the "rationalization of the economy."[89]

As pressure from the various groups in society grew, the opportunity for a written constitution to be constructed in order to control and direct the social dynamics unleashed by the reforms passed. Instead, the final and disastrous outcome of the reform period was the downfall of the adminis-tration—leading to the revolution of 1848.

In drawing this conclusion, Koselleck once again left the reader with the impression that he believed that it was extremely difficult, if not impossible, to handle the political and social energies let loose by the French Revolution in such a way that a durable political order could be established. This raises the question of whether Koselleck's study of the Prussian *Vormärz* was intended as a more or less direct continuation of the interpretation and the critique of modernity that he had launched in "Kritik und Krise". A letter written to Carl Schmitt in June 1959, when the project was in its early phase, suggests that this was originally the case. In his letter, Koselleck wrote:

> The crisis in Prussia and in Austria has in reality never entirely broken out. It was cut off by Napoleon and then directed into other channels: the ignorant German national-liberalism and the jammed German reac-tion were perhaps only illusory fronts. The cut off Prussian Enlightenment and the dead end of the German liberalism have led to a violent explosion: in Marx, who nevertheless did not find a real position in the nineteenth century and did not find his place at the British museum by mistake. It is

the unblown traits of the German nineteenth century that are the heritage to Lenin—and Hitler. The history of the crisis since 1789 is in fact still to be written. My studies of the *Vormärz* will hopefully lead me one step further.[90]

Koselleck's dialectical and pessimistic account of nineteenth century Prussian history in the passage above is evidently similar to his account of the European Enlightenment in "Kritik und Krise". Common to both is the assumption that the dynamics unleashed around the French Revolution led to permanent tension, crisis, and war, and prevented a stable and responsible social-political order in the modern age. However, nowhere in the article from 1962 does Koselleck portray the Prussian attempt at reform as a dialectical movement with a clear tendency toward crisis and disaster. On the contrary, by illuminating a variety of different aspects, actors and processes, Koselleck's picture of the transition to modernity in Prussia was considerably more complex and nuanced than the one found in "Kritik und Krise".

Moreover, in spite of the idealistic and utopian components present in the attempt of the Prussian bureaucrats to deal with the political and social processes of modernity, Koselleck was remarkably less hostile toward the bureaucrats than he had been in his dissertation toward the Enlightenment thinkers. Not only did he explicitly conceive of reform as unavoidable and necessary in the case of Prussia; he also sympathized with the attempt of the administrators to cope with this challenge through the measures of the *Beamtenstaat*. Hence Koselleck was remarkably positive toward the chosen *Mittelweg* and he additionally praised specific actions taken by the state—such as the attempts to improve conditions for the less privileged groups in society, educate its subjects, and prevent these from becoming alienated in "the technical world of labour."[91]

Even more important is Koselleck's implication that the reforms might have developed differently if the right ones had been implemented at the right time, and if it had not been for the unfortunate death of charismatic reform-leader—the Prussian Chancellor Hardenberg—in 1822. Koselleck described Hardenberg's death as crucial for the negative outcome of the reforms and for the course of Prussian history more generally. Indeed, according to Koselleck's account, it was with Hardenberg's death that the reformers lost control of the reform: The technically perfect machinery simply lost its political initiative and efficiency.

Along with the lack of direct ideological critique, the indications as to how the state might have handled the demand for changes more successfully, if certain factors related to the reform had fallen out differently, suggest that Koselleck had somewhat modified his previously critical attitude toward the processes of modernity. Was that the case? And, if so, how can we explain this change?

Although no direct proof exists, it may be that Koselleck presented a modified view of the processes of modernity as a reaction to the social-political developments taking place in Germany from the early 1950s to the early 1960s. In this period, the economy had been successfully modernized and liberalized via the so called *Wirtschaftswunder* (economic miracle); a successful democratic political system had been established, with a parliamentary democracy, a public sphere, and a democratization of its administrative spheres; and a set of new "Western" cultural and social norms, devoid of the authoritarian, nationalistic, and militaristic traits prevalent during National Socialism, had been taken up by the Germans. Against this background, it is possible that, as a result of his having experienced fifteen relatively stable years in the Federal Republic, like many of his fellow countrymen, Koselleck had gained greater trust in political reform and in the durability of a modern, liberal-democratic political system.

Another reason for the lack of modernity-critique is perhaps to be found in the strong reactions to "Kritik und Krise". Exactly how these reactions influenced Koselleck is difficult to say, but they may have convinced him not to refrain from participating directly in political debate or from expounding overtly negative views on modernity. The lack of ideological critique was presumably also affected by a need to adapt to certain standards within the program of structural history. Although Werner Conze and his associates were critical toward aspects of the modern world, it was not political criticism that they sought to be recognized for in the postwar period; it was for the scholarly quality of their work.

In his work on the Prussian *Vormärz*, Koselleck had to comply with the standards of Conze's program, even if this approach to history did not fit his analytical temperament, as he revealed was the case in a letter to the political scientist Wilhelm Hennis in June 1963. Giving Hennis a status report of his *Habilitation*, Koselleck wrote:

> My Prussians are marching into the final version, even if the uniform that I inflicted on them does not fit as well as it did in the old days. All in all a "neutralist" enterprise, for the current liberal and socialist critique reaches too short and the patriotic praise reaches too far, and when I appear to be "objective," I approach a sense of boredom that overcomes me in the process. The "social structure" is a way out, which neutralizes many things in the account, so that the specific flavour disappears. Anyway, I hope that I have not forgotten all of the old history in the grey area that lies in the direction toward social history.[92]

In the end, Koselleck managed, as we will see, to add an individual "flavour" to his social-historical study and to position himself vis-à-vis the other contributions to the field. However, overall, he conformed to the standards of Conze's social-historical approach—an approach that in his letter to Hennis he described as neutral, objective, and in the end somewhat boring, as it disallowed political and scientific critique. While writing social history was thus perhaps not the most intellectually stimulating experience for Koselleck, he learned many things from Conze's program that he was to draw on in his later work. In addition, by being affiliated with the program, Koselleck positioned himself as a politically and scientifically less controversial, more conventional and respected scholar within the historical profession. Conze's volume, including Koselleck's article, was met with positive responses among historians not only in Germany,[93] but also in the English-speaking part of the world. Having praised Koselleck's analysis, an American reviewer made the following remark on the overall study:

> Repeatedly the authors are brought back to the role of the bureaucracy. All over Germany its position was crucial. Surely, if a definitive study of Germany in the first half of the nineteenth century is ever to be written, it will almost inevitably have to shape itself around a history of the *Beamten*. The officials were at once the intermediaries between state and society, the inheritors of the traditions of the Enlightenment state, and the most progressive part of society itself. One must agree with the majority of these scholars that both more factual information and more analysis are needed for this pivotal group.[94]

This was exactly what Koselleck presented in *Preußen zwischen Reform und Revolution*, in which he attempted to reconstruct, through archival material, a state that consisted only of its administration, as will be shown below.

The Past and the Present:
the Prussian *Vormärz* and the Federal Republic

In his introduction to *Preußen zwischen Reform und Revolution*, Koselleck explained how the study temporally encompassed the period between 1791 and 1848—from the drafting of the Prussian Law Code until the outbreak of the bourgeois revolution that brought the reforms to their end. It was for this reason that he included the concepts of reform and revolution in his title. These two concepts, Koselleck stated, not only limited but also characterized the period: in constant friction, like so-called *Bewegungsbegriffe* (concepts of movement), they had pointed to-ward a future, which was still to be created. Koselleck announced that his focus was on the beginning of the larger societal change that the two concepts referred to: "the transition from a society that is still based on estates to an economically free society."[95]

During his work on the *Habilitation*, the topic of political reform had become increasingly topical in contemporary German social-political dis-cussions, and by the middle of the 1960s reform had manifested as a *Leit-begriff* (leading concept) in these discussions.[96]

In this decade, where a reform-euphoria was predominant, many Ger-man politicians and intellectuals felt that they were living in a time of rapid change. Striving for and expecting reforms, they contributed to what has been labeled a "dynamic time" in Germany in which attempts were made to reform practically every societal sphere in a more demo-cratic direction, so that the country's political, social, and cultural norms were increasingly "Westernized."[97]

Yet, the plans for reform were strongly debated, first of all between democratically and reform-minded forces, and more conservative and re-storative forces.[98] And from the mid 1960s onwards, when the Adenau-rian Christian Democratic Union-system of the *Wirtschaftswunder*-period was weakened due to economic crisis and on behalf of an increasing influ-ence of the Social Democratic Party, a wave of leftist movements and ac-tivists with revolutionary agendas joined the debate. While some of these primarily aimed at revolutionizing the structures of education,[99] others, such as the infamous Baader-Meinhof group, tried to overthrow the exist-ing social-political order by violent means. This happened in the 1970s, when Germany, along with many other European countries, entered a less prosperous era, and the political optimism disappeared.[100]

The themes of reform und revolution that Koselleck dealt with in *Preußen zwischen Reform und Revolution* had certain parallels to contem-porary events in Germany. However, in contrast to "Kritik und Krise", Koselleck did not use the Prussian past as a means to (directly) discuss or criticize affairs in the German present. Neither did Koselleck participate in or position himself in the intense discussion of the German constitu-tion that unfolded between the "Carl Schmitt-school" and the "Rudolf Smend-school" from the 1950s until the 1970s.[101]

In the early Weimar Republic, Schmitt and Smend had both showed themselves to be critics of legal positivism and liberal conceptions of con-stitutional thinking. However, due to their different views on constitu-tional issues and because of a strained and increasingly hostile personal relationship, they gradually staged themselves as scientific antipodes from the end of the 1920s onwards. Indeed, until Smend's death in 1975, their relation was characterized by personal competition. The main differences in Schmitt's and Smend's views were as follows: Whereas Schmitt focused on "decisionism" and developed his theories as polemical answers to political extremes, such as the civil war and the state of exception, the starting point for Smend's thinking was the vision of a peaceful and harmonic normal situation. Schmitt focused on the escalation of conflicts; Smend on how conflicts could be eliminated altogether.

In the postwar period, in their contribution to the postwar German academic and political constitutional debate, Smend and members of his school (primarily his students Ulrich Scheuner, Horst Ehmke, and Konrad Esse) eradicated the anti-liberal and conservative dimensions of Smend's earlier thinking and placed emphasis on the keywords of harmony, consensus, and pluralism. In this process, the earlier focus on the state was substituted with a focus on the constitution, which opened up to a less hierarchic and static relationship between state and society. This change had to do with the reception of Western liberal-democratic constitutional thinking among the members of the Smend-school, who supported the constitution of the Federal Republic through their academic and political activities.

Central for the members of the "Schmitt-school" was the nineteenth-century understanding of the state as a neutral and sovereign entity and a focus on conflict and decisionism. Early on, they positioned themselves as opponents of the "Western science of democracy." Two of the most prominent members of this strand of thinking, Ernst Forsthoff and Werner Weber, even defined themselves as "active enemies of the constitutional law" (although not in public). More generally, the academic and political activities of their school of thought were directed against countering what its members conceived of as an ongoing process of state-disintegration due to the increasing societal influence on the domain of the state.

Koselleck knew several members of the Schmitt-school, among them Ernst Forsthoff, whom he had encountered during his exams at the University of Heidelberg in the early 1950s.[102] From 1952, when Forsthoff was allowed to return to his position in Heidelberg, until he became emeritus in 1967,[103] he concerned himself with commenting on the Basic Constitutional Law of the Federal Republic and played a central role in the debates about the concepts of *Sozialstaatlichkeit* and *Rechtsstaatlichkeit*. Moreover, in the 1960s and 1970s, he organized the famous early summer event in Ebrach, where academics and intellectuals gathered to discuss current intellectual-political topics.[104] Koselleck was a regular participant in the early events in Ebrach,[105] and he also cooperated with Forsthoff on the editorial board of the journal *Die Verwaltung* in the period between 1970 and 1974.[106]

Besides a common scholarly interest in constitutional history, Koselleck shared with Forsthoff and members of the Schmitt-school a focus on moments of transition and disorder and the belief that radical societal revolutionaries should have no part in the construction of political order. However, Koselleck did not fit the ideological patterns and aims of the school nor did he join its academic-political activities. In fact with his conviction that a responsible political system is one in which powers are principally given not only to the state but also to societal interests, he was in normative terms closer to the Smend-school.

To this, it should be added that Koselleck did not pick up on a distinctive analytical theme that formed part of the Schmittian political view of history as a series of constitutional battles: This is the focus on the role of the army in the division of power in German constitutional attempts.[107] In fact, in Koselleck's work on Prussia, not a single reference can be found to Schmitt's writings on constitutional history (or to any other text of Schmitt's for that matter). Koselleck's understanding of the failure of the reforms was conceptualized along a very different axis. Taking into account his intimate knowledge of Schmitt's work, this might be interpreted as a conscious choice on Koselleck's part, as suggested by a letter from June 1976, in which he told Schmitt about the forthcoming second edition of *Preußen zwischen Reform und Revolution*.[108] Since Schmitt in an earlier letter had asked whether Koselleck had read his 1934 *Staatsgefüge und Zusammenbruch* (a deeply polemical book in which Schmitt blamed the German defeat in World War I for what he called "the defeat of the German army by the *Bürger* in 1871" and in which he praised National Socialism for finally revising this erroneous path in German history),[109] Koselleck seemingly felt obliged to comment on the differences between their approaches. He wrote: "It is of course inadequate to deal with Prussia without emphasizing its army-constitution (*Heeresverfassung*). I have only done that in important places, without placing the army-constitution as axis of the constitutional reality. Indirectly, there is a lot about the issue in my book: especially in the chapters on the corporate (*ständischen*) constitution on the level of districts and provinces."

As Koselleck portrayed the lack of focus on the relation between the army and society in his work on Prussia as inadequate, and while he simultaneously argued that it was a central theme in the book, his real message seems to have been a different one. In tune with the larger changes of the Federal Republic in the 1960s, over the course of his work on Prussia, Koselleck's normative stance had moved further away from Schmitt-inspired debates about, and notions of, the state and the constitution. In terms of his relations with Schmitt, Koselleck's analysis of the Federal Republic via his studies of Preussen was a departure which Koselleck remained reluctant to communicate directly, but which was conscious and definite.

The Conceptual Approach in
Preußen zwischen Reform und Revolution

The basic argument underlying the successes and failures of the Prussian reforms in Koselleck's *Habilitation* remained roughly the same as the one in his article from 1962. However, the study was amplified in terms of analytical range and depth, and the intimidating number of detailed analytical trajectories makes it very difficult to summarize the investigation in such a way as to do it justice. This is even more so because the investigation merged several different topics (the transition to political and social modernity; the role of the state in creating political, social, and economic changes; the origins and dynamics of class formation, etc.) and because, unlike "Kritik und Krise", it was dominated by a topical rather than a chronological design and by the constant repetition of one argument from a variety of angles rather than a progressive narrative.

What holds the study together is its focus on the activities of the Prussian bureaucrats—more specifically, on how the bureaucrats as main actors in the reforms sought to navigate within the space of possibilities that had been opened up on the threshold of "modernity." Against this background, the study constantly shows how the bureaucracy gradually became alienated from the rising society, thereby losing its authority as well as its ability "to act above estates (*überständisch zu handeln*)."[110]

With his focus on constitutional and bureaucratic issues, Koselleck wrote the project in two academic traditions: that of Brunner, Freyer, and Conze; and the work on Prussian bureaucratic and constitutional issues by the historians Otto Hintze and Hans Rosenberg. It should be added that the history of Prussia from 1640 had been the apogee of Protestant German historical writing in the nineteenth century, at least as far as the modern period was concerned. Luminaries of the discipline, most famously Ranke, Droysen, and Treitschke, had published widely distributed multi-volume histories of state and dynasty, and the institutional and economic history of Prussia had been covered by the Borussian school under the leadership of Gustav von Schmoller, who supervised the monumental source editions of the *Acta Borussica* and presided over his own journal, the *Forschungen zur brandenburgischen und preußischen Geschichte*. The biographical genre, too, was highly popular. Many prominent modernists published on the celebrated figures of Prussian political and cultural history, such as Gerhard Ritter on Freiherr vom Stein, Siegfried Kähler on Wilhelm von Humboldt, and finally Erich Marcks on Bismarck. This tradition continued well into the twentieth century. Nearly all the prominent modernists published monographs on Prussian matters. Taken as a whole, these works contributed to the enormous significance of Prussian history as a key period for a nationalist vision of German history; a vision that was after 1945 continued by scholars such as Gerhard Ritter and Hans Rothfels, and at the same time undermined by scholars such as Hans Rosenberg, who located the roots of National Socialism in traditions of Prussian authoritarianism, militarism, and nationalism.

Coming from a Prussian background, Conze's interest in Prussia was undoubtedly motivated by a deep sympathy for his topic. This did not, however, result in a narrative dominated by Prusso-centric nationalism. The same can be said of Koselleck's narrative. Rather than reproducing the patriotic eulogies of Prussia found in late-nineteenth and early twentieth-century historical writing or echoing the devastating critique of Prussia found in the work of Rosenberg, Koselleck aimed first of all at extending and innovating the analytical framework in Conze's approach to social history. Hence he acknowledged the institutional support and the supervision that Conze had provided during the working process in two explicit ways. First of all, in his foreword, he thanked Conze "for the stimulating thoughts and the continuing support he granted the present investigation."[111] Secondly, in the introduction, he described the nature of his method using Conze's terminology: "The applied method, in line with the question of research, belongs to the field of social history. It makes use—in a traditional way—of the given texts, but transcends them, and more so than biographical or political historical writing, in pursuit of supra-individual problems the texts do not always bring to words, at least never explicitly."[112]

In his search for such broader historical structures, Koselleck intended to make use of statistical data, but he also emphasized the need to subject the material to abstractions which went beyond the simply numerical, and he wanted to employ the historical-philological method in order to do so. Even statistics, he stated, do not speak for themselves. Historians always have to deal with and refer to texts, also social historians. In this way, he attempted to combine a hermeneutical and a social-historical method.

This analytical project was, as we have seen, one that Koselleck had begun in "Kritik und Krise", using conceptual history as a merging tool, and, as a continuation of this project, he stated in *Preußen zwischen Reform und Revolution* that hermeneutics and social history was to be combined "through word-, and occasionally through conceptual analysis." Likewise, he once again launched his conceptual-historical framework against the approach of historicism (in relation to which Koselleck presumably once again recalled Meinecke's book on *Die Idee der Staatsräson*), as he added: "It renounces *Geistesgeschichte*."[113]

It should be added that, during the 1960s, many historians had begun to criticize what they saw as thematic neglects and theoretical-methodological flaws in historicism, so the distance that Koselleck expressed to *Geistesgeschichte* in *Preußen zwischen Reform und Revolution* was less controversial than the critique he had launched at Meinecke in the early 1950s.[114] However, the lines of critique were the same: with the method of conceptual history, Koselleck wanted to make up for certain flaws that he detected in *Geistesgeschichte*. In the introduction, he wrote: "The resignation to conceptual history . . . has the advantage of staying near social history, though tracking the dynamics specific to language, in which historical experiences are accumulated and formulated." Moreover, in line with the framework of Conze's Arbeitskreis, Koselleck defined conceptual history as "a variant of social history."[115]

During his work on *Preußen zwischen Reform und Revolution*, Koselleck had developed his conceptual approach substantially. However, presumably not to challenge the boundaries of Conze's program with a too theoretical project, his description of the analytical framework and its implications was limited to these two sentences: "The ambiguous terms such as administration and constitution, estate and class refer to fierce controversies in the social and political domain, and in the end also to the differentiation of these areas in the nineteenth century. The conscious efforts to push through, implement, or impose a new political terminology belongs to the modern social movement."[116]

By highlighting the relation between social-political concepts and social-political contestation and change, Koselleck referred to a conceptual approach, which is connected to the birth of modern German conceptual history, as it was articulated in Brunner's social-constitutional studies from the 1930s and 1940s. To understand this approach, which became a central component in Conze's structural-historical framework, an introduction to Brunner and his work is needed.

Brunner was born in Austria in 1889.[117] Trained as a historian, he finished his dissertation in 1922 and his *Habilitation* in 1929, before he acquired a professorship in Vienna, where he later became the director of the Austrian Institute for Historical Research. At the end of World War II, he was barred from further teaching activities in response to his institutional affiliation with, and ideological affinities to, Nazism. However, in 1954 he was hired as the successor to Hermann Aubin at the University of Hamburg and came to play an important role in the German historical profession until his retirement in 1968. Brunner was involved in founding the Arbeitskreis für moderne Sozialgeschichte, and, until his death in 1982, he was one of the editors of the *Geschichtliche Grundbegriffe*.

Brunner rose to fame in the 1930s, when he argued for the need to distinguish historically between the concepts of today and those of the past. More concretely, according to Brunner, because concepts are always created in and belong to a specific situation, it is impossible to use specific concepts untranslated in other historical situations. It was working from this assumption, and through examples of how political and social concepts had lost their original meaning in the transition from early modern to modern times, that Brunner as a critic of 'historicism' claimed that only a scientific revision of the basic concepts could re-establish a proper understanding of the political and social structures of the past.

Brunner's aim to revise basic concepts also informed his most famous book: the 1939 *Land und Herrschaft*.[118] The book is a study of the social-political, constitutional *Stände*-order in the southeastern parts of the Old Reich from the Middle Ages onwards. It investigates the law-concepts, cases, and institutions, on which the public entities of power rested, from the early Middle Ages until the early seventeenth century, and which, according to Brunner, provided a stable and long-lasting basic political structure. Portraying the structure as one well-functioning, transparent, and responsible political order, Brunner's critique of the older literature on the state in the Middle Ages revealed that his aim to revise basic concepts was related not only to scientific concerns, but also to a critique of modernity. It thus represented an attempt to eliminate what he saw as a dangerous division between state and society, caused by modern society. In this respect, he followed, it has been said, "the arguments of national socialist constitutional theoreticians like Carl Schmitt or Ernst R. Huber, who back then propagated the overcoming of the liberal way of separating state and society (*Trennungsdenken*) and believed that it was possible to provide a constitutional order for a totalitarian *Volksgemeinschaft* and *Führerdiktatur*, with the concept of the concrete order."[119]

When Conze, making frequent references to Brunner, in the 1950s elevated the conceptual approach as a way to analyze a society's social-political constitution into an essential part of social history, he erased the political dimensions of Brunner's approach.[120] Already in 1954, in his famous article "Vom 'Pöbel' zum 'Proletariat,'" Conze presented an ideal example of how the conceptual approach should be practiced.[121] Focusing on the concepts of *Pöbel* and *Proletariat*, Conze sought to demonstrate a set of fundamental structural economic and social changes, including the origins of pauperism, which occurred in the German *Vormärz*. He wrote:

"Pauperism was seen with apprehension as a new phenomenon which was something quite different from the poverty question or the existence of the property-less and laboring classes in the traditional sense. This difference which was perceived in Germany during the 1830s and 1840s became articulated at the time in the notion of 'Pöbel' or at least in the latter word being used less frequently and with a narrower application. Both terms ultimately encapsulate everything that can help to explain the evolution toward pauperism."[122]

Brunner's conceptual approach appealed not only to Conze, but also to the latter's students. In an interview, Koselleck has described how, after Conze's arrival in Heidelberg, he was directly inspired by Brunner's semantic analysis of constitutional history.[123] First of all, on a general level, he found in Brunner's approach, which he would later speak of as a "consequent historicism," an analytical device to counter what he regarded as unhistorical dimensions of German historicism.[124] Secondly, the inspiration from Brunner shows in a more direct way in his work on Prussia. By arguing that the entire problem of the *Vormärz* was embodied in the tensions, conflicts, and fights surrounding the concept of the *Bürger*, he organized his attempt to understand the problems in drafting the Prussian social-political constitution within a conceptual analysis that was similar to Brunner's and Conze's.

More concretely, according to Koselleck, the constant ambiguity that surrounded the concept of *Bürger* demonstrates the successful implementation of certain reforms as well as the failure to implement others. The conceptual ambiguity had, he explained, begun already in the drafting of the Prussian Code, in which different concepts such as *Einwohner, Untertan, Mitglied,* and *Staatsbürger* (inhabitant, subject, member, and state-citizen) with seemingly broad or neutral connotations were used interchangeably. These concepts pointed simultaneously to the future and to the past: to the future, because they would liberate the Prussians as individuals; to the past, because the concepts were still in some respects bound to the old society of estates and its division of rights. Providing a typical example of the latter, Koselleck wrote: "As a member of the state one was subject to the monarch, but also the holder of certain rights and duties, depending on social position."[125]

Because it was vigorously resisted by the old estates, the reformers never managed to create a concept of *Bürger* that could bring about equal political and social rights for everybody. Instead, a new economic man was created, or liberated: "One was not a citizen of the state as political member of the state, but instead as partaker of the free economy—the modern society. Citizen of the state was in the proper sense the homo economicus; citizen of the state only to the extent to which the state was economically liberal."[126]

When equal political or social rights were occasionally given by the Prussian state, it was done only to serve the interest of the state: This was the case in the liberalization of access to the military, the administration, and the economic sector. In the private spheres, such as the family and the household, people entered a process of emancipation that was characterized by similar dynamics: They were liberated as free individuals, but they were not elevated to the status of *Bürger* through the granting of the same political and social rights as the members of the old estates possessed.

According to Koselleck, only one exception was made concerning the granting of political and social rights. This exception took shape through the economic reforms and created a new capitalist bourgeoisie, which managed to buy itself access to the nobility and to gain a share in their political and social rights. Due to the fact that this did not solve the problems connected to the societal structures in the Prussian *Vormärz*, but only intensified the political fight for the right to define the concept of *Bürger*, Koselleck described this change merely as a transition from an "*altständischen* to a *neuständischen* bourgeois society."

As such, without overtly theorizing the approach, Koselleck's conceptual analysis of the *Bürger* was vital to his account of how the Prussian *Vormärz* was characterized by an increasing opposition and tension between societal groups and between the state and society.

The Temporal Layers of the Prussian Reforms

Similar to his introduction to the conceptual historical approach, Koselleck elaborated little on what is to be considered his most original theoretical contribution to the program of structural history in *Preußen zwischen Reform und Revolution*. This contribution concerns the application of theories of historical time. While to some extent they already informed the article from 1962, during the conceptualization of the larger study, Koselleck had refined and enlarged his theories. This can be seen in the very beginning of the introduction, where he explained why, as reflected in the subtitle of the book, the study was divided into three parts: *Allgemeines Landrecht, Verwaltung, und Soziale Bewegung* (Prussian Law Code, Administration, and Social Movement). The three entities, Koselleck stated, constituted three temporally successive phases of the reform period. However, he added, the entities and the phases were inseparable, because the Prussian Code reacted to social unrest, the administration to both; and the social movements reacted to the reforms of the administration as well as to the Prussian Code.

Koselleck's intention was hence not to analyze the three entities separately. Instead, he aimed to organize the analysis along the temporally different planes on which historical movements take place. In a frequently quoted passage of the book, he elaborated on his temporal conception of history and its consequences for his investigation into the Prussian *Vormärz*: "The account consequently does not proceed along a linear conception of time. Theoretically, the investigation deals with different layers of historical time. The diverging durations, velocities and modes of acceleration of these layers caused the tensions of the epoch and thus characterize its unity."[127]

Koselleck's analysis, then, was guided by two temporal-theoretical aspects. Not only, as in the article from 1962, did he analyze conceptions of time as a way to understand the expectations of change, movement, and acceleration that sparked the reforms in Prussia; in addition, his analysis of the dynamics of the Prussian *Vormärz* was based on the theoretical presupposition that history does not unfold in *one* linear movement, but in the interaction among several different, but coexisting *Schichten geschichtlicher Zeit* (temporal layers), which are all characterized by diverse characteristics in terms of duration, speed, and intensity. Since after the *Habilitation* he made it his ambition to investigate in more depth how history—or rather histories—is created in the interaction between different layers of time, this presupposition was to be assigned a crucial role in Koselleck's work.

The presupposition was also important for the analysis in *Preußen zwischen Reform und Revolution*. It dictated not only the anti-chronological and multidimensional design of the analysis, but also connected directly to the overall argument made for the conceptual analysis of the *Bürger* that focussed on the two contradictory temporal-political layers that were condensed into the period between 1780 and 1848. One was connected to the emerging industrial and bourgeois society that, with a focus on the future and expectations of progression and change, worked for a growth-oriented economy and more democratic political structures; the other was connected to the past, to the old regime and the traditional agrarian society, and sought to hinder the massive social-political upheavals and changes taking place in the period. According to Koselleck, it was the interaction between these two temporal layers that caused the two contradictory movements within the processes of reform (the quickly-implemented and successful social-economic reforms and the much slower and considerably more problematic social-political reforms). The failure of the reforms was also rooted in the dynamics and opposition between these contradictory time layers.

The temporal-analytical framework with which Koselleck analyzed the expectations that sparked the reforms in Prussia can, as we will see in chapter 5, be interpreted as an attempt to develop Heidegger's idea of Being as a temporal phenomenon in a more historical-analytical context: as an attempt to analyze individual and collective self-understanding and action through analyzing historical actors' conceptions of time and "finality." Hence, as Koselleck rejected the idea of a unified and linear view of historical time and instead argued for a plurality of different and coexisting historical times, he sought to go beyond the temporal framework of *Sein und Zeit*.

This temporal framework alluded to and was to some extent inspired by a set of notions about historical time that have been outlined by the French historian Fernand Braudel (1902–1986). Already in 1949, in his celebrated work *La Méditerranée et le Monde Méditerranéen a l'époque de Philippe II*, Braudel put forward a theory of three different historical layers: (1) The slow, almost imperceptible history of man in relation to his geographical and climatic surroundings; (2) the somewhat more dynamic history of economic, social, and political structures; and (3) the history of events, which Braudel famously described as "surface disturbances, crests of foam that the tides of history carry on its strong back."[128]

In downplaying the traditional focus on politics, persons, and events in favor of long-term structures (geographic, social, and economic) as influential factors shaping history, Braudel's view on history had points of contact with that of Conze, who, by writing a highly positive review of Braudel's book in 1951 and inviting him to Heidelberg at the beginning of the 1960s, ensured that German historians became familiar with his work.[129]

Koselleck met Braudel during his visit in Heidelberg. Although he did not provide any references to the source of inspiration of his theory of historical time in *Preußen zwischen Reform und Revolution*, Koselleck retrospectively stated that he was inspired by Braudel's work on the issue.[130] In Koselleck's own words, his idea of the different layers of historical time is to be viewed as a continuation of Braudel's theories. Whereas Braudel worked with an ontological division between the three layers (the events, the structures, and the basic surroundings), Koselleck wanted to analyze the interaction among them. This analytical ambition became a central discursive feature in the unifying pattern and the common objective in Koselleck's writings, as it served to substantiate his critique of notions of history in the singular and as a very operational framework to thematize history in the plural.

Chapter 5 elaborates on how the framework was to occupy center stage in his work following the *Habilitation*, when, unconstrained by the conventions of the discipline, he declared it his aim to develop a theory of historical times. Bearing in mind that, by means of constructing and applying a theory of historical time, Koselleck went beyond the boundaries of Conze's structural history, we can move on to present another renewal that *Preußen zwischen Reform und Revolution* brought with it. This did not concern Koselleck's analytical framework, but his re-evaluation of the Prussian bureaucracy and of Prussian history more generally; it was, furthermore, a re-evaluation he announced only implicitly.

Koselleck vs. Rosenberg: The Role of the Administration

If we want to reach a full understanding of Koselleck's interpretation of the Prussian reforms, it is necessary to compare the study to the standard work in the field at that time. This is Hans Rosenberg's *Bureaucracy, Aristocracy and Autocracy: The Prussian Experience 1660–1815* from 1958,[131] which Koselleck referred to as a forerunner in the field in his introduction.

Born in 1904, Rosenberg was a deeply engaged Prussian-German left-liberal of Jewish origins, who was early on influenced by Eckart Kehr, a leftist student of Friedrich Meinecke. In the late 1920s, Rosenberg began to challenge the dominant methodologically and politically conservative German historiography with a focus on German foreign policy and economic systems. He achived his *Habilitation* with Johannes Ziekursch in 1932 in Cologne, before he was forced into exile in the 1930s in America, where he devoted his academic activities to investigating the history of the Prussian state and its political aristocracy.[132]

In his work on Prussia, Rosenberg was much more critical toward the country than his predecessors in the field had been. This was also the case in Rosenberg's famous study, *Bureaucracy, Aristocracy and Autocracy*, in which, using Prussia as his example, he sought to analyze the drift into political and administrative centralization and the growing importance of the professional classes in modern society. On the topic of the Prussian reforms, similar to Koselleck, Rosenberg observed that the bourgeoisie was too weak to demand democratic reforms. However, compared with Koselleck, he attributed less positive motives to the actions of the governmental ministers, the reform movement, and not least to the Prussian administrators in the process of reform.

More concretely, according to Rosenberg, in pursuit of their interests of power and prestige, the Prussian administration had early on entered a fatal authoritarian power triad with the *Junkers* (landlords) and the aristocratic army corps. The result of this alliance was, Rosenberg wrote, the triumph of bureaucratic absolutism—of centralized and authoritarian rule exercised through a growing bureaucracy. Moreover Rosenberg argued that by maintaining their political and societal positions in the transition to industrial society, the privileged groups assured the "perpetuation of pre-industrial values in Prussia." Rosenberg spoke of these values as "the blending of civil and military administration and personnel; the excessive militarization of social life; and the emergence of 'Prussian Puritanism', allied with the political docility and social quietism of orthodox Lutheranism."[133]

Whereas Koselleck approached the reforms from the perspective of the possibilities that opened up at the time of their inception, Rosenberg viewed them from the perspective of 1848, and he used his critique of what he portrayed as the conservative elements in German history to explain the preconditions of National Socialism. The rise of bureaucratic absolutism, Rosenberg thus explained, paved the way for a "long tradition of obedience to authority, centralized power in the hands of self-interested groups unwilling to learn the rules of democratic cooperation" and escaped "into a world of dangerous illusions and misconceptions and the immoderate use of high-sounding words."[134] Soon after, he added, the authoritarian leadership—informed by "habits of mind" crystallizing in Bismarck's nationalism and later in Ludendorff's militarism—"set out to salvage their political fortune and traditional social position in alliance with the totalitarian Nazi movement."[135] In this respect, according to Rosenberg, Prussia was exceptional.

By tracing the preconditions of National Socialism to the structures and dynamics of Prussian history, Rosenberg took up the argument about the *Sonderweg*, or special path, in German history. With origins in German anti-Enlightenment thought, the notion of a German *Sonderweg* had in Germany embodied positive values and developments in Germany history, especially in the tradition of Prusso-centric and nationalistic historical writing, and it been utilized as a means of propaganda in the period before and during World War I. However, in line with the work of Eckart Kehr, and in a way comparable to how politicians and scholars in other nations evaluated what they agreed was a special path in German history, Rosenberg filled the meaning of the notion with negative characteristics and values.[136]

Rosenberg's verdict undoubtedly belonged to the critiques of Prussian history that in Koselleck's opinion "reached too short." When Koselleck did not enter into a direct argument with Rosenberg's depreciation of Prussia and the Prussian bureaucracy was accused of "practicing the vices of self-glorification and group arrogance,"[137] it was seemingly in order not to overstep the disciplinary rules of the Arbeitskreis. However, *Preußen zwischen Reform und Revolution* is easily read as an indirect answer to *Bureaucracy, Aristocracy and Autocracy*. What Koselleck offered in the study was a somewhat more positive evaluation of the Prussian bureaucracy and history; an evaluation, which was in all probability partly motivated by Koselleck's own Prussian background.

Certainly, Koselleck did not reproduce the traditional patriotic eulogies of Prussia found in German historical writing. On the other hand, he did not attribute the collapse of the reforms to the administration's selfish power interest, and nowhere did he draw a connection between the organization, attitudes, and values of the Prussian administration and the authoritarian, nationalistic, and militaristic course of German history, culminating in National Socialism. In Koselleck's account, the administration is portrayed in more positive terms: Characterized by a necessary unity and spirit, it had made an admirable effort to mediate among the various social groups as to steer Prussia safely through the difficult transition to modernity.

But who, then, was responsible of the failure of the reforms? Although he pointed to the actions taken by the nobility, the new bourgeoisie and the proletariat to influence the reforms, in answering this question, Koselleck assigned much less guilt to specific actors than Rosenberg. Discussing this issue, an acute reviewer, the American historian Mack Walker, observed that what in Koselleck's account really worked against the reforms was not to be found in specific Prussian elements, but in the historical forces of modernity let loose by the French Revolution, which nobody was able to master—not even the Prussian bureaucrats. Once they began to initiate reforms, they became entangled in a process, in which all of their successes were simply bound to fail in the end.

From this observation, Walker went on to make the following comment:

> Whatever the arena of reform, the pattern is so invariable as to arouse the reader's uneasiness; a lesser book might have avoided that. Something in the nature of the "historical forces" was against the reform civil servants; some encompassing fate, tragic or ironic depending on the point of view, guided each alternative path to convergence in their own destruction. But again and again the author disarms—partly at least—congenital suspicion of historic forces and contradictions by that same mastery of details, for he composes his forces not with overt interpretations but with documents and with the aims and actions of believable people.[138]

With these reflections, Walker illuminated a key characteristic of Koselleck's dissertation and *Habilitation*. In these writings, modernity is—directly and indirectly—portrayed as a unified, destructive, and unstoppable force, which almost inevitably leads to tension, crisis, or war. Seen from this light, Koselleck did not live up to his ambition of writing a form of history devoid of historical-philosophical traits. But, as Walker also observed, Koselleck's arguments in *Preußen zwischen Reform und Revolution* are well-supported in terms of evidence and can certainly not be dismissed as pure teleology. To this we might add that by illuminating a variety of different factors from a variety of different angles, the *Habilitation* is considerably more theoretically and methodologically advanced than the dissertation. This multiperspective was related to the theory of historical times that Koselleck outlined in the study: a theory, which, similar to the anthropological categories, is based on the idea that history can unfold in different ways, depending on the interaction among the many different temporal layers that are always in play in the making of human events and lives.

Still, Koselleck's idea of history's open and pluralistic character is not thematized as explicitly in the *Habilitation* as in a variety of his contemporary writings, such as a remarkable 1965 article titled "Geschichtliche Prognose in Lorenz v. Steins Schrift zur preußischen Verfassung."[139] Written in relation to his work on the Prussian reform era, the aim of the text was to illuminate the life and work of the German scholar and bureaucrat, Lorenz von Stein (1815–1890), with a focus on Stein's ideas on state administration, constitutional issues, and historical writing. However, in the article Koselleck also sought to offer a set of didactic and constructive ideas on how historical-theoretical reflections can be included in political thought and planning. These reflections formed part of Koselleck's intellectual program in two ways. On the one hand, by means of portraying Stein as a figure who was out of tune with the times in which he lived, the article served as an argument against conceptualizing history as a temporally unified and uniform movement. On the other hand, by means of referring to Stein's work, it served as an appeal to rethink the fundamental conditions of possible history and historical writing.

Stein, Koselleck explained, lived in the age in which the role of history was changing in correspondence to the fundamental shift in the human conception of the relations among the past, the present, and the future. More concretely, as a new future was set free, a future that was expected to be radically different from the past and to run along a progressive and singular model, history, as the lessons of the past, lost its position as the teacher of life.[140]

In this turmoil, Koselleck stated, Lorenz von Stein was one of the few who managed to combine an erudite knowledge of historical dates and facts without forgetting the urgent demands of planning the future. But, according to Koselleck, Stein sought to view the present in a historical-critical perspective and refrained from a type of planning and prognosis that aimed at totality and was based on a punctual and accumulative chronology. In fact, it was Stein's theory of history that enabled him to break away from the idealistic, future-oriented, and utopian traits of contemporary thought: "He used it to open up all events: their enduring preconditions on the one hand, and the forces lending them motion on the other. Stein was a historical ontologist in the full and ambiguous sense of the word. He separated historical duration and historical contingency only theoretically and only to establish the uniqueness of given circumstances. This theoretical procedure has proved itself. He gained two mutually illuminating aspects without having to make either of them absolute."[141]

Due to his focus on the conditions of human history, Koselleck added, Stein was able to reveal the "movement as movement" and indicate the possibilities of its direction. More concretely, in relation to the Prussian constitutional question of 1852, by asking "for the concrete preconditions of a constitution, its conditions of possibility," Stein had allegedly managed to plan and to a certain degree predict the direction of future politics. Koselleck summed up Stein's achievement with the following words: "Stein . . . thought historically and not in a utopian fashion; he drew conclusions from a known present for the possibilities of tomorrow, moving from diagnosis to the prognosis, and not vice versa."[142]

Koselleck evidently not only sympathized but also identified with Stein's theory of the conditions of possible history, which had several similarities to the one that he himself had been developing since the early 1950s. With Stein, he staged himself as a theoretician of history, as someone who aimed to display the possibilities of the present and the future by analyzing the past and the conditions of the humanly possible. His message was a didactic and somewhat optimistic answer to how the challenges and dangers of modernity might be mastered through a structural-historical perspective. The *Habilitationsschrift* on Prussia marks, above all, the achievement of such a perspective. It was only through massive, concrete, and detailed historical research that Koselleck was able to keep some of the theoretical promises that "Kritik und Krise" had made. The pluralized conception of history, as theorized already in the mid 1950s, became palpable only in relation with the "temporal layers" of the Prussian *Vormärz* that Koselleck so painstakingly elaborated. The recognition of the complex and plural nature of a limited period in state and society allowed for a smooth departure from Schmittian macro-historical views that one-sidedly privileged conflict, state, and violent political action. In terms of Koselleck's normative political stance, modern politics was not bound to end in the disasters caused by utopian thought, if it remained prepared to theorize and to study and respect the limits and possibilities of human history. This was a belief that he was to more thoroughly reflect upon from the mid 1960s onwards, using the conceptual framework he had achieved through his *Habilitation*.

Revolution and Modernity: Political Geography Revisited

Preußen zwischen Reform und Revolution received a remarkably positive appraisal by almost all of its reviewers, both inside and outside of Germany.[143] Not only did they agree that the book was an unavoidable landmark in the field of nineteenth century history of Prussia; Mack Walker even suggested that it was "one of the half-dozen most important historical studies to appear in Germany after 1945,"[144] thus forecasting its later impact on the field of nineteenth century German history.[145]

In the late 1960s, however, *Preußen zwischen Reform und Revolution* not only earned Koselleck great respect within the historical discipline—it also earned him a position. After a short period as a professor in political science at the newly established University of Bochum in North Rhine-Westphalia, in 1967, two years after earning his *Habilitation*, Koselleck acquired a professorship in history at the University of Heidelberg. As a full member of the academic establishment, Koselleck was no longer, at least not to the same degree, required to adapt his historical writing to the norms of the profession or to the predominant intellectual discourses in Germany. This might explain why, in the last of his social-historical texts to appear in the 1960s, Koselleck decided to revisit the political-geographical framework and the more negative evaluation of modernity that he had left behind or toned down when he became an assistant to Conze.

The text referred to above was a contribution to the *Fischer Weltgeschichte* with the title "Das Zeitalter der europäischen Revolution 1780–1848," which Koselleck wrote together with the two French historians Louis Bergeron and François Furet.[146] The common aim of the three authors was to illuminate the various political, societal, technological, economic, and intellectual dynamics at play in the period of the European revolutions. Considering that, in the introduction to the book, the period was characterized as "replete with crisis" and moreover stated the methodological approach was one aiming to capture the interplay between long-term structures and individual events, thus avoiding a strict chronological narrative, the framework corresponded perfectly to Koselleck's conception of history.[147] His task in the project was to describe the continental dimension of European history from the year 1815 until the outbreak of the revolution of 1848 through four chapters on the Congress of Vienna, the agrarian constitutions of Europe, the revolution of 1830, and, finally, the rise and the structures of the bourgeois world.

What makes Koselleck's account of these events of special interest is his attempt to combine several of the theoretical and methodological elements as well as the various themes, arguments, and perspectives that are found in his various writings (including his letters to Schmitt) from the beginning of the 1950s until 1960. In other words, the text witnesses the high level of complexity, variety, but also unity in Koselleck's historical writing in this period. What contributes still further to make the text fascinating reading is its remarkable narrative style. Less constrained by the scientific norms of his surroundings, but obliged to communicate to a broader audience, Koselleck was in a freer position to voice his opinion on the past and the present, but was forced to do this in an easily understandable way. The result was a highly advanced, well-communicated, and almost apocalyptic account of European and global processes of modernity.

In the first chapter on the Congress of Vienna, restating the political-geographical themes, concepts, and arguments that had fascinated him so intensely in the mid 1950s, Koselleck portrayed the congress as a geopolitical fight for the redivision and reordering of the territories of Europe: a new *Raumordnung* (ordering of space).[148] Echoing his letter to Schmitt from 1956, Koselleck explained how the territorial reordering of Europe had been decided by the "the worldwide opposition between the maritime England and the great-continental Russia,", which had imposed their interests on the weaker powers, and he pointed to the persistence of the political discourses of Castlereigh and Alexander in the realm of contemporary international politics.[149] Again he sought to demonstrate the fundamental change of politics taking place in the period through tracing the change of the concept "legitimacy," which, he restated, "unnoticeably became a historical-philosophical concept that was changeable in time. It could serve different functions depending on parties and power."[150]

This time around, however, Koselleck described the consequences of the Congress of Vienna for the various European constitutions in more detail. In the case of Germany, the drafting of constitutions posed considerable problems, because the legitimacy of the old Reich had disappeared and the major European powers—as well as the competition between Germany and Austria—prevented the creation of a federation led by an emperor and comprised of constitutional organizations. Not least due to the motives and actions of the Austrian Foreign Minister, von Metternich, the German constitutions ended as problem-ridden compromises between new and old trends, characterized by the blurring of boundaries among territories as well as among state and federal structures and authorities. According to Koselleck, using the example of Prussia, this compromise remained an inescapable obstacle to later attempts to draft constitutions that might have been able to master and control the political and social energies let loose at the turn of the century.

The example of the German constitutions served to demonstrate what Koselleck conceived of as a key characteristic of modern politics: the increased convergence between domestic and foreign policy. At the beginning of the nineteenth century, Koselleck explained, Europe became a unity. When intellectual, political, and social forces were let loose in one country, they were bound to affect other European countries, as had happened with the dissemination of temporal expectations of rapid change, political ideologies, and revolutionary activities at the time of the French Revolution.

However, according to Koselleck, it was not only Europe, but the entire world that became united in the process of political modernity. Drawing on his earlier review of John Adams, Koselleck ended the chapter on the Congress of Vienna by pointing to how the United States introduced the famous Monroe Doctrine in 1823 as a reaction to events on European soil. This move proved to be vital, or rather fatal, for the political order of the modern world. By establishing the Monroe Doctrine as a reaction to the restoration in Spain imposed by the French, the United States had expressed an act of sympathy for the suppressed Spaniards—an act that stimulated the already ongoing dialectic between revolution and counter-revolution. This turned political modernity into a worldwide experience.

Having outlined these perspectives on the geographical dynamics of recent world history, in the following chapter, by describing the tensions between the old agrarian constitutions of Europe and the emerging industrial society as known from *Preußen zwischen Reform und Revolution*, Koselleck argued that two contradictory temporal-political layers were condensed in the period between 1780 and 1848. The existence of such contradictory layers he now described with the notion "*die Gleichzeitigkeit des Ungleichzeitigen*" (the simultaneity of the non-simultaneous), through which he argued that modernity was born in the conflict between these layers.[151]

The notion of *die Gleichzeitigkeit des Ungleichzeitigen* became a key term in Koselleck's attempt to describe the various different but coexisting temporal layers present in all human history. Philosophically, the basic

idea of the notion was influenced by Hegel (as a specific form of historical dialectic) and Heidegger, but it was the German Marxist philosopher
and atheist theologian Ernst Bloch (1885–1977) who made the expression of *Ungleichzeitigkeit* famous in his book *Erbschaft dieser Zeit* (Bequest
of this Time) from 1935, where he referred to it as a *Restsein aus früheren
Zeiten* (leftover from earlier times).[152] Without using the full notion of
die Gleichzeitigkeit des Ungleichzeitigen, but in a way similar to Koselleck,
Bloch referred to the temporal metaphor of *Schichten* (layers) to illustrate
what he conceived of as a basic characteristic of modernity: that social
and cultural structures of the present continue to flourish in the present
alongside existing ones and those pregnant with the future.

Koselleck knew of Bloch's writings and invited him in the 1960s to
give a talk at the University of Heidelberg.[153] Whether this means that
Koselleck was directly inspired by Bloch is difficult to say. Yet, it is evident that Koselleck's idea of *die Gleichzeitigkeit des Ungleichzeitigen*—like
his other ideas—was not created in an intellectual void.[154]

Moving to the main theme of "Kritik und Krise", Koselleck pointed to
one of the processes that the restorative powers were unable to prevent:
the increase of societal power. As competition, prestige, and influence
succeeded the old structural ties of the status layers and the personal rule,
Koselleck stated, toward the conclusion of the chapter, "power could appear in its naked form." To this, he immediately added, "that power is evil
in itself (Jacob Burckhardt) is a dictum of the nineteenth century."[155] According to Koselleck, as he proceeded to demonstrate in the subsequent
chapter, the "old European continuity" was finally destroyed in the period
between the July Revolution in 1830 and the Revolution of 1848. This
period witnessed not only the intensification in the movement of modernity, but also the birth of new and dangerous features, such as nationalism
and Marxism, in which Koselleck detected a hitherto unknown "historical-philosophical arrogance and brutality."[156]

The extreme historical philosophies were, Koselleck argued, a product
of the modern world: a world that was created by the bourgeoisie, the rise
and structure of which he described in the fourth and last chapter of the
text. Of fundamental importance, he wrote, was the emergence of a new
political generation around 1830, which brought with it a fundamental
break with the societal consciousness and values of old Europe. This generation found itself living in a new epoch, in which technological developments, together with a massive rise in population, not only made
the world appear smaller and more unified, but also suggested that it was
increasingly possible for human beings to shape and control it. Guided by
the experience of temporal acceleration and the expectation of progress,
and orientated toward historical-philosophical catchwords like "eman-

cipation" and "revolution," the new generation sought answers to the contemporary crisis through morally informed critique. According to Koselleck, this critique did nothing but reinforce the crisis.

Koselleck's account of the way in which the unstoppable social-political crises spread and intensified reached its climax in the final section of the chapter on the bourgeois world, which covered the period from 1830 to 1848. In the very last section of the chapter (and the book), describing the situation just before the revolution of 1848, Koselleck concluded: "As such, the crisis encompassed all areas of social, intellectual, economical and political life: it was a crisis, which marked the end of the natural circularities and for the first time unleashed a historical progress which we have not yet seen the end of."[157]

Koselleck's Intellectual Program: Pragmatism, Innovation, and Ambiguity

Having restated the pessimistic view of modernity, which had been virtually absent in his previous social-historical texts in the 1960s, Koselleck's text on the age of European revolution underpins the impression that this period saw him develop different but compatible layers of historical thinking that could be employed according to the norms of different academic and political circumstances as well as to his personal preferences.

In his first twenty years as a historian, in a remarkable way, Koselleck had managed combine a strategy of pragmatism with a constant exploration of new approaches, perspectives, and themes. Most importantly, he had learned to master, and in certain respects refine the approaches of historicism and of social history; he had created an anthropologically based concept of history, a theory of modernity, a theory of historical times, and a conceptual-historical approach; he'd created a number of theoretical and methodological catchwords with which he studied and described the past and the present; and he'd created a theory concerning the role of political geography in history. He had also managed to combine several of these perspectives in his analysis, as witnessed in the text on the "age of revolutions."

Koselleck's work drew on discursive features from several intellectual traditions and scholars, such as Schmitt, Conze, Löwith, and Heidegger, but also from a number of figures to whom he was less close in time and space, such as Fernand Braudel and perhaps Ernst Bloch. Meanwhile, he sharpened his arguments using Meinecke as a primary target of critique.

These were among the many scholars whose work Koselleck encountered in the course of his early career—a career that might seem pretty straightforward given that he was awarded a professorship in Heidelberg, where he wrote his dissertation and *Habilitation*. However, the course of his academic career and his work in the 1950s was in no way certain or easy to predict. That Koselleck ended up doing social history in Heidelberg with Conze and not sociology in Dortmund with Ipsen, Popitz, and Schelsky was to a certain extent a result of coincidences, unforeseen events, and choices. On the other hand, while Koselleck's work and career were partly formed by the dynamics and structures of his surroundings, it should be emphasized that within this process he also *chose* among different alternatives, and he was thus active in choosing where, by whom, and how he was formed. He chose for example Heidelberg and not Dortmund, because he could continue his career as a historian in Heidelberg in an intellectual atmosphere that he knew and appreciated.

At the same time, as he learned and refined analytical traditions, Koselleck was able to position himself vis-à-vis his surroundings and create a form of historical thought with unique features. For example, with his theories of historical time, which he coupled to a conceptual approach, he redefined what social history was and how it can be practiced. The theories of historical time became a key discursive feature in the unifying objective in Koselleck's work of deconstructing notions of history in the singular and thematizing histories in plural, even if his work was marked by the tension in his thought between a choice for the universal and for the pluralistic narrative. Another important and related discursive feature Koselleck developed in the 1950s was his idea concerning the relation among space, time, and history. This idea never came to occupy center stage in his writings in the form of a focused research project. Nevertheless it became an integral part of his analytical framework.[158]

In the period in question, Koselleck remained focused on human "finality" and on how the possibilities of human mass death had increased during the processes of modernity. This focus was linked to his attempt to develop the foundations for a more responsible and durable political order. As in "Kritik und Krise", Koselleck expressed a preference for a system in which political power is not one-sidedly accumulated but shared among different groups, representing both state and society. However, instead of outlining specific societal visions, he articulated his political positions within his theoretical project, by means of formalistic assumptions concerning how human life unfolds and how it can be studied.

In his writings on geopolitical issues and on Prussian social history from the mid 1950s to the mid 1960s, Koselleck's interpretations of the modern world and his theories of how its destructive elements might be countered were ambiguous. In some texts, he expressed the conviction that a critical historical analysis, based on a firm theory of the conditions of human history, might control the destructive forces of modernity and frame a more responsible political order. In other writings, he portrayed modernity as a permanent and dialectic movement of disaster that is fundamentally beyond human control and bound to trigger conflict, crisis, and war.

When, during the 1960s, Koselleck nevertheless to some extent modified his view of the processes of modernity, it presumably not only had to do with social-political developments taking place in Germany in the 1960s, or with his adaptation to Conze's research-program, but also with his newly developed analytical framework about history's temporal layers. While this analytical framework was not fully unfolded in his work on Prussia, it came to occupy center stage in his work following the *Habilitation*. The same was true of the conceptual-historical framework with which Koselleck analyzed the interaction between social history and language in *Preußen zwischen Reform und Revolution*. The following two chapters describe and analyze how Koselleck further developed his conceptual approach and his temporal-historical framework in relation to other scientific projects.

Notes

1. RW265-8135: 14/2 (1954). In a speech given in relation to the fiftieth anniversary of his *Promotion*, Koselleck talked in more detail about the exams with Gadamer and Kühn. Koselleck, "Dankrede am 23 November 2004," 45, 51.
2. He wrote: "Of course one may invoke the alleged neutrality of a scientific methodology in order to accuse me of being unscientific in the name of whatever other approach." RW265-8134: 29/11 (1953). These lines seem to attack the notion of "scientism": the belief in a stable and neutral method. If Kühn and Löwith would ask for a "proper method," Koselleck could seemingly only express a deep disagreement in response, since he believed that science is never neutral, but bound to pragmatic contexts, because it is always used to pursue certain aims.
3. RW265-8134: 29/11 (1953). Koselleck wrote: "I still must wait for the report from Professor Löwith, whose skepticism toward philosophy of history, as long as it does not stem from his emigration, my own work does not necessarily have to oppose." With the sub-clause, Koselleck seemingly expressed that he regarded Löwith's emigration as a separating experience that was not relatable to his own work.
4. Koselleck later explained that Kühn was in doubt whether the work should be given summa or magna cum laud, and that it was Löwith's decision to give the magna cum laud. Koselleck was happy merely with the fact that his dissertation was accepted at all. Koselleck, "Dankrede am 23 November 2004," 51.
5. RW265-8137/1: 7/6-1954. Moreover, whilst approving of what he called the "*geistigen Spitzenansatz*," Kühn criticized what he labeled the "naïve equation of Enlightenment and Bürgertum." See Ute Daniel, "Reinhart Koselleck," in *Klassiker der Geschichtswissenschaft, Bd. 2: Von Fernand Braudel to Natalie Z. Davis*, ed. Lutz Raphael, 171 (München, 2006). See also Koselleck's letter to Schmitt from November 1954 (RW265-8131/1: 5/11-1954) in which he referred to Kühn's proposal to publish the

dissertation. Kühn had two main suggestions for revisions: The first was to abandon the use of the notion of *Bürgertum* (see above). The second was to get rid of the notion of dualism, because, according to Kühn, this concept belonged in the history of religion and was not applicable to the political tendencies of the eighteenth century. Koselleck was unsure how to replace the two notions. Eventually, he deleted dualism from the headline, but continued to employ both notions in the analysis.

6. RW265-8135: 14/2 (1954). Koselleck mentioned a suggestion of Kühn's: "to work on a history of neo-Platonism in the modern age; something I certainly will not undertake, especially because [Jacob] Taubes has already worked through the field for the most part and probably still continues with it." Koselleck here referred to Taubes's book *Abendländische Eschatologie* (Bern, 1947), which is listed in the bibliography of "Kritik und Krise".

7. Helmut Schelsky (1912–1984) belonged to the most influential sociologists in postwar Germany until around 1970. Trained by Freyer in Leipzig, Schelsky was active within radical-conservative circles and supported National Socialism through his scholarly activities in the 1930s. In the post-war period, he trained a new generation of sociologists at the institute in Dortmund, and he was later the *spiritus rector* of the University of Bielefeld and a director of its Zentrum für Interdisziplinäre Forschung. When, in the end of the 1960s, attention was drawn to his activities at a student, Schelsky chose to resign from this post. In 1970, he nevertheless decided to take up a position as a professor in sociology in Bielefeld. Günther Ipsen (1899–1984) also studied in Lepzig, where in 1926 he achieved a professorship. In 1933, he went to Königsberg, where he, as we shall return to, became one of the fathers of *Volksgeschichte*. In 1939, he moved to Vienna, where he was discharged in 1945. In 1951, he got the position in Dortmund but had to leave in 1961, due to a problem-ridden relationship with his employees, including the two candidates for his succession, Helmut Schelsky and Richardt Behrendt. For these issues, see Etzemüller, *Sozialgeschichte als politische Geschichte*, 66, 140–44, 199–207.

8. Reinhart Koselleck, "Bristol, die 'zweite Stadt' Englands: Eine sozialgeschichtliche Skizze," *Soziale Welt* 6 (1955): 360–72.

9. Ibid., 362.

10. Ibid., 364.

11. Ibid., 362.

12. Ibid., 364.

13. Ibid., 365.

14. Ibid., 371.

15. Again, Koselleck arguably reproduced a specific set of polemical anti-British topoi from the period around World War I, although he freed his text from the moralizing overtones of nationalist war propaganda. The recurrence of these topoi in his work was most probably once again a result of his reception of Schmittian geopolitics, as we will return to.

16. Koselleck, "Bristol, die 'zweite Stadt' Englands," 374.

17. Ibid. In his letters to Schmitt, Koselleck indicated that in his opinion the peculiar relation between state and society was still omnipresent in England. He thus described how the university in Bristol was a "partly commercial institution (*halbes Wirtschaftsunternehmen*)" that was led with "pedagogical intentions" and fulfilled societal rather than social functions. To this he added that English academics gained their "self-confidence" via their particular "club life." RW265-8133/1: 8/7 (1953).

18. According to Schmitt, using the Treaty of Versailles and the League of Nations as examples, liberalism always defines its own wars as "just" and its opponents' as "crimi-

nal" and in this process, political language is replaced by a moral language that opens a path to wars against "enemies of humanity." The above account of Schmitt's work on international law draws extensively on Balakrishnan, *The Enemy*, 226–52.

19. In several of the letters, Koselleck referred to both recent and forthcoming visits to Plettenberg. For these visits, see also Mehring, *Carl Schmitt*, 512–14.

20. Carl Schmitt, *Gespräch über die Macht und den Zugang zum Machthaber* (Pfullingen, 1954).

21. For how the book related to Schmitt's strategy of portraying himself as having been disconnected from the circles of power between 1933 and 1945, see Mehring, *Carl Schmitt zur Einführung*, 90–91.

22. RW265-8138/1: 5/11 (1954).

23. Jeffrey Herf, *Reactionary Modernism: Technology, Culture, and Politics in Weimar and the Third Reich* (New York, 1986).

24. For the widespread skepticism toward technology in Germany in the 1950s, especially among conservatives, see Nolte, *Die Ordnung der deutschen Gesellschaft*, 273–318; and Schildt, *Moderne Zeiten*, 324–50.

25. Fritz Fellner, "Nationales und europäisch-atlantisches Geschichtsbild in der Bundesrepublik und im Westen in den Jahren nach Ende des Zweiten Weltkrieges," in *Deutsche Geschichtswissenschaft nach dem Zweiten Weltkrieg (1945–1965)*, ed. Ernst Schulin, 213–26 (München, 1989).

26. Most famous in this respect is Gerhard Ritter, *Machtstaat und Utopie: Vom Streit um die Dämonie der Macht seit Machiavelli and Morus* (München, 1940), which in the following six years was reprinted six times with the new title *Die Dämonie der Macht: Betrachtungen über Geschichte und Wesen des Machtproblems im Politischen Denken der Neuzeit*. See Cornelissen, *Gerhard Ritter*, 316–26.

27. Etzemüller, *Sozialgeschichte als politische Geschichte*, 268–96; Chung, *Das Bild der Moderne*, 85–104.

28. The book was read and referred to by scholars from many different fields and countries. See Müller, *A Dangerous Mind*, 87–103; Laak, *Gespräche in der Sicherheit*, 39 n. 106, 223–24.

29. Reinhart Koselleck, "Die Wiederentdeckung von John Adams," *Neue politische Literatur*, 1 Jg. (1956): 93–104. For another contemporary review that deals with similar themes, see Reinhart Koselleck, Review of *The Political Writings of James Harrington and of Richard Peters*, *Neue Politische Literatur*, 2 Jg. (1957): 288–93.

30. Koselleck, "Die Wiederentdeckung von John Adams," 95. It is interesting that Koselleck here used the notion of Erfahrungs*horizont*, thus merging the Gadamerian inspired conceptual pairs of Erfahrungs*raum* and Erwartungs*horizont* that he introduced in the 1970s. This is one of the clues indicating that Koselleck did not explore and develop Gadamer's hermeneutics in a systematic fashion before the 1960s. We return to the notions of *Erfahrungsraum* and *Erwartungshorizont* and Koselleck's reception of Gadamer in chapter 5.

31. Koselleck, "Die Wiederentdeckung von John Adams," 99–100.

32. Ibid., 102.

33. Ibid.

34. Reinhart Koselleck: "Review of *Christianity, Diplomacy and War*, by Herbert Butterfield", *Archiv für Rechts- und Sozialphilosophie*, no. 41 (1954/55): 591–95.

35. Ibid., 591.

36. Ibid., 592.

37. Ibid.

38. Ibid., 593.

39. Ibid.
40. Ibid., 595.
41. Ibid.
42. Koselleck discussed Butterfield's work in his letters to Schmitt. In a letter from April 1955, Koselleck wrote: "I have posted a review of Butterfield (Christianity, Diplomacy and War) to the ARSP and hope that I can send it to you shortly. I have not missed the opportunity to make two references to your book 'Der Nomos der Erde', in which what Butterfield more feels than demonstrates in his book is thoroughly analyzed." RW265-8140: 20/4 (1955). Koselleck had already mentioned the book to Schmitt in a letter from May 1954. Here Koselleck expressed the opinion that the book deserved a German translation and added that he planned to mention Schmitt's work to Butterfield on a forthcoming visit he was intending to pay the latter. RW265-8136/1: 28/5 (1954). In a letter to Schmitt from July 1955, Koselleck reported of a speech that Butterfield had recently given on the topic of "Die Rolle des Individuums in der Geschichte" at the University of Heidelberg. RW265-8145/2: 10/7 (1956). For the reception of Butterfield among (primarily national-conservative) German historians in the Federal Republic in the 1950s and 1960s, see Martina Steber, "Herbert Butterfield, der Nationalsozialismus und die deutsche Geschichtswissenschaft," Vierteljahrsheft für Zeitgeschichte 55 (2007): 269–307.
43. RW265-8135/1: 14/2 (1954).
44. RW265-8141/1: 6/7 (1955).
45. RW265-8142: 28/7 (1995).
46. In a letter from February 1954, he wrote that the position as assistant to Kühn was presumably not available for him, because Kühn was close to his retirement and had said nothing about it. RW265-8135: 14/2 (1954).
47. We will return to Koselleck's teaching experiences in Heidelberg in chapter 5.
48. RW265-8145/1: 10/7 (1956).
49. See first of all Carl Schmitt, Legalität und Legitimität (Berlin, 1932).
50. With this sentence, Koselleck seemingly addressed a historical transition from a universal notion (as informing historical progress, etc.) to a relativist one.
51. Koselleck, "Zeit, Zeitlichkeit und Geschichte," 10. In this interview, Koselleck explained how he eventually wanted to compare the temporal structures of the Congress of Vienna and the Treaty of Versailles.
52. RW265-8148: 6/7 (1958).
53. Ringer, The Decline of the German Mandarins.
54. Koselleck's last text on Anglo-Saxon themes was the review article "Zwei Denker der puritanischen Revolution [Harrington and Hobbes]", Neue politische Literatur, 2 Jg. (1957): 288–93. In the following years, Koselleck wrote a number of relatively short reviews, mainly in Das Historisch-Politische Buch, primarily of books dealing with Prussian social history. These include Review of Staat und Gesellschaft im Wandel unserer Zeit, by Theodor Schieder, The Economic History Review 12, no. 2 (1959): 325–26; Review of Freiherr vom Stein im Zeitalter der Restauration, by Werner Gembruch, Das historisch-politische Buch, Jg. IX (1961): 212; Review of Der neue Gebhardt, ed. Herbert Grundmann, Das historisch-politische Buch, Jg. IX (1961): 225–27; "Review of Staatsbildende Kräfte der Neuzeit, by Fritz Hartung, Das historisch-politische Buch, Jg. IX (1961): 301; Review of Die Struktur der europäischen Wirklichkeit, by Walter Felix Müller, Das historisch-politische Buch, Jg. IX (1961): 311; Review of Die Geschichte der Lage der Arbeiter unter dem Kapitalismus (vol. 8+9), by Jürgen Kuczynski, The Economic History Review, vol. 14, no. 2 (1961): 378-379; Review of Die deutsche verfassungsgeschichtliche Forschung im 19. Jahrhundert, by Ernst-Wolfgang Böckenförde, Das histo-

risch-politische Buch, Jg. X (1962): 10-11; Review of *Studien zur deutschen Geschichte des 19. und 20. Jahrhunderts*, by Siegfried A. Kaehler, *Das historisch-politische Buch*, Jg. X (1962): 111; Review of *Die letzten hundert Jahre. Gestalten, Ideen, Ereignissem*, by Kurt Seeberger, *Das historisch-politische Buch*, Jg. X (1962): 111; Review of *Die Rolle des Staates in den Frühstadien der Industrialisierung*, by Ulrich Peter Ritter, *Das historisch-politische Buch*, Jg. X (1962): 207; Review of *Das deutsche Kaiserreich von 1871 als Nationalstaat*, by Theodor Schieder, *Das historisch-politische Buch*, Jg. XI (1963): 306; Review of *Wilhelm von Humboldt und der Staat*, by Sigfried A. Kaehler, *Das historisch-politische Buch*, Jg. XIII (1965): 141. Koselleck used many of these books in relation to *Preußen zwischen Reform und Revolution*, as witnessed in the [Bibliography. Another two reviews from this period, which Koselleck authored in relation to preparing the publication of "Kritik und Krise", are Review of *Political Thought in England: Tyndal to Hooker*, by Christopher Morris, *Archiv für Rechts- und Sozialphilosophie*, Bd. XLI (1954/1955): 136–37; and Review of *Raynal et sa machine de guerre*, by Hans Wolpe, *Archiv für Rechts- und Sozial-Philosophie*, Nr. 45 (1959): 126–28.

55. The following is based on Jan Eike Dunkhase, *Werner Conze: Ein deutscher Historiker in 20. Jahrhundert* (Göttingen, 2010); Werner Lausecker, "Werner Conze," in *Handbuch der völkischen Wissenschaften: Personen, Institutionen, Forschungsprogramme, Stiftungen*, ed. Ingo Haar and Michael Fahlbusch, 93–103 (München, 2008); Etzemüller, *Sozialgeschichte als politische Geschichte*; Reinhart Koselleck, "Werner Conze. Tradition und Innovation," *Historische Zeitschrift*, Bd. 245 (1987): 529–43; Wolfgang Schieder, "Soziologie zwischen Soziologie und Geschichte. Das wissenschaftliche Lebenswerk Werner Conzes," *Geschichte und Gesellschaft*, Jg. 13. (1987): 244–66; and Jürgen Kocka, "Werner Conze und die Sozialgeschichte in der Bundesrepublik Deutschland," *Geschichte in Wissenschaft und Unterricht*, Jg. 10 (1986): 595–602.

56. Winfried Schulze and Otto Gerhard Oexle, eds., *Deutsche Historiker im Nationalsozialismus* (Frankfurt, 2000); Ingo Haar, *Historiker im Nationalsozialismus: deutsche Geschichtswissenschaft und der 'Volkstumkampf' im Osten* (Gottingen 2000); Peter Schöttler, ed., *Geschichtsschreibung als Legitimationswissenschaft. 1918–1945* (Frankfurt am Main, 1997); and Willi Oberkrome, *Volksgeschichte. Methodische Innovation und völkische Ideologisierung in der deutschen Geschichtswissenschaft 1918–1945* (Göttingen, 1993).

57. With the exception of Hans Rothfels. Due to his Jewish descent, Rothfels immigrated in 1938 after having been sacked from his academic positions and persecuted by the National Socialists.

58. Conze became a member of the Nazi party in May 1937 and since March 1933 had been a member of the SA.

59. The process through which Conze was hired is described in Etzemüller, *Sozialgeschichte als politische Geschichte*, 138–44. Etzemüller mentions here that Kühn put Conze on the list of his desired successors.

60. Werner Conze, "Die Strukturgeschichte des technisch-industriellen Zeitalter als Aufgabe für Forschung und Unterricht," *Werner Conze: Gesellschaft—Staat—Nation* (Stuttgart, 1992), 66–85.

61. In the following, the labels of "social history" and "structural history" will be used interchangeably.

62. Hans Freyer, *Theorie des Gegenwärtigen Zeitalters* (Stuttgart, 1955). The intellectual relations between Freyer and Conze are described in Dunkhase, *Werner Conze*, 129–34; and Etzemüller, *Sozialgeschichte als politische Geschichte*, 63–65. The following description of Freyer's book largely follows Etzemüller's account.

63. Etzemüller, *Sozialgeschichte als politische Geschichte*, 64.

64. Ibid., 64–65; Nolte, *Die Ordnung der deutschen Gesellschaft*, 287–90; Schildt, *Moderne Zeiten*, 346–48; Jerry Z. Muller, "'Historical Social Science' and Political Myth: Hans Freyer (1887–1969) and the Genealogy of Social History in West Germany," in *Paths of Continuity: Central European Historiography from the 1930s to the 1950s*, ed. Hartmut Lehmann and James Van Horn Melton, 197–229 (Cambridge, 1994); Jerry Z. Muller, *The Other God that Failed: Hans Freyer and the Deradicalization of German Conservatism* (Princeton, 1987).

65. For the reestablishment of the sociological profession in the 1950s, see Nolte, *Die Ordnung der deutschen Gesellschaft*.

66. For the history of "social" and "structural history," see Etzemüller, *Sozialgeschichte als politische Geschichte*.

67. As he wrote to Hans Rothfels in a letter from 18 October 1953 that is cited from Etzemüller, *Sozialgeschichte als politische Geschichte*, 97 n. 33. In the cited sentence, Conze also commented on the talk of Theodor Schieder. Brunner's talk should have been given in a separate section on social history headed by Conze, but the section was for a variety of reasons never realized.

68. As Theodor Schieder stated in his summary of Freyer's talk, "Zum Gegenwärtiges Verhältnis von Geschichte und Soziologe," *Geschichte in Wissenschaft und Unterricht*, 3. Jg. (1952): 28; see also Hans Freyer, "Soziologie und Geschichtswissenschaft," *Geschichte in Wissenschaft und Unterricht*, 3 Jg. (1952): 15–20.

69. Conze quoted in Etzemüller, *Sozialgeschichte als politische Geschichte*, 161.

70. The parallels drawn here concern Conze's historical thinking after 1945, when it was more or less disconnected from, modified, or at least concealed the radically anti-democratic, authoritarian, and violent aspects that informed his scientific contributions to the Nazi *Volkstum- und Bevölkerungspolitik* before 1945. For an account of Conze's "order-thinking" in the period before and after 1945, see Etzemüller, *Sozialgeschichte als politische Geschichte*, 268–310.

71. Dunkhase, *Werner Conze*, 78–166; Etzemüller, *Sozialgeschichte als politische Geschichte*, 149–60; and Koselleck,"Werner Conze", 540–42 (Koselleck lists the entire fifteen organizations that Conze founded, directed or influenced).

72. As stated by Schieder in "Soziologie zwischen Soziologie und Geschichte," 244–45. See also Junker, "Theorie der Geschichtswissenschaft," 169.

73. Quoted in Etzemüller, *Sozialgeschichte als politische Geschichte*, 155.

74. Werner Conze, ed., *Staat und Gesellschaft im deutschen Vormärz, 1815–1848* (Stuttgart, 1962).

75. The volume was the outcome of a 1958 conference at which the contributors presented their initial thoughts on their topics. Etzemüller, *Sozialgeschichte als politische Geschichte*, 169–70.

76. Werner Conze, "Das Spannungsfeld von Staat von Gesellschaft im Vormärz," in *Staat und Gesellschaft im deutschen Vormärz 1815–1848*, ed. Werner Conze, 207–70 (Stuttgart, 1962). For excellent comments on Conze's essay, see Chung, *Das Bild der Moderne*, 195–98.

77. Conze, "Das Spannungsfeld von Staat von Gesellschaft im Vormärz," 247.

78. Reinhart Koselleck, "Staat und Gesellschaft in Preußen 1815–1848," in *Staat und Gesellschaft im deutschen Vormärz 1815–1848*, ed. Werner Conze, 79–112 (Stuttgart, 1962). For excellent comments on Koselleck's essay, see Chung, *Das Bild der Moderne*, 194–95.

79. Werner Conze, "Die Stellung der Sozialgeschichte in Forschung und Unterricht," *Geschichte in Wissenschaft und Unterricht*, Jg. 3 (1952): 655. We will return to the importance of Brunner's work for Conze's program.

80. Koselleck, "Staat und Gesellschaft in Preußen 1815–1848," 79.
81. Ibid., 81.
82. Ibid., 88.
83. Ibid., 109.
84. Ibid., 109.
85. Freyer, *Theorie des Gegenwärtigen Zeitalters*, 206–20. In fact, Freyer referred to Löwith's book, as he outlined the idea (207).
86. Examples are found in, among other places, Conze, "Die Strukturgeschichte des technisch-industriellen Zeitalter," 73; and "Das Spannungsfeld von Staat von Gesellschaft im Vormärz," 211–12.
87. Koselleck, "Staat und Gesellschaft in Preußen 1815-1848," 86.
88. Ibid.
89. Ibid., 99.
90. RW265-8151/11: 8/7 (1959).
91. Koselleck, "Staat und Gesellschaft in Preußen 1815-1848," 107.
92. Quoted in Schlak, *Wilhelm Hennis*, 249 n. 28.
93. Etzemüller, *Sozialgeschichte als politische Geschichte*, 170.
94. Leonora O'Boyle, Review of *Staat und Gesellschaft im deutschen Vormärz 1815–1848*, ed. By Werner Conze, *Journal of Modern History* 35, no. 3 (1963): 299. See also the praise in Thomas T. Helde, Review of *Staat und Gesellschaft im deutschen Vormärz 1815–1848*, ed. Werner Conze, *Journal of Economic History* 23, no. 3 (1963): 351–52.
95. Koselleck, *Preußen zwischen Reform und Revolution*, 13.
96. Silke Hahn, "Zwischen Re-education und Zweiter Bildungsreform: Die Sprache der Bildungspolitik in der Öffentlichen Diskussion," in *Kontroverse Begriffe: Geschichte des öffentlichen Sprachgebrauch in der Bundesrepublik Deutschland*, ed. Georg Stötzel and Martin Wengeler, 185–87 (Berlin, 1995); and Steger, "Sprache im Wandel," 24.
97. Axel Schildt, "Materieller Wohlstand—pragmatische Politik—kulturelle Umbrüche: Die 60er Jahre in der Bundesrepublik," in *Dynamische Zeiten: Die 60er Jahre in den beiden deutschen Gesellschaften*, ed. Axel Schildt, Detlef Siegfried, and Karl Christian Lammers, 21–53 (Hamburg, 2000). See also Wolfrum, *Die geglückte Demokratie*, 187–283; Wolfrum, *Die Bundesrepublik Deutschland 1949–1990*, 242–356.
98. See Axel Schildt, Detlef Siegfried, and Karl Christian Lammers, eds., *Dynamische Zeiten: Die 60er Jahre in den beiden deutschen Gesellschaften* (Hamburg, 2000).
99. We will return to these issues in chapter 5.
100. Wolfrum, *Die geglückte Demokratie*, 327–56; Wolfrum, *Die Bundesrepublik Deutschland 1949–1990*, 416–45.
101. The following draws on Frieder Günther, *Denken vom Staat her: Die Bundesdeutsche Staatsrechtslehre zwischen Dezision und Integration 1949–1970* (München, 2004).
102. For Forsthoff's life and work, see Christian Schütte, *Progressive Verwaltungsrechtswissenschaft auf konservativer Grundlage: Zur Verwaltungsrechtslehre Ernst Forsthoffs* (Berlin, 2006); Peter Caldwell, "Ernst Forsthoff and the Legacy of Radical Conservative State Theory in the Federal Republic of Germany," *History of Political Thought*, vol. XV (1994): 615–40; Laak, *Gespräche in der Sicherheit*, 240–46.
103. Forsthoff chose to become emeritus prematurely, after, with reference to his past, he was heavily attacked in relation to the prospect of receiving an honorary doctorate at the University of Vienna in 1965.
104. Mehring, *Carl Schmitt*, 514–15; Laak, *Gespräche in der Sicherheit*, 200–08.

105. For Koselleck's participation in Ebrach, see Angela Reintal and Reinhard Mußnug, ed., *Briefwechsel Ernst Forsthoff—Carl Schmitt (1926–1974)* (Berlin, 2007), 438–39 [(no. 144), 505 (no. 292), 518 (no. 317); and Mehring, *Carl Schmitt*, 535, 553.

106. Together with Klaus von der Groeben, Franz Meyer, Franz Ronneberger, and Roman Schnur, they were members of the journal's founding editorial board in 1970. With Roman Schnur, Forsthoff was co-editor-in-chief until his death in 1974. Koselleck left the journal in 1978; he never contributed articles to it. Florian Meinel has described Koselleck's and Forsthoff's common interest in historical and contemporary issues of public administration and public law as follows: "The German historian Reinhart Koselleck, another adept of Carl Schmitt and a friend of Forsthoff from their common Heidelberg days, has analysed in his classical study on Prussia in the aftermath of the French Revolution the role of a clever bureaucracy in preventing social revolt. Koselleck focused on the time after 1789, while Forsthoff's moment of truth came in 1914. In a world devastated by war, the role and burden of the administration had to be reconsidered. For both scholars, it appeared that the administration was then expected to be the last resort of order against chaos." Florian Meinel, "Review essay—Ernst Forsthoff and the Intellectual History of the German Administrative Law," *German Law Journal* 8 (2007): 798.

107. For this view and for how his associates adopted it, see Mehring, "Carl Schmitt and His Influence on Historians," 1653–64.

108. RW265-8171/1: 24/6 (1976). In the letter, Koselleck ventured into a longer explanation of how to place the "Heeresverfassung" in his account of the Prussian *Vormärz*. He moreover described the later course of German history as a result of the failed attempt to create a constitution around 1848.

109. Carl Schmitt, *Staatsgefüge und Zusammenbruch des Zweiten Reiches: Der Sieg des Bürgers über den Soldaten* (Hamburg, 1934). Already in the 1920s, Schmitt had outlined a historical argument concerning what he argued was the dangerous legacies of the recent "blurry" and "unclear" German constitutions, in which forces of the German society had "robbed" the German state of its sovereignty. His prime example was what he referred to as the "non-transparent" and "dangerous" compromise that had been made in the German constitution in 1871. It was this argument that Schmitt sharpened in *Staatsgefüge und Zusammenbruch des zweiten Reiches*. His interpretation of events was severely (and courageously) criticized by the historian Fritz Hartung, who in the early 1930s became Hintze's successor at the University at Berlin, where Schmitt was also teaching at the time. Hans-Christoph Kraus, "Soldatenstaat oder Verfassungsstaat. Zur Kontroverse zwischen Carl Schmitt und Fritz Hartung über den preußisch-deutschen Konstitutionalismus (1934–1935)," *Jahrbuch für die Geschichte Mittel- und Ostdeutschlands*, Bd. 45 (1999): 275–310. For Hintze and Hartung's reviews of Schmitt's *Verfassungslehre* (1928), see Hans-Christoph Kraus, "Verfassungslehre und Verfassungsgeschichte: Otto Hintze und Fritz Hartung als Kritiker Carl Schmitts," *Staat—Souveränität—Verfassung. Festschrift für Helmut Quaritsch zum 70. Geburtstag*, ed. Dietrich Murswiek, 637–61 (Berlin, 2000).

110. Koselleck, *Preußen zwischen Reform und Revolution*, 637.

111. Ibid., Vorwort. Koselleck also thanked his two colleagues from the historical and juridical seminars in Heidelberg, the social historian Wolfgang Schieder, and the jurist and constitutional historian Ernst Wolfgang Böckenförde, for suggestions and criticism.

112. Ibid., 17.

113. Ibid.

114. In chapter 5, I will deal in more depth with the critique of historicism in the 1960s and 1970s.
115. Koselleck, *Preußen zwischen Reform und Revolution*, 17.
116. Ibid.
117. For more on Brunner's life and work, see Reinhard Blänkner, "Von der 'Staatsbildung' zur 'Volkwerdung': Otto Brunners Perspektivenwechsel der Verfassungshistorie im Spannungsfeld zwischen völkischem und alteuropäischem Geschichtsdenken," in *Alteuropa oder Frühe Moderne. Deutungsmuster für das 16. bis 18. Jahrhundert aus dem Krisenbewußtsein der Weimarer Republik in Theologie, Rechts- und Geschichtswissenschaft*, ed. Luise Schorn-Schütte, 87–135 (Berlin, 1999); Gadi Algazi, "Otto Brunner—'Konkrete Ordnung' und Sprache der Zeit," in *Geschichtsschreibung als Legitimationswissenschaft 1918–45*, ed. Peter Schöttler, 166–204 (Frankfurt am Main, 1999); and Otto Gerhard Oexle, "Sozialgeschichte—Begriffsgeschichte—Wissenschaftsgeschichte. Anmerkungen zum Werk Otto Brunners," *Vierteljahrschrift für Sozial- und Wirtschaftsgeschichte*, no. 71 (1984): 305–41.
118. Otto Brunner, *Land und Herrschaft: Grundfragen der territorialen Verfassungsgeschichte Südostdeutschlands im Mittelalter* (Baden bei Wien, 1939).
119. Lutz Raphael, *Geschichtswissenschaft im Zeitalter der Extreme: Theorien, Methoden, Tendenzen von 1900 bis zur Gegenwart* (München, 2003), 94. With reference to "the Germanic thinking in the Middle Ages," which Schmitt in *Über Drei Arten des rechtswissenschaftlichen Denken* (Hamburg, 1934) claimed was a "through and through concrete order thinking," Schmitt attempted to establish a basic juridical thinking that the Nazis could use without taking the existing norms and rules into account.
120. See Werner Conze, "Sozialgeschichte" [1966], *Gesellschaft—Staat—Nation*, (Stuttgart, 1992), 86–95.
121. Werner Conze, "Vom 'Pöbel zum 'Proletariat': Sozialgeschichtliche Voraussetzungen für den Sozialismus on Deutschland," *Vierteljahrschrift für Sozial- und Wirtschaftsgeschichte*, 41 (1954): 333–68.
122. Conze, "Vom 'Pöbel zum 'Proletariat'," 336 [cited from official translation (CFOT)].
123. Koselleck, "Zeit, Zeitlichkeit und Geschichte," 10–11. See also Reinhart Koselleck, "Begriffsgeschichtliche Probleme der Verfassungsgeschichtsschreibung," *Der Staat. Beiheft 6. Gegenstand und Begriffe der Verfassungsgeschichtsschreibung* (1983): 13.
124. Koselleck, "Begriffsgeschichtliche Probleme," 13. Koselleck also commented on how Brunner forgot to historicize his own position.
125. Koselleck, *Preußen zwischen Reform und Revolution*, 56.
126. Ibid., 60.
127. Ibid., 14.
128. Fernand Braudel, preface to *La Méditerranée et le Monde Méditerranéen a l'époque de Philippe II* (Paris, 1949).
129. Wolfgang Schieder, "Wir können keine Kommentare erzwingen, denn schließlich waren wir nicht das hohe Gericht," in *Versäumte Fragen: Deutsche Historiker im Schatten des Nationalsozialismus*, ed. Rüdiger Hohls and Konrad H. Jarausch, 293 (München, 2000); Lutz Raphael, "Trotzige Ablehnung, Produktive Missverständnisse und verborgene Affinitäten: Westdeutsche Antworten auf die Herausforderungen der 'Annales'-Historiographie (1945–1960)," in *Geschichtswissenschaft um 1950*, ed. Heinz Duchhardt and Gerhard May, 75–80 (Mainz, 2002); Etzemüller, *Sozialgeschichte als politische Geschichte*, 54-49; Lutz Raphael, "Trotzige Ablehnung, Produktive Missverständnisse und verborgene Affinitäten: Westdeutsche Antworten auf die Herausforderungen der 'Annales'-Historiographie (1945–1960)," in *Geschichtswissenschaft um 1950*, ed. Heinz Duchhardt and Gerhard May, 75–80 (Mainz, 2002).

130. Koselleck, "Zeit, Zeitlichkeit und Geschichte," 11. The first direct reference to Braudel in Koselleck's work is found in "Über die Theoriebedürftigkeit der Geschichtswissenschaft," 23.

131. Hans Rosenberg, *Bureaucracy, Aristocracy and Autocracy: The Prussian Experience 1660–1815* (Cambridge, 1958).

132. William W. Hagen, "Descent of the Sonderweg. Hans Rosenberg's History of Old-Regime Prussia," *Central European History* 24, no. 1 (1991): 24–50; Hans August Winkler, "Ein Erneuerer der Geschichtswissenschaft: Hans Rosenberg: 1904–1988," *Historische Zeitschrift*, Bd. 248 (1989): 259–52; and Gerhard A. Ritter, "Hans Rosenberg 1904-1988," *Geschichte und Gesellschaft*, Bd. 15 (1989): 282–302.

133. Rosenberg, *Bureaucracy, Aristocracy and Autocracy*, 22.

134. Ibid., 25, 23.

135. Ibid., 25.

136. We will deal in more depth with the notion of a German *Sonderweg* in chapter 6.

137. Rosenberg, *Bureaucracy, Aristocracy and Autocracy*, 23.

138. Mack Walker, "Review of Preußen zwischen Reform und Revolution," *Journal of Social History* 2/3 (1969–1970): 184. Walker's somewhat different view on Prussian history can be seen in *German Home Towns: Community, State and General Estate, 1648–1871* (Ithaca, 1971), in which he argues for the persistence of local institutions, traditions, and regulations that remained outside the state's administrative sphere.

139. Reinhart Koselleck, "Geschichtliche Prognose in Lorenz v. Steins Schrift zur preußischen Verfassung," *Der Staat*, Bd. 4 (1965): 469–81.

140. We shall later return to the topos of "Historia Magistra Vitae."

141. Koselleck, "Geschichtliche Prognose," 473 (CFOT).

142. Ibid., 476.

143. See Karl-Georg Faber, Review of *Preußen zwischen Reform und Revolution*, by Reinhart Koselleck, *Neue politische Literatur*, no. 3 (1968): 396–400; Ernst Klein, Review of *Preußen zwischen Reform und Revolution*, by Reinhart Koselleck, *Das Historisch-Politische Buch*, XVI (1968): 298–99; Hans Joachim-Schoeps, Review of *Preußen zwischen Reform und Revolution*, by Reinhart Koselleck, *Zeitschrift für Religions- und Geistesgeschichte* 20 (1968): 88–91; and W. H. Simon, Review of *Preußen zwischen Reform und Revolution*, by Reinhart Koselleck, *The English Historical Review* 84, no. 330 (1969): 194–95. See also Arnold H. Price, Review of *Preußen zwischen Reform und Revolution*, by Reinhart Koselleck, *The American Historical Review* 73, no. 4 (1968): 1178–79; Donald G. Rohr, Review of *Preußen zwischen Reform und Revolution*, by Reinhart Koselleck and also of *Staat und Gesellschaft im deutschen Vormärz, 1815–1848*, ed. Werner Conze, *Central European History* 1, no. 3 (1968): 285–88; Hans Herzfeld, Review of *Preußen zwischen Reform und Revolution*, by Reinhart Koselleck, *Jahrbuch für die Geschichte Mittel- und Ostdeutschlands* 18 (1969): 377; Eberhard Schmeider, Review of *Preußen zwischen Reform und Revolution*, by Reinhart Koselleck, *Schmollers Jahrbuch für Wirtschafts- und Sozialwissenschaften* 90, Hf. 3 (1970): 357–58; Jürgen Kocka, Review of *Preußen zwischen Reform und Revolution*, by Reinhart Koselleck, *Vierteljahrschrift für Sozial und Wirtschaftsgeschichte*, Bd. 75 (1970): 121–25; and Jonathan Sperber, "State and Civil Society in Prussia: Thoughts of a New Edition of Reinhart Koselleck's 'Preußen zwischen Reform und Revolution'," *Journal of Modern History* 57, no. 2 (1985): 278–96. Also three entirely negative reviews appeared. The first does not find Koselleck's analysis satisfactory. Arthur Schweitzer, Review of *Preußen zwischen Reform und Revolution*, by Reinhart Koselleck, *Political Science Quarterly* 85, no. 1 (1970): 158–59. The second, published in a GDR-journal, denounces Ko-

selleck from a Marxist perspective as being a proponent of bourgeois and restorative forces in West German society. Helmut Bleiber, Review of *Preußen zwischen Reform und Revolution*, by Reinhart Koselleck, *Zeitschrift für Geschichtswissenschaft* XIX Jg., Hf. 1 (1971): 112–15. The third, published also in a leftist journal, likewise criticizes the book for being an example of "bourgeois historiography." Heiner Christ, Review of *Preußen zwischen Reform und Revolution*, by Reinhart Koselleck, *Das Argument*, no. 2 (1970): 141–42. Quite critical is also Herbert Obenaus, Review of *Preußen zwischen Reform und Revolution*, by Reinhart Koselleck, *Göttingschen Gelehrte Anzeiger*, 222 Jg., 1970: 155–67.

144. Walker, Review of *Preußen zwischen Reform und Revolution*, by Reinhart Koselleck, 184.

145. Koselleck's work has first of all inspired Thomas Nipperdey's famous *Deutsche Geschichte 1860–1866: Bürgerwelt und starker Staat* (München, 1985). See Jonathan Sperber, "Master Narratives of Nineteenth-Century German History," *Central European History* 24 (1991): 69–91.

146. Louis Bergeron, François Furet, and Reinhart Koselleck: "Das Zeitalter der europäischen Revolution 1780–1848," *Fischer Weltgeschichte* (Frankfurt am Main, 1969).

147. Bergeron, "Das Zeitalter der europäischen Revolution," 7.

148. Ibid., 202.

149. Ibid., 206.

150. Ibid., 208–09.

151. Ibid., 285.

152. Paul Nolte, "Gleichzeitigkeit des Ungleichzeitigen," in *Lexikon Geschichtswissenschaft: Hundert Grundbegriffe*, ed. Stefan Jordan, 134–36 (Stuttgart, 2002). The specific notion has its origins in the cultural sciences of the 1920s, where it was often used to explain the different perceptions at play between generations temporally. See Jureit, *Generationenforschung*, 20–21.

153. Koselleck, "Die Diskontinuität der Erinnerung," 213. Koselleck was critical of Bloch's work. For example, a critique of Bloch's idea of "hope" as a central category for human existence, and an attempt to outline a number of additional categories that could together compose a human theory of action, can be found in Reinhart Koselleck, "Zur Begriffsgeschichte der Zeitutopie," *Begriffgeschichten: Studien zur Semantik und Pragmatik der politische und soziale Sprache* (Frankfurt am Main, 2006), 267–68.

154. The similar notion of *Gleichzeitigkeit des Nicht-Gleichzeitigen* was used in postwar writings by conservative social-theorists such as Hans Freyer. See Nolte, "Gleichzeitigkeit des Ungleichzeitigen," 134–36.

155. Bergeron, "Das Zeitalter der europäischen Revolution," 260.

156. Ibid., 295.

157. Ibid.

158. See, for example, Reinhart Koselleck, "Raum und Geschichte," *Zeitschichten: Studien zur Historik* (Frankfurt am Main, 2000), 78–96, which is based on the concluding talk that Koselleck gave at the Historian's Conference in Trier in 1986.

4

PROGRAM—PROJECT—STRAIGHT JACKET
The *Geschichtliche Grundbegriffe*

In 1957, when Werner Conze was appointed as professor in Heidelberg, he approached Koselleck in order to discuss the latter's academic plans. One of Koselleck's proposals was to make a lexicon of central historical concepts. Soon the idea was taken up in Conze's working group for modern social history, where, with the support of Otto Brunner and Günther Ipsen, it was agreed upon to launch a project in which concepts were to be studied as indicators and factors of the social and political language.[1]

To begin with, the lexicon project was supposed to include only around 10 contributors, all from the University of Heidelberg, and the aim was exclusively to illuminate conceptual changes in the nineteenth century. However, the project gradually grew in terms of scope and ambition. The final result was the enormous lexicon *Geschichtliche Grundbegriffe: Historisches Lexikon zur politischen-sozialen Sprache in Deutschland*, consisting of 119 articles collected in 7 volumes, the first of which was published in 1972 and the last in 1992.[2] Written by 109 contributors from a range of different disciplines, the articles cover the histories of social and political concepts—such as state, revolution, and democracy—through time spans of often more than 2,000 years, from Ancient Greece to the Weimar Republic.

The *Geschichtliche Grundbegriffe* has been a highly successful enterprise. Widely celebrated as a supreme source of knowledge and an important attempt to renew the study of language and history, the lexicon has in the last thirty years inspired uncounted conceptual studies across many different academic disciplines and countries. Koselleck's activities in relation to the lexicon were crucial to this development. Not only was he the central theoretical, methodological, and editorial driving force behind the project,[3] but he also contributed a number of renowned articles to the various volumes.[4] Consequently, Koselleck's name is inextricably linked with the *Geschichtliche Grundbegriffe*, which is regarded by many as his most important and innovative scholarly achievement.

The aim of the present chapter is to illuminate the dimension of conceptual history in Koselleck's work. The focus is primarily on the *Geschichtliche Grundbegriffe*. What are the central theoretical-methodological features of the conceptual approach that Koselleck outlined and practiced in relation to the lexicon? How did he develop his approach, and what were his aims with it? What are the relations between the lexicon and Koselleck's earlier work? And how did Koselleck's work on the lexicon and the reception of it influence his position and reputation in German and international academia?

This chapter is structured around two broad aims. The first is to show how Koselleck's conceptual approach in the *Geschichtliche Grundbegriffe* represents both a continuation and a renewal of his earlier work. On the one hand, the lexicon draws to a large extent on discursive features from *Kritik und Krise* and *Preußen zwischen Reform und Revolution*. This is first of all the case with the normative aim of the lexicon framework: to criticize the modern historical-philosophical notions of history in the singular. On the other hand, because Koselleck developed and systematized his analytical framework, the approach in the lexicon is in many ways more nuanced and advanced than the approaches in the dissertation and the *Habilitation*. Relevant to this is first of all the way in which Koselleck reduced the tension in his work between a universal narrative and pluralism by means of a more elaborate conceptual-political approach with which he attempted to counter the so-called ideologization and politicization of social-political concepts.

The second aim is to demonstrate how Koselleck's involvement in the *Geschichtliche Grundbegriffe* was instrumental in changing his status and reputation in the field. We will thus see how, with the lexicon, Koselleck not only became known as an innovative and respected scholar who moved on the theoretical-methodological forefront of the field, but also as an employer who facilitated the careers of other scholars by means of creating something like an industry of conceptual history that came to influence research agendas in many countries, in spite of the criticism leveled against his approach.

The Program Articles and the Guidelines

While the approach to *Begriffsgeschichte* that Koselleck outlined in *Geschichtliche Grundbegriffe* was broadly in accordance with the approach of his earlier work, it differed in crucial respects from the traditional ways of practicing and defining conceptual history in Germany.

The first use of the word *Begriffsgeschichte* is often traced to Hegel's *Vorlesungen über die Philosophie der Geschichte* from 1837.[5] However, Hegel did not speak of the study of concepts, but of any form of historical writing that refers to a certain level of abstraction in the "transition to a philosophical world history." Before the coinage of *Begriffsgeschichte*, the study of concepts and their form was practiced in relation to the many dictionaries that were published during the Enlightenment. The aim of these dictionaries was first of all to list the various meanings and forms of words belonging to the past.

Around 1800, philologists and philosophers began to focus increasingly on the origins, changes, and functions of words, with the hope that such reconstructions would lead to a more concise use of language. It was against this background that two famous dictionaries were published in the late nineteenth century: R. Eucken's *Geschichte der philosophischen Terminologie* (1879), and R. Eisler's *Wörterbuch der philosophischen Begriffe* (1899). During the 1920s, the philosopher Erich Rothacker (1888–1965) attempted to revise and update Eisler's dictionary, which was steeped in contemporary expectations of scientific progress and the national significance of the project, which was encompassed in the ambition of producing an encyclopedia that matched those produced in other countries. These expectations were still present in Rothacker's project that was continued and revised in one of the two major conceptual-historical enterprises that emerged in Germany during the 1950s and 1960s, after a period in which scholars, such as Carl Schmitt and Otto Brunner, who were studying concepts had focused on uncovering what they considered the original meaning of those concepts.

The most important media for the discipline in the 1950s and 1960s was the journal *Archiv für Begriffsgeschichte*, founded by Rothacker in 1955. It was in this journal that two conceptual-historical enterprises were announced in 1967: *das Lexikon politisch-sozialer Begriffe der Neuzeit*, launched by Brunner, Conze, and Koselleck; and the *Historisches Wörterbuch der Philosophie*, initiated by the philosopher Joachim Ritter.[6]

Both lexicons sought to demarcate themselves from earlier approaches in the field of conceptual history. Yet the approach practiced in the *Historisches Wörterbuch der Philosophie* (which was first conceptualized as a new and reworked edition of Eisler's dictionary) remained close to the tradition of history of philosophy that had emerged in Germany during the nineteenth century.[7] Hence, it aimed at a history of philosophical concepts, which did not relate conceptual changes to the social-political position of the users of the respective concepts or to societal changes.

To probe the relation between social history and language was one of the fundamental ambitions of the *Geschichtliche Grundbegriffe*. In this endeavor it departed from the tradition of German academic philosophy, in which the analysis of semantic developments was aimed at a systematic clarification of the essential meanings of philosophical concepts. This departure was announced already in the 1967 program article in *Archiv für Begriffsgeschichte*, which described the project. The article was authored by Koselleck, who in an introductory note stated that the text had been written already in 1963, following an editorial meeting between the three editors and their initial cooperators on the project. Moreover, Koselleck stated that the announced title of the lexicon—*das Lexikon politisch-sozialer Begriffe der Neuzeit*—was only a preliminary working title that was likely to change during the preparation of the first volume. This volume was expected to be ready for publication during the winter of 1967–1968.

Whereas the assertion about the title of the lexicon proved to be correct, expectations concerning the publication of the first volume turned out to be too optimistic: When the first volume finally appeared in 1972, the lexicon had been renamed as *Geschichtliche Grundbegriffe: Historisches Lexikon zur politischen-sozialen Sprache in Deutschland*.[8] The revised and official program article, which is included in the first volume, shows that Koselleck, Conze, and Brunner had also changed parts of the approach.[9] However, a close comparison of the two programs suggests that the original framework of the project had primarily been modified and rearranged, rather than substantially changed in the years between 1967 and 1972.[10] Outlining the analytical guidelines for the entire framework, the 1972 program firstly described the overall aim of the lexicon; the heuristic principles and hypotheses; the theoretical-methodological approach; key assumptions and definitions; the source basis; and the structure of the articles.

The overall aim of the lexicon was announced at the beginning of the article: "The primary concern (*leitende Fragestellung*)," Koselleck wrote, "is to investigate the dissolution of the old world and the rise of the modern through the history of their conceptual framing."[11] The lexicon was, he specified, to be restricted to investigations of the German language area, though set against the background of European linguistic traditions, and it was to deal only with concepts that had been changed, coined or in other ways influenced by the political, social, and industrial revolutions characterizing the period.

In line with this, the basic heuristic principle of the lexicon was that a change of concepts took place during what Koselleck labeled the *Sattelzeit* (saddle period). The notion refers to how, in the period between 1750 and 1850, deep-seated societal-political changes went hand in hand with fundamental changes in the conceptual topography, so that basic social and political concepts acquired meanings that no longer need to be translated in order to be understood today.[12] On the one hand, many old concepts were given new meanings, which was the case for the concept of revolution, for example; on the other hand, a variety of new concepts were coined, such as liberalism and socialism.

Koselleck described the selected concepts as "leading concepts of the historical movement," which as "indicators" and "factors" at the same time registered and effected the transition to the modern world.[13] He moreover announced that the transition to the modern world was to be investigated through four working hypotheses concerning how the meaning, status, and use of basic social and political concepts changed during the *Sattelzeit*.

The first of these hypotheses is labeled the *Demokratisierung* (democratization) of concepts; it refers to the assumption that concepts were no longer used only by the elite (the aristocracy, the lawyers, and the learned), but had spread throughout all layers of society. The second hypothesis is labeled the *Verzeitlichung* (temporalization) of concepts; it refers to the assumption that social and political change was no longer interpreted through patterns of repetition and recurrence, but through a focus on the future and expectations of change and progress, so that concepts in this process were structured around historical-philosophical ideas of history, as a unified and progressive movement, running along a fixed scheme and toward an ultimate social-political end and meaning. The third hypothesis is labeled the *Ideologisierbarkeit* (ideologization) of concepts; it refers to the assumption that an increase of the level of abstraction in concepts made them utilizable according to interests and aims of various groups and movements. Finally, the fourth hypothesis is labeled the *Politisierung* (politicization) of concepts; it refers to the assumption that the increase in the number of people who were able to use and be mobilized by concepts led to an increase in the use of concepts as slogans in the making of political and societal positions.

These hypotheses, Koselleck stated, were to be tested through a specific conceptual method grounded in a specific "historical method" and aimed to make conceptual history fruitful for the historical and social sciences. Koselleck wrote: "This method aims neither at a history of words nor at a history of facts, events, ideas or problems, but it makes use of these as auxiliaries. The method is first of all historical-critical."[14]

As central features of the historical-critical method, Koselleck first of all listed a number of social-historical questions concerning in which social-political contexts, with which intentions, and by whom the respective concepts were coined, used, and acquired their meanings. He also outlined a methodological principle of framing the analysis through a diachronic and a synchronic perspective: the synchronic dimension concerns the specific situation in which a protagonist uses a concept and the diachronic dimension involves tracing the meanings of a concept over time. With these measures, Koselleck stated, conceptual history aimed at analyzing the various temporal and social structures in history, including *die Gleichzeitigkeit des Ungleichzeitigen*.[15]

But how did Koselleck in fact define the focal point of the lexicon—the concept? To clarify this issue, he distinguished between a word and a concept:

> A word can be unambiguous in use due to its ambiguity. The concept, on the other hand, must retain multiple meanings in order to be a concept. The concept is tied to a word, but it is at the same time more than the word. According to our method, a word becomes a concept, when the full richness of a social and political context of meaning, in which, and for which, a word is used, is taken up by the word. Concepts are thus concentrations of multiple meanings.[16]

To this, Koselleck added: "The theoretical premise of our method is that history is coined into specific concepts (*niederschlägt*) and only becomes history in the first place in the ways it is conceptualized."[17] What appears from these passages is that, according to Koselleck, a concept is not a concrete and narrowly defined linguistic expression; rather it belongs to the epistemic sphere, though this sphere can seemingly not be separated entirely from the linguistic. In addition, the concept was for Koselleck something that is present in the mind, and it helps the mind grasp the input it gets from the world. Basically, this notion of the concept emerges from a Kantian tradition rather than from modern linguistic thought. What is important to point out about Koselleck's definition is that a concept always interrelates with broader semantic fields and with a social reality. Hence, in relation to the cited passages, he announced that conceptual history has the convergence of concept and history as its theme. This convergence should not be understood as one of identity between language and history, but as a more dynamic relation characterized by constant interaction and change: "Semantic change and social change, a change of situation and a need for redefinitions correspond in different ways with each other."[18] As such, he specified, conceptual history as practiced in the *Geschichtliche Grundbegriffe* aimed to avoid *Geistesgeschichte* both in the form of a mere history of ideas and in the form of a history of material processes.[19]

Having outlined the basic aim, the heuristic principles and hypotheses, the theoretical-methodological method and assumptions of the lexicon, Koselleck finished the 1972 program article by describing the material basis and the intended structure of the conceptual analysis. In respect to the material, he listed a broad, or plural perspective comprised of three types of sources: the classic writings of the philosophers, the lawyers, and the literary writers; sources from everyday life (such as newspapers, diaries, and letters); and standard dictionaries. As for the structure, he announced that all articles were to be composed in three parts. They were to begin with a section covering the period from Antiquity to pre-modernity; then move on to cover in depth conceptual changes in modernity; and finally end with a perspective on the contemporary use of language. As such, Koselleck had outlined the basic analytical framework and guidelines for the *Geschichtliche Grundbegriffe*.

The described framework and the guidelines' encompassed sociological and theoretical dimensions obviously went far beyond earlier traditions of conceptual history. In respect to the sociological dimensions, the aim was not merely to record the variety of meanings or recover the original meaning of concepts, but to register the rise of modernity using social-political concepts as analytical instruments. On the one hand, this involved the assumption that all social-political concepts are prone to constant change; on the other hand, the sociological approach amounted to an analytical model according to which concepts are characterized both by unique characteristics and by common developmental traits. This model drew on a theoretical and interdisciplinary framework that combined discursive features from many different disciplines—from history, sociology, and linguistics, and from the work of many different scholars.

Before we elaborate on the theoretical-methodological foundations of the lexicon, two examples will be provided of a typical Koselleckian conceptual-historical investigation. These are drawn from two paradigmatic articles dealing respectively with the concepts of history and revolution. Both articles were published before the first volume of the *Geschichtliche Grundbegriffe* appeared: The article on history was published in a 1967 Festschrift (honorary publication) to Karl Löwith; the 1969 article on revolution was published in the journal *Studium Generale*.[20] The texts should thus be considered as proclamations of how the conceptual approach was ideally to be practiced in the lexicon.[21]

The Paradigmatic Examples: History and Revolution

It is not a coincidence that Koselleck's article on history was published in Festschrift to Karl Löwith. The study dealt with the main theme of Löwith's work: the changes in human consciousness from the natural cosmos of Ancient Greece to the Christian certainty of salvation and to the modern secularized claims for salvation made possible by a substitution of Christian eschatology with historical philosophy.

Koselleck elaborated on this theme via an analysis of the relation between the rise of historical philosophy and the modern concept of history. As reflected in the title of the article "Historia Magistra Vitae: Über die Auflösung des Topos im Horizont neuzeitlich bewegter Geschichte," Koselleck's main argument in the text was that history had lost its status and function as the "teacher of life" in the transition to the modern world. The reason was, he stated, that modern people (in contrast to the Greeks, who thought of life as repetitive and recurrent in its structure, and the Christians, who believed in the Apocalypse, the second coming of Christ and the final judgment) began to imagine history as a phenomenon that unfolds through a sequence of new and singular events. Therefore, it was no longer thought possible to draw useful pedagogical, moral, or political teachings from historical examples and narratives.

According to Koselleck, this change in the human historical consciousness was symbolized by the replacement of the concept of *Historie* with that of *Geschichte*. Because the new concept of history was a construction that encompassed all of history and was referred to both as an object and as a subject, there was no longer talk of histories in plural, but only of history in singular—*Die Geschichte*. Koselleck therefore labeled this conceptual form a *Kollektivsingular* (collective singular). About this conceptual form, he wrote:

> The collective singular permitted yet another step. It made possible the attribution to history of the latent power of human events and suffering, a power that connected and motivated everything in accordance with a secret or evident plan and to which one could feel responsible, or in whose name one could believe oneself to be acting. This philological event occurred in a context of epochal significance: that of the great period of singularization and simplification which was directed socially and politically against a society of estates. Here, Freedom took the place of freedoms, Justice that of rights and servitudes, Progress that of progressions (*les progrès*, the plural) and from the diversity of revolutions, "The Revolution" emerged.[22]

The coinage of *die Geschichte* and its impregnation with historical-philosophical ideas of history as a schematic and progressive movement was, Koselleck added, connected to the discovery of a specifically historical world: "This involves what one might call a temporalization of history, which has since that time detached itself from a naturally formed chronology."[23] One result of this denaturalization of historical time was a separation of the temporal dimensions of past and future in the historical consciousness of modern man: "It is not only because transpired events cannot be repeated that past and future cannot be reconciled. Even if they could, as in 1820 with the revival of the revolution, the history that awaits us deprives us of the ability to experience it. A concluded experience is both complete and past, while those to be had in the future decompose into an infinity of different temporal perspectives."[24]

In line with this, Koselleck defined the human belief in the *Machbarkeit der Geschichte* (feasibility of history) as another key characteristic of modern historical consciousness: "Since the future of modern history opens itself as the unknown, it becomes possible to plan—indeed it must be planned."[25] According to Koselleck, the separation of the past and the future and the eagerness to plan and create the future also had consequences for the writing of history. Because it no longer concerned the past but only the future, historical writing became impossible to falsify and was therefore easily subjected to the utopian ideas and aspirations of social-political groups and individuals—as was the case in the writings of nineteenth century "teachers of revolution," like Karl Marx.

Koselleck did not further pursue the issue of how the concept of *Geschichte* had been ideologized and politicized in the twentieth century. Instead, he ended his article with a brief discussion concerning the possibilities of developing a concept of history in which ideas about progress and the future could be considered along with experience of the past. However, Koselleck did not offer concrete ideas on this issue, and the article on history is thus—as will be discussed in more detail below—an example of how his early conceptual historical writings aimed to undermine notions of history in singular and to confirm the existence of histories in plural rather than theorizing how these histories might be written.

Koselleck's study of history is generally regarded as one of his most important investigations in the field of conceptual history—and was also similarly seen by Koselleck himself. He thus once remarked that his approach to conceptual history took form with his discovery of how *Geschichte* during the *Sattelzeit* changed from a plural to a singular concept— to a so-called *Kollektivsingular*.[26] Soon after, he began to use this discovery to describe the developmental patterns of many other social-political concepts on the threshold to modernity.

The notion of *Kollektivsingular* is consequently also applied in the 1969 article on revolution. Where the article on history focused mainly on processes of *Ideologisierbarkeit* and *Verzeitlichung* taking place during the *Sattelzeit*, the revolution-article focused more on the processes of *Politisierung* and *Demokratisierung*. Koselleck began the article with the following passage: "There are few words so widely diffused and belonging so naturally to modern political vocabulary as the term 'revolution.' It also belongs, of course, to those widely used forceful expressions whose lack of conceptual clarity is so marked that they can be defined as slogans. Quite clearly, the semantic content of 'revolution' is not exhausted by such sloganistic usage and utility. Instead, the term 'revolution' indicates upheaval or civil war as well as long-term change, events and structures that reach deep into our daily life."[27]

Revolution, Koselleck elaborated, clarifying the history of the concept, belongs to the group of already existing concepts, which acquired radically new meanings during the *Sattelzeit*. Having its roots in the Latin word *revolutio*, until the rise of the modern world, the concept referred in a political context to the natural and unbreakable circulation between the classical political systems (as in Hobbes), while in a scientific context, it referred to the circular movements of the celestial bodies, as was the case in Copernicus's *De revolutionibus orbium caelestium* from 1542.

Enlightenment thinkers, however, gave the concept of revolution a new meaning when they used it to interpret all events and processes, including the domains of law, religion, politics, economy, and cultural traditions from the perspective of change and alteration. "Everything in this world is revolution," the French author Louis Sébastian Mercier exclaimed, for example, in 1772.[28] At this time, Koselleck argued, the concept of revolution assumed the form of a *Kollektivsingular* that comprised the idea of *the Revolution* as an irreversible and permanent movement that is bound to occur in the future, and it changed from referring not only to a political, but also to a social revolution that included all human beings and a total change in the social structure. According to Koselleck, these changes led to a situation in which those who managed to define the specific content of the concept acquired one of the most effective, but also one of the most dangerous, weapons in modern politics.

Toward the end of the article, Koselleck ventured into a direct critique of the status and the (mis)use of the concept of revolution in modern politics. He wrote:

> Applied to our present international political situation, the question arises how the hypostatized legitimacy of civil war relates to the background legitimacy of permanent world revolution. Since the end of the Second World War, our planet has seen a raging succession of civil wars, burning on between the great power-blocks. From Greece to Vietnam and Korea,

from Hungary to Algeria to the Congo, from the Near East to Cuba and again to Vietnam—limited civil wars, whose awfulness is, however, boundless, stretch around the globe. We have to ask whether these numerous, regionally limited but globally conducted civil wars did not long ago consume and replace the concept of legitimate and permanent world revolution. Has not the "world revolution" been reduced to an empty formula which can be appropriated pragmatically by the most diverse groups of countries and flogged to death?[29]

With this ending of the revolution article, Koselleck fulfilled one of the three declared ambitions of the *Geschichtliche Grundbegriffe*: that of providing a "semantic check" of the contemporary use of language.[30] More concretely, in the 1972 program article, he expressed the hope that the conceptual analyses in the lexicon might lead to a sharpening of consciousness "that leads from historical clarification to political clarity."[31]

The aim to provide a semantic check of the social-political language is another feature that distinguishes Koselleck's conceptual history in the *Geschichtliche Grundbegriffe* from earlier approaches to language in the German cultural sciences, not least the approaches of Erich Rothacker and Friedrich Meinecke. More generally, for Koselleck, as for other scholars of his generation who contributed to the conceptual-historical projects that emerged in the 1960s and 1970s, conceptual analysis involved what he understood as a necessary evaluation of the available scientific and social-political language. In other words, he wanted to identify and deconstruct the ideological-politically hypostatized vocabularies that had led to the "German catastrophe" and to outline the contours of a plurality of less destructive and more responsible semantic meanings and practices. This aim represents another line of continuity in Koselleck's work from *Kritik und Krise* to the *Geschichtliche Grundbegriffe*.

While Koselleck once remarked in retrospect that he was not a specialized conceptual historian when he studied in Heidelberg, all of his early writings—including *Kritik und Krise*; his unfinished project on the Congress of Vienna; *Preußen zwischen Reform und Revolution*; and his concept of history—make use of conceptual frameworks.[32] And while he substantially elaborated on his framework in the *Geschichtliche Grundbegriffe*, the lexicon drew to a great extent on discursive features that he had discovered and applied in these earlier writings.

This was first of all the case with the chief aim of the lexicon. Although *Kritik und Krise* and *Preußen zwischen Reform und Revolution* were not designed as fully-fledged conceptual investigations, both studies focused on central or "leading" concepts (respectively *Kritik/Krise* and *Bürger*) to illustrate the transition to the modern world taking place in the period between 1750 and 1850.[33] To a large extent, the analyses in the dissertation and the *Habilitation* likewise thematize the processes of *Demokratisierung, Verzeitlichung, Ideologisierbarkeit,* and *Politisierung* of the social-political language that, according to Koselleck, characterized the *Sattelzeit.* Moreover, the historical-critical method that he announced in the *Geschichtliche Grundbegriffe,* including the ambition to study the relation between social history and language, was closely related to the conceptual approach that he had developed as critiques of historicism in the early 1950s.

The substantial difference between the conceptual approach in Koselleck's earlier work and the lexicon thus resides not in the basic analytical framework, but rather in the systematically developed character of the approach and the idea of framing this in a vocabulary of suggestive analytical notions, such as the four conceptual hypotheses, the notion of *Kollektivsingular,* and that of the *Sattelzeit.*

Since the 1970s, the notion of the *Sattelzeit* has been one of the most famous terms to arise from Koselleck's entire oeuvre. In retrospect, Koselleck stated that the notion was a *"Kunstbegriff"* (artificial concept) and a *"Schlagwort"* (catchword) that he first coined with the intention of raising money for the project and which then turned out to be useful to describe the fundamental structural-historical and linguistic changes taking place in the period from 1750 to 1850.[34] As Koselleck was aware, the notion of *Sattelzeit* resembles notions such as *Zeitschwelle* and *Strukturbruch,* which scholars such as Schmitt and Freyer had used in the 1920s to describe the massive transformations (political, social, economical, but also mental and intellectual) taking place around 1800. But how, more precisely, did Koselleck's approach to conceptual history as practiced in the *Geschichtliche Grundbegriffe* relate to the work of other scholars? That is, in which ways did he draw upon the work of and demarcate himself from other actors in the field in the creation of his analytical framework?

Social History and Linguistics—
Hermeneutics, Experience, and Time

When asked to explain the intellectual context in which his approach to conceptual history originated, Koselleck once listed four different traditions that he considered as precursors and sources of inspiration for his project.[35] The first was the tradition related to Otto Brunner and Werner Conze, who founded modern conceptual history as an approach to social history. The second was the tradition related to the history of philosophy, which goes back to Hegel, and which in the twentieth century was refined by Erich Rothacker, Martin Heidegger, and Hans-Georg Gadamer, who all practiced a method of tracing conceptual changes back in time through the writings of key philosophers. The third tradition was the conceptual approach, focused on religious language, which Koselleck's supervisor Johannes Kühn had practiced in *Toleranz und Offenbarung*. And the fourth and last tradition was the way of questioning the meaning of concepts from a political-juridical perspective as practiced by Carl Schmitt.

While it is possible to illuminate much of Koselleck's conceptual-historical framework with reference to these four traditions, some of these are easier to trace and locate than others in his texts, in terms of discursive features. Arguably, the tradition that is most difficult to relate directly to the program-articles of the *Geschichtliche Grundbegriffe* is that represented by Kühn. To be sure, the introduction to *Toleranz und Offenbarung* contains a number of reflections on conceptual history, first of all concerning how the meanings of concepts depend on the aims and intentions of the agents using them, which are in accordance with and perhaps inspired Koselleck's approach.[36] And Friedrich Wilhelm Graf is probably right in suggesting that the bias toward the language of Protestantism in contrast to that of Catholicism in the *Geschichtliche Grundbegriffe* also has to do with Kühn's influence on Koselleck.[37] However, the inspiration that Koselleck found in Kühn did not leave the same traces in the form of specific assumptions, hypothesis, or notions, as did the other traditions that Koselleck drew on.

It is, for example, much easier to detect the social-historical tradition founded by Brunner and Conze in the program articles. These texts are first of all informed by the analytical principle practiced by Conze: that any investigation of the modern world must include perspectives on the larger societal processes, movements, and tendencies in the transition to the modern world and their effect on all layers of society. This ambition is pursued through the hypothesis of *Demokratisierung* and through the aim of uncovering what Koselleck labeled the *Strukturwandel der Geschichte* in the medium of concepts.[38] Here Koselleck obviously continued and elaborated on the conceptual-historical approach that he had practiced in *Preußen zwischen Reform und Revolution* through his analysis of the concept of *Bürger*. In the *Habilitation*, Koselleck also anticipated another basic idea of the *Geschichtliche Grundbegriffe*: that of studying conceptual changes in relation to changes in the political, social, and economic structures—an ambition that was based on the belief that social structures and language both condition and influence each other.

What characterized this ambition is the pragmatic approach to theorizing that Koselleck adopted at the time of the *Habilitation*. Significantly, as opposed to many of the scholars who became associated with the so-called linguistic turn in the 1960s and 1970s by means of theorizing language and narrative arrangements as crucial factors in human history, Koselleck's theoretical efforts were always aimed at, and limited to, the historical issues he wanted to investigate. Even in the 1970s, when he began to focus in more depth on theoretical issues, he remained, as Jan Ifversen has noted, more of a "historian" than the "theoreticians" who embraced the linguistic turn. As a general characteristic of Koselleck's position toward and approach to language and social history, Ifversen writes: "He does not work with texts *en tant que tel*, but with sources. He does not only work with the immediate contexts, but with more over-arching societal contexts. He does not work with philosophical contexts or with concepts that are first of all interesting from a normative political-theoretical perspective, but with concepts that have been significant for political and social change."[39]

Still, Koselleck's focus on language diverged strongly from the social science-inspired approach to history of *Gesellschaftsgeschichte* that emerged in the same period.[40] And in contrast to other scholars at the time, for Koselleck, the gap between language and history was a challenge to be met theoretically and methodologically, and he did this by thinking of the two dimensions as in convergence.[41] But how, more exactly, did Koselleck define these two dimensions and the interaction between them?

To answer this question, it is necessary to return to the linguistic dimensions of the framework and to the definition of the *Grundbegriff*. In the 1972 program article, Koselleck presented these issues via discussing and introducing discursive features from the field of linguistic theory and structural linguistics.[42] The latter field was at the time heavily influenced by the Swiss linguist Ferdinand de Saussure and his distinction between language (*langue*), which he identified as a system composed of signs that are defined by their relation to other signs, and the *use of* language (*parole*). From a structuralist perspective, Saussure was more interested in studying *langue* than *parole*. Hence, the historical and temporal dynamics, including the social negotiation, contestation, and struggle, at play in the production of language, were downplayed in his framework.

In response to this tendency, Koselleck avoided the distinction of *langue* and *parole*, and explicitly rejected the triple distinction—then popular in structural linguistics in order to grasp the different aspects of meaning—of *Wortkörper* (the word as a form of sound), *Bedeutung* (the concept that the word expressed), and *Sache* (the object referred to).[43] In line with this, even if he announced the use of synchronic/diachronic and semasiological/onomasiological methods, it was not a primary concern for Koselleck to construct an elaborate and bullet-proof linguistic theory.[44] What interested him, and what he referred to as basic concepts, were ultimately words in which a complex and diverse cluster of political and social contexts, experiences, and meanings are brought to a particularly intense level of linguistic condensation.[45] Hence, as we have seen, he distinguished a concept from a word from the perspective of social context, and not by referring to notions from linguistic theory. Besides stating that "a word becomes a concept when the full richness of a social and political context of meaning, in which and for which the word is used, is taken up in the word," he explained that a concept "assembles the plurality of historical experiences as well as a series of theoretical and historical issues in one single whole, which is only given in the concept and which only can be experienced there."[46]

These definitions of a concept, and of how the concept relates to the linguistic system and the social context, have been criticized, especially by linguists, as unclear and inadequate.[47] In line with this, as stated by Jan Ifversen, the social (which is in the lexicon loosely defined via a variety of shifting notions, referring to both broad and concrete social contexts, experiences and expectations and temporal structures) and the linguistic sphere represent for Koselleck two different worlds that meet and depart, but the question of how language and context influence each other is nowhere elaborated in his approach, except for in the abstract reference to the convergence between history and concept, and the status given to concepts as indicators and factors of historical change.[48]

The theoretical vagueness in these aspects of the framework should partly be explained with reference to Koselleck's pragmatism in respect to defining the status and the function of a concept—a pragmatism that was explicitly announced in the 1972 program article and involved the blurred merging of (or oscillation between) notions from linguistic theory and the contextual perspective.[49] Seen retrospectively, his references to linguistic theory come across as an attempt to turn conceptual history into a science with methods and theories that were acceptable for the increasingly influential field of linguistic sciences. Hence, although he gave occasional and approving references to the Romanian linguist Eugenio Coseriu (1921–2002), who confronted Saussure's rigid dichotomy of *langue* and *parole* by returning to Wilhelm von Humboldt's concept of language as *energeia* understood as the speaker's creative activity, linguistic theory plays a very limited role in Koselleck's work.[50]

It is, then, no coincidence that the notion of *Grundbegriff* is defined without the use of notions from linguistic theory in the foreword to the seventh volume of the lexicon, in which Koselleck discussed the criticism leveled against the approach since the publication of the first volume and specified aspects of the framework. Here, he provided a purely contextual definition of the basic concept that is not only less ambiguous than the one in the 1972 program article, but also makes it more comprehensible why this phenomenon ought to be privileged over a variety of other phenomena of political language: "In a historical context, one can speak of a basic concept, when all conflicting social layers and political parties are using it to communicate their different experiences, interests, and party-political programs. Basic concepts demand their use, because they comprise those minimal similarities that are necessary for making experiences, and without which there can be neither conflict nor consensus. A basic concept is thus found, when it can be interpreted and used according to different perspectives in order to gain insight or facilitate capacity to act."[51]

This notion of a *Grundbegriff* informed the *Geschichtliche Grundbegriffe* from the beginning, even if it was at first defined in a less lucid way. It entailed a specific stance on linguistic matters: the claim that there is a specific type of linguistic expression that is interconnected with the social in a privileged manner, and that it is this type of expression that matters most historically. Hence Koselleck sorted out the relation between language and society in a way that differed strongly from what many other proponents of the linguistic turn have put forward: He gave up the idea that language ought to be treated as a unified whole and he insisted that there are provinces of language that are inconceivable without the social.

Koselleck's perspective encompassed context in a very broad sense as organized in different layers. In particular, in the 1972 program article, he portrayed three of these layers as especially important. The first of these was the structural perspective on the larger changes in the political, social, and economic structures, which he drew from Brunner and Conze; the second was a perspective on experience, expectation, and temporality that he developed from the philosophical tradition represented by Gadamer and Heidegger; and the third was a perspective on the concrete social contexts and contestations that he outlined in a dialogue with the work Schmitt. Each of the three contextual perspectives are embedded in a number of theoretical assumptions and principles about language that are not derived primarily from the field of linguistic science, but which instead issue from the field of hermeneutics.

One of the key hermeneutic principles was related to Koselleck's encounter with the tradition of conceptual history that he learned from Brunner and Conze. More concretely, as Koselleck stated in a 1982 article, his approach was in a theoretical-methodological perspective deeply inspired by Brunner's plea for "a consequent historicism," that is, the need to distinguish historically between the concepts of today's politics and science and those of the past.[52] The inspiration from Brunner was forcefully expressed in a famous passage in the 1967 program article where Koselleck announced the practice of a "solid historicism": "Exactly how the social and political world before '1789' was conceived," he explained, "can only be shown, when you embark on the concepts of the period."[53]

Koselleck's announcement of a "solid historicism" was in epistemological accordance with Gadamer's call for a "radical historicism" in *Wahrheit und Methode*.[54] Drawing on Heidegger's analysis of Being in *Sein und Zeit*, Gadamer argued that human historical understanding is fundamentally conditioned by human "finality." According to Gadamer, caught in their temporality between life and death, the historically-affected consciousness of human beings can never fully understand the past. A truly historical consciousness must therefore not pursue a position of objectivity, but instead recognize the otherness of the past and engage in a dialogue with historical texts on these premises. This was exactly what Koselleck emphasized in the introduction to the *Geschichtliche Grundbegriffe*.

In line with this, Koselleck's conceptual framework in the lexicon followed the key hermeneutical assumption that informs Gadamer's investigation into the conditions of human understanding in *Wahrheit und Methode*: that all understanding is linguistically mediated. A fundamental premise in Koselleck's conceptual history is thus that history and historical consciousness is layered in and communicated through language. Where Gadamer claimed that nothing exists except through language, Koselleck assumed that history is only what has been conceptualized. More concretely, in the 1972 program article, Koselleck spoke of the close relation between "*Begrifflichkeit und Begreifbarkeit*," and of how concepts layer and express changes of "experience" and of "expectation."[55]

These definitions point to a hermeneutic style of historical inquiry that focuses on the temporal structures and the processes of linguistic reception and formation that form the self-understanding of historical actors. However, Koselleck's notion of experience differs from Gadamer's in that it comprises a way of conceptualizing social context (that is different from, but relates to, social systems and structures). Melvin Richter has in relation to this observed that the *Geschichtliche Grundbegriffe* attempted to "shift conceptual history away from a philosophical and hermeneutic method toward another sort more acceptable for historians."[56] This was a conscious move on Koselleck's part. He himself underlined this on various occasions, including an interview from 2005, in which he gave a very clear reasoning for why he used a concept of history that was less bound to language than Gadamer's:

[L]anguage is always ambiguous. It is at the same time receptive and productive. On the one hand, it indicates social change and on the other hand it is an essential factor that allows us to become conscious of changes in reality. Gadamer did not accept this ambiguity in language. For him, following Heidegger's footsteps, language implicitly contains the totality of experience. There is no doubt that in the process of transferring many concepts from Greek into German philosophy, Gadamer's hermeneutical philosophy transformed language into the key to all human reality. There is a very strong argument backing up this position, but for me, as a historian, it is simply impossible to accept it as a unique and exclusive truth. As a historian, I cannot limit myself to the linguistic domain, that is, to what was in fact said, I must also occupy myself with that which could be said.[57]

In the quotation, Koselleck pointed out not only his deviation, but also his innovative contribution to the hermeneutical tradition of conceptual history. His point is that Heidegger and Gadamer tended to regard language as a form containing all possible human experience. In this way, they lost a perspective on concrete languages (or provinces of languages) and their historicity, their function as indicators and agents of historical change. This is to say, they did not regard languages as limited, as setting conditions for what is sayable at a certain time and place—and, consequently, they did not realize that such limits are changeable. In Koselleck's eyes, the changeability of these limits means that there must be experience beyond language. This seems to be the theoretical deviation he expressed in the quoted passage.

Nonetheless, this deviation may be described as a contribution to, rather than a radical departure from the hermeneutic tradition, because it retains the basic assumptions about human historicity from Gadamer's and Heidegger's works. These assumptions were central for the theory of historical times that Koselleck developed from the late 1960s and for the temporal-analytical framework that he outlined in the lexicon, first of all via the hypothesis of temporalization. The hypothesis refers, as mentioned, to the assumption that political and social change was no longer interpreted through patterns of repetition and recurrence, but through a focus on the future and expectations of change and progress, and that concepts in this process became structured around historical-philosophical ideas of history. Like many other features in the lexicon, this hypothesis is easily read as a series of elaborations on ideas that Koselleck had outlined in *Kritik und Krise*, where Löwith's book *Meaning in History* served as the central point of reference. What differentiates the lexicon from the dissertation is the more explicit character of the lexicon's temporal framework, and the related series of analytical notions, such as *Verzeitlichung*, *Machbarkeit der Geschichte*, and *Kollektiv-Singular* with which he sought to investigate the rise of modern historical consciousness.

These ideas and notions were used in relation to the set of assumptions about human historicity that Koselleck drew from the hermeneutical-philosophical tradition. These assumptions concern how, according to the hermeneutic tradition, Being is a temporal and historical phenomenon: that for humans, *to be* is *to be in time*, as a result of which all human understanding and interpretation has an ongoing, open, and changing character that ultimately depends on our conceptions of time. Where Heidegger viewed human existence and the ways in which we make sense of ourselves, our world, and our relations with others as a temporal self-projection in the dimension of the past, present, and future, Gadamer argued that these issues depend on our variable experiences, expectations, and horizons.

In line with the hermeneutical-philosophical tradition, Koselleck sought in the lexicon to focus on the human awareness of time as a way to analyze how human beings have configured and reconfigured their ways of understanding themselves and the world. While broadening the use of the hermeneutic temporal categories in the direction of analyzing how not only individuals, but also communities and societies have conceptualized and acted in the world, he focused specifically on the changes in the relation among past, present, and future and among experience, expectation, and horizon taking place in the *Sattelzeit*. In doing so, in the introduction to the lexicon, Koselleck anticipated the famous argument from his 1977 article "Erfahrungsraum und Erwartungshorizont" concerning how the human "horizon of expectation" in the *Sattelzeit* had been disconnected from the "space of experience," so that the social-political language was no longer oriented toward the past, but increasingly loaded with future-oriented expectations.

"Erfahrungsraum und Erwartungshorizont" was written in relation to Koselleck's ambition of developing a theory of historical time that he pursued in various texts from the late 1960s onwards. While this ambition also informs the *Geschichtliche Grundbegriffe*, it is not given center stage in the framework, and the Heideggarian and Gadamerian notions are not theorized and systematized to the same extent in the lexicon as in Koselleck's later and more specific texts on historical time. We will therefore postpone the more detailed analysis of Koselleck's reception of *Sein und Zeit* and *Wahrheit und Methode* and the role they played in his writings, including those dealing with conceptual history, until the next chapter.

What is important to understand about the temporal framework in the *Geschichtliche Grundbegriffe* is that it served as a way to illustrate larger social-historical dynamics, processes, and contexts. As such, it relied on a mode of analysis that not only viewed language as bound to time and time as bound to language, but instead portrayed social reality, time, and language as three interrelated dimensions in human life. It therefore mediated between the social-historical and the philosophical tradition of practicing conceptual history.

Seen in relation to the common objective of his work, Koselleck's conceptual approach, as it was practiced in relation to the lexicon, is to a certain extent informed by the schematic account of the modern world that he outlined in *Kritik und Krise*. This account is an indispensable part of the analytical framework, which points back to the worldview shared by the three editors in the 1960s, when the lexicon was conceptualized. However, as we have seen, Koselleck softened up his schematic picture of the transition to modernity during the 1960s, and in his conceptual historical writings from this period there is less of a tension between a choice for the universal and the pluralist narrative. This is because, in the late 1960s and early 1970s, he enlarged the plural dimensions and connected these more directly to his ambition of deconstructing history in the singular, as we will elaborate on below.

The Sociology of Concepts and the Conceptual-Political Intention

What Koselleck aimed at in his conceptual analysis was to criticize the linguistic components of the modern utopian and historical-philosophical ideas of history by means of demonstrating the plural, diverse, and contested nature of all language and politics. In this respect, he thus attempted to inscribe a perspective on the more concrete social contexts and contestations in the framework. For this purpose, he continued his dialogue with, and demarcation from, the tradition of conceptual history as practiced by Carl Schmitt.

Schmitt's work is, as mentioned, characterized by an investigation of changes in meanings of concepts in the transition from early modern times with the aim of establishing and fighting intellectual and political positions. This focus and Schmitt's work more generally played an important role for the arrival of conceptual history in twentieth century German historical scholarship, as it was articulated in Otto Brunner's work in the 1930s and 1940s. Brunner's plea for a "revision of the basic concepts" in history and Schmitt wish for a "concrete order thinking" in the field of law were both rooted in a critique of modernity and represented an attempt to eliminate what they saw as a dangerous division between state and society in modern times.

On the one hand, as we will see below, Koselleck found great inspiration in Schmitt's and Brunner's conceptual approaches. On the other

hand, from the beginning he demarcated his approach from the normative, static, and decisionistic traits in their approaches to concepts. There
are thus not only, as we will return to below, differences in the values with
which Koselleck charged concepts, but also in the way he viewed the
concepts. Instead of conceiving of concepts as units of meaning with an
original core and essence that can be discovered and recovered, Koselleck
analyzed them as contentious and transforming, changing with social
powers and social conflicts.[58] Thus, he rejected the idea that conceptual
frameworks simply mirrored the structure of the world and in this manner Koselleck approached a constructivist position regarding the stock of
concepts in a society at a given time. This also means that he decoupled,
localized, and historicized the conflicts latent in conceptual oppositions
from those basic dichotomies he continued to accept as a universal foundation of the anthropological conditions of human existence.

Koselleck's attempt to bring in social reality, struggle, and changeability was not only aimed against the essentialism in Schmitt's approach to
concepts. It was also indirectly aimed at Heidegger's essentialist views on
language as the frame of all human existence and at Gadamer's related
views on language as the key to all human reality. At the end of the day,
this was a crucial dimension in the conceptual set-up of Koselleck's pragmatic historical approach to language, diverging from that of his sources
of inspiration at a very basic level.

Beyond the conceptual issues drawn to frame the approach, Schmitt
was a source of inspiration on other levels. It was Schmitt who initially
spurred Koselleck to use dictionaries and encyclopedias to subject political and social concepts to a historical analysis. Koselleck also drew several
other theoretical-methodological assumptions from Schmitt to develop
a conceptual approach to history that should account for the flaws in
the traditional historicist approach to the history of ideas, as practiced
by Friedrich Meinecke. Following Schmitt, Koselleck worked from the
assumption that it is necessary to analyze ideas and concepts in relation
to concrete human action and social-political contexts, and in Schmitt's
writings he found various discursive features that helped him in this en-
deavour.

In addition, Koselleck often drew attention to Schmitt as one of the
intellectual fathers of the *Geschichtliche Grundbegriffe* and once spoke of
his work as "methodologically brilliant" conceptual history.[59] This situation has been explored in an article by Reinhard Mehring that shows
how Koselleck was to a large degree inspired by Schmitt's theoretical
and methodological approach to concepts.[60] According to Mehring, Koselleck drew inspiration first of all from Schmitt's fundamental theoretical
notion: that entire periods, or epochs, can be understood and interpreted

through what Schmitt in *Politische Theologie* spoke of as *Begriffssoziologie* (sociology of concepts).[61] The idea encapsulated in *Begriffssoziologie*'s concepts is that an entire epoch's political and in certain cases also religious, intellectual, and societal thinking can be deciphered through a focus on the key concepts of the respective epoch. Schmitt took this idea to its extremes in his famous 1929 essay "Das Zeitalter der Neutralisierungen" by arguing that the European *Zeitgeist* during the past four centuries has moved through stages in which the human consciousness has been permeated by a "theological," "metaphysical," "humanitarian-moral," and then "economic" concept.[62]

How the theoretical fundament in *Geschichtliche Grundbegriffe* is based similarly in *Begriffssoziologie* is clear first of all from its aim to study "the dissolution of the old and the rise of the new world within the history of their conceptual origins and structure." The focus on "lead concepts in the historical movement" in *Geschichtliche Grundbegriffe* was, as we have seen, already present in *Kritik und Krise* in which Koselleck used the concepts of "critique" and "crises" to decipher the *Zeitgeist* of the Enlightenment. "The expression of 'crisis,'" he wrote in the book, "is through its diagnostic and prognostic content an indicator of a new consciousness."[63]

In *Kritik und Krise*, Koselleck moreover drew on another idea characterizing Schmitt's conceptual analysis: the idea that historical agents can use concepts to create and shape history. This idea is elaborated upon in the program articles of *Geschichtliche Grundbegriffe* that present a methodological focus of political conflict and polemical counter-concepts, including the friend/enemy relation. "Concepts," Schmitt once wrote, are constituted through "concrete oppositions." All "political concepts" are thus "polemical" concepts; they acquire their "intellectual force and historical significance" through the meeting with an "enemy," a "concrete antithesis," a "counter concept."[64] In the methodical programs of *Geschichtliche Grundbegriffe*, Koselleck echoed this train of thought with his focus on "the situational given context that gives the concept its social and political force" and by arguing that concepts can only be understood through counter-concepts, that is, through a sociological analysis of the individuals and groups that use and position themselves via a certain concept. "Does the speaker include or exclude himself, when he uses a certain concept?" Koselleck moreover asked. "Who is it aimed at?"[65] Strikingly similar ideas concerning the importance of studying in which contexts and by whom concepts are used can be found in several of Schmitt's writings, including *Der Begriff des Politischen*: "Words such as state, republic, society, class, as well as sovereignty, constitutional state, absolutism, dictatorship, economic planning, neutral or total state, and so on, are incomprehensible if one does not know exactly who is to be affected, combated, refuted or negated by such a term."[66]

How Koselleck's ambition to analyze concepts in relation to concrete social context and interaction was inspired by Schmitt (and in demarcation to Meinecke) is an issue that we have already dealt with in relation to his critique of historicism. In respect to the *Geschichtliche Grundbegriffe*, it is, as also pointed out by Reinhard Mehring, of great importance to emphasize that Koselleck distanced himself in a more explicit manner from Schmitt's conceptual-political intention. Whereas Schmitt used concepts with a clear polemical and ideological intention, Koselleck's conceptual history was primarily knowledge-oriented. He recognized with Schmitt the latent totality and escalation of "the political." But with an eye for the dangerous potential of language, he used conceptual history to plea for a reflective and careful use of language.

A striking example of this is found in Koselleck's famous 1975 article "Zur historisch-politischen Semantik asymmetrischer Gegenbegriffe", which is constructed as a historical investigation of the friend/enemy categories.[67] Koselleck began the article with the statement that all concepts have a counter-concept and that some concepts are asymmetrical in such a way that they exclude mutual recognition. If, for example, *Arbeitgeber* (employer) and *Arbeitnehmer* (employee) are substituted with *Ausbeuter* (exploiter) and *Menschenmaterial* (human material), the conceptual pairs have become asymmetrical. Koselleck then exemplified this statement by investigating three asymmetrical counter-concepts that have claimed to embody the whole of humanity at different times in history—those of Hellene/barbarian, Christian/heathen and human/nonhuman—and, even if the article does not investigate one single concept, the analysis of these counter-concepts is in many ways typical of the way in which he studied language and history.

Here four factors are especially important. The first is the integration of a Schmittian conception of an essentially political society in permanent conflict (and a normative notion of how such conflicts can be contained). The second is the concrete social-historical perspective: the idea that concepts must be studied as changeable entities that are shaped in specific historical situations through the interaction between social and political units of action. The third is that all concepts acquire a history of reception that survives the original situation in which they were coined. One of the arguments of the article is thus that argumentative forms of filling out asymmetrical counter-concepts survived from Antiquity into the era of Christianity and that Christian discursive features determined parts of the horizons of modernity. Hence, Koselleck used the conceptual approach to thematize and measure what he called *die Gleichzeitigkeit des Ungleichzeitigen.*

The fourth dimension is the plea for a semantically controlled language that aims at pluralism and recognition instead of exclusion, intolerance, and exaggerated friend/enemy relations. This dimension relates to the main purpose of the article, which is to show how, in contrast to the earlier concepts Hellene/barbarian and Christian/heathen, the concepts of human/humanity from the Enlightenment, and their dichotomies "unhuman/non-human," undermined the possibility of mutual recognition and respect among political groups. The consequences of this development, Koselleck argues, reached their most extreme point in National Socialism's ideologization of rationality, leading to euthanasia and genocide.

Toward the end of the article, to propose a way out of the modern destructive ideologization of dichotomies, Koselleck brings into play Schmitt's "friend/enemy" dichotomy. Schmitt's "scientific achievement," Koselleck writes, is to have provided a "formalistic" political antithesis without filling out the categories beforehand by means of the dichotomy of "friend" and "enemy." [68] If the contesting groups want peace, Koselleck argues, this can be reached by filling out Schmitt's dichotomy in such a way that mutual recognition and respect between the political groups is established. In this formalistic redefinition of the friend/enemy dichotomy, we touch simultaneously upon a fundamental similarity and difference in Koselleck's and Schmitt's understandings of and approaches to history and politics. On the one hand, they both viewed the presence of friends and enemies as a primary existential condition for man's existence and made the dichotomy a cardinal point in their scientific analysis. On the other hand, whereas Schmitt continually attempted to ideologize and politicize the dichotomy, Koselleck tried to counter the ideologization and politization of all social-political concepts.

The Reception of the *Geschichtliche Grundbegriffe*

"Zur historisch-politischen Semantik asymmetrischer Gegenbegriffe" shows on a more general level how Koselleck's attempt to historicize the conflicts inherent in conceptual oppositions was related to his ambition of providing a "semantic check" of the contemporary language and how the analytical framework thematized not only issues of the past, but also of the present. In the 1960s and the 1970s, when the lexicon-project was launched, an intense and highly ideological battle to define the social-political vocabulary was raging in German academic and public debates.

Here conceptual history as practiced in the lexicon offered itself as a scientific style of inquiry with which the dynamics of semantic struggle could be analyzed and discussed without the scholar necessarily having to identify with one of the opposed parts in the debate. Postponing the presentation of these debates, and Koselleck's position in them, what follows illustrates how the anti-ideological or neutral potential of conceptual history provides one of the reasons for its remarkable success in German academia.

The lexicon was from the beginning very positively received in postwar German academia (apart from an early critique of the lexicon launched by Hans-Ulrich Wehler, also discussed in the following chapter). This positive reception, it seems, was the result of a variety of factors or conditions. The first is that Koselleck and his fellow editors had simply managed to create an innovative and interesting project that appealed to and attracted other scholars. Some of these attractive features were pointed out in the enthusiastic reviews of the first lexicon volumes that appeared in the 1970s. The reviewers emphasized three achievements of the lexicon in particular.[69] Firstly, the lexicon was praised for the fact that its huge amount of information provided a new kind of interdisciplinary work not only for historians, but also for "sociologists, political scientists, philologists, linguists, philosophers, lawyers, and theologians."[70] Secondly, the interdisciplinary ambitions of the project were seen as a much needed attempt at "overcoming the often deplored theoretical deficit in the historical discipline."[71] Finally, the conceptual approach in the *Geschichtliche Grundbegriffe* was interpreted as a new form of ideological critique, which, in contrast to other forms of ideological critique, embraced the possibility "to unfold historically the dialectic between the social and the conceptual sphere."[72]

Having launched a project that seemed to offer a way out of the theoretical-methodological and political deadlocks of the discipline and that promised to reassert the study of history as relevant vis-à-vis other disciplines, Koselleck and his fellow editors managed to attract a remarkable number of established and upcoming scholars to participate in making the lexicon.[73] Among these was the rising literary scholar Hans Ulrich Gumbrecht, who has vividly described the allegedly euphoric atmosphere that surrounded the various conceptual historical projects in the 1960s and 1970, as well as the experience of his participation in the *Geschichtliche Grundbegriffe* (and in other conceptual historical lexicons that emerged in this period) as a crucial and honorable step on his way to becoming a respected scholar.[74]

Gumbrecht's remarks here point to the second condition that facilitated the emergence of lexicon as a successful enterprise in post-World War

II academia: The institutional facilities provided and the funding secured by the editors, first of all by Conze, enabled them to host conferences, hire contributors, and publish the volume—that is, to carry out the project and to turn the *Geschichtliche Grundbegriffe* into an academic industry in which scholars' careers were made by means of acquiring academic recognition, merits, and contacts. In launching the lexicon, Koselleck thus not only secured his reputation as an innovative scholar, but also as a potential employer of his fellow scholars, whom he and the editorial group would contact if they were considered capable of contributing to the lexicon.

Wilhelm Hennis was one of the many scholars who were contacted by the editorial group already in the 1960s.[75] During the 1950s Hennis had published a number of eminent writings on issues related to the state, sovereignty, and the public sphere, and he was consequently invited to attend the first meetings and conferences in the Arbeitskreis für moderne Sozialgeschichte in which the *Geschichtliche Grundbegriffe* was conceptualized in the early 1960s. In a letter from Conze in 1962, Hennis was assigned the prominent concepts of *Moral*, *Politik*, and *Öffentlichkeit*, and he wanted, to begin with, to author a number of further entries. However, Hennis soon abandoned these plans, as he lost interest in writing articles devoted exclusively to concepts. In a letter to Koselleck from November 1962, he gave up the concept of *Moral*, and, after suggesting co-authoring the entry on *Politik* with Koselleck, he eventually gave that up too, along with the entry on *Öffentlichkeit*. However, Hennis was full of praise of the *Geschichtliche Grundbegriffe* when it was finally launched in the 1970s. In a letter written to Koselleck in October 1977, Hennis reported how he had made an "enthusiastic commercial" (*eifrig Reklame*) for the lexicon at the New School in New York, where Hennis was a guest professor at the time. "I really think that both enterprises [the *Geschichtliche Grundbegriffe* and the *Historisches Wörterbuch der Philosophie*] belong to the most impressive achievements of the German historical discipline in recent years. And the real engine behind the entire project was of course, next to Conze, nobody else than you," he said.[76]

Hennis's letter to Koselleck illuminates how the *Geschichtliche Grundbegriffe* won Koselleck a new position and reputation in the German historical profession in the 1970s. Instead of being known as an outsider, as had been the case in the 1950s, or as someone working within the framework of his professor's program, as in the early 1960s, he now became known as a scholar who had launched an innovative and promising research project and possessed the institutional resources to carry it out.

In line with this, when conceptual history as practiced in the *Geschichtliche Grundbegriffe* became a subject of interdisciplinary discussion in Germany in the 1970s, it was partly because Koselleck established contact with scholars from other disciplines in order to discuss certain theoretical-methodological features and problems in the approach. Most importantly, Koselleck began a dialogue with the linguists, who showed interest in the project, even if, as mentioned, they found his definition of a concept and its relation to the linguistic system and the social context insufficient and unclear.[77] It has been said that these issues in Koselleck's framework are characterized by a "pragmatic insecurity."[78] Arguably, this pragmatic insecurity characterizes not only the lexicon framework, but Koselleck's attitude toward theoretical-methodological issues more generally. On the one hand, he was deeply interested in discussing and applying theoretical-methodological features in his work. On the other hand, he was not interested in establishing a theoretical-methodological system with a fixed number of analytical features that were defined and applied in a definite and mutually ordered fashion and could be applied in a straightforward way to any historical analysis. While he reflected carefully on the strengths and the limitations of the discursive features that he applied in his frameworks, his analysis did not begin from such a system, but from a number of related and compatible hypotheses and assumptions that seemed to open new ways of investigating the past and its relations to the present. In this sense, as to be discussed in more detail in the following chapter, Koselleck was indeed theoretically-methodologically eclectic and pragmatic.

However, his pragmatism did not result in a rejection of the approach. Instead, it was instrumental in facilitating a discussion among scholars from many different disciplines concerning the problems and possibilities of conceptual history. This discussion has now been going on for more than three decades, during which several German scholars have found inspiration in the *Geschichtliche Grundbegriffe* to construct other conceptually focused projects and writings. Among these scholars belong the students of Conze and Koselleck: Otto Dann, Christof Dipper, Jörg Fisch, Lucian Hölscher, and Horst Stuke, who contributed to the lexicon the 1970s and 1980s and pursued conceptual-historical themes in their dissertations and *Habilitationen* with reference to the lexicon-framework or to Koselleck's later writings in the field.[79] As a result of the contributions of these and other scholars, the field has experienced further growth and institutionalization and has branched into many different directions that are no longer associated exclusively with the *Geschichtliche Grundbegriffe* or with Reinhart Koselleck.[80] However, until his death Koselleck remained a key figure who was habitually referred to and consulted when new projects or discussions were launched in the field. He was therefore for a long time known primarily as a "conceptual historian" among his colleagues.

This was also the case abroad, where, from the late 1980s onwards, the reception of Koselleck's conceptual history has been substantial, first of all in the Netherlands and in Finland, but also in Italy and Spain, and in the various Scandinavian countries. It was the American historian of ideas, Melvin Richter, who was the first to make the *Geschichtliche Grundbegriffe* known to an international audience, when he published a series of articles in American journals in the mid 1980s.[81] Richter's aim was to introduce the lexicon to Anglo-Saxon scholars and to compare Koselleck's approach to the theories and methods of the so-called Anglophone approach to the study of political thought. Richter identified the "Anglophone" approach with the work of the historians Quentin Skinner and John Pocock, who are known for their studies of the rise of republican political thought and for studying linguistic expressions as part of a broader discursive context.

Richter's proposal to merge perspectives from the two approaches has been pursued both in the Netherlands and in Finland. In the Netherlands, a larger research project resulted, among other things, in the anthology *History of Concepts: Comparative Perspectives* from 1998, which contains focused conceptual studies as well as discussions and comparisons of the "German" and the "Anglophone" approaches.[82]

In Finland, the reception of Koselleck and the institutionalization of conceptual history have been even stronger, not least due to the activities of the political scientist Kari Palonen.[83] Together with Richter, in 1998 Palonen established the international network History of Political and Social Concepts Group, which has its own journal, *Contributions to the History of Concepts*, and in 1995 it began a summer school in conceptual history that is now an independent research school. Palonen also contributed to the renaming of the *Finnish Yearbook of Political Thought* into *Re-descriptions: Yearbook of Political Thought and Conceptual History*; he contributed to the Finnish lexicon of political concepts that appeared in 2003; and he has in several writings tried to develop new approaches to the study of political language with a focus on concepts.[84]

Similar to Richter's, Palonen's aim is to merge perspectives from writings of Koselleck and Skinner as a way to develop a new approach to the study of language and concepts, and with the 2004 book *Die Entzauberung der Begriffe*, he has provided the most convincing attempt to compare and connect the two approaches to date.[85] Palonen detects a basic similarity in their opposition to all ahistorical and apolitical understandings of concepts: according to Palonen, they both emphasize that all concepts have a history; that concepts are prone to change; and that there will always be a fight to define their meanings. The main difference between the two is, Palonen argues, that Skinner studies conceptual changes through a focus on how historical agents, often famous political philosophers with changing intentions, perform so-called rhetorical redefinitions of certain concepts, whereas Koselleck studied concepts in a more structural perspective, often with the aim of discerning the beliefs, experiences, and expectations of societies and epochs in a temporal perspective. Palonen concludes that Skinner's and Koselleck's perspectives on conceptual change are respectively "rhetorical" and "temporal."

The comparisons with Skinner certainly boosted Koselleck's international reputation from the 1980s onwards. However, the reception of his conceptual history in the English-speaking part of the world, including with the Anglophone scholars, has been rather limited—and vice versa. In fact, the dialogue between the protagonists of the two approaches, Koselleck and Skinner/Pocock, were for the most part characterized by mutual criticism and demarcation. For example: Whereas Skinner and Pocock stressed the differences rather than the similarities between the approaches, questioned an approach to the study of language with an exclusive focus on concepts, and categorically rejected the idea that the experience of modernity as found in the German approach holds any relevance for their objects of study, in an interview a few months before his death Koselleck labeled Skinner a "conventional historian" with an "excessively normative" approach to the study of language.[86] It is difficult to estimate whether these mutual reservations were the result of different theoretical-methodological convictions, academic interests, personal temperaments, or political views—or rather a mixture of all these dimensions. What is certain is that the reservations have set limits to the reception of Koselleck's conceptual history in the English-speaking part of the world.

Still, to speak of the Koselleck's approach to conceptual history (and the conceptual historical projects that emerged from the 1960s onwards) as an intellectual trend of the past that disappeared without having realized its grand ambitions, as Hans Ulrich Gumbrecht recently did, does not hold in the light of the many ongoing discussions, projects and institutions inspired by and connected to the approach.[87] The issue is rather what form, or forms, investigations of conceptual history will take in the future. Hence, it is in response to Gumbrecht that Helge Jordheim has pointed out that the reception of Koselleck's work has moved away from the methodological and disciplinary issues of *Begriffsgeschichte* and toward a focus on the more theoretical dimensions of Koselleck's writings.[88] This shift of interest from methodological to theoretical concerns in Koselleck's work has been documented by Kari Palonen.[89] However,

Koselleck himself also thematized the shift by pointing out that it would be wrong to view his conceptual approach to history as a stable and unchangeable entity. In a speech in the beginning of the 1990s, reflecting on his work in the field since the conceptualization of the *Geschichtliche Grundbegriffe*, he stated:

> Publication of that lexicon has been going on for two decades by now and, for me at least, its theoretical and methodological presuppositions, first formulated some twenty-five years ago, have grown into an intellectual straightjacket. While it was necessary to maintain these suppositions in relatively unchanged form in order to be able to proceed with the collaborative project of the *Geschichtliche Grundbegriffe*, my own approach has kept changing. It should therefore not surprise you, if the positions I shall be defending in this paper are somewhat different from the one that originally inspired *Geschichtliche Grundbegriffe*. Indeed, it would be dreadful and depressing if years of reflection had not led to significant change in my approach to conceptual history.[90]

This quotation brings us to conclude the chapter by means of pointing to a paradoxical element in respect to the *Geschichtliche Grundbegriffe*. On the one hand, the lexicon helped Koselleck position himself intellectually and institutionally in German academia, and it is regarded by many as Koselleck's most innovative scholarly achievement. On the other hand, the lexicon was not as innovative as often assumed, as it relied to a great extent on discursive features that he had already outlined in his earlier work, and its rigid theoretical and methodological presuppositions made it impossible to further renew with the framework.

At the end of the day, as a work that was to be accomplished by a group of authors rather than by Koselleck alone, the *Geschichtliche Grundbegriffe* did not fit well with the individualized, continuously emerging oeuvre he was pursuing simultaneously. In a way, the nature of the lexicon as a communal work seems to have fit badly with Koselleck's habit of dwelling on the margins of the discipline and his bent toward constant innovation. Although the achievement of the *Geschichtliche Grundbegriffe* was a major success for Koselleck as a science manager, it is characteristic of the pattern of his career and of his self-image that his position as an outsider to the mainstream of the discipline ultimately prevailed, as will be described in the following chapter.

Notes

1. Koselleck, "Begriffsgeschichte, Sozialgeschichte, Begriffene Geschichte," 187–88. For the origins of the *Geschichtliche Grundbegriffe*, see also Christof Dipper, "Die Geschichtliche Grundbegriffe: Von der Begriffsgeschichte zur Theorie der historischen Zeiten," *Historische Zeitschrift*, Bd. 279, Hf. 2 (2000): 281–309; Etzemüller, *Sozialgeschichte als politische Geschichte*, 171–76; and Melvin Richter, *The History of Political and Social Concepts: A Critical Introduction* (Oxford, 1995), 27–51.
2. The lexicon also contains a register volume that appeared in 1997.
3. Koselleck was the only contributor to outlive the project; Brunner died in 1982 and Conze in 1986. Conze's role as a "science manager," providing the institutional settings, securing funding, etc., was crucial for the project. Moreover, until his death, Conze was involved in editing the various volumes and contributed to sixteen entries. Brunner, on the other hand, did not contribute significantly to the editorial process, and he wrote only one entry to the lexicon—the one for *Feudalismus*.
4. Koselleck contributed a total of twelve entries—*Bund*, *Demokratie*, *Emanzipation*, *Fortschritt*, *Geschichte*, *Herrschaft*, *Interesse*, *Krise*, *Revolution*, *Staat und Souveränität*, *Verwaltung*, and *Volk/Nation*. He also spent considerable periods of time revising and rewriting the articles of other contributors.
5. For historical perspectives on *Begriffsgeschichte*, see Hans-Ulrich Gumbrecht, "Pyramiden des Geistes: Über den schnellen Aufstieg, die unsichtbaren Dimensionen und das Abebben der begriffsgeschichtlichen Bewegung," *Dimensionen und Grenzen der Begriffsgeschichte* (München, 2006), 7–36; Palonen, *Die Entzauberung der Begriffe*, 227–29; Richter, *The History of Political and Social Concepts*, 9–57; and H. G. Meier, "Begriffsgeschichte," in *Historische Wörterbuch der Philosophie*, Bd. 1, ed. Joachim Ritter, 788–808 (Stuttgart, 1971).
6. Reinhart Koselleck, "Richtlinien für das Lexikon politisch-sozialer Begriffe der Neuzeit," *Archiv für Begriffsgeschichte*, Bd. XI (1967): 81–97; and Joachim Ritter, "Leitgedanken und Grundsätze eines Historischen Wörterbuch der Philosophie," *Archiv für Begriffsgeschichte*, Bd. XI (1967): 75–80. A few years before, Ritter had presented his project in "Zur Neufassung der 'Eisler'—Leitgedanken und Grundsätze eines Historischen Wörterbuch der Philosophie," *Zeitschrift für philosophische Forschung* 18, no. 4 (1964): 704–08.
7. For a comparison of the *Historischen Wörterbuch der Philosophie* and the *Geschictliche Grunbegriffe*, see Richter, *The History of Political and Social Concepts*, 9–25. The most thorough introduction to and discussion of the *Geschichtliche Grundbegriffe* is in Palonen, *Die Entzauberung der Begriffe*, 227–63.
8. The first volume covered concepts beginning with the four letters A, B, C, and D.
9. Reinhart Koselleck, "Einleitung," *Geschichtliche Grundbegriffe*, Bd. 1 (Stuttgart, 1972), XIII-XXVII.
10. For excellent comparisons of the two texts, see Steinmetz, "Nachruf auf Reinhart Koselleck," 422–23; and Palonen, *Die Entzauberung der Begriffe*, 229–35.
11. Koselleck, "Einleitung," XIV.
12. The notion was in the 1967 article written with a hyphen (*Sattel-Zeit*) and designated a longer time span, the period between 1700 and 1900.
13. Koselleck, "Einleitung," XIII.
14. Ibid., XX.
15. Ibid., XXI.
16. Ibid., XXII.

17. Ibid., XXIII.
18. Ibid.
19. Ibid., XXIV.
20. Reinhart Koselleck, "Historia Magistra Vitae: Über die Auflösung des Topos im Horizont neuzeitlich bewegter Geschichte," in *Natur und Geschichte: Karl Löwith zum 70. Geburtstag*, ed. Hermann Braun and Manfried Riedel, 196–219 (Stuttgart, 1967); and Reinhart Koselleck, "Der neuzeitliche Revolutionsbegriff als geschichtliche Kategorie," *Studium Generale* 22 (1969): 825–38.
21. Both concepts were later included in the *Geschichtliche Grundbegriffe*.
22. Koselleck, "Historia Magistra Vitae," 205 (CFOT).
23. Ibid., 207.
24. Ibid., 208.
25. Ibid., 209.
26. Koselleck, "Begriffsgeschichte, Sozialgeschichte, Begriffene Geschichte," 197. In the interview, Koselleck explained that he had already written down this discovery as a student.
27. Koselleck, "Der neuzeitliche Revolutionsbegriff," 825 (CFOT).
28. Ibid., 831.
29. Ibid., 837.
30. The two other ambitions were to provide information on the history of concepts to the social and linguistic sciences and to illuminate the processes of transition to the modern world.
31. Koselleck, "Einleitung," XIX.
32. Koselleck, "Begriffsgeschichte, Sozialgeschichte, Begriffene Geschichte," 187.
33. The concepts *Bürger* and *Krise* are also included in the *Geschichtliche Grundbegriffe*.
34. Koselleck, "Begriffsgeschichte, Sozialgeschichte, Begriffene Geschichte," 199. In a more recent interview, Koselleck gave the following explanation of the origin and the meaning of the term: "First of all, concerning Sattelzeit, I have to tell you that I invented the term and used it for the first time in commercial advertisements created to promote the GG—to sell more issues. Although I am happy that [I] succeeded in providing the lexicon with some money, I do not particularly like the term, mainly because it is very ambiguous. As you know, one of the meanings of the Sattel refers to the equestrian world, another refers to the situation experienced when one climbs to the top of a mountain and from there can contemplate a larger view. But in the end it does not allude in any specific way to the acceleration of time, which is the crucial aspect of the experience of the modern world. Therefore, from a theoretical point of view, Sattelzeit is a very deficient term." Reinhart Koselleck, Javier Fernández Sebastián, and Juan Francisco Fuentes, "Conceptual History, Memory, and Identity: An Interview with Reinhart Koselleck," *Contributions* 2 (2006): 120.
35. Koselleck, "Begriffsgeschichte, Sozialgeschichte, Begriffene Geschichte," 187.
36. See, for example, Kühn, *Toleranz und Offenbarung*, 2: "If one wants to assess the importance of tolerance or intolerance historically, one has to move from the general concepts to the specific forces that determine and define the concepts in particular situations. In other words, one must investigate what was actually challenged and defended in the name of tolerance and intolerance. Because they are only relational concepts, tolerance and intolerance are not, as history shows, challenged or defended for their own sake, but for the sake of the forces that stand behind them."
37. Graf, "Die Macht des Schicksals entschuldigt gar nichts." To this, Graf added that the concept of *Bildung* in Koselleck's later writings was inspired by Kühn's *Bildungsprotestantismus*.

38. Koselleck, "Einleitung," XXIV.
39. Jan Ifversen, "Begrebshistorien efter Reinhart Koselleck," *Slagmark*, no. 48 (2007): 87.
40. The following chapter situates Koselleck's work more closely vis-à-vis these two disciplinary trends.
41. Thus Helge Jordheim, "Thinking in Convergences—Koselleck on Language, History and Time," *Ideas in History* 2, no. 3 (2007): 65–90.
42. Koselleck, "Einleitung," XXI-XXIII. See also Ifversen, "Begrebshistorien efter Reinhart Koselleck," 87; and Jordheim, "Thinking in Convergences."
43. Koselleck, "Einleitung", XXII.
44. These terms denote respectively the study of all the meanings of a given word, term, or concept, and the study of all names or terms in a language for the same thing or concept. See Koselleck, "Einleitung," XXI-XXII.
45. See Gumbrecht, "Pyramiden des Geistes," 18–19.
46. Koselleck, "Einleitung," XXII, XXIII.
47. For lines of the critique, see Ifversen, "Begrebshistorien efter Reinhart Koselleck." Several articles in the *Geschichtliche Grundbegriffe* have also been criticized for reproducing the classical tradition of *Geistesgeschichte* by not relating the concepts to social-political contexts and by focusing mainly on the intellectual elite. This criticism was primarily leveled against Koselleck's collaborators. Even if they are rarely as detailed as in his study of the Prussian *Vormärz*, Koselleck's analyses are all set on contextual backgrounds.
48. Ifversen, "Begrebshistorien efter Reinhart Koselleck," 87.
49. Koselleck, "Einleitung," XXII.
50. Jordheim, "Thinking in Convergences," 74–75; and Gumbrecht, "Pyramiden des Geistes," 19.
51. Reinhart Koselleck, "Vorwort," in *Geschichtliche Grundbegriffe. Historisches Lexikon zur politisch-sozialen Sprache in Deutschland*, Bd. VII, ed. Otto Brunner, Werner Conze, and Reinhart Koselleck (Stuttgart, 1992).
52. Koselleck, "Begriffsgeschichtliche Probleme der Verfassungsgeschichtsschreibung," 13.
53. Koselleck, "Richtlinien für das Lexikon," 91. In a later interview, Koselleck spoke instead of a "reflective historicism." Koselleck, "Begriffsgeschichte, Sozialgeschichte, Begriffene Geschichte," 188.
54. For an excellent introduction to these dimensions of Gadamer's thought, see Richard Bernstein, *Beyond Objectivism and Relativism: Science, Hermeneutics and Praxis* (Oxford 1984), 109–70.
55. Koselleck, "Einleitung," XV, XVI.
56. Richter, *The History of Political and Social Concepts*, 35.
57. Koselleck, "Conceptual History, Memory, and Identity," 126. As mentioned earlier, it was in Gadamer's seminar in Heidelberg that Koselleck met Heidegger, who, Koselleck wrote to Schmitt in January 1977, by comparing the concepts of Hegel and Kant and tracing concepts back to Leibniz, Thomas, and Augustine to Aristotle, could make "*Geschichte hörbar*" (history hearable). See RW265-8172: 3/1 (1977).
58. Bo Stråth, Review of *Futures Past*, By Reinhart Koselleck, *European Journal of Social Theory* 8, no. 4 (2005): 528. These are also among the reasons why Dipper, in "Die Geschichtliche Grundbegriffe" (287), has asserted that the main legacy of Brunner and Schmitt is located in the title of the lexicon, that is, in the label of *Grundbegriff*.

59. Koselleck, "Begriffsgeschichte, Sozialgeschichte, Begriffene Geschichte," 187. See also Koselleck, "Begriffsgeschichtliche Probleme," 33.
60. Mehring, "Begriffssoziologie, Begriffsgeschichte, Begriffspolitik," 31–50. The following is based on Mehring's excellent article, with a number of new examples added.
61. Schmitt, *Politische Theologie*. Focussing on the relation between theological and political concepts, Schmitt argued that the metaphysical conception of a certain epoch corresponds to its political organization, and he described *Begriffssoziologie* as a key to decipher the "metaphysical picture" of an epoch.
62. Carl Schmitt, "Das Zeitalter der Neutralisierungen" [1929], *Der Begriff des Politischen* (München 1932), 79–95.
63. Koselleck, *Kritik und Krise: Ein Beitrag*, 134.
64. Carl Schmitt, *Hugo Preuss: Sein Staatsbegriff und seine Stellung in der Deutschen Rechtslehre* (Tübingen, 1930), 5.
65. Koselleck, "Richtlinien für das Lexikon," 87; Koselleck, "Einleitung," XX.
66. Schmitt, *Der Begriff des Politischen*, 31 (CFOT).
67. Reinhart Koselleck, "Zur historisch-politischen Semantik asymmetrischer Gegenbegriffe," in *Positionen der Negativität: Poetik und Hermeneutik VI*, ed. Harald Weinrich, 65–105 (München, 1975).
68. Koselleck, "Zur historisch-politischen Semantik," 103–04. In *Nomos der Erde*, Schmitt outlined a shorter but similar analysis of the dynamics at play in the definitions and uses of the asymmetrical counter-concepts that Koselleck deals with in his article. See Schmitt, *Der Nomos der Erde*, 71–75.
69. See, for example, Peter von Polenz, Review of *Geschichtliche Grundbegriffe: Historisches Lexikon zur politisch-sozialen Sprache in Deutschland*, Bd. I, ed. by Otto Brunner, Werner Conze, Reinhart Koselleck, *Zeitschrift für germanistische Linguistik*, Bd. 1 (1973): 235–41; Dieter Dowe, Review of *Geschichtliche Grundbegriffe: Historisches Lexikon zur politisch-sozialen Sprache in Deutschland*, Bd. I, ed. by Otto Brunner, Werner Conze, Reinhart Koselleck, *Archiv für Sozialgeschichte*, Bd. XIV (1974): 720–22; Thomas Wüttenberger, Review of *Geschichtliche Grundbegriffe: Historisches Lexikon zur politisch-sozialen Sprache in Deutschland*, Bd. I, ed. by Otto Brunner, Werner Conze, Reinhart Koselleck, *Archiv für Rechts- und Sozialphilosophie*, Bd. LXI/4 (1975): 589–91; Helmut Berding, "Begriffsgeschichte und Sozialgeschichte," *Historische Zeitschrift*, Bd. 223 (1976): 9–110; Wolfgang Zorn, *Geschichtliche Grundbegriffe: Historisches Lexikon zur politisch-sozialen Sprache in Deutschland*, Bd. I, ed. by Otto Brunner, Werner Conze, Reinhart Koselleck, *Archiv für Kulturgeschichte*, Bd. 59 (1977), 243–47; Michael Stürmer, "Begriffsgeschichte oder der Abschied von der schönen neuen Welt," *Der Staat*, 17 (1978): 270-272; Joachim Rohlfes, "Das Lexikon 'Geschichtliche Grundbegriffe,'" *Geschichte in Wissenschaft und Unterricht*, Bd. 21 (1980): 525–30.
70. Dowe, Dowe, Review of *Geschichtliche Grundbegriffe*, 720.
71. Berding, "Begriffsgeschichte und Sozialgeschichte," 99.
72. Stürmer, "Begriffsgeschichte oder der Abschied von der schönen neuen Welt," 279.
73. For the academic backgrounds and affiliations of the authors, see Dipper, "Die Geschichtliche Grundbegriffe," 291–92.
74. Gumbrecht, "Pyramiden des Geistes," 8. Gumbrecht contributed to the fourth volume of the *Geschichtliche Grundbegriffe* with the entry on "Modern, Modernität, Moderne." After holding his first professorships in Germany, since 1989 he has been a professor in literature at Stanford University. He has long been a proponent of an approach to the study of language inspired by Hans Blumenberg's *Metaphorologie*.
75. The following is based on Schlak, *Wilhelm Hennis*, 61–62.

76. Cited in ibid., 61.
77. See, for example, Reinhart Koselleck, ed., *Historische Semantik und Begriffsgeschichte* (Stuttgart, 1979).
78. Dietrich Busse, *Historische Semantik. Analyse eines Programms* (Stuttgart, 1987), 54–55.
79. See Dipper, "Die Geschichtliche Grundbegriffe," 290–91.
80. Concerning the reception of Koselleck in Germany, first of all among his students, see Jeppe Nevers, "Nyere bidrag til begrebshistorien," *Nyt fra historien*, no. 1 (2007): 1–12.
81. See the references in Richter, *The History of Political and Social Concepts*, vii.
82. Ian Hampsher-Monk, Karin Tilmans, and Frank Van Vree, eds., *History of Concepts: Comparative Perspectives* (Amsterdam, 1998).
83. Jeppe Nevers, "Spørgsmålets politik: Kari Palonen og den nyere begrebshistorie," *Slagmark*, no. 48 (2007): 123–37.
84. Nevers, "Spørgsmålets politik." Palonen also co-edited the Festschrift to Koselleck; Kurunmäki, ed. *Zeit, Geschichte und Politik.*
85. Palonen, *Die Entzauberung der Begriffe.* Palonen also highlights a list of further similarities that suggests the two historians may well be closer related than hitherto presumed. Among these are a critique of the increasing de-politicization of politics; sympathy for the lost, the forgotten, and the demarcated in history; and the perception of history as a continuous *Umschreiben der Geschichte.*
86. Koselleck, "Conceptual History, Memory, and Identity," 109.
87. Gumbrecht, "Pyramiden des Geistes."
88. Jordheim, "Thinking in Convergences," 67–70.
89. Kari Palonen, "An Application of Conceptual History to Itself: From Method to Theory in Reinhart Koselleck's Begriffsgeschichte," *Finnish Yearbook of Political Thought* 1, no. 1 (1997): 39–69.
90. Reinhart Koselleck, "Some Reflections on the Temporal Structure of Conceptual Change," *Main Trends in Cultural History: Ten Essays*, ed. Willem Melching and Wyger Welema (Amsterdam, 1994), 7. A letter that he wrote to Conze in August 1974 shows that Koselleck also had fundamental worries about his approach. See Dunkhase, *Werner Conze*, 151.

5

THEORIZING HISTORICAL TIME AND HISTORICAL WRITING

In the late 1960s and early 1970s, there was widespread talk of an identity crisis in the German historical discipline. This identity crisis was related to developments both inside and outside of the profession. The gradual disintegration of the traditional profile of the discipline, with its focus on great personalities, ideas, and politics, spurred an internal discussion about how the disciplinary profile should be defined after the demise of historicism. However, when the discussion developed into a fundamental questioning of what history is and why it should be practiced, this was because extra-disciplinary developments (such as the student revolts, the expansion of the social sciences, and broader societal changes) prompted the members of the profession to justify the scientific and societal relevance of their craft vis-à-vis other crafts.[1]

These developments took place against the background of a series of political changes in the Federal Republic during the 1960s. In this decade, due to economic recessions and changes in the political climate, the Adenauerian and by the Christian Democratic Union (CDU)-led system of the *Wirtschaftswunder* period was weakened in favor of an increasing influence of the Social Democratic Party (SPD). Having spent the entire postwar period in opposition, in 1966 the SPD joined a grand coalition led by Chancellor Kurt Georg Kiesinger (CDU) and in 1969 formed a new government with the Free Democratic Party (FDP). This government was led by Chancellor Willy Brandt (SPD) and promoted the slogan *Mehr Demokratie wagen* (Dare more democracy). One of its aims was to reform the educational systems, which were perceived as perpetuating a veritable *Bildungskatastrophe* (educational disaster) of authoritarianism and social exclusivity. The ensuing call to enlarge and restructure the various educational institutions was justified by referring to the both necessity of improving the country's competitiveness and the right to equal societal opportunities.

As education was assigned a key role in the processes of economic and social reform, large sums were invested to expand and modernize the university system.[2] One of the results was the founding of numerous new universities, the first six of which were established in the 1960s: Bielefeld, Bochum, Dortmund, Düsseldorf, Konstanz, and Regensburg. At some of the new universities, first of all at those in North Rhine-Westphalia (Bielefeld, Bochum, Dortmund, and Düsseldorf), where an SPD-FDP coalition had already come to power in 1966, there were also substantial moves toward structural changes of the university system. Most importantly, the old "professor University" was substituted by a model of "group university," according to which the university was supposed to be run in cooperation among the academic and the non-academic staff and the students. It was also in North Rhine-Westphalia that the contemporary plans of establishing so-called *Gesamthochschulen* were pursued most extensively, when, in 1972, as part of a practical reform model, five new *Gesamthochschulen* were established in Duisburg, Essen, Paderborn, Siegen, and Wuppertal. In line with the overall educational aim of the Federal State, this model aimed to democratize the entry requirements at the universities; create an integrative, organizational unity among universities, *Fachhochschulen* and *Pädagogische Hochschulen*; integrate the various programs of study in broad departments; integrate teaching and research; and integrate the scientific personnel (teachers and researchers) into a functional unity. This program was imitated in other federal states with SPD-led governments and came to be identified with the progressive potential of the party. It created a novel system of political lines of contestation that dominated the educational system in Germany for decades.

The processes of university expansion and reform were important for the discipline of history in several respects.[3] First of all, they stimulated discussion of the identity and relevance of history in modern society. Secondly, the idea that society could be reformed through education spawned a flood of theories, plans, and programs as to how the university system, including the history curriculum, could be modernized through institutional and educational restructuring. Thirdly, the reforms resulted in a huge rise in the number of historians (professors as well as students) and in the creation of institutional space where new approaches could be cultivated within the overall spirit of reform.

One of the ambitions of the present chapter is to illuminate how Koselleck as a historian and a university professor reacted to the various changes and challenges facing the historical profession in the late 1960s and early 1970s. The first part of the chapter accordingly illuminates how he responded to the self-questioning and the redefinition of the discipline by introducing one of the most famous themes in his work: the project of developing a theory of historical time.

In the analysis of how he pursued this project, attention is first paid to how, from the 1950s to the 1980s, Koselleck began to focus less on deconstructing history in the singular and more on how histories in plural can be written. The chapter then deals with his attempts, in a variety of essays, written from the late 1960s to the late 1980s, to describe various theoretical-methodological conditions of historical writing. The focus here is on what will be described as the somewhat unsystematic character of his analytical framework that went hand in hand with a position toward historical writing that will be labeled cautiously constructive and pluralistic in its attitude toward theoretical-methodological matters.

The second part of the chapter deals with Koselleck's academic activities at the University of Bielefeld, as a hub of the upheavals of educational reform, and the institutional and social constellations he entered there. The aim of this part of chapter is to show how, through his affiliation with a large number of institutions and projects, during his time in Bielefeld, Koselleck became an increasingly established scholar, while at the same time he positioned himself as a somewhat marginalized figure at the department and in the historical profession more generally. This final part of the chapter also demonstrates that, in spite of his eventual manifestation as a famous and influential scholar, Koselleck continued to think of himself as an academic outsider.

The chapter begins with a view on the reconfigurations of the German historical discipline beginning in the 1960s. This brings us to Koselleck's activities in the working group Poetik und Hermeneutik and at the University of Heidelberg in the late 1960s and early 1970s, where he launched his project of developing a theory of historical time.

Gesellschaftsgeschichte, 1968, and the Historical Discipline in the Late 1960s and Early 1970s

One factor for the changes taking place in the disciplinary profile during the 1960s and 1970s was the rise of a new generation of scholars, including the social historians Hans-Ulrich Wehler and Jürgen Kocka, the historian of National Socialism Hans Mommsen, the theoretician Jörn Rüsen, and historians whose work is more difficult to subsume under one label, such as Wolfgang Mommsen, Wolfgang Schieder, and Heinrich-August Winkler. None of these historians had been trained by the older generation of German historians to which Friedrich Meinecke and Gerhard Ritter belonged, but had been taught by the middle-generation, first of all by Werner Conze and Theodor Schieder. And while they for various reasons refrained from confronting Conze and Schieder with their activities in the period between 1933 and 1945, they were severely critical toward both the political dimensions and the (lack of a) theoretical-methodological fundament in the historical writing of the older generation.[4]

The new generation of historians followed partly in the footsteps of Fritz Fischer (1908–1999), who was the first to attack a number of the dominant assumptions and beliefs in the German historical profession. In his famous *Griff nach der Weltmacht* (1961) Fischer had argued that Germany had deliberately launched World War I in an attempt to become a world power. He had furthermore suggested that there was continuity in German foreign policy aims from Wilhelm II to Hitler, thus indicating that Germany was responsible for both world wars.[5] For many German historians at this time, it was acceptable to believe that Germany had caused World War II, as World War I was widely regarded as a war forced upon Germany or resulting from a complicated process in international politics in which all participating governments were equally guilty. Fischer's work caused deep controversy in the German historical profession and inspired other historians, such as Gerhard Ritter and Karl-Dietrich Erdmann (1910–1990), to write books and articles in response to his arguments.[6]

Although Fischer's work challenged traditional interpretations within the profession, his method did not challenge the one of traditional *Diplomatiegeschichte*. *Griff nach der Weltmacht* was a work of narrative history, focusing on political events and devoid of explicit appeals to theory. However, the controversy aroused by Fischer's work made it easier for the younger historians, who entered the profession in the period of university expansion in the late 1960s and early 1970s, to formulate approaches that combined a critique of the traditional nationalistic historical writing with attempts to redefine the theoretical-methodological fundament of the discipline.

The most famous and comprehensive attempt in this direction was launched by a group of social historians headed by Hans-Ulrich Wehler and Jürgen Kocka. Similarly to members of the middle-generation, such as Conze, these historians aimed to substitute the traditional focus on

politics, personalities, and ideas with a focus on social structures and processes. However, their comprehensive and programmatic research program, often referred to as *Gesellschaftsgeschichte*, encompassed a variety
of theoretical-methodological features and societal-political values that
are not found in Conze's program.[7] Among these features were an explicit
normative binding to the social-political values of the West (and to the
social democratic reform agenda); a commitment to combine historical
writing with political pedagogic and ideological critique; a theoretical-
methodological approach based on a merging of Weberian sociology with
American social science and with the work of the two exiled German
left-wing social historians Eckart Kehr and Hans Rosenberg; and a focus
on the thesis about a German *Sonderweg*, that is, a special German path
into modernity that deviates from a presumed Western European model.
This focus included an examination of the specific German elements that
lead to Hitler's rise to power.[8]

In the discussion about the disciplinary profile, from the late 1960s
onwards, Wehler and Kocka promoted *Gesellschaftsgeschichte* as a properly
scientific and empirical approach that in their eyes was superior to and
ought to replace the unscientific and ideologically tainted historicism of
previous generations.[9] The *Gesellschaftshistoriker* enjoyed a considerable
success, especially in the 1970s and the 1980s when they achieved a certain discursive dominance and constructed one of the most powerful institutional networks of the discipline. This was partly because in different
ways their approach had been in tune with changes taking place both
inside and outside the historical discipline from the late 1960s onwards.
Most importantly, it was in accordance with the broader societal developments and expectations in the direction of reform and modernization.
It was compatible with research agendas of many other historians, both
inside and outside of Germany, who similarly wanted to substitute the traditional disciplinary focus with a more interdisciplinary and theoretical
approach that takes into account social structures and processes in history.[10] It matched the most fashionable contemporary trend within the
social-political disciplines: the projects launched at the Frankfurt School
to create a critical theory that should enable human beings to emancipate
themselves from forms of domination.[11] And it was, in line with this, not
alien to the demands for theoretical reflection, societal emancipation,
and ideological critique launched by the new generation of students that
emerged at universities all over the world in the late 1960s: a generation
that retrospectively became known as the 68ers.[12]

At several German universities in the late 1960s and early 1970s the
68ers took part in protests against what they considered a paternalistic,
reactionary, and repressive educational and societal system. In their at-

tempts to gain influence over university reforms, the student activists not only used verbal argumentation; they also launched demonstrations, strikes, and rallies, and took other kinds of physical action. Many humanities and social science departments at German universities were consequently taken over by students. This was the case in Berlin and in Frankfurt, where, in accordance with a set of left-wing societal-political beliefs and visions, the inaugurations of the "critical" and "political" university were respectively proclaimed.[13]

The 68ers not only mobilized in protest against the contemporary educational and societal system, but also against social, political, and economic structures, and the authority of the state more generally, as well as against the Vietnam War and the brutal police strikes against demonstrators that climaxed in the killing of the 26-year-old Benny Ohnesorg on 2 June 1967, when the Persian head of state visited West Berlin. While some of the 68ers were mainly interested in integrating social and political concerns more closely into the curriculum, others saw the university revolts as a platform for broader and more radical societal changes, which in their eyes necessitated various means, including violence. As such, the 68ers represented many different levels and directions of protest and revolt.

The 68ers became key actors in the contemporary battle to redefine the social-political vocabulary. Their attempts to define words and concepts according to left-wing values and visions prompted various politicians and intellectuals, who were positioned further to the right on the political spectrum, to react with counter-measures aimed at preserving or redefining the meaning of words and concepts so that they corresponded to a more conservative agenda.[14] The 68ers—"68" was the symbol of the events, processes, and conflicts unfolding in the late 1960s and early 1970s—consequently divided most scholars in German academia into opposed camps that were informed by conflicting interpretations of the political issues involved around the year 1968.

On the one hand, according to members of the left-wing camp, 68 represented a much needed confrontation with the authoritarian and undemocratic social-political structures that continued to dominate Germany after 1945. In fact, one of the leftist aims in the late 1960s was to end the presence of former National Socialists in the German intellectual and political elite. On the other hand, part of the right-wing camp interpreted the radicalism, language, and tactics of the 68ers as a continuation of the totalitarian ideological warfare that had been at the core of National Socialism and Stalinism. In between these positions were various liberal and conservative scholars, some of whom sympathized with and supported the demands for social and political reform in the 1960s, although the increasing radicalism of the 68ers caused some of these scholars to move toward the political right around 1968.[15]

At this time, the 68ers had come to dominate the student bodies at the German universities, where they organized themselves in a multitude of groups informed by different (and often for the outsider indistinguishable) aims, theories, and sources of inspirations. Several 68ers were steeped in the vocabulary of critical theory, dialectical Marxism and psychoanalysis, as found in the work of Herbert Marcuse, Theodor Adorno, and Max Horkheimer, and some of these encountered in Habermas a young, left-liberal and theoretically-minded scholar, who, to begin with, sympathized with their demands for social-political, institutional, and intellectual reform.[16] There was no equivalent to Habermas among the historians. Here the 68ers were met with different kinds of reactions, depending on generational identities, intellectual-political orientations, and personal temperaments.[17] As most of the older professors had difficulties understanding and generally depreciated the 68ers, they left it to their younger professors and assistants to deal with them. One group of these assistants was made up of Hans-Ulrich Wehler, Helmut Berding, and Wolfgang Mommsen, who all worked as assistants to Schieder in Köln in the 1960s. They were considerably more sympathetic toward and allegedly succeeded in establishing a dialogue with the 68ers.[18]

This was not the case for a group of young professors that included Thomas Nipperdey, Andreas Hillgruber, and Ernst Nolte, who were a few years older and known to be more conservative than Wehler, Berding, and Mommsen. They were all targeted by the student protests, and perceiving the left-wing students as representatives of an antidemocratic, utopian, and dangerous mode of thought, they consequently took steps to counter the public influence of their demands and activities.

Especially active were Nipperdey and Nolte, who both joined the Bund Freiheit der Wissenschaften, a group founded in 1970 by conservative and liberal university professors who wanted to address the politicization of the university by the 68ers, because they saw in this a dangerous threat toward the freedom of research and teaching. The aim of the group was more specifically to defend "a positivist and technocratic university settlement (one that rejected tying scholarship explicitly to political goals), as well as affecting to speak on a wide range of educational matters pertaining to all levels of the system."[19] Eventually, the Bund Freiheit der Wissenschaften came to represent a distinctly neo-conservative position.

Among other things, as chairman of the group, in the early 1970s, Nipperdey wrote a critique of the Hessian guidelines for school politics together with the philosopher Hermann Lübbe.[20] The aim of the guidelines was to dissolve history as an independent subject in high school by integrating it in the new subject *Gesellschaftslehre*. Nipperdey and Lübbe heavily criticized this plan, along with the fact that the guidelines, with reference to the German constitution, placed a critical evaluation of societal structures in the center of its learning targets. More concretely, they argued that an overemphasized call for criticism might lead to a pseudo-critical consciousness in which every element of societal consensus would be ignored on behalf of a focus on conflict and in which vague moral categories are misused to construct ideological societal interpretations that merely generate further criticism and conflict.

Nipperdey echoed many of his concerns toward the Hessian guidelines for school politics in his famous controversy with Hans-Ulrich Wehler in the early 1970s. The controversy began when, in a 1973 review of Wehler's *Das deutsche Kaiserreich*, Nipperdey took issue with Wehler's approach of *Gesellschaftsgeschichte*.[21] Nipperdey criticized the approach for being too deterministic in its reliance on the *Sonderweg* thesis and too narrow in its focus on social factors. Furthermore, he portrayed Wehler's attempt to perform political pedagogy (through a relentless criticism of various actors, institutions and traditions in German history) as ahistorical. Instead of creating a position "beyond historicism," as was the aspiration of the social-historians,[22] Nipperdey wanted to renew the hermeneutical-historicist approach, which for him meant renouncing the historian's supposed duty to carry out political-pedagogical criticism. His research projects were often theoretically-methodologically advanced and thematically broad: He found room not only for social and structural history, but also for the history of politics, mentality, and art.[23]

Nipperdey's review of *Das deutsche Kaiserreich* appeared in the first issue of the journal *Geschichte und Gesellschaft* in 1975. This journal was edited by Hans-Ulrich Wehler, Jürgen Kocka, and Wolfgang Mommsen, among others, and came to function as a publishing platform for the *Gesellschaftshistoriker*.[24] It was also in the first issue of *Geschichte und Gesellschaft* that Wehler first took issue with the position of Andreas Hillgruber and Klaus Hildebrand, two conservative historians, who were both steeped in the classical tradition of political-diplomatic history and thus fundamentally opposed to *Gesellschaftsgeschichte*. Where Wehler favored the *Primat der Innenpolitik*, emphasized the need for theoretically-based research, and focused on societal issues, Hillgruber and Hildebrand defended the traditional *Primat der Aussenpolitik* approach to diplomatic history with a focus on the records of the foreign ministry and on the decision-making elite.[25]

In their defense of an autonomous approach to political history, Hillgruber and Hildebrand criticized *Gesellschaftsgeschichte* for being inadequate due to its neglect of political processes. They furthermore portrayed the launching of the approach as a politically leftist claim to exclusive power in the German historical profession. These charges were denied by Wehler, who frequently described his approach as progressive and democratic, and as opposed to the allegedly reactionary and conservative approach of his opponents. Whereas Nipperdey took the position that it is the quality of the research rather than the political background of the researcher that matters, Hillgruber bluntly denied the existence of labels such as reactionary and progressive within research. As such, in the discussions of whether history should be redefined into a critical *Gesell-schaftsgeschichte*, the various positions as roughly represented by Wehler and Kocka on one side, and by Nipperdey, Hillgruber, and Hildebrand on the other side, formed two opposed and fundamentally irreconcilable poles, even if Nipperdey's research agenda was thematically considerably broader and theoretically-methodologically more advanced than Hillgruber and Hildebrand's.

Koselleck in Poetik und Hermeneutik and at the University of Heidelberg

Koselleck also emerged as a key figure in the discussion about the historical discipline in the late 1960s and early 1970s. If placed vis-à-vis the competing programs of historical writing, there can be no doubt that, in terms of theoretical-methodological standpoints, research projects, and specific interpretations, he was much closer to Nipperdey than to Hillgruber and Hildebrand or to Wehler and Kocka, with whom he became colleagues in Bielefeld in 1973.

To be sure, Koselleck's work had little to do with that of Hillgruber and Hildebrand, whose research-program of a modern political history he undoubtedly found theoretically-methodologically and thematically too narrow. In line with this, Koselleck surely agreed with Wehler and the *Gesellschaftshistoriker* on the need to go beyond the *Primat der Aussenpolitik* and practice a more theoretical, interdisciplinary, and social-historical approach that involved a broader and more critical examination of the intellectual-political conditions and discourses that had led to the "German catastrophe." This was, broadly speaking, a type of approach that Koselleck had called for and tried to develop since the early 1950s.

However, the differences between Koselleck and the *Gesellschaftshistoriker* evidently outweighed the similarities. To begin with, whereas Wehler and his associates found inspiration in Weberian sociology and American social science, Koselleck was more oriented toward reading (and cooperating with) philosophers, literary theorists, and theologians. Whereas the former focused on social structures, Koselleck was more interested in language, mentality, and the historicity of the political. In addition, whereas the *Gesellschaftshistoriker* aimed at discursive and institutional power in the profession, embraced a polemic style of argumentation, and declared a position as left-liberal, Koselleck avoided identifying himself with any political position and tried to withdraw from the ideologically loaded debates of the time in order to pursue his research agendas. And even if, similar to the *Gesellschaftshistoriker*, Koselleck wanted to use lessons deduced from the past to improve social-political conditions in the present, he evidently nurtured a deeper skepticism concerning the usability of history and envisioned a tie between science and politics that was not as close as the one they saw. More generally, *Gesellschaftsgeschichte* entailed a certain scientific claim that the more hermeneutically minded Koselleck simply renounced.[26]

In this respect, Koselleck was in line with Thomas Nipperdey, who in the 1960s and 1970s pursued research projects that were to some extent similar to Koselleck's. Both sought to renew the historicist-hermeneutic approach, explored the possibilities of developing a historical anthropology (although, they had two different conceptions of anthropology), and pioneered the study of monuments and iconography.[27] However, their theoretical-methodological visions, research projects, and normative positions were in many respects dissimilar, and, in the debate about *Gesellschaftsgeschichte*, Koselleck sided neither with Nipperdey nor with Wehler/Kocka or Hillgruber/Hildebrand.[28]

Koselleck's choice of not taking a position in the debate not only had to do with the lack of compatibility between his position and those represented in the debate or with his lack of taste for the open conflicts in the discipline; it was also a result of the fact that he appeared on the discussion scene and made his name in the discipline before the debate about *Gesellschaftsgeschichte* began. As we have seen, the limits and purposes of historical writing in modern society were issues that had deeply interested Koselleck since he was a student in Heidelberg, and which he had been discussing in the Arbeitskreis für moderne Sozialgeschichte and in the interdisciplinary working group Poetik und Hermeneutik in the 1950s and 1960s. It was rather in forums of this kind, and not by means of polemical public exchanges, that Koselleck preferred to discuss his work. It is characteristic of both forums that they pursued interdisciplinary agendas, and that they had a humanities rather than a stringent social science outlook. Whereas the Arbeitskreis (of which also Wehler and Kocka eventually became members) aimed at a social history that connected to economics, law, sociology, and ethnography, Poetik und Hermeneutik housed scholars from the more hermeneutically oriented disciplines such as philosophy, literature, and theology.

The group was formed in the early 1960s on the initiative of the literary scholars Hans Robert Jauss (1921–1997), Clemens Heselhaus (1912–2999), and Wolfgang Iser (1926–2007), and the philosopher Hans Blumenberg (1920–1996). Their ambition was to break down the increased specialization within the humanities by creating a forum in which the newest literary theories should be related to classical aesthetic topics in the (Gadamerian) hermeneutic tradition and where theological, historical, and philosophical questions could be discussed in relation to each other. The outcome was, it has been said, the making of a center of postwar (German) intellectual history in which the presumably most successful series of conferences in the humanities after 1945 took place.[29]

One key to the success of Poetik und Hermeneutik is arguably to be found in how its conferences were structured along a certain principles that became somewhat unique in contemporary scientific culture. Among other things, instead of planning the conference themes years ahead, each conference ended with a meeting during which the theme of the next session was decided upon; instead of giving a lengthy presentation at the conferences, the participants submitted their contributions as texts beforehand, so that after a brief summary there was time for a two-hour discussion of each text during the meetings (in the various conference volumes, the discussions were published alongside the talks); and instead of finding the participants by announcement, they were found through co-option.

Koselleck participated in nine out of twelve conferences from the early 1960s until the mid 1980s, where themes related to, for example, *Die nicht mehr schönen Künste, Geschichte—Ereignis und Erzählung*, and *Identität* were on the agenda.[30] Koselleck deeply appreciated the academic culture, the research themes and his collaborators in Poetik und Hermeneutik. Among these were, besides Jauss, Heselhaus, Iser, and Blumenberg, for example also the literary scholar Karlheinz Stierle, and the philosophers Odo Marquard, Hermann Lübbe, and Dieter Henrich, who all pursued projects that overlapped with Koselleck's and held his work in high esteem.

This was evident already during the discussions at the first meeting, in Gießen in 1963, where, in the discussions, Koselleck presented his later famous argument concerning the modern concept of history as a collective singular.[31] The relation between *Geschichten und Geschichte* was discussed in more detail at the 1970 conference that focused on *Geschichte—Ereignis und Erzählung* and was co-organized by Koselleck. It was on this occasion, when Koselleck also presented his project of developing a theory of historical time, that Jacob Taubes labeled him a "partisan of histories in plural."

The specific type of philosophical approach to aesthetics, poetics, and history that Koselleck practiced in Poetik und Hermeneutik obviously represented an intellectual tradition that related science to politics less directly than the program of *Gesellschaftsgeschichte*. The members of Poetik und Hermeneutik did not view or profile themselves as polemics with a specific ideological or political agenda that was to be legitimated and substantiated via a scholarly analysis. Instead, they aimed at a (new) style of inquiry that allowed for a deconstruction of ideological-political vocabularies, mindsets, and positions in the past and the present, without aiming at outlining an alternative ideological position.[32] The discussion of the relation between history and histories at the 1970 conference provides one of many examples of this. All this notwithstanding, there were certain divisions within the circle. To bracket or to bridge these divisions were a genuine and considerable achievement. After all, Poetik und Hermeneutik was mainly taken up by a generation that had undergone the violent conflicts and divisions of the 1930s and 1940s in full measure, and on various sides. Arguably, the group was in part driven by a shared attachment to a tradition of scholarship in the humanities that most of the participants also recognized as tainted and compromised by its extreme ideological subservience in the Nazi period. Still, they hoped, in some cases perhaps rather despairingly, that their scholarly work would help to counter, or even depart from, the atrocious past. This basic attitude recognized the problems raised by the past that most other debates in German historical writing and related fields lacked during this period. This might be part of the lasting appeal of Poetik und Hermeneutik.

By the time Koselleck took up his professorial chair in history in Heidelberg in 1968, on the basis of his activities in the Arbeitskreis and in Poetik und Hermeneutik he was known as a scholar who moved on the theoretical-methodological forefront of the historical discipline.[33] In Heidelberg, he was able to draw on a substantial teaching experience, accumulated from the early 1950s onwards in Bristol and as an assistant to Kühn and Conze in Heidelberg.[34] In the mid 1950s, Koselleck had complained to Schmitt that, due to being socialized during and after World War II, the young generation of (German) students was characterized by a fundamentally a-political stance and an inclination to view the study of history merely as a required university education.[35] In contrast, during his five years as a professor in Heidelberg he was to encounter a generation of students that he found too politicized. These students were of the generation of 68ers.[36]

At the department of history in Heidelberg, the demands of the 68ers resulted in ongoing discussions about the discipline and an increase of courses dealing with historical-theoretical issues.[37] However, the 68ers also launched a wave of physical activism that prompted members of the historical seminar to temporarily cease their teaching activities in the summer semester of 1971. A few years earlier, the most prominent member of the faculty, Werner Conze, had been a target of the student protests, when he, against the advice of his assistants, attempted to be elected as the first rector of the new group university in 1969.[38] Already in 1968, Conze had been rejected by his colleagues as a rector candidate for being too progressive, and when he (also in 1969) became rector in short transitory period to the new group university, he remained unpopular among his colleagues as a result of his support of the new university structure. However, Conze was even more unpopular among the left-wing students, who found him reactionary. When he ran for the rector candidature, they began to dig into and expose his Nazi past and bombarded him with eggs and tomatoes during his speeches.[39] In addition, the left-wing students heavily criticized his famous social-historical lectures, because these circumvented any debate concerning the Marxist view of history. Conze, on the other hand, had difficulties understanding the events taking place around 1968: Deprecatingly, he paralleled these with the political events leading to the breakdown of the Weimar Republic.

Koselleck took more of a middle-position toward the left-wing students. On the one hand, he had no sympathy for and warned against the most radical assumptions, demands, and activities of the 68ers. He did so by means of comparing their vision of history as a totality and their attempts to moralize and politicize historical writing to the historical-philosophical visions and projects of the most extreme Enlightenment thinkers, thus using 1968 as a negative reference point against which he defined his own scientific and political positions. In response to the fact that the 68ers aimed to create societies in which all distinctions between public and private, friend and enemy, master and slave, science and politics were to be eliminated, Koselleck argued that such attempts were plainly impossible and bound to have disastrous consequences. Tellingly, when, in an earlier cited interview, he moreover explained how, since his experiences of World War II, he had maintained a skeptical attitude in order to counteract utopian aspirations, he added: "also the utopian aspirations of the 68ers."[40]

On the other hand, Koselleck was not unsympathetic toward all demands for intellectual, institutional, and social change in the late 1960s, and he once explained how his relation to the 68ers was different than Conze's in that, without being known as a leftist intellectual, he was accepted as an interlocutor by the left-wing students with whom he was willing to engage in discussions.[41] In the interview, Koselleck explained his mediating position in the conflict unfolding in the late 1960s and early 1970s with reference to specific generational experiences and expectations that in his view always characterize and divide societies:

> As for generational relations, I believe that the issue is comparable to an accordion: sometimes they are further removed from each other. As a member of the war generation, I was for example closely associated with Werner Conze, who was born in 1910. The war still functioned like glue that was specific for those who lived through it and was based on analogous experience. However, when the student revolts and, at the same time, the radical investigation of the NS-period began, I was off the hook. Unlike Conze, who to some extent had been a convinced National Socialist, coming from the grand bourgeoisie, but supporting the *Volksgemeinschaft*, I had never assumed responsibilities in the Third Reich. And then the generational gap was large; suddenly the thirteen years between us marked a huge distance.[42]

Koselleck's understanding of the generational problem was evidently based on assumptions from his temporal thought, in that he described himself, Conze, and the 68ers as located in different, dynamic temporal layers, as a large arrangement of *Ungleichzeitigen* (non-simultaneousness) that was prone to generate conflict. Koselleck was rather content to avoid conflict, and his mediating position and his theoretical thought of the period seemingly represent an attempt to make things more dialogical and complex and thereby tacitly undermine the foundations of the lines of conflict at the time. This interpretation is in accordance with the ways in which friends and colleagues of Koselleck have described how he came to function as a mediator between the generation of predominantly conservative scholars, who had been socialized in the 1920s and 1930s and who were commonly uninterested in theoretical questions, and the generation of theoretically interested left-wing students that grew up after 1945 and revolted against the older generation during the late 1960s and early 1970s. One example is found in a recent speech given by Lucian Hölscher. Looking back at his first encounter with Koselleck, he said:

> When I, coming as a member of the student institute from Freiburg, for the first time saw Reinhart Koselleck at the historian's conference in Cologne in 1970, I was captivated by the brilliance of his concluding talk *Wozu noch Historie?*, but also of his human attitude (*Menschlichkeit*). The conservative board of the Association of Historians would not allow a discussion, whereon Christian Meier, back then a historian of Antiquity in Cologne, invited the interested students to his seminar, with his characteristic provocative frankness. Then we were 20 students discussing with Koselleck until the early morning—about what? —Of course about Marx. I

was far from convinced by Koselleck's conservative way of reading Marx. .
. . What nevertheless drew me to Koselleck was his way of leading a discussion: strong in his convictions, but listening; open, yet critical.[43]

While many young historians were attracted to Marxism, critical
theory or Gesellschaftsgeschichte, others, such as Hölscher, were attracted
to Koselleck, who in the late 1960s and 1970s appeared as one of the
few established historians with whom they could communicate and from
whom they could hope for a renewal of the discipline.[44] In contrast to
other current debaters, Koselleck did not stage himself as a polemicist
or an ideologist, but as an open-minded and theoretically acute scholar,
who was primarily interested in challenging the established assumptions
within the discipline. On these grounds he had a certain appeal, also for
the left-wing students. While nurturing deep reservations toward some of
Koselleck's analytical assumptions, such as his anthropological categories,
they felt challenged and inspired by his style of thinking and arguing.[45]
In addition, they shared his conviction that history was in need of theory
and should occupy itself with societal-political questions, if it was to regain its relevance and survive as a science. This was the key argument
in two programmatic texts in the beginning of the 1970s, titled "Wozu
noch Historie?" and "Über die Theoriebedürftigkeit der Geschichtswissenschaft," with which Koselleck directly addressed the discussion about
the identity crisis in the historical profession.

A Message to the Historical Profession and a Personal Program

"Wozu noch Historie?" was—as mentioned by Lucian Hölscher—first presented as the final talk at the Historikertag in Köln in 1970 and then published in Historische Zeitschrift in 1971; "Über die Theoriebedürftigkeit der
Geschichtswissenschaft" was first presented as a talk at a 1969 conference
in the Arbeitskreis für moderne Sozialgeschichte and then published in
the volume Theorie der Geschichte und Praxis der Geschichtsunterricht from
1972.[46]

The two articles are structured around the same basic themes, assumptions, and arguments. First of all, they begin with a perspective on the
crises that marked the discipline and manifested in the discussion concerning the relevance of history. According to Koselleck, while this discussion had intensified the so-called "crisis of historicism" of the 1920s
and 1930s, it referred not only to the problems related to the worldview
and the relativism of historicism; it referred also, as he wrote in "Wozu
noch Historie?" to a crisis in "history as a stringent branch of research."[47]

The crisis, Koselleck argued, was connected to a process of de-historicization within the human and social sciences since the 1920s; a process in which history had been increasingly isolated from the other disciplines. While they had developed their own theories, objects of study, and areas of societal relevance, history had been relegated to a sub- or ancillary science, defined only by its method. What Koselleck consequently asked for in his two articles was thus a specific object of study through which history could regain its relevance vis-à-vis the other sciences and the surrounding society.

On his way to present such an object, and by means of recapitulating his analysis of the modern concept of history, in "Wozu noch Historie?," Koselleck listed five formal analytical criteria to characterize what historical research is and what it can achieve: "[t]he turn toward concrete detail; the need to draw upon the theoretical premises of the related sciences; the alienating effect of historical declarations; the ideological-critical implications of the historical-philological method and the impossibility of gaining any immediate benefit from historical knowledge. The list can be expanded, but I believe it is sufficient for us to see a positive aspect in respect to the question: Does history still have a role to play in science and education?"[48]

Koselleck then returned to the issue that is missing in the list: the specific object that would allow history to regain its scientific and societal relevance. He did so by stressing what he labelled *Theoriebedürftigkeit* (the need for theory) in historical science. In an attempt to provide a new and useful theoretical fundament, he referred to the concept of historicity from Heidegger's *Sein und Zeit*. More concretely, on the first pages of "Über die Theoriebedürftigkeit der Geschichtswissenschaft," he proposed to develop Heidegger's notion of historicity into a *Historik* that eschews the problems of historicism. Echoing the argumentative line from his 1953 letter to Schmitt, he proposed to expand Heidegger's notion of historicity with a list of further categories in order to outline the formalistic conditions that allegedly condition and structure history. In line with this, while he recognized the difficulties in applying such metahistorical categories in actual research, Koselleck claimed that historical writing can only survive as a science if its theoretical premises are clarified.

It was against this background that Koselleck in the articles launched his programmatic statement: that the discipline of history should concentrate on developing a specific theory—a theory of historical times. In "Wozu noch Historie?," he wrote: "We are simply lacking a theory, which—if possible—will distinguish our science from the theories of the other social sciences: a theory of historical times. . . . The task will then be to uncover temporal structures that are shaped in accordance with the multiple kinds of historical change. The temporality of historical events and the structures of historical processes can thus organize historical writing—as they organize history itself."[49]

Such a theory of historical times, Koselleck further argued, was needed to clarify the relation among "history as such" and the many "histories in plural," in order to illuminate the "*Gleichzeitigkeit des Ungleichzeitigen*" and to allow the application of concepts such as acceleration, progress, and movement and even history within the sciences. In other words, according to Koselleck, a theory of historical times was to be regarded as *the* subject matter with which history should regain its relevance in relation to the other sciences as well as its societal status as *magistrae vitae*.[50]

Seen retrospectively, "Wozu noch Historie?" and "Über die Theoriebedürftigkeit der Geschichtswissenschaft" are both easy and difficult to place within the discussion of the historical discipline in the early 1970s. On the one hand, they provided a very accurate description of the atmosphere within the profession, where Koselleck was only one among many to identify a crisis in the discipline and to propose theory as a remedy against the crisis. In addition, by asking the question "what for, history?" and by emphasizing the "need for theory," he coined suggestive catchphrases that were recurrently referred to in the debate.[51]

On the other hand, besides being a message for the historical profession, the texts communicated a personal project that no other German historian was to pursue: the project of developing a theory of historical time. This was a project that Koselleck had in fact already begun in the 1960s, and which he continued to work on in the following decades. So, while the project was launched as a reaction to the educational-political situation of the late 1960s and 1970s, its origins and further development evidently transcended this situation.

In contrast to his catchphrases, Koselleck's specific theoretical program initially received limited attention. To be sure, in the early 1970s, stimulated first of all by Braudel's and Koselleck's writings, historical time was on occasion thematized in the discussions of the historical discipline. This was, for example, the case in a 1972 volume of essays titled *Soziologie und Sozialgeschichte*, in which Koselleck dealt with historical time in a text focusing on the relation between conceptual history and social history.[52] In his contribution to the volume, Hans-Ulrich Wehler also stressed the need for theories of historical time in the study of history, while he criticized the lack of reflections on historical time among sociologists.[53] This critique was indirectly responded to in the text by the sociologist Niklas Luhmann, who made an elaborate and complex effort to theorize historical time as an analytical tool in the study of history and societal systems.[54]

However, no other contribution to the debate of historical time reached the level of Luhmann's and Koselleck's texts, and soon the issue disappeared from the discussions of the historical discipline.[55] There seem to be a least two reasons for this development. First of all, the issue of historical time was simply overshadowed by other themes and projects. Secondly, many scholars did not know what to expect from Koselleck's program or where to place it in relation to the other programs and positions in the profession. Although his theoretical ambitions were in the early 1970s frequently referred to and on occasion discussed in more detail, both inside and outside the historical profession,[56] the discussants found it difficult to debate Koselleck's project in depth before he had qualified his theoretical ambitions by means of (further) empirical and theoretical studies.[57] The following sections describe how Koselleck did this in his attempt to develop a theory of historical time.

Past, Present, Future—Experience and Expectation

To begin with, when discussing the place of historical time in Koselleck's scholarly production, it should be remembered that he had worked with time as an analytical tool right from the beginning of his career. This is, as we have seen, evident in *Kritik und Krise*, *Preußen zwischen Reform und Revolution* and the *Geschichtliche Grundbegriffe*, and it was against the background of and in relation to these projects that during the 1960s he made it his ambition to develop a more elaborate theory of historical time.

It is also important to emphasize that Koselleck's theory of historical time was never based on a paradigm similar to the one of *Gesellschaftsgeschichte*—that is, on an approach largely defined by one theme, one period, and one method. Instead, his theory of historical times took into account many different themes, periods and methods, including methods from art history, as we will see in the chapter on his studies of war memorials.

It should finally be mentioned that Koselleck never wrote one exhaustive and overarching treatise on the topic. Instead, he wrote a number of smaller outlines, which, as contributions to his overall ambition of developing a theory of historical time, draw on a number of compatible assumptions, arguments and keywords that were aimed at empirical research rather than at forming a closed and fixed theoretical system. In fact, as pointed out by Jens Busck, due to the unsystematic character of his writings, it is difficult to establish a definite list of what Koselleck subsumed under his theory of historical time.[58]

The most important theoretical outlines and empirical articles are included in the two collections of essays *Vergangene Zukunft* from 1979 and *Zeitschichten* from 2000.[59] With a focus on these two collections, the following argues that Koselleck's work on historical time crystallized in two lines of research, which, in spite of their common overall ambition of deconstructing histories in singular and thematizing histories in plural, were directed toward different objectives that can be distinguished from each other via the keywords informing the respective analytical frameworks. The first line of research was especially central in Koselleck's writings from the late 1960s until the late 1970s as documented first of all in *Vergangene Zukunft*, and the other became increasingly important from the 1980s onwards as documented primarily in *Zeitschichten*.

The theoretical ambition in *Vergangene Zukunft* is outlined in the foreword in which Koselleck firstly discussed the possibilities of developing a theory of historical time that is not derived from nature, but from human history. In a crucial sentence, he wrote: "Historical time, if the concept has a specific meaning, is bound up with social and political actions, with concretely acting and suffering human beings and their institutions and organizations."[60] In investigating the possibilities of developing a theory of historical time, Koselleck's project responded to the efforts made by philosophers, from Wilhelm Dilthey (1883–1911) to Martin Heidegger, to reflect on the temporal structures of human existence in order to determine what history is and how it unfolds.[61] In particular, he followed in the footsteps of Martin Heidegger, who had in 1916 questioned the distinctiveness of the concept of time within historical writing and found the answer in the difference between a quantitative concept of time within the natural sciences and a historical concept of time that concerns the uniqueness of qualitative human time.[62] Hence, the theoretical framework that Koselleck further outlined in *Vergangene Zukunft* draws to a great extent on Heidegger's terminology. However, in the center of the framework is not the notion of finality, but instead the related notions of past, present, and future that are also found in *Sein und Zeit*. When Heidegger stated that Being is essentially a temporal and historical phenomenon, he moreover argued that human time unfolds in the interaction between the three temporal dimensions of the past, the present, and the future. David Carr has written the following to clarify what Heidegger aimed at with his reflections on the human temporal condition:

> For Heidegger human existence is a temporal self-projection in which past, present, and future are understood in terms of each other. This hermeneutical circle is not merely a matter of self-understanding and self-interpretation but also ultimately one of self-constitution: our selfhood is the

temporal construction of our own lives. In the process the sense we make, not only of ourselves but also of our world and our relations with others, is derived more from our projected future than from the past. The past, too, is part of what we are, but even it is something we give structure to by means of our projects. Thus for Heidegger the prime dimension of human temporality is the future: possibility has priority over actuality. In *Sein und Zeit* Heidegger is able to draw from his theory an ironic consequence for the discipline of history. Because its subject-matter is persons and their lives and actions, it must treat what is ultimately constitutive of them as persons, their possibilities and their future. Thus the subject-matter of history is in an important sense not fact but possibility, not past but future; or, more precisely past possibilities and prospects, past conceptions of the future: futures past.[63]

Koselleck often emphasized that Heidegger's temporal interpretation of Being was important for his own theories of historical time. "I have learned so much from him," Koselleck said in a 2003 interview. "The stimulus to a historical theory of time also comes from my reading of *Sein und Zeit*.[64] This shows in *Vergangene Zukunft*, where investigations of futures past (*Vergangene Zukunft* literally means "futures past" or "passed futures") are placed at the center of the investigation with the aim of rediscovering the Heideggerian notions of human self-understanding, self-interpretation, and self-constitution historically and empirically.[65] Koselleck pursued this aim by developing the notion of Being as an essentially temporal phenomenon, unfolding in the interaction between past, present, and future, into a theory of historical time that analyzes individual and collective self-understanding and action by focusing on historical actor's conceptions about time and finality. In his introduction to the essays in the collection, Koselleck wrote:

> They direct themselves to texts in which historical experience of time is articulated either explicitly or implicitly. To be more precise, texts were sought out and interrogated that, explicitly or implicitly, deal with the relation of a given past and a given future. . . . All testimony answers to the problem of how, in a concrete situation, experiences come to terms with the past; how expectations, hopes or prognoses are projected into the future become articulated in language. These essays will constantly ask: how, in a given situation, are the temporal dimensions of past and future related? This query involves the hypothesis that in differentiating past and future, or (in anthropological terms) experience and expectation, it is possible to grasp something like historical time.[66]

The cited passage demonstrates not only the importance of Heidegger's temporal assumptions and terminology in *Vergangene Zukunft*, but points also to how, in constructing his analytical framework, Koselleck also found inspiration in the concepts of experience, expectation, and horizon from Gadamer's *Wahrheit und Methode*.[67] In the book, Gadamer defined horizon as being the visual field that encompasses and constitutes everything that is visible from a certain point of view. According to Gadamer, everybody has a limited horizon, because all horizons are bound to the temporal conditions of human finality. Yet every horizon is dynamic; it is bound to constant change, and can broaden or shrink, according to our experiences. As for the notion of experience, Gadamer defined real experience as the point at which people become aware of their own finality as the fundament of their existence and possibilities and find the limits for their rational ability to realize their expectations and plans for the future.

The Gadamerian notions of horizon, experience, and expectations are applied in the analytical framework in virtually all of the essays in *Vergangene Zukunft*. Yet nowhere is their importance for the theory of historical time that Koselleck developed in the 1970s sketched out in as detailed a way as in the essay "Erfahrungsraum und Erwartungshorizont" from 1976.[68] That article is linked to Koselleck's plea for the need for theorizing historical writing in the 1970s in that it opens with the argument that historical research must always clarify its analytical categories. With reference to Augustine, Heidegger, and Gadamer, Koselleck subsequently presents experience and expectation as metahistorical categories, which as pre-linguistic and anthropological conditions create and structure all human history, given that the fundamental temporal distinction in human life between sooner and later will always express itself in a difference between experiences and expectations. There can, he argued, simply be no history that is not constituted by the experiences and expectations of acting and suffering human beings.

Unlike other conceptual pairs, Koselleck added, experience and expectation are not opposed or mutually exclusive categories. On the one hand, there is no experience without expectation or vice versa. On the other hand, the categories do not describe the concrete content of the specific experiences and expectations that have shaped history. However, the two categories are, according to Koselleck, fundamentally different. He defined experience as "present past" and expectation as "futures projected in the past." In other words, Koselleck described experience as the dimension of the past that due to its presence in the present orients the interpretations and actions of human beings. When experience is directed toward future actions, he further argued, they turn into expectations. Expectations are existentially different than experiences, because they are located outside the realm of the latter. In line with this, according to Koselleck, human beings not only orient themselves toward their experiences, but also toward the unknown future. They have expectations and might produce plans and prognosis for what is to come. Working from this theoretical premise, at the end of the article Koselleck qualified his theory of modernity: In modern times, he wrote, the *Erwartungshoriz-ont* (horizon of expectation) was disconnected from the *Erfahrungsraum* (space of experience) so that the social-political language was no longer oriented toward past experience but became increasingly loaded with future-oriented expectations.

Following the theoretical outlines in the foreword and in "Erfah-rungsraum und Erwartungshorizont," the ambition of the essays in *Vergangene Zukunft* is to decipher the changes in the relation among past, present, and future and between experience and expectation during the *Neuzeit*. While some of the essays are methodologically connected through the approach of conceptual history, other essays follow different methodological trajectories. This is for example the case with the opening essay, "Vergangene Zukunft der frühen Neuzeit."[69] The latter illuminates changes in the human historical consciousness from the sixteenth century onwards with a focus on the experience of art, and it is informed by the Gadamerian perspective on the act of creating and translating a piece of art as a negotiation between different temporal horizons (a perspective that is also found in Koselleck's later studies of political iconography).

The specific object in focus in "Vergangene Zukunft der frühen Neuzeit" is Albrecht Altdorfer's early sixteenth-century painting titled "The Battle of Issus." For Koselleck, the painting comprises a specifically premodern view of history in the way it brings together different historical times. While Altdorfer carefully reconstructed the various details of the battle, such as the number of the combatants, in his painting the Persians strikingly resemble the Turks, who the same year unsuccessfully tried to besiege Vienna. Likewise, the persons of Alexander and Maximillian, one of Altdorfer's patrons, "merge in exemplary manner."[70]

According to Koselleck, besides referring to the past and the present, in line with the pre-modern view of history, "The Battle of Issus" pointed to a certain vision of the future. This vision was based the belief of a battle between light and darkness, leading up to an apocalyptic struggle between Christ and the Anti-Christ. Whereas there was widespread disagreement (for example between the Pope and Luther) as to who represented the Christ and the Anti-Christ, everybody shared the conviction that the future would crystallize on the day of judgment and that this event was inevitable and beyond human control.

This vision, and the fusion of different temporal horizons, was, Koselleck argued, absent in the historical consciousness that Friedrich Schlegel expressed three centuries later in his reactions to the picture.

What instead characterized Schegel's reaction was first of all a historical-critical distance. Where Altdorfer had merged and emphasized the sameness between the temporal dimensions of the past, the present, and the future, Schlegel instead emphasized the difference between his own time, the time in which the picture was painted, and the time it represented. One of the ways in which Schlegel demarcated himself temporally from the picture was by labeling it the "the greatest feat of the age of chivalry." This reaction exemplifies for Koselleck how history had won a specifically temporal dimension for Schlegel that was missing in Altdorfer's time: "Formulated schematically, there was for Schegel, in the three hundred years separating him from Altdorfer, more time (or perhaps a different mode of time) that appeared to have passed for Altdorfer in the eighteen hundred years or so that lay between the Battle of Issus and his painting."[71]

Koselleck explained this temporal change with the rise of modern historical philosophy, which transformed history into something characterized by its changeability, newness, and progression, so that it was no longer thought possible to learn from the stories of the past. Individuals and societies consequently try to compensate for the lack of experience with ever-increasing expectations and plans for the future that give birth to radical fictions such as the "Thousand-year Reich" and the "classless society."

Focusing on the notions of past, present, and future, experience and expectation, "Vergangene Zukunft der frühen Neuzeit" shows the inspiration that Koselleck found in Heidegger and Gadamer in constructing the analytical framework for his theory of historical time. Furthermore, it demonstrates how he reworked and broadened their categories to fit his own project. In adapting the temporal categories from *Sein und Zeit* to a historical analysis, Koselleck not only left behind the historical-philosophical implications of Heidegger's analysis of Being, but also shifted the focus from individual to social temporality: to empirical investigations of how communities and societies have conceptualized the relations between their own future, present, and past.

Evidently, this shift away from the individual that is built into Heidegger's conceptions bears some similarity to what Löwith did in his dissertation and should be understood as a continuation of Koselleck's project of revising Heidegger's analysis of Being into a larger anthropological system of the human existence that emphasizes the importance of social relations in human life. This ambition is also at play in Koselleck's transformation of Gadamer's categories of experience, expectation, and horizon.[72] It should firstly be emphasized that Koselleck used the spatial metaphor 'space of experience'. He thereby defined experience as something

shared by many people, who at a given time, and in a given place constitute a political or social unit of action. Likewise, he viewed expectations
in a social collective perspective: Together, the expectations constitute
a horizon, which the social actors appraise as a group. Koselleck consequently used Gadamer's hermeneutic approach to convey larger social-
historical arguments that are not only constructed through the study of
texts and pieces of art, but via analysis of social-historical dynamics and
processes. In addition, Koselleck combined the categories of Heidegger
and Gadamer with a variety of further analytical categories as witnessed
first of all in Zeitschichten. The result was an attempt to theorize historical
time and an analytical framework that is neither Heideggerian of Gadamerian, but distinctly Koselleckian.

Temporal Layers and Repetitive Structures

Where many of the temporal-theoretical perspectives in Vergangene Zukunft were anticipated in Kritik und Krise and the Geschichtliche Grundbegriffe, the reflections on historical time that Koselleck unfolded in Zeitschichten were anticipated in Preußen zwischen Reform und Revolution and in
Das Zeitalter der europäischen Revolution.[73] Hence, where the focus in Vergangene Zukunft is on the temporal dimensions of the past, the present,
and the future, on experience and expectation, and on the singularity of
the Neuzeit, the emphasis in Zeitschichten is on analytical keywords such
as the Gleichzeitigkeit des Ungleichzeitigen and Wiederholung (repetition),
Dauer (durability) and Struktur (structure). These keywords provide the
pillars of the main argument of the volume: the idea that history consists
of and unfolds in the interaction among various Zeitschichen (temporal
layers).

As we have seen, Koselleck had already thematized this idea in his
writings from the late 1960s onwards. However, with reference to, first
of all, the French historian Fernand Braudel, the idea in Zeitschichten is
developed into a elaborate theoretical framework according to which all
types of history can be studied as temporal layers or structures that are
characterized by repetition as well as change.[74] It is with the purpose of
encapsulating this assumption that Koselleck employs the metaphor of
Zeitschichten. In the programmatic article also titled "Zeitschichten", Koselleck explained: "'Zeitschichten' refers to geological formations, which
reach back in time with different breadth and depth, and which in the
course of the so-called history of the Earth have changed and been moved
apart at different speeds. The retranslation into the domain of human,
political, or social history, as well as structural history, makes it possible

to distinguish analytically between different temporal layers, where persons move and events unfold, or where their preconditions can be investigated."[75]

As observed by Kari Palonen, due to the problems involved in grasping the "temporal" and the "historical" in linguistic terms, Koselleck used many and shifting analytical expressions in his attempts to define historical time.[76] However, he seemed to have been particularly satisfied with the metaphor of *Zeitschichten*. Indeed, this notion became increasingly vital for his attempt to theorize historical time in the last decades of his career. This points to a more general change taking place in Koselleck's work from the 1950s to the 1980s: Whereas he first focused primarily on deconstructing histories in singular, he began to focus more on how histories in plural could be written in practice.

The analytical framework behind the geological metaphor is first of all described in the mentioned programmatic article *Zeitschichten*. Here Koselleck outlined the assumption that all history contains at least three different layers of temporal structures. The first layer is that of events, such as the revolutions of 1789 and 1989, which human beings habitually experience as *singular*. Koselleck thus presented history as a series of *singular* events that are continuously inscribed in various levels of *recursive* structures that represent the second layer of history's temporal structures. More concretely, Koselleck argued that the *singular* is conditioned by *recursive* or repetitive structures. This does not mean that history is simply repeating itself, but rather that certain *recursive* patterns provide events with common features, and at the same time the events are always characterized by a *singular* dimension.

To demonstrate this argument, Koselleck used an example from everyday life: receiving a letter. On the one hand, this event can be of *singular* and decisive significance for the receiver. On the other hand, the delivery and the reception of the letter only become possible because the mail carrier carries out his daily work according to the established structures of the mail services. In this way, Koselleck argues, the *singular* and the *recursive* are related.

Next to the *singular* events and the *recursive* structures, Koselleck introduced a third temporal layer that concerns a type of repetition that is biological and anthropological in nature and goes beyond generational and individual experience. It concerns, in other words, the structures *transcending* history that are encompassed in his anthropological categories. What the description of these three temporal layers amounts to in *Zeitschichten* is a theoretically framed structural history that takes account of events as well as changes. That is, a history that investigates the relations between the *singular* events and the different levels of movement and change taking place within the *recursive* and *transcending* structures.

The theory of historical times as described in *Zeitschichten* is not to be viewed as a rupture in Koselleck's historical thinking, but rather as a shift of interest that encompassed new ways of approaching and evaluating certain themes and issues. Some of these changes can be illustrated via a comparison of two articles on the same theme written in different decades. The first essay, "Neuzeit," is written in 1977 and included in *Vergangene Zukunft*; the second essay, "Wie neu ist die Neuzeit?," is written in 1989 and included in *Zeitschichten*.[77] In the first essay, Koselleck described the *Neuzeit* as an epochal change in respect to how history and time are suddenly conceptualized as future-oriented and as unfolding in one, singular, and unique way. In the second essay, he echoed this interpretation, but at the same time relativized the extent to which the *Neuzeit* allegedly represented a new time. For this purpose, he unfolded what he called a semantic and a prognostic argument.

In respect to the semantic argument, Koselleck pointed out that the notion of *Neuzeit* is somewhat unclear and ambiguous in that it suggests that earlier epochs were not new. According to Koselleck, this suggestion is in a certain sense wrong, because all histories are experienced as new by those involved. In respect to his prognostic argument, he relativized the notion of "new" by arguing that history not only consists of singular events, but always encompasses repetitive structures that condition all singular events. The repetitive structures are, he added, found in all areas of human life: in time tables, in law, and in language. In fact, even human prognoses are preconditioned by history's repetitive structures.

Koselleck exemplified this argument by referring to a political prognosis made by Diderot in 1772 that it would require nothing but a random event to set free the overthrowing of the current political system; that the people would revolt to claim its rights, but because it had no specific aim or plan, anarchy would soon reign, only to be succeeded by two political parties in the state dividing the people in two; that whereas these parties would be distinguishable from each other only by their names, they would both be driven by ambition and greed, leading to a situation characterized first by conspiracies and plots and then by a civil war. This situation would, according to Diderot, be brought to an end by a modern sovereign to whom the people would pledge their loyalty, and the revolution would afterwards continue along lines that he found difficult to predict.[78]

Koselleck labeled Diderot's prognosis a classical one "that begins with a conditional if-then sentence and reckons with past reality as structurally repeatable in the future."[79] According to Koselleck, Diderot's prognosis was based on a theory of the repetition of possible histories that the latter knew from his reading of Cromwell and Tacitus's thoughts on resistance against tyranny and civil war: "It was this knowledge about a singular, passed reality that enabled him to extrapolate structural and repeatable possibilities into the future."[80]

Following up his relativization of the notion of *Neuzeit*, Koselleck ended the article by explaining more exactly how the *Neuzeit*, in his eyes, after all represented a change in terms of being a "new time." He referred here to how certain temporal-structural changes taking place around the French Revolution outdated traditional interpretative and prognostic models. At this time, according to Koselleck, it for example became impossible to interpret social-political developments through the traditional model of *Verfassungskreislauf* (constitutional cycles). The contemporaries had no problems understanding the empirical chain of events, but struggled to comprehend the enormous acceleration of the speed with which the events unfolded. According to Koselleck, the specifically modern in the *Neuzeit* is located exactly in the temporal acceleration of the political processes. He concluded: "We historians must therefore learn to distinguish between different layers: those, who can change fast, those, who only change slowly, and those, who are more endurable and contain recurring possibilities. Then it is possible to redefine the epoch, in such a way that the modern is recognized, but without excluding other epochs as being totally different."[81]

This passage demonstrates how Koselleck's theory of *Zeitschichten* not only encompassed a shift of interest, but also an elaboration of his conception of history. With its assumption of history as an open, diverse, and contingent process composed of various *histories*, the notion of *Zeitschichten* softened up the more schematic account of history as composed by radically different epochs found in his earlier work.

That Koselleck was aware of this change in his historical writing can be seen on the first page on the earlier mentioned text *Zeitschichten*. Here he wrote that historians usually conceptualize time in two ways—either as a linear and irreversible model, as the Christians did, or as a recurrent and circular model, as the Greeks did—and that it is necessary to develop a concept of time that surpasses these models and the imagined opposition between them. It is tempting to read this sentence partly as an indirect criticism of Löwith's embrace of the Greek cosmos and tendency toward a radical detachment from history, and partly as an act of self-criticism pointed at Koselleck's early work. Hence the sentence arguably points to the tension between the universal and the plural notion of history in Koselleck's work—a tension that he tried to solve by turning his attention from the universal historical perspectives that he took from *Meaning in History* toward the possibilities for historical writing that he found in Löwith's analysis of the human *Miteinandersein*.

These possibilities featured an ideological-critical dimension that is also encompassed in the idea of *Zeitschichten* as can be seen for example in the 1994 article "Diesseits des Nationalstaates: Föderale Strukturen der deutschen Geschichte."[82] Focusing on *Wiederholung* and *Struktur* in history, in the article Koselleck pointed to federal political structures as a dimension that distinguishes German history from the history of other European countries. He did not argue that federal structures are a unique German achievement, but rather that certain structures for a long period made federalism possible in Germany—until these structures were discarded with Hitler's compensatory slogan "One people, one Reich, one Führer." With reference to this slogan, and with an eye on contemporary and future political order in Europe, Koselleck added that, similar to the national state, federal structures should never be understood as a *telos* in history. Federalism, he claimed, is rather one among several political options to be pursued within the formalistic structures, or layers of history. However, like everything else in life, these structures cannot be formed entirely according to our wishes.[83]

The theory of *Zeitschichten* required slight ramifications of Koselleck's anthropological notions. In several texts, the temporal and the anthropological framework are developed as two integrated features in Koselleck's departure from Heidegger's *Sein und Zeit*'s notions of temporal being and of finality, respectively. Koselleck insisted that historical times cannot be reduced to an existence, the conditions of an individual being. In this way, he echoed his earlier criticism of Heidegger's notion of finality as having to be expanded into conceptual pairs giving ample room to the social. And he brought his theory of historical times in tune with the conceptual pairs. It seems fair to say, then, that these were different strands of thought that needed to be harmonized and did not emerge from each other—in spite of the fact that they both emerged from the reception of Heidegger.

Yet, Koselleck does not seem to have pursued the task of developing a theory of historical time, or to have systematically utilized the temporal notions from *Sein und Zeit* before, at some point in the 1960s. It is from the end of this decade that temporal assumptions and notions from *Sein und Zeit* (alongside temporal notions from other discourses) take center stage in his work. One example is found in a passage in "Wozu noch Historie?" in which Koselleck stated that the past, present, and future are always interrelated in human life and added that human self-understanding, self-interpretation, and self-constitution are always constructed in the interaction among these temporal dimensions: "The past has passed, irrevocably—and it has not: the past is present and contains future. It restraints and opens up future possibilities, it is preset in our language, it influences our consciousness as well as the unconscious, our attitudes, our institutions the way we criticize them."[84]

In "Wozu noch Historie?" and "Über die Theoriebedürftigkeit der Geschichtswissenschaft," the anthropological pairs and the theory of historical times were for the first time presented together: the anthropological pairs as a meta-theory of the conditions of possible history required for any historical analysis, and the theory of historical time as the object that is to be given primacy in historical research. In many ways this reflects how Koselleck approached the two dimensions and the relation between them in his work from the late 1960s onwards. While he emphasized different things at different times, according to what the particular analytical situation required, the discursive features involved in the theory of historical time were referred to and applied more frequently in his texts than the anthropological pairs. This happened without apparent tensions, as temporal categories such as *Erfahrungsraum und Erwartungshorizont* or *Zeitschichten* not only connected to, but also further took Koselleck's counter-conceptually based attempt at reworking Heidegger's temporal analysis of Being in *Sein und Zeit* into a theory of human history.

Still, the precise relation between the two frameworks remains elusive. One might assume that the anthropological categories are conceived of as being conceptually prior to the temporal layers; and that thus, in a conceptual fashion, they stand outside time. Yet, this would imply that the temporal layers depend on a specific set of (counter-) concepts rather than the free play of social experience and this seems a doubtful interpretation of Koselleck's intentions. Alternatively, one might suppose that the anthropological categories are supposed to be conceptually posterior to the temporal layers, and that they constitute a specific, mostly invariant and basic layer of time. Yet, in this case the static character of the categories would be in danger of invalidating the creative force and the contingency of other layers of time, which also seems like a doubtful interpretation of Koselleck's intentions. At the end of the day, these matters are difficult to discuss, because Koselleck never clarified the issues at stake in his writings, nor did he develop sufficient conceptual tools to achieve such a clarification.[85]

This points to an important feature characterizing his intellectual temperament and interests: for Koselleck, theory was evidently something that needed to be discussed and defined, but if the various theoretical frameworks and notions proved useful as a starting point for a historical analysis, he saw no reason to integrate the notions into a systematic and unified framework or to explain the exact relation among them.

Objectivity and Partisanship—Experience and Method

Koselleck's attempt to develop a theory of historical time is today regarded as one of the most important and innovative contributions to historical writing in Germany after World War II, and his work has been instrumental in placing the issue of historical time on the agenda in German and international historiography.

However, in the early 1970s when the historical discipline was in debate, Koselleck's theoretical ambitions were, as mentioned, overshadowed by other scientific projects, first of all by the program of *Gesellschaftsgeschichte*. In this period, as the market for history books grew, not least due to the expansion of the subject of history at the universities, they launched no less than four publication series related to the approach: the journal *Geschichte und Gesellschaft*, the encyclopedia *Deutsche Historiker*, and the two monograph series *Deutsche Geschichte* and *Kritische Studien zur Geschichtswissenschaft*.[86]

These publications presented the theoretical and empirical program of *Gesellschaftsgeschichte* and moreover provided a history of modern German historiography that portrayed the approach as the natural successor of historicism. More concretely, the works described the emergence of *Gesellschaftsgeschichte* as a necessary development from a methodologically narrow and conservative historical writing that focused on and promoted the nation state, to a more theoretical, rational, and scientific form of historical writing that served emancipatory, ideological-critical, and democratic aims.[87]

This line of reasoning neither discussed Koselleck's theory of historical times nor the essays on questions related to theoretical-methodological aspects of historical writing that he wrote from the late 1960s to the late 1980s. Similar to his theory of historical time, Koselleck's take on historical writing is difficult to place in relation to the discussions and trends in the German historical discipline in this period. This can be exemplified with reference to the earlier cited passage in "Wozu noch Historie?" in which Koselleck stressed that history holds a profound ideological-critical potential but also argued that historical knowledge can never be immediately applied in the present. This assumption did not fit with any of the competing programs of historical writing launched by Wehler and Kocka, Hildebrand and Hillgruber, or Nipperdey. Rather it mediated among and even went beyond these programs.

Like his essays on historical time, most of Koselleck's essays on historical writing were written on different occasions and then included in *Vergangene Zukunft* and *Zeitschichten*. In these essays, Koselleck did not aim to construct an all-encompassing and definite theoretical-methodological system. Instead, he offered something like a toolbox of compatible assumptions and ideas of what historical writing is and what can be done with it. All of his texts communicated the conviction that historical research is an extremely complex field involving several problems and dilemmas that set fundamental limits on what historians can discover about the past and on how historical knowledge can be applied in the present. At the same time, he argued that these dilemmas entail possibilities through which valuable and usable insights and knowledge can be reached, and he articulated some of these possibilities in strong and powerful fashion. As such, Koselleck articulated a position on historical writing that was neither downright pessimistic nor entirely optimistic: It was rather what might be called cautiously constructive.

In order to outline some of the central assumptions in Koselleck's theoretical-methodological universe, the following sections take a closer look at two of his famous articles: "Standortbindung und Zeitlichkeit" from 1977 and "Erfahrungswandel und Methodenwechsel" from 1988.[88] Both articles were written in the framework of Theorie der Geschichte, a working group that was formed in the early 1970s on the initiative of Theodor Schieder and Reinhard Wittram and that met on six occasions between 1975 and 1988 to discuss theoretical-methodological questions in historical writing. Along with Wolfgang Mommsen, Jörn Rüsen, and Jürgen Kocka among others, Koselleck was a regular member of the group, and he was also present when the group first met in 1975 to discuss the relation between objectivity and partisanship in historical writing. The members of the group generally agreed that objectivity and partisanship are not mutually exclusive in historical writing, but they did not establish a common consensus as to the precise relation between the two poles.

Koselleck began his contribution "Standortbindung und Zeitlichkeit" by outlining objectivity and partisanship as two poles of a seemingly unsolvable dilemma in historical writing. "Contemporary historical science is," he wrote, "subject to two mutually exclusive demands: to make true statements, while at the same time to admit and take account of the relativity of these statements."[89] He then ventured into historicizing the dilemma by illustrating how the emergence of partisanship as historical relativism had to do with the discovery of the modern world.

According to Koselleck, until the eighteenth century, historical writing had been characterized by a "scientific postulate of nonpartisanship, in the sense of nonadherence to a party, abstinence or neutrality." An important role in this understanding of history had been played by the eyewitness, whose presence guaranteed authenticity and truth: "The signs of authenticity," Koselleck wrote, "were centered on the eyewitness; whenever possible, the acting or participating agent, be it for the history of revelation, or for the continuing history of church or worldly events."[90]

However, the status of the eyewitness changed, when, in the Renaissance, the discovery of positional commitment became a precondition of historical knowledge. According to Koselleck, the eighteenth-century German theologian and historian Chladenius (1710–1759) was the first to argue that the position of non-partisanship is impossible for historians. While believing in the authenticity of eyewitnesses, Chladenius made a crucial distinction between future *Geschichten* and ancient *Geschichten*. With this distinction, Koselleck stated: "It is no longer a given temporal order—for instance, a God-given order—of all history that arranges the material of history, but instead the history of the future and the history of the past are determined by desires and plans, as well as the questions, which arise in the present. The experiential space of contemporaries is the epistemological kernel of all history."[91]

According to Koselleck, Chladenius deduced two things from his assumption that every temporal arrangement of history is dependent on the position one occupies within history: the relativity of all intuitive judgments and experience, and the perspective of later investigation and representation. Where the first dimension relativized the privileged position of the eyewitness, the other pointed to how the historian is always forced to choose the events and the metaphors with which he or she constructs his narrative. However, although Chladenius illustrated how positional commitment is a presupposition of historical knowledge, he did not argue that perspective necessarily led to a partisan account in which events and knowledge are intentionally obscured. According to Koselleck, he pointed instead to how the sources of the past "display a resistance and retain a weight that is not susceptible to displacement ex post through a partisan evaluation, whether positive or negative."[92]

However, Koselleck added, this insight was lost in the eighteenth century. Here the modern philosophy of progress impregnated historical time with a new mode of temporal experience, so that today was conceived as distinctly different than yesterday and tomorrow as distinctively different than today. This created a situation in which historical writing was only possible through the critical review of previous historiography and in which truth and temporal perspective were no longer separable, leading to the final exclusion of the eyewitness from its privileged position.

The notion of partisanship was, according to Koselleck, radicalized in the period around the French Revolution, where the experience of the acceleration of time made it impossible to establish any kind of viewpoint from which a history of the past could be written that might be relevant in the present or in the future. To counter this development, different measures were proposed. On the one hand, the advocate for liberal politics, Gervinus, argued for a methodologically required impartiality, while he nonetheless regarded the historian as a partisan of progress and freedom. On the other hand, Ranke made a plea for objectivity through a disregard of the present to reach a strictly objective science. Koselleck argued that it was these two positions that continued to represent the dilemma in the present discussions of objectivity and partisanship.

In the final pages of his investigation, Koselleck turned to offer some theoretical remarks in order to make the outlined dilemma "more bearable, if not altogether dispensable."[93] He began by shifting the discussion to the viewpoint of investigative practice, where, he argued, the problems inherent in the dilemma between objectivity and partisanship become less critical. According to Koselleck, the historian can always, as suggested by Chladenius, start out by relying on the historical method to ensure results that are "universally communicable and verifiable independent of the position of the historian" and as such "offers a solid barrier against arbitrary claims made by those convinced by their own certainty."[94] It was on this background that Koselleck famously spoke of a *Vetorecht der Quellen*, meaning that sources possess a power of veto, which forbids the historians from providing interpretations "that can be shown on the basis of a source to be false or unreliable."[95]

At the same time, Koselleck argued that there is always more at stake in historical writing than what is contained in the sources and that historians are therefore always in need of theory to make their sources speak. Koselleck thus spoke of the formation of judgement as a "productive tension, which the historian should see himself confronting . . . between a theory of history and the given sources."[96] He added to this a sentence that ultimately placed the dilemma in an entirely new light: "Partisanship and objectivity cross one another in a new fashion within the force field between theory formation and source exegesis. One without the other is worthless for research."[97]

"Standortbindung und Zeitlichkeit" is in many ways typical for Koselleck's articles dealing with theoretical-methodological questions related to the practice of historical writing. Common to these texts is the attempt to outline a pragmatic and constructive position between difficult dilemmas and conditions in the historian's craft by means of softening up strong analytical dichotomies. This position is established partly by drawing on themes and arguments from earlier writings and partly through a habit of recovering and rephrasing arguments from largely forgotten figures, such as Chladenius, into strong hypotheses, such as *Vetorecht der Quellen*. This was a suggestive, but somewhat obtuse course of argumentation that oscillated between precision and vagueness and eschewed clear instructions regarding application as well as an elaborate theoretical systematic. Nevertheless, Koselleck offered historians a set of platforms and starting points from which they could carry out their research with a certain confidence. In addition, he emphasized that these starting points and platforms must always be combined with theory, but he never recommended a specific theoretical model according to which all historical research and writing must be practiced. Instead, he left it to the theoretical self-reflection and thematic interest of each historian to figure out more exactly how he/she should approach a specific investigation. As such, Koselleck staged himself as a proponent of perspectival plurality in historical writing.

Koselleck's pluralistic position was based on the conviction that thematic interest and theoretical orientation is highly dependent on individual experience. This is one of the key messages in "Erfahrungswandel und Methodenwechsel." In common with "Standortbindung und Zeitlichkeit," the text was aimed at delineating certain conditions of historical writing through reflections on two seemingly opposed, but nevertheless related notions: those of experience and method. Where "Standortbindung und Zeitlichkeit" stated that historical writing is neither exclusively composed by partisanship nor by objectivity, "Erfahrungswandel und Methodenwechsel" argued that historical writing is neither only a matter of experience nor one of pure method. In the opening lines of the article, Koselleck wrote:

> What is sought after, found, and represented as historical truth never depends solely on the experiences that a historian has, or solely on the methods that he uses. Certainly, as a historical work is being written, experience and method interrelate with one other. However, determining their relation is difficult, first because in the course of history it has constantly changed, and second, because as yet we have neither an anthropologically grounded history of historical experience nor a comprehensive history of historical methods. The following answer is therefore a proposal that seeks more questions than it supplies answers.[98]

In his attempt to further probe the relation between the opposed notions at issue, Koselleck presented three different forms of experience and method. The first form of experience relies on the assumption that histories are told and written because human beings experience something unexpected. Koselleck labeled this form of experience "singular." However, he also pointed to how certain singular experiences demand to be told via and integrated into existing patterns of experience. For Koselleck, these patterns represent a second form of experience that is obtained, stabilized, and handed over via so-called "units of action." Common to the singular acquisitions of experience and the stabilizing structures of collective experiences is that people can immediately relate to them. This distinguishes them from the third type of experiences introduced by Koselleck. These are the experiences that transcend persons and generations and therefore only can be recaptured retrospectively through historical reflection.

These three forms of experience are all included in the three forms of method that Koselleck subsequently listed in "Erfahrungswandel und Methodenwechsel." The first form of method concerns history written as an immediate recording or retelling of experiences, presenting history as a form of cognition, which is related to the experience of something singular that has to be preserved in memory through being written down and reflected upon. Because historical writing is always a reworking of experience, the question of *what happened?*, Koselleck continued, will always be connected to the question of *how could it happen?* In other words, the singular is only surprising because existing experiences and expectations are somehow challenged.

Koselleck thereby arrived at the second form of historical writing: the continuing of history. This level concerns the method through which earlier and contemporary experiences are written into a history of continuation. According to Koselleck, the confrontation between earlier and contemporary experience can lead to the third form of method: the so-called rewriting of history. About this method, he stated: "The rewriting of history is as unique as the very first time history is written. It is certainly innovative because it moves in a conscious opposition to the previously reported or written history. It follows provisionally that this corresponds to a change of experience that amounts to a new experience."[99]

Having thus drawn the conclusion that experience and method is always intertwined, Koselleck ended the article by reflecting on Marx's famous dictum that history is written by the victors. His reply to Marx is that this is true in the short run, but because the victors are only interested in illuminating the immediate causes of their victory, it is left to the vanquished to analyze the long-term causes for why things did not happen in the way they had planned and hoped. He wrote: "If they [the vanquished] reflect at all, they face a greater burden of proof to explain why something happened in this and not the anticipated way." To this assumption, he added the following hypothesis: "If history is made in the short run by the victors, historical gains in knowledge stem in the long run from the vanquished."[100]

This hypothesis was in the last pages of the article exemplified with reference to Herodotus, Tocqueville, and Marx, among others, who allegedly all drew from their experiences of defeat to produce methodological innovations in the writing of history.

However, as mentioned above, the phrase "Erfahrungswandel und Methodenwechsel" should also be read as an autobiographical statement, referring to Koselleck's own experience during and after World War II and to his subsequent attempt to explain the reasons for his defeat through a revision of the existing understandings of and approaches to history. Such autobiographical musing was an inseparable dimension of the reflections on theoretical-methodological issues in historical writing that Koselleck authored between the 1960s and the 1990s. The visits related to, or rather formed part of his habit of destabilizing otherwise strong hypotheses with skeptical and ironic comments, thus pointing to what he saw as the many limits, paradoxes and even absurd dimensions of history and historical writing. One instance of this appears in the very last lines of "Erfahrungswandel und Methodenwechsel." Here Koselleck summarized the teachings of the investigation as follows:

> Historical change feeds on the vanquished. Should they survive, they create the irreplaceable primary experience of all histories: that histories take another course than that intended by those involved. This always unique experience cannot be chosen and remains unrepeatable. Yet it can be processed through the search for the causes, which last for a middle- or long-term period, and thus are repeatable. This is what distinguishes methods. They can be abstracted from the unique event; they can be applied elsewhere. Once experience has been methodologically transposed into knowledge by the vanquished—and which victor does not finally belong to them?—it remains accessible beyond all change of experience. This might offer some comfort, perhaps a gain. In practice, it would mean saving us from victories. Yet every experience speaks against it.[101]

The quoted passage illuminates that the oblique autobiographical references ultimately point to an ethical foundation of Koselleck's notion of historical writing: In the long run, suffering and defeat are universal (though survival is not), and they are the incentives for writing and re-writing history. They are ethical incentives because they respond to something that ought not to have happened, to a disturbance, not simply of expectations, but of a moral order that is disturbed by the pretence of victory. This ethical foundation is something of a blind spot in Koselleck's theoretical writings. He did not make it explicit and distrusted it, as the last sentence indicates: here, his skeptical perspective turns against the hope of being "saved" from victories. This perspective reached much further than the passage indicates. In a way, it turned against his theoretical course of argumentation as a whole, because it casts what the text identified as the foundations of historical writing in the light of absurdity. The quoted passage thus illuminates in exemplary fashion how, in spite of his thorough analysis of various assumptions and notions, Koselleck remained ambivalent about their status and usability. This ambivalence was symptomatic of his diffidence toward his own theorizing, leading to a certain tendency toward the paradoxical.

The quoted passage also comments on the question of the usability of historical writing. Koselleck emphasized that a certain level of abstract historical research that succeeds in identifying long-term historical conditions may have direct relevance for present-day decisions. But at the same time, he claimed that this theoretical notion seemed to have no precedent in historical experience of historical research; it is not spared from the degree of complexity and absurdity that characterizes all human affairs and that makes it practically impossible for the historian to arrive at insights about the human past that can be utilized to improve conditions in the present and the future.

There is, however, one issue that is never portrayed as absurd in Koselleck's texts on historical writing: the aim of deconstructing ideas of history in singular and thematizing histories in plural. According to Koselleck, this aim can only be pursued by means of a plurality of perspectives on historical writing. Along with the substantial degree of skepticism and relativism, this call for a plurality of perspectives is a discursive feature that distinguishes his reflections on historical writing from the reflections made by many other German historians between the 1960s and the 1980s. It was in particular a discursive feature with which Koselleck reacted against and positioned himself outside the more scientific, unambiguous, and uniform social-historical discourses in the discipline.

This does not mean that Koselleck was in agreement with those scholars who, in relation to the linguistic turn in the 1960s and 1970s, questioned the possibility of writing a scientific mode of history that referred to an actual past. In the broadest sense, the linguistic turn can be described as a product of a European philosophical tradition that evolved from Friedrich Nietzsche, Ludwig Wittgenstein, and Martin Heidegger and called for new and more varied approach to history with a focus on the role of language and linguistic representation in human affairs.[102] The scholars that have been associated with the linguistic turn are many and diverse. Often portrayed as decisive for the linguistic turn in the humanities are scholars such as Michel Foucault, Richard Rorty, Jacques Derrida and Hayden White, who shared a constructivist epistemology and a critique of positivist beliefs of language as a mirror of nature and of the assumed certainty of scientific, or objective, efforts to explain reality.

To some extent, Koselleck was also a product of some of the philosophical traditions and concerns that led to the linguistic turn. In light of this, it is understandable that he felt a certain affinity to some of the scholars associated with the turn—and vice versa.[103] The key example here is Hayden White, a scholar primarily renowned for his book *Metahistory* (1973) that argues for the importance of narrative arrangements, modes of emplotment and tropes for all historical writing.[104] From the 1980s onwards, White made a significant effort to promote Koselleck's work internationally. In 1987, he wrote an enthusiastic review of the English translation of *Vergangene Zukunft*, stating that, alongside the writings of scholars such as Paul Ricoeur, Frank Ankersmit, and Dominick La Capra, Koselleck's work pointed to "a new era in the conceptualization of not only what 'history' means for Western culture but also for what Western culture means for 'history,'"[105] and in the foreword to *The Practice of Conceptual History*, a collection of Koselleck's essays that were translated into English in 2002, he introduced his German colleague as "one of the most important theorists of history and historiography of the last half-century."[106]

Already in 1986, Koselleck had written a similarly enthusiastic foreword to the German translation of White's *Tropics of Discourse*.[107] Whereas White connected Koselleck's work to current international trends, Koselleck related White's book to a German philosophical tradition represented by the work of Hans-Georg Gadamer and Hans Blumenberg. This comparison is an indication of Koselleck's admiration for White's inquiries into the linguistic conditions of representing historical experience. What Koselleck found appealing about White's project was presumably not only the latter's plea that historians should question their use of language, but also his identification with an ironic mode of historical writing that allows for certain elements of absurdity and contradiction.

However, the comparison with Gadamer and Blumenberg also points to the limits that Koselleck saw in White's approach. Recalling his search for a concept of experience less bound to language than Gadamer's, in his foreword to *Tropics of Discourse*, Koselleck argued that White's strong interest in the metaphorical language of historical writing left little space for the domain of social reality. He also maintained that White's focus bypassed systematic investigations of the role of theory and method in representing historical experience. In addition, in a later interview he criticized White for ignoring source criticism as a check (*Kontrollinstanz*) on historical writing that distinguishes it from fiction.[108] In sum, he staged himself as a more social-historically oriented and less relativistic historian than White.

However, in his foreword to *Tropics of Discourse*, Koselleck distinguished White from French post-structuralists, who, Koselleck wrote, "want to dispose of the historical (*historische*) text as a historical (*geschichtliche*) mediator of truth." This was a variant of relativism to which Koselleck was opposed, just as he was opposed to the rigorous claims to scientism that were articulated in the social-historical discourses.[109]

As Koselleck stated in his 1989 article "Sprache und Ereignisgeschichte," he was interested in those linguistic-turn discussions that questioned "the strong dichotomy between reality and thought, existence and consciousness, history and language," and he sought to replace these with softer dichotomies such as "meaning and experience" and "text and context."[110] In virtually all of his research projects, Koselleck attempted to think of these dichotomies in convergence,[111] either alone or in collaboration with scholars who belonged neither to the social science nor to the linguistic turn discourse. One of these scholars is the historian, Christian Meier (b. 1929), a long-time friend of Koselleck's, to whom the cited article "Sprachgeschichte und Ereignis" is dedicated.[112] A specialist in the Classic Athens and the late Roman Republic, Meier's work is similar to Koselleck's in that it combines broad thematic interests (including studies of constitutional history, "the political," and parliamentary democracy) and generalizing interpretations of historical epochs with reflections on the narrative dimensions of historical writing. Meier was also a member of Poetik und Hermeneutik and Theorie der Geschichte, and, due to his expertise in the Classic Athens and the late Roman Republic, he became one of Koselleck's key collaborators on the *Geschichtliche Grundbegriffe*.

While Koselleck was attempting to navigate between what he saw as too scientific or relativistic approaches to historical writing, he collaborated in various projects from the 1960s to the 1980s with several like-minded scholars. However, in this period, he was arguably the representative of the historical profession in Germany (and perhaps even internationally), who most systematically tried to carve out a position that insisted on both the scientific and the relativistic character of historical writing. Interestingly, in contrast to the way in which he conceptualized most other theoretical matters, in respect to the theory of historical writing, Koselleck did not make use of his familiar household sources of inspiration—his teachers in a broad sense, ranging from Heidegger and Schmitt to Gadamer and Löwith. Instead, he predominantly referred to an entirely different range of scholars, from Chladenius to Christian Meier. Still, it is perhaps appropriate to point out that one of the group of teachers articulated views that are very similar to Koselleck's: Johannes Kühn, who had taught him the methods of source criticism. Consider for example the following passage from Kühn's *Toleranz und Offenbarung*:

[My] work deviates perhaps in composition and aim from other historical works of the more narrow discipline. It does not intend, though, to develop something like a "new method." Besides the indispensable philological fundament, I am convinced that there is no such a thing as "the method," but that the ways depart and branch out depending on whether the scholar focuses on the stage of history, its characters and its tremors, or rather on historical "causalities" or general "trends" or on invariable forms of historical life etc. They all have their legitimacy and their limits. It is not about finding "the right method," but to remain conscious of the limits of the method that has been chosen with good reason and with respect to the subject matter and the scholarly aim.[113]

The idea of methodical "tolerance," as one might put it, that Kühn formulated in these lines seems very akin to Koselleck's insistence on pluralism and the continuous search for conceptual models that are specifically adapted to the sources of a particular historical project. The passage lays open a subtle process of reception that marks Koselleck's theoretical position as one of tolerance, too. For both scholars, the particular conditions and needs of particular projects called for different conceptualizations; there were no valid models of conceptual thought that all historical writing could follow, and there was no alternative to a pluralism of methods.

Reinhart Koselleck at the University of Bielefeld

Koselleck's essays on historical writing have been increasingly referred to by German historians since the 1980s, but were also out of tune with the disciplinary discussions and trends in the 1970s. This was not least the case at the University of Bielefeld to which Koselleck transferred in 1973. Focusing on the intellectual-institutional activities and the academic-social constellations that he entered, the following sections illuminate the ways in which his stay in Bielefeld was important for his identity in the discipline, his modes of self-representation, and his work. We begin with a brief introduction to the foundation of the university in the late 1960s, and then follow a perspective on Koselleck's various activities at the institution and on his disagreements with the *Gesellschaftshistoriker* at the department of history in the 1970s. Finally, this chapter offers a view on how Koselleck's status in German and international academia changed from the 1980s onwards while he maintained the same style of self-representation.

The University of Bielefeld was founded in 1969 in relation to the contemporary processes of reform of the German university sector. As proposed by its *spiritus rector*, the sociologist Helmut Schelsky, and the founding commission, the purpose of the university was to practice a different form of organization and teaching than that which characterized the established universities. The main aims were to create a stronger unity between research and teaching, to focus on the theory of the various disciplines and to promote interdisciplinary work. The latter was to be facilitated by the so-called Zentrum for Interdisciplinäre Forschung (ZIF) and a university architecture that encloses all faculties in one great structure, constructed in a typically 1960s mode in concrete.[114]

The department of history was also to be given an innovative profile. One of the central actors in defining this profile was Werner Conze, who was a member of the founding commission from 1965 until 1968, when, due to his rector candidature at the University of Heidelberg, he withdrew from the commission. Conze was replaced by Koselleck, who also was the chairman of the advisory board for the department of history.[115] In a 1979 status report on the first decade of the department, Koselleck has described how the planners agreed on a disciplinary profile that was broadly in tune with the main developments in the German historical profession that had been taking place since the late 1950s: "There was an agreement that the historical science in Bielefeld was not to be oriented toward the pure history of events, that the questions of the traditional history of politics and ideas were not to be in the center of its research and that the traditional hermeneutic approaches were to be complemented through social-scientific methods. This was a conscious scientific-political decision that gave the faculty its profile."[116]

With this profile as its basis, the faculty was officially founded on 17 April 1973. Taking up what was at the time the only existing chair in Germany in historical theory,[117] Koselleck stayed in Bielefeld until he retired in 1988, and his fifteen years as a professor there were in many ways successful. On the one hand, through his institutional activities, both within the department and in the ZIF, he was instrumental in making the department of history in Bielefeld a renowned institution in Germany and around the world. On the other hand, by means of various research projects, including the *Geschichtliche Grundbegriffe*, his work on theories of historical time, and his studies of war memorials, he managed to substantially enlarge and develop his scholarly production. Accordingly, together with Hans-Ulrich Wehler, the sociologist Niklas Luhmann, the literary scholar Karl-Heinz Bohrer, and the pedagogue Hartmut von Hentig, Koselleck is today remembered as one of the outstanding scholars in the history of the University of Bielefeld.[118]

However, the fifteen years in Bielefeld also included many frustrating and disappointing experiences for Koselleck. This was first of all the case in respect to the processes of institutional reform in the 1970s. In the beginning of the decade, Koselleck made a passionate contribution to the discussion of how the university system, including the history curriculum, could be renewed and improved.[119] However, at the same time, as he told Carl Schmitt in a letter from July 1973, he was uncertain what to expect from what he labeled the "the comprehensive university (*Gesamthochschule*) forced by the SPD-government."[120] One of the problems that Koselleck saw in the university plans was that the increased teaching obligations might turn the professors into mere *Studienräte im Hochschuldienst* (schoolteachers).[121] "During my time in Bielefeld," he consequently wrote to Schmitt, "it has come to seem more and more questionable to me, whether it will be possible to maintain the concept of a research-intensive university."

After only a few years in Bielefeld, Koselleck saw his apprehensions on this issue justified, as he in the earlier cited status report described the increased teaching obligations as harmful for the department, because, along with the time-consuming processes of administration, they had severely undermined the dimension of research.[122] At this time, Koselleck was moreover deeply disappointed that several of the planned institutional arrangements had been subject to change or never realized. Of the many divergences from the founding concepts, the cancelation of the planned chair in art history was purportedly the greatest blow for him.[123]

While it is evident that Koselleck was dissatisfied with the direction that the university reforms took in the 1970s, it is also obvious that he was more interested in studying modern bureaucracy than being part of it. Koselleck felt much more at home as a scholar in the seminar or the archive than as an administrator in the meeting room, and in comparison with many of his colleagues, he was more interested in pursuing his own research than in designing the department according to his personal interests.

This brings us to another source of frustration for Koselleck in Bielefeld: his many disagreements with his colleague Hans-Ulrich Wehler. Koselleck had actively supported hiring Wehler as a professor with a special focus on the nineteenth and twentieth century. In the late 1960s, Wehler had with some difficulties acquired his first position as a professor of American history at the Free University in Berlin. Nevertheless, when he was offered the position in Bielefeld in the early 1970s, he was happy to leave Berlin for Bielefeld, where he would be able to participate in designing a departmental profile without being bound to the usual auspices of tradition.[124] In Bielefeld, Wehler teamed up with Jürgen Kocka, who in 1973 took up the chair in modern history. As they attempted to redefine the profile of the historical profession, scholars in Germany and abroad soon began to associate the department of history in Bielefeld with a so-called Bielefeld School of *Gesellschaftsgeschichte*.[125]

However, the department was in reality composed of several different schools, or directions. Koselleck was not considered (and never considered himself) a member of the Bielefeld School. His initial motivation for inviting Wehler to Bielefeld was presumably that he saw in the latter a scholar, who, like himself, sought to go beyond a pure history of events and politics and practice a more theoretical, interdisciplinary and social-historical approach. However, it soon turned out that the disagreements between their projects and personalities by far overshadowed the similarities and ultimately prevented close academic cooperation between the two. In fact, according to a 1998 interview with Koselleck, he and Wehler taught separate seminars, pursued different research projects, ran different publication series, and worked with two largely separate groups of assistants and students.[126]

Wehler and Koselleck did little to hide the reservations they nurtured toward each other's academic activities. Most famously, at the moment Wehler was positioning himself in the discipline, he warned in his *Krisenherde des Kaiserreichs* (1970) of certain dangers that he saw in the contemporary conceptual-historical projects. More specifically, relating the approach in the conceptual lexicons to that of historicism, Wehler stated that the hermeneutic approach of conceptual history diverts attention away from the real problems in society, and he polemically prophesied that: ". . . an exaggerated conceptual history, just like the history of ideas after The First World War, according to its scientific-political function will lead to a renewed escape from the real problems of history into the world of ideas. It will be a road to a cul-de-sac, of which one clearly can see the end."[127]

The publication of the first volumes of the *Geschichtliche Grundbegriffe* did not make Wehler change his opinion: He still detected in conceptual history an old-fashioned, naïve, and politically irresponsible way of historical writing. He thus republished the above-cited passage, and this time with direct reference to Koselleck and the *Geschichtliche Grundbegriffe*, in Habermas's famous anthology *Stichwörter zur geistigen Situation der Zeit* from 1979.[128] The aim of the anthology was to counter how the so-called *Tendenzwende* taking place in the 1970s had allegedly strengthened the conservative intellectual-political camp in Germany, symbolized for instance by the influence of Carl Schmitt on the contemporary debates.[129] In addition, in a 1969 essay, Wehler had already criticized the group of scholars, including Koselleck, who had contributed to the Schmitt-Festschrifts (Wehler called these publications a scandal).[130] Finally, in the 1980s, in the first volumes of his *Deutsche Gesellschaftsge-*

schichte, Wehler refuted Koselleck's idea in *Preußen zwischen Reform und Revolution* that the state played a key role in shaping civil society in the German *Vormärz*.[131]

Seen from Wehler's perspective, historicism, Carl Schmitt, and the Prussian attempt to deal with modernity all formed parts of the dangerous German *Sonderweg* from which nothing valuable could be retrieved.[132] Seen from Koselleck's perspective, things were more complex, and he disagreed strongly with Wehler's *Sonderweg* thesis. In fact, this thesis constituted one of the centers of conflict between the two.

As earlier mentioned, after Germany's defeat in World War II in 1945, the term *Sonderweg* gradually lost its positive connotations. As scholars began to probe the origins of the "German catastrophe" by examining why German democracy failed during the Weimar Republic and National Socialism arose, many historians came to the conclusion that the failure of a strong and authoritarian Germany to develop firm democratic institutions in the nineteenth century should be considered a cause of special national developments.[133]

In the 1960s, Wehler emerged as one of the staunchest critics of what he saw as the negative characteristics of a unique German *Sonderweg*. In line with Hans Rosenberg and Eckart Kehr, he criticized Prussian-German militarism and the persistent social and political influence of the reactionary Prussian Junkers in a rapidly industrializing German Empire. According to Wehler, unlike France and the United Kingdom, Germany had experienced only partial modernization, in that industrialization was not followed by changes in the political and social spheres. Instead, these spheres continued to be dominated by the pre-modern aristocratic elite, who tried to compensate for the lack of democracy and transcend deep social and political divisions by promoting popular hostility toward internal and external enemies. Wehler further claimed that the peculiarities of this German *Sonderweg* led to the failure of the Weimar Republic in the twentieth century and moreover paved the way for the dictatorial structures and the exaggerated quest for glory and power characterizing National Socialism.

After this line of interpretation in the 1970s developed into something like a new orthodoxy in the writing of German history, it was challenged from several sides.[134] Among the staunches critiques of the *Sonderweg* thesis were the two British historians Geoff Eley and David Blackbourn, who argued that there is no normal path of social and political change: that the experience of France and Britain was not, as the *Gesellschaftshistoriker* believed, the norm for Europe.[135] In particular Eley and Blackbourn contested the *Gesellschaftshistoriker*'s idea of a failed bourgeois revolution, which implies that all modern societies must pass through a bourgeois revolution of the British or French type, thus suggesting a necessary connection among bourgeois domination, industrial modernization, and liberal politics. Instead, they argued that even if the liberal bourgeoisie was disempowered at the national political level, it dominated the social, economic and cultural life of nineteenth-century Germany, and that this embourgeoisement of German social life was greater than in Britain and France, where aristocratic values were more widespread than was the case in Germany.

Thomas Nipperdey launched a counterpart to Blackbourn and Eley's critique of the *Sonderweg* thesis by questioning the portrayal of the German bourgeoisie as weak and feudalized and by stressing the Empire's potential for democratic and liberal reform.[136] Finally, from the late 1970s onwards, a number of scholars, including the American historian James Sheehan, sought to counter the *Sonderweg* thesis by arguing "that the leitmotif of German history was a persistent struggle between centripetal and centrifugal forces—the former tending toward national unification, the latter reinforcing Germany's traditional fragmentation and decentralization."[137]

Overlapping with the other critiques launched at the thesis, Koselleck's disagreements with the *Sonderweg* thesis were of three kinds. On the level of interpretation, he placed a much stronger emphasis on the European character of modern German history, and he evaluated certain aspects of this, such as the Prussian attempt to deal with modernity, from a much more positive perspective than the *Gesellschaftshistoriker*. On a normative level, he thought it possible to salvage usable insights from this and other experiences in recent German history, as well as from politically compromised figures such as Schmitt and Heidegger, whom the *Gesellschaftshistoriker* unequivocally denounced as components of the German *Sonderweg*. Finally, on a theoretical level, Koselleck disagreed with the conceptualization of history that is embodied in the *Sonderweg* thesis.

Koselleck's theoretical disagreement was closely related to his temporal theorizing. One might even go so far as to claim that the *Sonderweg* thesis of the Bielefeld *Gesellschaftsgeschichte* provided a decisive reason for him to prioritize the theory of historical times in his research from the 1970s onwards. In this way, the landscape of polemics, centered on Bielefeld, contributed immensely to his scholarly oeuvre. However, it was only much later, in 1998, when he attacked Wehler and Kocka in an interview and in a published text, that he made this connection explicit. In the interview, Koselleck stated that, in his discussions with the *Gesellschaftshistoriker* in Bielefeld, he simply denied the existence of a German *Sonderweg*, and in the text he moreover expressed his profound reservations both toward the notion and its creators by labeling the *Sonderweg* thesis an "ideology of 68."[138]

The text at issue is the article "Deutschland—eine verspätete Nation?"[139] As indicated in the title, the article is not structured around a direct polemic with the *Gesellschaftshistoriker*, but around a discussion of Helmut Plessner's famous work *Das Schicksal des deutschen Geistes im Ausgang seiner bürgerlichen Epoche* from 1935, which in 1959 was republished with the new title *Die verspätete Nation*.[140] While Koselleck praised Plessner's attempt to place German history in relation to European history, he was critical of the new title of the book: *Die verspätete Nation*. More concretely, he disliked the temporal assumptions encapsulated in the title, because he found it impossible to determine whether something occurs too early or too late, and to argue that Germany's development was *verspätet* (belated) which presupposes the existence of a pre-given timetable, destination, and aim in history, toward which nations can always orient themselves. Refuting the existence of such teleological ideas of history, Koselleck labeled *Die verspätete Nation* a theoretically weak, but morally and normatively effective category: "It proclaims an exclusive theology ex post, which only allows two options: completion or failure. This coerced alternative has on top of that the argumentative advantage that those who use it will always be right."[141]

According to Koselleck, in his search for sociological and cultural explanations for the German development, Plessner had in fact avoided such a teleological, normative, and theoretically weak conception of historical writing. As such, his analysis had implicitly distanced itself from what Koselleck with deep antipathy labeled an ideology that "after 1968 proliferated without any criticism in Germany: the ideology of the German *Sonderweg*."[142]

Koselleck continued this polemic against the *Gesellschaftshistoriker* with a harsh critique of what he saw as three fundamental theoretical weaknesses in the *Sonderweg* thesis. He first argued that the idea of a German *Sonderweg* necessitates the conclusion that all national histories have followed a unique path, given that all nations are characterized by chains of events that differ from those of other nations. Secondly, according to Koselleck, if various nations are compared in order to identify certain structural differences or similarities, the result can never be an entirely unique *Sonderweg*, as minimal structural similarities must always be presupposed to establish differences. Thirdly, the *Sonderweg* thesis is, he stated, devoid of a theoretical imperative as to how far back in history in terms of events and personalities one must go to construct such a special path. He wrote: "From a theoretical perspective, there is no mandatory beginning of a causal chain that can be constructed ex ante. For each event and for each chain of events there can be summoned as many reasons as there has been events and as there can be made connections between them."[143]

In the opinion of Koselleck, all these theoretical insufficiencies of the *Sonderweg* thesis amounted to a fatal moral insufficiency. More concretely, according to Koselleck, the proponents of the thesis to some degree free the perpetrators in modern German history from responsibility for their actions by placing them within a causal and pre-given model of history that exclude the possibility of alternative developments and of individual agency: "As such," Koselleck concludes, "the moral challenge that the *Sonderweg* thesis is supposed to answer, crumbles completely."[144]

As in the earlier mentioned article "Diesseits des Nationalstaates," Koselleck proposed in "Deutschland—eine verspätete Nation?" to replace the *Sonderweg* thesis with a focus on federal structures as a feature that distinguishes German history, because they prevented the foundation of a national state, similarly to those of the neighboring countries. This proposal, and the critique of the *Sonderweg* thesis more generally, served not only as a continuation of Koselleck's ambition to replace ideas of history in the singular with an idea of history's formalistic and pluralistic structures, but also as a line of interpretation that carved out a space for the more positive interpretation of certain aspects in modern German history that is also present in his other writings. This is to say that both articles illustrate that just like Wehler and Kocka, Koselleck remained strongly focused on problems of German national history. Indeed, the entire *Sonderweg* debate was located not beyond, but indeed still on this side of the national state. This helps to account for the intense, tenacious, and partly politicized character of the polemics that surrounded the issue.

However, representing by far the most polemic critique that Koselleck ever launched in public against other scholars, the article should presumably not only be read as an expression of his disagreements with the *Gesellschaftshistoriker*, but also as a reaction to the critiques that had been launched against his work and to the more personal tensions at Bielefeld, where Koselleck in the 1970s felt marginalized by the *Gesellschaftshistoriker* and out of tune with broader disciplinary developments.[145] However, Koselleck also helped to construct a position that fell outside the boundaries of the more fashionable programs of the period. A vital decision that he took in this respect was to downplay the dimensions of his work that connected to the more traditional forms of historical writing and to the current trends, such as the social-historical approach unfolded in *Preußen zwischen Reform und Revolution*, on behalf of research projects that did not connect to mainstream historical writing and hence made it difficult for other historians to communicate with him. Hence, observing the growing gap between Koselleck's projects and mainstream historical writing during the 1970s, Christian Meier recently questioned "if it was necessary and right to leave the entire conventional terrain of historical science due to the challenge of the social sciences in order to focus on the historical times."[146]

Meier views the increasing specialization in Koselleck's work as related to a defensive position vis-à-vis the disciplinary developments in the 1970s. It might thus also be possible to interpret the specialization as a means with which Koselleck tried to overcome the ideological tensions and polemical confrontations of the period and cope with the disappointing experience of moving from Heidelberg, the center of philosophy, hermeneutics and *Bildung*, to Bielefeld, where the social sciences were held in higher esteem. To be sure, as stated by Stefan Ludwig Hoffman: "Heidelberg, more than Bielefeld, remained his intellectual home for most of his life."[147]

Correspondingly, it is possible to interpret both Koselleck's later reputation as an outsider and his contemporary reflections on the role of the "vanquished" in history as related to his experiences in Bielefeld.[148] However, even if such links can be made, it should be emphasized that Koselleck was in fact a very established scholar in German academia in the 1970s and 1980s, when, in collaboration with a wide range of scholars, he was involved in several research projects and institutions, both in and outside Bielefeld. As for the latter, he remained a very active member of the Arbeitskreis für moderne Sozialgeschichte, in which the successful enterprise *Geschichtliche Grundbegriffe* was flourishing; he continued to participate in conferences organized by Poetik und Hermeneutik; he was until 1978 on the editorial board of the journal *Die Verwaltung*; he was in the 1970s and 1980s a member of Theorie der Geschichte; and together with an interdisciplinary group of scholars, including François Furet, Hans Robert Jauss, Hermann Lübbe, Thomas Luckmann, and Christian Meier, he edited the publication series *Sprache und Geschichte* with Klett-Cotta in Stuttgart.

In Bielefeld, Koselleck not only pursued his academic interests at the department, but also in colloquiums hosted in his villa (in the borough Stieghorst) and in the ZIF, of which he was a director from 1975 until 1979.[149] Moreover, in between 1971 and 1988, he was involved in organizing no less than thirteen events within the ZIF: eight so-called research groups, two research-years, and three author-colloquiums. The first event was an author-colloquium featuring Norbert Elias in April 1971 titled "Soziologie und Geschichte" that Koselleck organized with the sociologist Othein Rammstedt; the last was another author-colloquium in June/July 1988 titled "Zeit der Geschichte—Geschichte der Zeit" that was organized by Lucian Hölscher and in which Koselleck's work was at debate.

As for the eleven events taking place in the period between the two author-colloquiums, Koselleck either organized these alone and/or in co-operation with scholars outside of the department or outside of Biele-feld—never with his colleagues from the department. Among his collabo-rators were the art historians Max Ihmdahl and P. A. Riedl with whom he in 1976 organized a research group on "Todesbilder und Totenmale"; the natural scientists Ludwig Streit and Phillippe Blanchard with whom Koselleck in 1982 arranged a research group focusing on "Die Neutron-enwaffen";[150] and his former student Rolf Reichardt with whom in 1985 he organized the research group "Die Französische Revolution als Um-bruch des gesellschaftlichen Bewußtseins".[151] All in all, Koselleck's many activities in the ZIF testify to the broadness of the topical interests that he cultivated from the 1970s to the 1990s, as well as to the way in which his academic network in this period extended far beyond the department of history at Bielefeld.[152]

Among those colleagues at the department with whom Koselleck did collaborate was Klaus Schreiner, who held a chair in medieval history. Sharing Koselleck's interest in the history of art and language, Schreiner contributed to the *Geschichtliche Grundbegriffe* and together with Ko-selleck, he edited the 1994 volume *Bürgerschaft*.[153] The volume was part of a larger research project on the *Sozialgeschichte des neuzeitlichen Bürger-tums*, which was conceptualized in the Arbeitskreis für moderne Sozial-geschichte and carried out in a research project in the ZIF under the aus-pices of Jürgen Kocka in 1987 and 1988. While Wehler and Kocka dealt with social-historical aspects,[154] Koselleck and Schreiner focused on the semantics of the *Bürgertum*, and in addition Koselleck edited a volume titled *Bildungsgüter und Bildungswissen* that focused on cultural aspects of the *Bildungsbürgertum*.[155]

Many of the students whose dissertations and/or *Habilitationen* Ko-selleck had supervised since the late 1960s contributed to his volumes on the *Bürgertum* and the *Bildungsbürgertum*. Among these students were Ute Daniel, Jörg Fisch, Jochen Hoock, Lucian Hölscher, Michael Jeismann, Heinz-Dieter Kittsteiner, Josef Mooser, Martin Papenheim, Ulrike Spree, Monica Wienfort, and Willibald Steinmetz. Several of these figures col-laborated in various projects with Koselleck and pursued in their own work a range of themes, theories, and methods from his oeuvre, which was met with increasing interest among scholars both in Germany and abroad during the 1970s and 1980s.

This development had to do with larger structural shifts taking place in the cultural and human sciences in many countries. Whereas scholars had primarily been oriented toward the social sciences in the 1960s, the advent of the so-called linguistic and cultural turns in the 1970s meant that it became increasingly fashionable to stress the importance of language and culture in human affairs and to work from a more constructivist epistemology.[156] The interest in topics related to language was pioneered first of all by Michel Foucault, Hayden White, Jacques Derrida, Quentin Skinner, and John Pocock. The interest in cultural history was likewise pioneered by a diverse group of scholars, including the anthropologist Clifford Geertz, the sociologist Pierre Bourdieu, and historians such as Emmanuel Le Roy Ladurie, Natalie Zemon Davis, and Carlo Ginzburg, who portrayed cultural phenomena, such as rituals and so-called social capital and mentalities, as integral to human thought and action.

The linguistic and cultural turns were also met with a growing interest among German historians from the early 1980s onwards. Together with his students and his colleagues, Koselleck helped spur this interest—in Bielefeld and beyond. Koselleck's position in Bielefeld in these years might have been that of an outsider, seen from the point of view of the social historians. But at the same time his work on the role of language, identity, and political iconography became crucial orientation points for a younger generation of scholars in Germany. It was to a great extent in dialogues with Koselleck and his work that this younger generation, with whom Koselleck increasingly interacted as the older colleagues died away, attempted to challenge and go beyond the dominance of social scientific approaches as well as older forms of writing history.

The social historians were also challenged by representatives of the ethnological-anthropological framed approach known as *Alltagsgeschichte*.[157] The approach was a part of an international trend or movement of historical writing that began in the 1970s as a political and a scientific project in history workshops. These workshops aimed at a detailed reconstruction of the social practices, beliefs, and feelings of those individuals and groups, primarily from the lower classes, which had been neglected in the systematic research of political events and social structures. The *Alltagshistoriker* questioned universal interpretational models and notions of progress in human history. Instead of focusing on quantitative material and on overarching analytical explanations for historical change, they welcomed a return to narrative in historical writing and put an emphasis on discontinuity and contingency in history. These programmatic features reflected some of the broader changes in international historiography taking place in the 1970s and 1980s, when the interest in social history decreased because of a tighter focus on themes related to the cultural and linguistic turn.[158]

After a German debate about *Alltagsgeschichte* began at the 1984 *Historikertag* in Berlin, Wehler and Kocka soon after argued that the approach was characterized by both a lack of relevance, theoretical-methodological inadequacies and potential political dangers. However, they could not prevent the ending, in Germany as in other European countries, of an era of social-science oriented history in the mid 1980s.

Koselleck was also critical toward some of the new trends, such as the radical relativism voiced by linguistic-turn scholars or the unwillingness among historians of everyday life to connect micro-perspectives to broader generalizations. Yet his work communicated better with the disciplinary changes than Wehler and Kocka's, and the increased focus on language and culture helped prepare the ground for a more favorable attitude toward his work in German and international academia. His reputation as an innovative scholar was consequently boosted and broadened from the late 1970s onwards, in the sense that his oeuvre was no longer merely connected to conceptual history and the *Geschichtliche Grundbegriffe*.

Important for this development was first of all the publication of *Vergangene Zukunft* in 1979. Although the concerns of the book did not fit mainstream German historical writing, *Vergangene Zukunft*, it received much praise and recognition among the reviewers. And even if they did not all agree with Karl-Georg Faber, who labeled the essay collection "the most important German contribution to a theory of historical writing (*Geschichtswissenschaft*) in the last two decades," the book made it difficult not to count Koselleck among the most important and innovative German historians of his time.[159]

This was also the case outside Germany, where Koselleck's writings were read by scholars from many different disciplines during the 1980s.[160] In fact, when Koselleck turned sixty-five in 1988 and was therefore forced to retire from his professorial chair in Bielefeld,[161] his work had won a degree of international admiration that enabled him to begin something like a second career as a guest professor and lecturer at academic institutions in a various countries around the world such as the United States, France, and Israel.

However, in spite of his increased fame and the many awards and memberships that he received by various scientific boards and societies, Koselleck continued to portray and think of himself as an outsider in the field: as someone whose work was and had always been out of tune with that of his colleagues in the profession. This self-conception was first of all articulated in a famous 1993 talk that he gave in the Weimar Goethe-Gesellschaft titled "Goethes unzeitgemäße Geschichte" and later published in an enlarged book version.[162] Although Koselleck spoke exclusively about Goethe, the talk was clearly dosed with a subtle, but nevertheless tangible autobiographical subtext that he communicated via his subject. Koselleck had on earlier occasions qualified arguments by bringing into play figures such as Lorenz von Stein, with whom he felt intellectually affiliated. This time around, however, Koselleck went a step further in stressing historical parallels, using Goethe as a mirror in which he reflected himself by means of unfolding a comprehensive interpretation and evaluation of his lifelong activities as a historian.

The procedure, it should be emphasized, had a deeper cultural meaning, as with his speech Koselleck embraced a long-standing German tradition of describing oneself through analyzing Goethe. This tradition was present in literature, very prominently for instance in the case of Thomas Mann, as well as in historical writing—for instance in the case of Friedrich Meinecke, whose *Historismus* study culminated in a lengthy description of Goethe's oeuvre as the culmination and achievement of historical thought.[163] This was a very important tradition of identification with the Enlightenment world of thought of classical Germany; and it was a tradition that was very bourgeois. In the 1950s, Koselleck would presumably have been very skeptical of it. But at the time of his Goethe speech, this skepticism appears mitigated. Thus, he entirely avoided taking issue with Meinecke or with other predecessors in the field. Still, the main aim of his speech was to dissociate Goethe from all the movements, schools, and directions of his time. More concretely, Koselleck sought to illuminate how Goethe had experienced, lived and understood history, in ways that were in various ways *unzeitgemäß* (untimely), that is, out of tune with the time in which Goethe lived.

The first part of the speech focused on the relation between Goethe's life and the history of his time, and Koselleck began this part by stating that viewed from outside it might appear as if Goethe's life story, his upbringing in the *Bürgerstand*, and his successful career in the government of Sachsen-Weimar had by and large been timely. However, according to Koselleck, because of his skeptical attitude toward the French Revolution, Goethe was soon deemed untimely by his contemporaries: "From the perspective of those who were insignificant before the French Revolution, but grew with it, Goethe belonged to the conservative, counter-revolutionary, anti-patriotic corner. In modern terms, he was ideological-critically labeled as untimely."[164]

According to Koselleck, the contemporary judgment of Goethe as a conservative counter-revolutionary had to do with the rise of historical philosophy and the related trend of accusing people for thinking and acting in ways that was deemed wrong. Whereas other Enlightenment thinkers evaluated the past and the present by means of strong dichotomies and as necessary transition phases to a better future, Goethe viewed the contemporary developments from the perspective that every death was one too many, regardless of the political orientation of the deceased. And because Goethe, who repeatedly uttered statements claiming all history is chaotic and absurd, refrained from teleological interpretations of history that were motivated by a particular political viewpoint, it was allegedly impossible to subject Goethe to ideological critique. This was, Koselleck argued, one of the ways in which Goethe was *unzeitgemäß*.

Goethe's untimely quality, Koselleck added, was related to his ability to reflect on his life and work. According to Koselleck, the decisive insight that Goethe drew from these reflections was that history must continually be rewritten, because changing conditions and experiences repeatedly generate new questions and answers, and because words continually change their meanings, even after they have been written down. It was with this insight in mind, Koselleck stated, that Goethe always aimed at controlling and questioning his own history as *Wirkungsgeschichte* (a history of reception).

In the second part of the speech, Koselleck turned to thematize how Goethe's ways of interpreting and understanding of history had been untimely. Here Koselleck pointed to how, instead of developing an elaborate methodological system, Goethe embedded his *Erkenntnistheorie* (epistemology) in anthropological assumptions. More concretely, Goethe worked with conceptual parts that were dynamically related to each other. Among the central categories that allowed Goethe to perceive history as both singular and repetitive and thereby describe new historical constellations, without subscribing to a finalistic vision of history, were "formal oppositional pairs: inside/outside, above/below, sooner/later, with which Goethe deciphered all conditions of possible history."[165]

In addition, according to Koselleck, Goethe did not exclude the possibility of progress, but knew "neither the progress of history nor a history of progress."[166] And when Goethe refrained from commenting on current political events, Koselleck added, it was because his anthropologically based conception of history rather focused on long durations and repetitive structures. Goethe thus uncovered social and political changes as ruptures in geological layers that encompass repetitive structures, allowing for a prognosis for the future, but not a total prediction of later events. In line with this, aiming to uncover deeper mental and social structures, such as the murderous mechanisms at play during civil wars or the disintegration of bourgeois society, Goethe's historical writing was in fact political, but in a less activist and self-assured way than his contemporaries. In Koselleck's estimation, Goethe's conception of historical writing was likewise less self-confident and more complex than the conceptions of his contemporaries. Goethe saw historical writing composed not by fundamental oppositions between fact and fiction, past and present, objectivity and partisanship, but as created in mediation between these dichotomies. This was yet another reason why Goethe, in Koselleck's opinion, had been untimely in comparison to his contemporaries.

Listing all Goethe's untimely qualities altogether clearly points to an interpretation of the speech as a document to Koselleck's self-conception in the early 1990s, showing how he interpreted his (lack of) ideological-political position, his theoretical-methodological framework, his themes and interpretations, his concern for human death, and his reflections on the relation between historical experience and historical writing as features that had always been out of tune with the contexts in which he moved and the times in which he lived.

Although it is devoid of reflections on the many coincidences and changes involved in his academic career and historical writing, Koselleck's self-interpretation in the speech seems in several ways fitting. However, his strong insistence on having been untimely comes across as somewhat striking. Hence, it would certainly be possible to argue that Koselleck was not always an untimely outsider in the German historical profession. This was for example not the case within the Arbeitskreis in the later 1950s and during the 1960s, where his work in fact sat well with the mainstream. Even in the 1970s, when discursive features from the social sciences were taken up in the historical profession and Koselleck felt marginalized at the department of history at Bielefeld, he had an ongoing and fruitful communication and collaboration with a huge number of scholars both inside and outside of the university and influenced a number of significant research agendas. In light of this, he was not always as *unzeitgemäß* as he later claimed.

Notes

1. For overviews of the discussions related to the identity crisis, see Arnold Sywottek, *Geschichtswissenschaft in der Legitimationskrise: Ein Überblick über die Diskussion um Theorie und Didaktik der Geschichte in der Bundesrepublik Deutschland 1969–1973* (Bonn-Bad Godesberg, 1974); and Günter Heydemann, *Geschichtswissenschaft im geteilten Deutschland. Entwicklungsgeschichte, Organisationsstruktur, Funktionen, Theorie- und Methodenprobleme in der Bundesrepublik Deutschland und in der DDR* (Frankfurt am Main, 1980).
2. For a broad view of the German education system since 1945, see Christof Führ and Carl-Ludwig Furck, eds., *Handbuch der deutschen Bildungsgeschichte, Bd. VI. 1945 bis zur Gegenwart. Erster Teilband. Bundesrepublik Deutschland* (München, 1988).
3. See Etzemüller, *Sozialgeschichte als Politische Geschichte*, 328–35.
4. See Hohls, *Versäumte Frage*.

5. Fritz Fischer, *Griff nach der Weltmacht: Die Kriegszielpolitik des kaiserlichen Deutschland 1914–18* (Düsseldorf, 1961).
6. See Klaus Große Kracht, *Die Zankende Zunft: historische Kontroverse in Deutschland nach 1945* (Göttingen, 2005), 47–67.
7. Sometimes other labels were used to name the approach. Wehler for example often spoke of his approach as a *Historische Sozialwissenschaft*, while Kocka spoke of his as *Sozialgeschichte*.
8. See Thomas Welskopp, "Westbindung auf dem 'Sonderweg': Die deutsche Sozialge-schichte vom Appendix der Wirtschaftsgeschichte," in *Geschichtsdiskurs. Bd 5. Globale Konflikte, Erinnerungsarbeit und Neuorientierungen seit 1945*, ed. Wolfgang Küttler, Jörn Rüsen, and Ernst Schulin, 191–237 (Frankfurt am Main, 1997). Welskopp outlines all in all ten characteristics of *Gesellschaftsgeschichte*.
9. Wehler also polemicized against what he saw as Conze's insufficient conception of society and social history. See Hans-Ulrich Wehler, "Geschichtswissenschaft Heute," in *Stichwörter zur Geistigen Situation der Zeit. Bd. 2*, ed. Jürgen Habermas, 714–26 (notes) (Frankfurt Am Main, 1979).
10. For the international expansion of social history between the 1950s and the 1980s, see Christoph Conrad, "Social History," in *International Encyclopaedia of the Social and Behavioural Sciences*, vol. 21, ed. N. J. Smelser and P. B. Baltes, 14299–306 (Oxford, 2001); Raphael, *Geschichtswissenschaft*, 173–95.
11. Rolf Wiggershaus, *The Frankfurt School: Its History, Theories and Political Significance* (Cambridge, 1995); and Martin Jay, *The Dialectical Imagination: A History of the Frankfurt School and the Institute for Social Research 1923–1950* (Berkeley, 1996).
12. Norbert Frei, *1968: Jugendrevolte und globaler Protest* (München, 2008).
13. Moses, *German Intellectuals*, 186–88.
14. Martin Vengeler, "'1968' als sprachgeschichtliche Zäsur," in *Kontroverse Begriffe: Geschichte des öffentlichen Sprachgebrauchs in der Bundesrepublik Deutschland*, ed. Georg Stötzel and Martin Vengeler, 383–404 (Berlin, 1995).
15. One prominent example is the political scientist Wilhelm Hennis. See Schlak, *Wilhelm Hennis*, 117–87. For an account of the reactions toward '68' in German academia, see Moses, *German Intellectuals*, 186–218.
16. At an SDS congress after the death of Benny Ohnesorg, Habermas characterized the voluntaristic strategies of direct actions as proposed by the student leader, Rudi Dutsche, as "left fascism," and as such distanced himself from the radical measures taken by the 68ers.
17. The following draws on the informative account of the developments within the discipline around 1968 in Kracht, *Die Zankende Zunft*, 69–90.
18. Hans-Ulrich Wehler, "Historiker sollten auch politisch zu den Positionen stehen, die sie in der Wissenschaft vertreten," *Versäumte Fragen: Deutsche Historiker im Schatten des Nationalsozialismus*, ed. Rüdiger Hohls and Konrad H. Jarausch, 252–53 (Stuttgart, 2000).
19. Thus, Moses, *German Intellectuals*, 205–06. The above account of the *Bund Freiheit der Wissenschaften* follows Moses's excellent overview.
20. Between 1963 and 1969, Lübbe was professor in Bochum. From 1966, he also held a cultural-ministerial post in North Rhine-Westphalia, but resigned in 1969 after his education reform proposal was amended against his will. The same year he became secretary of state at the prime minister (a position he gave up in 1970) and became a professor in philosophy at the University of Bielefeld. From 1971 until he became emeritus in 1991, he was a professor in philosophy and political theory at the University of Zürich. A professor in Gießen (1962), in Karlsruhe (1963), at the Free

University in Berlin (1967) and in München (1971), Nipperdey is today first of all remembered for his earlier mentioned three-volume *Deutsche Geschichte 1800–1918*. In spite of what is often described as a conservative outlook and affiliations, he was a member of the SPD.

21. See Kracht, *Die Zankende Zunft*, 6–90, on which the following account of the discussions among the *Gesellschaftshistoriker* and Nipperdey and Hillgrüber/Hildebrand is based.

22. Thus, Wolfgang J. Mommsen, *Die Geschichtswissenschaft jenseits des Historismus* (Düsseldorf, 1971).

23. See Thomas Nipperdey, *Gesellschaft, Kultur, Theorie: Gesammelte Aufsätze zur neueren Geschichte* (Göttingen, 1975).

24. For the founding (and the further history) of the journal, see Lutz Raphael, "Nationalzentrierte Sozialgeschichte im programmatischer Absicht: Die Zeitschrift 'Geschichte und Gesellschaft. Zeitschrift für Historische Sozialwissenschaft' in den ersten 25 Jahren ihren Bestehens," *Geschichte und Gesellschaft* 25 (1999): 5–37; Olaf Blaschke and Lutz Raphael, "Im Kampf um Positionen: Änderungen im Feld der französischen und deutschen Geschichtswissenschaft nach 1945," *Neue Zugänge zur Geschichte der Geschichtswissenschaft*, ed. Jan Eckel and Thomas Etzemüller, 104–06 (Göttingen, 2007).

25. These differences were already apparent in relation to the Fischer controversy, where, in line with Fischer, Wehler charged the German elite of the period from 1870 to 1945 for having been solely responsible for launching World War I, while Hillgruber rejected Fischer's perspective.

26. See also Frank Becker, "Mit dem Fahrstuhl in die Sattelzeit? Koselleck und Wehler in Bielefeld," in *Was war Bielefeld? Eine ideengeschichtliche Nachfrage*, ed. Sonja Asal and Stephan Schlak, 89–110 (Göttingen, 2009).

27. In addition, Nipperdey contributed to the first volume of the *Geschichtliche Grundbegriffe* (with Reinhard Rürup, he wrote the article on *Antisemitismus*), and his *Deutsche Geschichte 1800–1914* was, as earlier mentioned, greatly inspired by Koselleck's *Preußen zwischen Reform und Revolution*.

28. It should be added that Koselleck was a specialist of the eighteenth and early nineteenth centuries, whereas the others were nineteenth and early twentieth century specialists and thus dealt with different themes and subfields.

29. See Jürgen Kaube, "Zentrum der intellektuellen Nachkriegsgeschichte," *Frankfurter Allgemeine Zeitung*, 18/6 (2003). See also Oliver Müller, "Subtile Stile: Hans Blumenberg und die Forschungsgruppe 'Poetik und Hermeneutik,'" in *Kontroverse in der Literaturtheorie/Literaturtheorie in der Kontroverse*, ed. Ralf Klausnitzer and Carlos Spoerhase, 249–64 (Bern, 2007).

30. See the following published volumes: Hans Robert Jauss, ed., *Poetik und Hermeneutik III: Die nicht mehr schönen Künste. Grenzphänomene des Ästhetischen* (München, 1968); Reinhart Koselleck and Wolf-Dieter Stempel, eds., *Poetik und Hermeneutik V. Geschichte—Ereignis und Erzählung* (München, 1973); and Odo Marquard and Karlheinz Stierle, eds., *Poetik und Hermeneutik VIII. Identität* (München, 1979). According to Bernard Giesen, Koselleck continued to appear as an occasional guest. "Nachruf auf Reinhart Koselleck (1923–2006)," *Berliner Journal für Soziologie*, Bd. 17 (2007): 265.

31. Hans Robert Jauss, ed., *Poetik und Hermeneutik I. Nachahmung und Illusion* (München, 1964), 187–95.

32. According to Hans Robert Jauss, the group "embarked on an intellectual project that opposed any tendency to return to the idea of nationality or race as meaningful vectors in the human sciences." Olender, "The Radical Strangeness," 144.
33. Koselleck succeeded Rudolf von Albertini, who in 1967 returned to the University of Zürich.
34. In Heidelberg, Koselleck taught on topics related to the history of historical writing, the history of National Socialist concentration camps, conceptual history, and historical theory and methodology. For the titles of some of these courses and when they took place, see Altemos, "Lehrende und Lehrprogramm", 36–85; Conze, "Das historische Seminar," 148.
35. Koselleck described the generational difference that he detected between himself and his students in a letter to Schmitt from November 1955, in which he referred to his experience of war as a crucial dividing line. Koselleck wrote: "Sociologically speaking, one may perhaps divide the students into two groups: Those who have been shaped by education from 1945 onwards, and those who have been spared this education or reeducation; whether because of parental influence or because they were refugees or grew up in old, structured circumstances. In any case, almost all of them lack the experience of actual war; and therein lies the decisive distance between the students and me. The fall of Danzig is for nearly all of them something that only their parents remember" RW265-8144: 28/11 (1955). (Koselleck referred here to the city of Danzig, under the administration of the League of Nations since 1919 and claimed by both Germany and Poland. In 1939, it came to play a role in the German military aggressions leading to the invasion of Poland, as Hitler demanded that it should be returned to Germany, which Poland refused to do). Koselleck elaborated on the consequences of these generational differences in a letter to Schmitt in July 1956, when he was somewhat irritated with the efforts of his students. Koselleck complained that some of the students wandered around aimlessly, merely focusing on the exam. Due to having been socialized during and after the war, he added, "[m]any students are entirely lacking the sociological organ and the heritage of the classical, 'political' historical writing of the previous century" RW265-8145: 10/7 (1956).
36. The following is based on Christian Peters, "Lehrangebot und Geschichtsbild. Ein Beitrag zu einer Sozialgeschichte des Faches Geschichte an der Heidelberger Universität," in *Eine Studie zum Alltagsleben der Historie. Zeitgeschichte des Faches Geschichte an der Heidelberger Universität 1945–1978*, ed. Robert Deutsch, Heilwig Schomerus, and Christian Peters (Heidelberg, 1978), 32–33. The student movement arose relatively late in Heidelberg. Among its first aims were to lower the tram-prices and to secure student influence on issues related to university-administration. For (three very different) perspectives on the student revolts in Heidelberg, see Wolgast, *Die Universität Heidelberg*, 182; Buselmeier, *Auch eine Geschichte*; and Jürgen Hoppe, "Heidelberg Sommer," *Deutsche Universitäten: Berichte und Analysen*, ed. Ernst Nolte (Marburg, 1969).
37. See Peters, "Lehrangebot und Geschichtsbild," 26–27, which has divided the teaching activities at the University of Heidelberg between 1945 and 1975 into three phases: 1) a phase that runs from 1945 until 1957 in which *geistesgeschichtliche* themes dominated; 2) a phase running from 1957 until 1970 dominated by themes related to social and economic history; and 3) a phase running from 1970 until 1975 dominated by themes related to historical theory and method.
38. The following is based on Dunkhase, *Werner Conze*, 94–105; Etzemüller, *Sozialgeschichte als politische Geschichte*, 338; Hans Mommsen, "Daraus erklärt sich, daß es niemals zuvor eine derartige Vorherrschaft alter Männer gegeben hat wie in der Zeit

von 1945 bis in die 60er Jahre," *Versäumte Fragen. Deutsche Historiker im Schatten des Nationalsozialismus*, ed. Rüdiger Hohls and Konrad H. Jarausch (Stuttgart, 2000); and Schieder, "Wir können keine Kommentare erzwingen," 288–89.

39. See Dunkhase, *Werner Conze*, 101, and the picture in Buselmeier, ed. *Auch eine Geschichte*, 443. Conze lost the subsequent election.

40. Koselleck, "Ich war weder Opfer noch befreit."

41. Koselleck, "Formen der Bürgerlichkeit," 80.

42. Ibid.

43. Hölscher, "Abschied von Koselleck," 86-87. Another description of Koselleck's dialogue with the 68ers is found in Christian Meier, "Gedenkrede auf Reinhart Koselleck," in *Reinhart Koselleck 1923–2006: Reden zur Gedenkfeier am 24. Mai 2006, Bielefelder Universitätsgespräche und Vorträge*, vol. 9, ed. Neithart Bulst and Willibald Steinmetz (Bielefeld, 2007), 33: "He [Koselleck] also engaged enthusiastically in discussions with the 68ers, all night long, patiently, equal to equal, and he has taken them seriously (and occasionally even defended them, which some colleagues held against him), even though he did not sympathise with their utopianism."

44. Thus Steinmetz, "Nachruf auf Reinhart Koselleck," 421.

45. Hölscher, "Abschied von Reinhart Koselleck," 87.

46. Reinhart Koselleck, "Wozu noch Historie?," *Historische Zeitschrift* 212 (1971): 1–18; and "Über die Theoriebedürftigkeit der Geschichtswissenschaft," in *Theorie der Geschichtswissenschaft und Praxis des Geschichtsunterrichts*, ed. Werner Conze (Stuttgart, 1972), 10–28.

47. Koselleck, "Wozu noch Historie?," 1.

48. Ibid., 12–13.

49. Ibid., 15.

50. Ibid., 16, 17.

51. See, for, example Jürgen Kocka, "Geschichte—wozu?," *Sozialgeschichte. Begriff—Entwicklung—Probleme* (Göttingen 1977), 112–31; Thomas Nipperdey, "Wozu noch Geschichte?," in *Die Zukunft der Vergangenheit*, ed. G. D. Kaltenbrunner, 34–57 (München, 1975); Willi Oelmüller, ed. *Wozu noch Geschichte?* (München, 1977).

52. Reinhart Koselleck, "Begriffsgeschichte und Sozialgeschichte," in *Soziologie und Sozialgeschichte. Aspekte und Probleme*, ed. Peter Christian Ludz (Köln, 1972), 116–31.

53. Hans-Ulrich Wehler, "Soziologie und Geschichte aus der Sicht des Sozialhistorikers," in *Soziologie und Sozialgeschichte: Aspekte und Probleme*, ed. Peter Christian Ludz, 60–80 (Köln, 1972). With reference first of all to Braudel, Wehler listed four temporalities that he argued must be considered in a historical analysis.

54. Niklas Luhmann, "Weltzeit und Systemgeschichte. Über Beziehungen zwischen Zeithorizonten und sozialen Strukturen gesellschaftlicher Systeme," in *Soziologie und Sozialgeschichte: Aspekte und Probleme*, ed. Peter Christian Ludz, 81–115 (Köln, 1972).

55. As also observed by Jürgen Osterhammel, "Gesellschaftsgeschichte und Historische Soziologie," in *Wege der Gesellschaftsgeschichte*, ed. Jürgen Osterhammel, Dieter Langewiesche, and Paul Nolte (Göttingen, 2006), 94 n. 46. For a comparison of Luhmann's and Koselleck's use of temporal theories, see Jens Gunni Busck, *Koselleck og Luhmann. En teorisammenligning* (unpublished MA thesis, Roskilde University Center, 2008).

56. For reactions outside the profession, see Taubes, "Geschichtsphilosophie und Historik"; Wolfhart Pannenberg, "Erfordert die Einheit der Geschichte ein Subjekt?" in *Poetik und Hermeneutik V. Geschichte—Ereignis und Erzählung*, ed. Reinhart Koselleck, Wolf-Dieter Stempel (München, 1973), 478–90; M. Rainer Lipsius, "Bemerkungen zum Verhältnis von Geschichtswissenschaft und Soziologie," in *Theorie der Geschichts-*

wissenschaft und Praxis des Geschichtsunterrichts, ed Werner Conze, 59–60 (Stuttgart, 1972). For reactions inside the profession, see Karl-Georg Faber, *Theorie der Geschichtswissenschaft. Dritte erweiterte Auflage* (München, 1974), 227–38; Winfried Schulze, *Soziologie und Geschichtswissenschaft. Einführung in die Probleme der Kooperation beider Wissenschaften* (München, 1974), 197–209; Alfred Schmidt, "Zum Problem einer marxistischen Historik" in *Wozu noch Geschichte?*, ed. Willi Oelmüller (München, 1977), 154–59; Heydemann, *Geschichtswissenschaft im geteilten Deutschland*, 116–20; and the references to Koselleck in Karl-Georg Faber and Christian Meier, eds., *Historische Prozesse: Theorie der Geschichte. Beiträge zur Historik*, Bd. 2 (München, 1978).

57. See for example Faber, *Theorie der Geschichtswissenschaft*, 228; Jürgen Kocka, "Theorien in der Sozial- und Wirtschaftsgeschichte," *Geschichte und Gesellschaft*, 1. Jg. (1975): 22 n. 22.

58. Busck, *Koselleck og Luhmann*, 21.

59. Most of the articles in the two volumes had been published before—those in *Vergangene Zukunft* in the period between 1967 and 1977, and those in *Zeitschichten* between 1982 and 1999.

60. Koselleck, *Vergangene Zukunft*, 9 (CFOT).

61. For the German tradition of reflecting the temporal structures of human existence, see David Carr, *Time, Narrative and History* (Bloomington, 1986).

62. Martin Heidegger, "Der Zeitbegriff in der Geschichtswissenschaft," *Zeitschrift für Philosophie und philosophische Kritik*, Nr. 160 (1916): 173–88.

63. David Carr, Review of *Vergangene Zukunft*, by Reinhart Koselleck, *History and Theory* 26, no. 2 (1987): 198. There does not yet exist any in-depth analysis of Koselleck's use of Heidegger. However, excellent perspectives on the issue can be found in Carr's review and in Taubes, "Geschichtsphilosophie und Historik."

64. Koselleck, "Formen der Bürgerlichkeit," 76.

65. As observed by Keith Tribe, "Introduction," Reinhart Koselleck, *Futures Past: On the Semantics of Historical Time* (New York, 2004), XI.

66. Koselleck, *Vergangene Zukunft*, 11–12 (CFOT).

67. The following draws extensively on Jan Ifversen's excellent account of Gadamer's key concepts and of how Koselleck reworked these for his own purpose, "Om den tyske begrebshistorie," *Politologiske studier* 6, no. 1 (2003): 18–34.

68. Reinhart Koselleck, "'Erfahrungsraum' und 'Erwartungshorizont': Zwei historische Kategorien," in *Soziale Bewegung und politische Verfassung. Beiträge zur Geschichte der modernen Welt. Werner Conze zum 65. Geburtstag*, ed. Ulrich Engelhardt, Volker Sellin and Horst Stuke, 13–33 (Stuttgart, 1976).

69. Partly based on Koselleck's 1965 inaugural lecture in Heidelberg, the text was first published in a Festschrift to Carl Schmitt. Reinhart Koselleck, "Vergangene Zukunft der frühen Neuzeit," in *Epirrhosis, Festgabe für Carl Schmitt, Bd. 2*, ed. Hans Barion et al. , 549–66 (Berlin, 1968).

70. Koselleck, "Vergangene Zukunft der frühen Neuzeit," 550 (CFOT).

71. Ibid., 19.

72. Ifversen, "Om den tyske begrebshistorie," 23–27.

73. See also Reinhart Koselleck, "Geschichte, Geschichten und formale Zeitstrukturen" and "Ereignis und Struktur," in *Poetik und Hermeneutik V*, 211–22, 560–71.

74. Koselleck referred also to Herder to as a theoretical forerunner in the field. See Reinhart Koselleck, "Zeitschichten," *Zeitschichten: Studien zur Historik* (Frankfurt am Main, 2000), 20 (first published in *Zeit und Wahrheit*, ed. Heinrich Pfusterschmid-Hardtenstein, 95–100 (Wien, 1994)).

75. Koselleck, "Zeitschichten," 19.

76. As observed by Palonen, *Die Entzauberung der Begriffe*, 279–84.
77. Reinhart Koselleck, "'Neuzeit': Zur Semantik moderner Bewegungsbegriffe," *Vergangene Zukunft: Zur Semantik geschichtlicher Zeiten* (Frankfurt am Main, 1979), 260–77 (first published in Reinhart Koselleck, ed., *Studien zum Beginn der modernen Welt*. Bd. 20 (Stuttgart, 1977) 264–99; and [Reinhart Koselleck, "Wie neu ist die Neuzeit," *Zeitschichten. Studien zur Historik* (Frankfurt am Main 2000), 225-239.
78. While Diderot's prognosis was meant as a warning against how events might unfold in France, according to Koselleck, he camouflaged the context by referring to events in Sweden.
79. Koselleck, "Wie neu ist die Neuzeit?," 233.
80. Ibid., 236–37.
81. Ibid., 238–39.
82. Reinhart Koselleck, "Diesseits des Nationalstaates: Föderale Strukturen der deutschen Geschichte," *Transit. Europäische Revue*, no. 7 (1994): 63–76 (later included in *Begriffsgeschichten*, 486–503).
83. In the last passage of the text, Koselleck embraced European federalism: "Whatever Europe may be, there is a federal minimum that must be achieved, not merely economically, but also politically and that we must preserve, if we wish to continue living on this continent." Koselleck, "Diesseits des Nationalstaates," 76.
84. Koselleck, "Wozu noch Historie?," 13.
85. See also Palonen, *Die Entzauberung der Begriffe*, 297–304.
86. Blaschke, "Im Kampf um Positionen," 93–106.
87. Contributions to this line of reasoning include, for example, also: Hans Mommsen, *Die Geschichtswissenschaft jenseits des Historismus*, "Historical Scholarship in Transition: The Situation in the Federal Republic of Germany," *Daedalus*, no. 100 (1971): 458–508; and Georg G. Iggers, ed., *Neue Geschichtswissenschaft: vom Historismus zur historischen Sozialwissenschaft* (München, 1978). The narrative culminated in Horst Walter Blanke, *Historiographiegeschichte als Historik* (Stuttgart-Cannstatt, 1991).
88. Reinhart Koselleck, "Standortbindung und Zeitlichkeit. Ein Beitrag zur historiographischen Erschließung der geschichtlichen Welt," in *Objektivität und Parteilichkeit in der Geschichtswissenschaft. Beiträge zur Historik. Bd. 1*, ed. Reinhart Koselleck, Wolfgang J. Mommsen, and Jörn Rüsen, 17–46 (München, 1977); and Koselleck, "Erfahrungswandel und Methodenwechsel." Moreover, as co-editors, Koselleck, Wolfgang J. Mommsen, and Jörn Rüsen co-authored the introduction to the first volume of *Theorie und Geschichte*, "Einführung," in *Objektivität und Parteilichkeit in der Geschichtswissenschaft. Beiträge zur Historik*, Bd. 1, (München, 1977), 11–14; and, to a later volume, Koselleck added the article "Fragen an den Formen der Geschichtsschreibung," in *Formen der Geschichtsschreibung*, ed. Reinhart Koselleck, Heinrich Lutz, and Jörn Rüsen, 9–13 (München, 1982).
89. Koselleck, "Standortbindung und Zeitlichkeit," 128 (CFOT).
90. Ibid., 133.
91. Ibid., 134.
92. Ibid., 136.
93. Ibid., 130.
94. Ibid., 149.
95. Ibid., 151.
96. Ibid., 149.
97. Ibid., 151.
98. Koselleck, "Erfahrungswandel und Methodenwechsel," 45 (CFOT).
99. Ibid., 65.

100. Ibid., 76.
101. Ibid., 83.
102. The term "linguistic turn" became famous with the publication of the anthology Richard Rorty, ed., *The Linguistic Turn: Essays in Philosophical Method* (Chicago, 1967).
103. See Jordheim, "Thinking in Convergences," 74. The following draws on Jordheim's excellent account of Koselleck's stance on the issues raised by the linguistic turn.
104. Hayden White, *Metahistory: The Historical Imagination in Nineteenth Century Europe* (Baltimore, 1973).
105. Hayden White, Review of *Vergangene Zukunft*, by Reinhart Koselleck, *American Historical Review* 95, no. 5 (1987): 1175–76.
106. Hayden White, Foreword to *The Practice of Conceptual History: Timing History, Spacing Concepts*, by Reinhart Koselleck (Stanford, 2002), ix.
107. Reinhart Koselleck, "Vorwort," in Hayden White, *Auch Klio dichtet oder die Fiktion des Faktischen: Studien zur Tropologie des historischen Diskurses* (Stuttgart, 1986) (republished in Koselleck, *The Practice of Conceptual History*, 38–44).
108. Dutt, "Geschichte(n) und Historik," 267.
109. Koselleck's stance on radical relativism is excellently described by White: "Koselleck insists that . . . relativism provides no ground for nihilism or a crippling skepticism. Historical relativism, he concludes, avoids Pyrrhonism by virtue of its substitution of the relative certainly of our knowledge we can have of our society and culture for the absolute certainty promised by all forms of idealism. The concept of history includes a concept of historical knowledge that knows itself to be always provisional and open to revision. As historical knowledge dissolves the myths, lies, and falsifications of history, it secures a stable base from which to asses and augment that 'space of experience' in which men build a notion of a human reality that is both always changing and ever more becoming itself." Foreword to *The Practice of Conceptual History*, xiv.
110. Reinhart Koselleck, "Sprachwandel und Ereignisgeschichte," *Merkur*, no. 8 (1989): 657.
111. I am here recapitulating the key argument in Jordheim's "Thinking in Convergences..
112. For the affiliations between the two, see Meier, "Gedenkrede auf Reinhart Koselleck," 11. For Koselleck's admiration for Meier's work, see the references in *Vergangene Zukunft* and *Zeitschichten*.
113. Kühn, *Toleranz und Offenbarung*, IX.
114. Peter Lundgreen, ed., *Reformuniversität Bielefeld: 1969–1994: Zwischen Defensive und Innovation* (Bielefeld, 1994).
115. The board also included Max Imdahl, Günther Kahle, Christian Meier, Gottfried Schramm, and Rudolf Vierhaus.
116. Reinhart Koselleck, "Geschichtswissenschaft in Bielefeld: Die neue Orientierung eines alten Faches," in *Zwischenstation*, ed. Karl Peter Grotemeyer (Bielefeld, 1979), 70.
117. Koselleck did not make the final decision to take up the position in Bielefeld before 1972. Neithart Bulst, ["Koselleck], in *Reinhart Koselleck 1923–2006: Reden zur Gedenkfeier am 24. Mai 2006, Bielefelder Universitätsgespräche und Vorträge*, vol. 9, ed. Neithart Bulst and Willibald Steinmetz, 45–50 (Bielefeld, 2007).
118. Becker, "Mit dem Fahrstuhl in die Sattelzeit?"
119. Reinhart Koselleck, "Erläuterungen zum Bielefeld Modell für das Geschichtsstudium," *Geschichte und Sozialwissenschaften, Sonderheft 6 der Neuen Sammlung* (1974): 36–40.

120. RW265-8167: 14/7 (1973).

121. *Studienrat* is a title that schoolteachers (in the Gymnasium) acquire once they reach a certain (career st)age: Continuing his letter with the sentence: "Die Gleichheit wird dann neue Blüten treiben—die Oberstudienräte, die Oberststudienräte, Generalstudienräte, Generaloberst usw," Koselleck poked fun at how the *Gleichheit*-jargon of the Social Democratic Party would lead to nothing but new bureaucratic hierarchies. RW265-8167: 14/7 (1973).

122. Koselleck, "Geschichtswissenschaft in Bielefeld," 78. Koselleck also occasionally complained about issues of administration in his letters to Carl Schmitt—for example in a letter from October 1975 in which he reported that he had become *geschäftsführender Direktor* of the ZIF, "which drew along a quagmire (*Rattenschwanz*) of administration and administrative quarrels." RW265-8170: 1/10 (1975).

123. As stated by Bulst, ["Koselleck], 48.

124. Hans-Ulrich Wehler, *Eine lebhafte Kampfsituation: Ein Gespräch mit Manfred Hettling und Cornelius Torp* (München, 2006), 65. Wehler earned his *habilitation* in 1960 with a work on *Sozialdemokratie und Nationalstaat (1840–1914)* written under Theodor Schieder in Cologne. Soon after, he became an assistant for Schieder in the historical seminar, but [traveled in the summer of 1962 to the United States to prepare his *Habilitation*, titled "Aufstieg des amerikanischen Imperialismus 1865–1900," which he submitted in Cologne in 1964, only to have it rejected by the jury. The same was close to happening, when Wehler in 1968 submitted his second work, "Bismarck und der Imperialismus." Only after a marginal vote in favor, he was finally awarded his degree. See Wehler, "Historikern sollten auch," 246–48.

125. For a typical example, see Roger Fletcher, "Recent Developments in West German Historiography: The Bielefeld School and Its Critics," *German Studies Review* 7, no. 3 (1984): 451–80. For a recent example, see Chris Lorenz, "'Won't You Tell Me, Where Have All The Good Times Gone?': On the Advantages and the Disadvantages of Modernization Theory for Historical Study," in *The Many Faces of Clio: Cross-Cultural Approaches to Historiography*, ed. Franz Leander Fillafer and Edward Q. Wang, 104–27 (Oxford, 2007).

126. Koselleck, "Begriffsgeschichte, Sozialgeschichte, Begriffene Geschichte," 197–200. Koselleck was part of the editorial board that founded *Geschichte und Gesellschaft*, but he never authored an article to the journal and only rarely participated in the conferences organized within its framework. See Blaschke, "Im Kampf um Positionen," 106; and Raphael, "Nationalzentrierte Sozialgeschichte," 15. The reservations between Kocka and Koselleck seem to have been of less severe character. Besides writing a positive review of *Preußen zwischen Reform und Revolution*, Kocka contributed to the first volume of the *Geschichtliche Grundbegriffe* with an article on "Angestellte," and he later wrote a very sympathetic obituary in Koselleck's honor. Moreover, Kocka saw less of an opposition between *Gesellschaftsgeschichte* and the structural-historical approach of Conze and Koselleck than Wehler. However, Kocka and Koselleck never collaborated directly on larger projects. See Kocka, Review of *Preußen zwischen Reform und Revolution*; by Reinhart Koselleck; Jürgen Kocka, "Wir sind ein Fach, das nicht nur für sich selber schreibt und forscht, sondern zur Aufklärung und zum Selbstverständnis der eigenen Gesellschaft und Kultur beitragen sollte," in *Versäumte Fragen. Deutsche Historiker im Schatten des Nationalsozialismus*, ed. Rüdiger Hohls and Konrad H. Jarausch, 390–91 (Stuttgart, 2000); and Kocka, "Die Zukunft der Vergangenheit."

127. Hans-Ulrich Wehler, *Krisenherde des Kaiserreichs 1871–1918* (Göttingen, 1970), 320.

128. In the article, Wehler also compiled a list of historians who supposedly shared his reservations toward the *Geschichtliche Grundbegriffe*. "Geschichtswissenschaft Heute," 725 n. 2.

129. Jürgen Habermas, "Einleitung," in *Stichwörter zur geistigen Situation der Zeit*. Bd. 1 (Frankfurt am Main, 1979), 7–35.

130. Hans-Ulrich Wehler, "Absoluter und Totaler Krieg. Von Clausewitz zu Ludendorff," *Politische Vierteljahrschrift*, Jg. X (1969): 236–37 n. 26.

131. Hans-Ulrich Wehler, *Deutsche Gesellschaftsgeschichte*, Vol. 1. 1700–1815, and Vol. 2. 1815–1845/1849 (Stuttgart, 1987). For an account of Wehler's criticism, see Sperber, "Master Narratives of Nineteenth-Century German History," *Central European History* 24 (1991): 69–91.

132. Whereas, according to Wehler, historicists had been incapable of warning against the German *Sonderweg* in the first decades of the twentieth century, Schmitt had contributed intellectually to the authoritarian, aggressive, and militaristic dimensions of the *Sonderweg*. See, for example, Wehler, *Krisenherde des Kaiserreichs*, 85–113 (in which Wehler blamed Hans Freyer, Ernst Jünger, Carl Schmitt, and Ernst Forsthoff for having intellectually paved the way for the "total state" and the "total war").

133. For how German historians articulated the German *Sonderweg* in the period before, during, and after World War I, see Bernd Faulenbach, *Ideologie des deutschen Weges: Die deutsche Geschichte in der Historiographie zwischen Kaiserreich und Nationalsozialismus* (München, 1980).

134. Thus, James Sheehan, Review of *Gesellschaft, Parlament und Regierung. Zur Geschichte des Parlamentarismus in Deutschland*, ed. Gerhard A. Ritter and *Regierung und Reichstag im Bismarckstaat, 1871–1880: Cäsarismus oder Parlamentarismus*, by Michael Stürmer, *Journal of Modern History* 48, no. 3 (1976): 567.

135. See David Blackbourn and Geoff Eley, *The Peculiarities of German History: Bourgeois Society and Politics in Nineteenth-Century Germany* (Oxford, 1984).

136. Thomas Nipperdey, *Religion im Umbruch: Deutschland 1870–1918* (München, 1988).

137. Cited in Abigail Green, "The Federal Alternative: A New View on German History," *The Historical Journal* 46, no. 1 (2002): 188.

138. Koselleck, "Begriffsgeschichte, Sozialgeschichte, Begriffene Geschichte," 198–99.

139. Reinhart Koselleck, "Deutschland—eine verspätete Nation?," jn *Zeitschichten: Studien zur Historik* (Frankfurt am Main, 2000), 359–80. (The article first appeared in Dutch and was also included in Reinhart Koselleck, *Europäische Umrisse deutscher Geschichte: Zwei Essays* (Heidelberg, 1999) 37–78.

140. Helmut Plessner, *Das Schicksal des deutschen Geistes: im Ausgang seiner bürgerlichen Epoche* (Zürich, 1935), and *Die verspätete Nation: Über die politische Verführbarkeit bürgerlichen Geistes* (Stuttgart, 1959).

141. Koselleck, "Deutschland—eine verspätete Nation?," 363. For the Hegelian traits informing the program of *Gesellschaftsgeschichte*, see also Lorenz, "'Won't You Tell Me,'" 115.

142. Koselleck, "Deutschland—eine verspätete Nation?," 376.

143. Ibid., 378.

144. Ibid., 379. As in several other texts, Koselleck instead argued that German history has since the Middle Ages been characterized by its federal structures, which have prevented a foundation of a national state similar to those of the neighboring countries.

145. According to Giesen, Koselleck was regarded as a "conservative bohemian" by many of his departmental colleagues. "Nachruf auf Reinhart Koselleck," 265.

146. Meier, "Gedenkrede auf Reinhart Koselleck," 22.

147. Hoffmann, "Reinhart Koselleck," 478.
148. See for example Bo Stråth, Review of Zeitschichten, by Reinhart Koselleck, European Journal of Social Theory, 4 (2001): 535. There, Stråth suggests that Koselleck's reflections on the "vanquished" in history refers to the latter's "experiences as something like a marginalized loser . . . at Bielefeld in the 1970s [when he] was looked down on from the victorious bandwagon of Gesellschaftsgeschichte."
149. For the colloquiums taking place in Stieghorst, see Bulst, ["Koselleck], 46, 49. For the events and research groups in ZIF, see Zentrum for Interdisziplinäre Forschung, "Gesamtliste ZIF Veranstaltungen zwischen 1968 und 1996," http://www.uni-bielefeld.de/ZIF/Forschung/Gesamtliste-Veranstaltungen.pdf, accessed 23/7 (2011).
150. Philippe Blanchard, Reinhart Koselleck, and Ludwig Streit, eds., Taktische Kernwaffen: Die fragmentierte Abschreckung (Frankfurt am Main, 1987).
151. Reinhart Koselleck and Rolf Reichardt, eds., Die Französischen Revolution als Bruch der gesellschaftlichen Bewusstseins (München, 1988).
152. Koselleck's network at the university included also scholars from other departments. Among these were Ernst-Wolfgang Böckenförde, who between 1969 and 1977 held a chair at the law faculty, and Wilhelm Voßkamp, who between 1972 and 1987 held a chair in the faculty of literature, and who was a director of the ZIF between 1978 and 1982. There Voßkamp organized a seminar, "Funktionsgeschichte der literarischer Utopien in den frühen Neuzeit," which took place between September 1980 and September 1981 and in which Koselleck participated. Voßkamp, on the other hand, contributed to a 1988 conference in Poetik und Hermeneutik that Koselleck organized with Reinhart Herzog.
153. Koselleck, Bürgerschaft.
154. Koselleck, "Begriffsgeschichte, Sozialgeschichte, Begriffene Geschichte," 199.
155. Koselleck, ed., Bildungsbürgertum im 19. Jahrhundert.
156. Raphael, Geschichtswissenschaft, 156–271; and Georg G. Iggers, Historiography in the Twentieth Century: From Scientific Objectivity to the Postmodern Challenge (Middletown, 1997), 97–140.
157. For introductions to Alltagsgeschichte, see Alf Lüdtke, "Alltagsgeschichte," in Lexikon Geschichtswissenschaft. Hundert Grundbegriffe, ed. Stefan Jordan, 21–24 (Stuttgart, 2002); Alf Lüdtke, ed., Alltagsgeschichte. Zur Rekonstruktion historischer Erfahrungen und Lebensweisen (Frankfurt am Main, 1989); Iggers, Historiography, 101–17; Thomas Lindenberger, "'Alltagsgeschichte' oder: Als um die zünftigen Grenzen des Faches noch gestritten wurde," in Zeitgeschichte als Streitgeschichte, ed. Martin Sabrow, Ralph Jessen, and Klaus Große Kracht, 74–91 (München, 2003).
158. Alltagsgeschichte was related to the rise of so-called Green politics that focused on ecological and environmental issues, pacifism, and social justice and encouraged the practice of a grass-roots participatory democracy. From the late 1970s onwards, Green politics were institutionalized in political parties: the German Green party was founded in 1979/1980.
159. Karl-Georg Faber, Review of Vergangene Zukunft, by Reinhart Koselleck, Neue politische Literatur, 2 (1980): 621. See also Helmut Berding, Review of Vergangene Zukunft, by Reinhart Koselleck, Zeitschrift für Philosophische Forschung, Bd. 34, Hf. 3 (1980): 461-464; Claudia Albert, Review of Vergangene Zukunft, by Reinhart Koselleck, Das Argument, 127 (1981): 423-424; Hans Ulrich Gumbrecht, Review of Vergangene Zukunft, by Reinhart Koselleck, Poetica, Bd. 13 (1981): 345-359; Rudolf Lüthe, Review of Vergangene Zukunft, by Reinhart Koselleck, Philosophischer Literaturanzeiger, 34/1 (1981): 27-31; Arno Seifert, Review of Vergangene Zukunft, by Reinhart Koselleck, Historischen Jahrbuch, Jg. 101 (1981): 276-277; Stefan Smid, Review of Vergangene

Zukunft, by Reinhart Koselleck, *Archiv für Rechts-und Sozialphilosophie*, Bd., LXXI (1985): 564-567.

160. For reviews of *Futures past*, see White, Review of *Futures Past*, by Reinhart Koselleck; David Carr, *Futures Past*, by Reinhart Koselleck, *History and Theory*, vol. 26, nr. 2 (1987): 197-204; Richard T. Vann, "Historians' Words and Things", *Journal of Interdisciplinary Studies*, vol. 18, nr. 3 (1988): 465-470; Peter Burke, *Futures Past*, by Reinhart Koselleck, *History of European Ideas*, vol. 8 (1987): 744-745.

161. Koselleck referred to his retirement as a *Zwangsvergreisung* (forced senilification). See Jeismann, "Geschichte und Eigensinn."

162. Reinhart Koselleck, "Goethes unzeitgemäße Geschichte," *Goethe-Jahrbuch*, Bd. 100 (1993): 27–39; and *Goethes unzeitgemäße Geschichte* (Heidelberg, 2001). The following citations are from the book version.

163. On the reception of Goethe in Germany, see Karl Robert Mandelkow, *Goethe in Deutschland: Rezeptionsgeschichte eines Klassikers*, Bd. 1 and 2 (München, 1980/1989). For an authoritative perspective on Goethe, see Nicholas Boyle, "Geschichte und Autobiographik bei Goethe (1810–1817)," *Goethe-Jahrbuch* 110 (1993): 163–72.

164. Koselleck, *Goethes unzeitgemäße Geschichte*, 11.

165. Ibid., 27.

166. Ibid., 23.

6

COMMEMORATING THE DEAD
Experience, Understanding, Identity

During the 1970s, Reinhart Koselleck added yet another theme to his oeuvre, as he began to investigate how war, violence, and terror have been experienced, and how, or if, we as human beings and historians can understand, cope with, and commemorate such experiences. In the following decades, using dreams, war memorials, and personal experiences as his source-material, he explored this theme in various studies and contributed to pioneer the field of historical memory, and identity.

My ambition in this chapter is to illuminate the key discursive features in Koselleck's writings on the experience of war, violence, and terror, and to position these writings within the broader spectrum of his scholarly production. For three reasons, this body of texts represents the most difficult part of his oeuvre. First, it comprises a range of very different texts that were written over a period of about thirty years. Second, this was an area of Koselleck's work that remained unfinished: In the introduction to *Zeitschichten*, Koselleck announced a volume on historical memory and monuments, which was supposed to draw together the common objectives of his work in the field, but the volume is yet to appear. Third, his reflections on the epistemological and moral questions in the field remained characterized by a degree of ambiguity and hesitance that is not found elsewhere in his work.

The following analysis illustrates not only the unfinished and ambiguous aspects of Koselleck's writings on the experience of war, violence, and terror, but also that all of these texts were connected by means of a discursive feature with which he sought to deconstruct ideas of history in the singular and thematize histories in the plural from a new perspective. This perspective was based on an attempt to describe the ways in which the limits of the human condition were experienced by the victims of World War II and National Socialism and on an interpretation of the Holocaust as a radical break in history, which, according to Koselleck, with its extreme violence and suffering, questioned every notion of meaning in history and posed new challenges to how experienced reality can be mastered, communicated, and understood. Indeed, as we will see, Koselleck's aim was to demonstrate that human beings interpret and make sense of their most extreme experiences in different or plural ways that cannot be fully understood or shared by others.

The chapter also shows that Koselleck's new perspective on history in the plural came to involve an analytical change of focus from the collective to the individual that went hand in hand with a defense of the individual experience against overarching notions of collective memory. It also went hand in hand with a change of identity in his mode of argumentation. These changes were related: When, as we will see, in academic and public debates in the 1990s, Koselleck argued for the "veto-right of the personal experience" he argued not only as scholar, but also as a former soldier and prisoner of war. As such, he drew his analytical framework and normative principles from personal experience, and, as the following section illustrates, Koselleck's merging of identities into a "partisan for personal experience and against collective memory" conflicted in certain ways with his earlier work as a "partisan for histories in the plural and against history in singular".

This chapter approaches Koselleck's writings on war, violence, and terror roughly in chronological order. It begins by illuminating his texts on dreams, war memorials, and caricatures that were written from the 1970s onwards. It then describes his interventions in the German memorial debates in the 1990s and presents an autobiographical text from the mid 1990s in which he described his experiences in World War II. This autobiographical text leads us to Koselleck's critique of the theoretical assumptions in the field of memory studies in the 1990s and to a final discussion of some of the dilemmas that inform his writings in the field.

Experiences of National Socialism:
Communicating the Incommunicable

One of Koselleck's first texts in the field at issue was the outline "Terror und Traum," which he presented at various conferences from 1971 onwards and later published in *Vergangene Zukunft*.[1] The text related to his contemporary essays on historical writing, as it opened with reflections on a set of themes that the linguistic turn had placed on the agenda in the 1960s and 1970s: the relation between history and poetry, fact and fiction, past events and our interpretations of these. However, Koselleck approached these issues from a new angle, analyzing accounts of dreams written down by persecuted Jews in Germany during the first years of National Socialism and in the extermination camps during the 1940s. His specific aim was to illuminate the ways in which experiences of National Socialism and concentration camps influenced modern humans' historical consciousness and experience of time.

Due to the extreme character of the events taking place in this period, Koselleck described this as a difficult task: "Thus we have here experiences that are not directly communicable . . ." and ". . . what happened in concentration camps is in written form barely comprehensible, can scarcely be grasped in descriptive or imaginative language."[2] However, Koselleck added, whereas the experiences of the people in the camps tend to escape the usual written sources and historical methodology, their dreams offer a range of metaphors and symbols that make it possible to illuminate aspects of what happened to the human consciousness during the Nazi terror. In the words of Koselleck, constituting a field "within which *res factae* and *res fictae* are mingled in an extraordinary fashion dramatic fashion," dreams "testify to a past reality in a manner which perhaps could not be surpassed by any other source." He added: "Terror is not only dreamed; the dreams are themselves components of the terror."[3]

More concretely, according to Koselleck, dreams contain a temporal and prognostic dimension that allows a perspective on the psychic life of the dreamer, and it was by focusing on this dimension that he unfolded one of the key arguments of the essay: Whereas the dreams written down by the persecuted in the 1930s correspond to the reality experienced by most people, the dreams of the victims in the concentration camps show that they lost touch with reality as a consequence of their extreme experiences and sufferings. As terror surpassed reality and hence no longer could be dreamed, it was replaced by utopian camp dreams in which the usual temporal points of orientation in life were reversed, so that the dreams of the future moved in the temporal perspective of past life; they were fed by a happy memory of past life, out of which all wishes and hopes

272 • Niklas Olsen

were deduced. Because these dreams became increasingly frequent among the inmates, while the chances of survival fatally decreased, Koselleck labeled them "precursors of death." He wrote the following on these conditions and on the brutality and absurdity of the concentrations camps more generally: "The inner evidence of the chance of survival evident in the spontaneous behavior of the inmate and in his dreams is not commensurable with the statistical frequency with which gassing took place. In this way, those destroyed were deprived of a final meaning, that of being a sacrifice; absurdity became event."[4]

It was with reflections such as these that Koselleck in "Terror und Traum" introduced one of the discursive features that came to inform all of his writings about experiences of war, violence, and terror from the 1970s onwards: the attempt to describe and reflect upon how the limits of the human condition were experienced by the victims of World War II and National Socialism. This attempt went hand in hand with the argument that the experiences of this period represent a "domain in which human understanding appears to break down, where language is struck dumb" in such a way that the "loss of reality" suffered by the victims is difficult, if not impossible to understand for others.[5] In other words, what Koselleck introduced in "Terror und Traum" was an interpretation of the Holocaust as a radical break, or something like another *Sattelzeit* in history, which posed new and perhaps insurmountable challenges to how experienced reality can be understood, communicated, and mastered.

In order to understand the implications of this discursive feature, it should be noted that Koselleck's thematization of the Nazi terror and the Holocaust in "Terror und Traum" in itself represented a significant new feature that he introduced in his writings during the 1970s. Until then, even if these issues had motivated and indirectly been dealt with in his work, similarly to most other historians of his generation, Koselleck had not dealt directly with them.[6] To be sure, his generation was not unique in this respect. Until the generational revolt at the end of the 1960s, and arguably, in a different form for a long time afterward, there was a widespread silence about these issues in German academia and society more generally.[7]

In "Terror und Traum," Koselleck for the first time thematized the Nazi terror and the Holocaust directly and in a fashion that was highly unusual for the 1970s and 1980s. At this time, most scholars focused either on intellectual, social, and political pre-histories and structures of the Nazi regime or on its perpetrators, while the director of the Munich Institut für Zeitgeschichte, Martin Broszat, in the mid 1980s famously argued for a historicization of the Nazi period by analyzing it as part of broader structures in German history.[8] Koselleck's position in "Terror und Traum" was arguably incompatible both with the dominant research trends and with Broszat's suggestion, in that Koselleck neither attempted to provide explanatory frameworks nor defended the analytical prevalence of the perpetrators, of broader parts of German history, or, for that matter, of his own war experiences. Instead, Koselleck's analysis was based on the belief that a study of National Socialism has to start from the perspective of the victims of the Nazi terror and to focus on the hopelessness, loss of meaning, and incommunicability that marked their experiences. Koselleck maintained this belief, and it became more explicit in his writings on war, violence, and terror in the 1980s and 1990s.

In a set of methodological remarks, outlined in the last section of "Terror und Traum," Koselleck explained his analytical choice by arguing that in any historical analysis it "is necessary to proceed in a synchronic as well as a diachronic fashion; not only to explain *post eventum*, but also to show *in eventum* how something happened the way it did."[9] However, in later texts, he related his choice not to write a synthesis of National Socialism with reference to a reason that was not explicitly stated but undoubtedly informed the methodological remarks in "Terror und Traum." The reason was that the phenomena of National Socialism posed analytical challenges that he simply did not know how to deal with. Koselleck first described the nature of these challenges in a letter that he wrote to the prominent historian of National Socialism, Saul Friedländer, in 1989:

> I consider that the history [of the "Final Solution"] is confronted by demands that are moral, as well as political and religious, and which altogether do not suffice to convey what happened. The moral judgment is unavoidable, but it does not gain in strength through repetition. The political and social interpretation is also necessary, but it is too limited to explain what happened. The escape into a religious interpretation requires forms of observance which do not belong either to the historical, the moral or the political domain. In my thoughts on this issue up to the present day, I did not manage to get beyond this aporetic situation. In any case, these considerations point to a uniqueness which, in order to be determined, creates both the necessity of making comparisons as well as the need to leave these comparisons behind.[10]

When, in the 1999 article "Die Diskontinuität der Erinnerung," Koselleck developed these considerations into reflections on how the Nazi crimes resist all attempts to grasp them scientifically or morally, or atone for them through religion, he added that all three explanatory modes in different ways lead to "the aporia."[11] He specified: "And exactly this, the aporia, must be maintained in memory. Metaphorically speaking, every step leads to the door of the gas-chamber, but no step leads inside."[12]

This line of reasoning also informs the analysis in "Terror und Traum." What Koselleck aimed at in the text was evidently not to explain the history of National Socialism, but to illuminate the way its victims experienced it. The only possibility that Koselleck saw in this respect was to give voice to the victims and to do so on their own terms, that is, by means of an introvert and reticent narrative from which both explanatory models and moralizing lessons are left out.[13]

With this mode of historical writing, Koselleck both continued and diverged from the basic principles that had informed his work since the early 1950s. On the one hand, his insistence on giving the victims of war, violence, and terror their own story can be interpreted as yet another attempt to thematize histories in the plural. On the other, by arguing that human beings interpret and make sense of their experiences in ways that cannot be fully understood or shared by others, he opened the door to a radical form of pluralism that is not found in his earlier work. This form of pluralism came to be based on a defense of the personal memory and questioned the possibility of transforming the individually-made experiences of war into a narrative form of writing history that included generalizations. It is within this perspective that his reflections in "Die Diskontinuität der Erinnerung" should be understood and, following a view on some of the texts on war, violence, and terror published in between "Terror und Traum" and "Die Diskontinuität der Erinnerung," we will return to this point.

War Memorials and the Justification of Violent Death

All of Koselleck's texts on war, violence, and terror are informed by the discursive features concerning World War II and National Socialism that are found in "Terror und Traum." Presumably, he conceptualized these features in the late the 1960s, when he taught courses at Heidelberg on the history of the National Socialist concentration camps and war memorials. Whereas Koselleck never went on to thematize the concentration camps in a more direct fashion than in "Terror und Traum,"[14] the theme of war memorials moved to center stage in his work from the mid 1970s onwards. Here, with the support of students and collaborators, he began to photograph a huge number of war memorials in Germany and abroad. "To go 'hunting' memorials with a camera and a notepad," Willibald Steinmetz has written of his teacher's immense interest in the theme, "remained since then one of Koselleck's passions. No excursion and no trip abroad without visiting memorials."[15]

In an interview, Koselleck once dated the beginning of his research on war memorials back to the student revolts in 1969/70, when he proposed to the "revolutionary" students a seminar on the social history of art that dealt with representations of death in revolution and war.[16] While they allegedly found the topic too bourgeois, Koselleck continued his research into the field. In 1976, after his transfer to Bielefeld, and in collaboration with the art historians Max Imdahl and P. A. Riedl, he gave a seminar on the topic in the ZIF, and, in 1979, in the Poetik und Hermeneutik volume on *Identität*, he finally published his first article in the field, titled "Krieg-erdenkmale als Identitätsstiftungen der Überlebenden."[17]

With its focus on war memorials, "Kriegerdenkmale als Identitätsstif-tungen der Überlebenden" was influential in pioneering the field of mem-ory studies that was to become vastly popular among historians from the 1980s onwards. However, the article overlapped with studies in the field of national monuments and symbols that had emerged since the 1960s. The most famous German text in this field was Thomas Nipperdey's 1968 article "Nationalidee und Nationaldenkmal in Deutschland im 19. Jah-rhundert."[18] Analyzing artistic symbols of German national memorials as a way to decipher the structures of national movements and ideas of the nation in the nineteenth century, Nipperdey's article presented five dominant memorial ideal-types of the period: the national-monarchical, in which the nation-state is represented in the shape of a ruler; the monu-ment-church (which was never built); the monuments representing the German *Bildungs- und Kulturnation*; the national monument of the demo-cratically constituted nation (which was never built in its ideal form); and the national monument of the national unity or concentration.

According to Nipperdey, all of these ideal-types represent attempts at creating a national identity by means of clear and permanent symbols. More concretely, they were meant to represent and create a common identity and idea about the German nation by means of appealing to, for example, a shared national history, loyalty, enmity, struggle, suffering, aim, and destiny. Reflecting on the political implications of these means of identity, Nipperdey ended his article with observations on the ways in which the German national monuments during the Second Empire came to be dominated by an appeal to power and heroism that symbolized the contemporary sense of inner and outer threats. However, as his analy-sis stopped before the 1930s, he did not illuminate the relation between monument types and nationalism in the Nazi regime.

This relation was dealt with in another famous text on national monu-ments that appeared before Koselleck's article: George Mosse's 1975 book *The Nationalization of the Masses: Political Symbolism and Mass Movements in Germany from the Napoleonic Wars through the Third Reich.*[19] In this work

Mosse sought to demonstrate how, since the French Revolution, people had come to worship themselves as the nation, and how a new politics sought to express and mobilize national feeling and unity "through the creation of a political style, which became, in reality, a secularized religion."[20] This new style was based upon a use of myths, symbols, and monuments that allowed people to participate directly in national worship, and which, by fusing nationalism and mass democracy, gave rise to a visually and participatory counter-political alternative to liberal parliamentarianism. According to Mosse, this new political style appealed to emotions and desires and not to rationality.

Mosse described the origins of the new political style as a broader European phenomenon with roots in the French Revolution. However, he focused especially on the political style that developed in Germany during the nineteenth century and reached its most radical expression in the 1930s and 1940s, when National Socialism called upon the people to worship themselves in a national community of myths, symbols, and monuments, thereby creating a national cult. Although Mosse pointed to certain continuities in the political style from the wars of liberation against Napoleon to National Socialism, he did not seek to present *the* factor that caused the Third Reich. He was "rather concerned with the growth and evolution of a political style which National Socialism perfected" and which "provided merely one among a great variety of factors which went into the making of the Third Reich."[21]

Koselleck's study "Kriegerdenkmale als Identitätsstiftungen der Überlebenden" did not directly address Nipperdey's "Nationalidee und Nationaldenkmal in Deutschland im 19. Jahrhundert" or Mosse's *The Nationalization of the Masses.*[22] However, there were several analytical overlaps between the three studies, some of which point to broader analytical trends that came into fashion with the cultural turn in the 1970s. One such example was the portrayal of historical memory as a resource of symbolic power that can be marshalled as material power.[23] Like Nipperdey, Koselleck was interested in the means of political identity offered by nineteenth-century memorials (of which war memorials were a subgenre). Like Mosse, he argued that the visual expressions of democratization and nationalization produced by modern war memorials began to offer "identifications in ways that could not have been offered before the French Revolution."[24]

By means of this argument, "Kriegerdenkmale als Identitätsstiftungen der Überlebenden" connected to the aim of illuminating the transition to modernity that Koselleck had pursued since the 1950s. It was hence by drawing on the assumptions encapsulated in the notion of the *Sattelzeit* that he described the ways in which a process of so-called functionalization and democratization of violent death changed the known shapes and functions of war memorials. In the pre-modern period, Koselleck argued, war memorials had been characterized by otherworldly references; by a differentiation by estate in the representation of the violent death; and by an absence of individual soldiers in the depiction. These characteristics disappeared around the French Revolution. At this point, according to Koselleck, the number of memorials increased; they were moved into open spaces; the individual soldier killed in action became entitled to a memorial; and remembrance was increasingly shaped to serve political aims within this world. More concretely, when the memory of the dead soldier was shifted into an inner-worldly context that aimed only at the future of the survivors, death was put into the service of units of political action, which turned the practice of remembering into a pursuit of their aims. The memorials were, Koselleck added, now supposed to "attune the political sensibility of surviving onlookers to the same cause for whose sake the death of the soldiers is supposed to be remembered."[25]

It is on account of arguments such as these that Stefan Goebel has labelled Koselleck a representative of a so-called functionalist position—a position characterized by a focus on the war memorial as a political tool.[26] According to Goebel, Georg Mosse, whose 1990 book *Fallen Soldiers* is "an account of great war remembrance and its nineteenth-century precursors extending the work of Koselleck," represents the same position.[27] Goebel contrasts the functionalist positions of Koselleck and Mosse to a so-called grief school, represented by the American historian Jay Winter. This is, Goebel explains, "a historiographical school which assesses the cost of war at much more intimate levels than historians interested in nationalism and identity politics" and places "emphasis on the personal instead of the political."[28]

It is certainly true that in "Kriegerdenkmale als Identitätsstiftungen der Überlebenden" Koselleck analyzed war memorials as functional tools for political mobilization. However, he was also interested in the cost of war at the intimate and personal level. In fact, his work joined a focus on functionalization and grief, and it did so by means of applying discursive features that also inform other parts of his work, namely anthropological categories. In the beginning of the article, Koselleck thus identified memorials to the dead as corresponding to a "fundamental state of being, pregiven to human beings, in which death and life intertwine in whatever ways they are referred to one another."[29] According to Koselleck, what separates memorials to natural death from those to violent death is that the latter (as a question of "*Sein zum Totschlagen*" (Being toward beating to death)) stands in need of justification and demands to be considered worthy of remembrance.[30] Violent death must have a special reason and meaning attached to it, which offers an identity not only to the death, but also to the living in order to make their survival meaningful.

Related to the notions *Sein zum Tode* (Being toward death) and *Sein zum Totschlagen* (Being toward beating to death), *Totschlagenkönnen* (the ability to kill) was one of the anthropological categories that Koselleck had developed from the 1950s onwards. The fact that it resurfaces in his writings on war memorials suggests, firstly, that this category was linked to his actual lived experience in a way that was different than the other anthropological categories; and, secondly, that *Totschlagenkönnen* was a key element in his attempt to distinguish his ideas from Heidegger's notion of finality. Ultimately, his insistence on the need to account for the social on the level of theory might be interpreted as a consequence of the fact that it requires at least two people, i.e. a social setting, for one person to be able to kill the other. If this interpretation is valid, this might well be one of the most direct connections between Koselleck's war experience and his theorizing, even if he did not make it explicit in "Kriegerdenkmale als Identitätsstiftungen der Überlebenden."

In the text, Koselleck instead related his perspective on *Totschlagenkönnen* to the construction of meaning that is related to violent death. This construction of meaning, he argued, is always shaped by certain anthropological constraints. Most importantly, the meanings connected to war memorials, which bond the living to the dead, will always be constructed by the survivors—never by the dead. Hence the survivors cannot recover the meaning that the deceased may have found in their deaths. In addition, according to Koselleck, during the passage of time, the intended meaning of the monuments will also elude the control of those who erected the memorials. With the purpose of describing this condition, Koselleck outlined the main argument of his investigation: "The thesis that I want to demonstrate from history is this: the only identity that endures clandestinely in all war memorials is the identity of the dead with themselves. All political and social identifications that try to visually capture and permanently fix the 'dying for . . .' vanish in the course of time. For this reason, the message that was to have been established by a memorial changes."[31]

To illustrate this argument, toward the end of his study, Koselleck described the ways in which twentieth-century wars have changed the memorial practices of commemorating violent death. According to Koselleck, one important change took place in relation to World War I, when technical mass death on an industrial scale made it impossible to find and lay the dead to rest. This condition, he wrote, left the survivors with "an obligation to search for justifications that were hard to create with traditional metaphors and concepts."[32] However, with its even more extreme measures of annihilation, World War II posed even greater challenges to the memorial practice. These challenges resulted in what Koselleck described as a "transformation in the iconographic landscape that also changed political sensibility."[33] More concretely, the experiences of this period called for a new political function of monuments, which, rather than visualizing a bond or an identity between the living and the dead, concerned only the question of the meaning of death. Koselleck wrote: "Although not everywhere and not universally, a tendency has thus grown in the Western world to represent death in foreign or civil war only as a question and no longer as an answer, only as demanding meaning and no longer as establishing meaning. What remains is the identity of the dead with themselves; the capability of memorializing the dead eludes the formal language of political sensibility."[34]

The discursive features in these reflections echoed the interpretation of World War II as a *Sattelzeit* in the history of human experience that Koselleck had outlined in "Terror und Traum." However, in "Kriegerdenkmale als Identitätsstiftungen der Überlebenden" he expressed a deeper or more explicit skepticism about the possibilities of representing and communicating the experiences and meanings related to violent death. And he related this skepticism to an assumption about the relation among violent death, meaning, and politics that is not found in "Terror und Traum," but which came to inform his later writings in the field. This assumption is that all attempts to explain, legitimize, or use modern violent death politically are doomed to fail or to express pure ideology, because the only meanings that can be recaptured from violent death are various forms of inexpressible existential suffering.

This assumption also informs the article "Daumier und der Tod," which Koselleck published in a 1985 Festschrift for his friend, the art historian Max Imdahl (1925–1988), whose approach to political iconography Koselleck's work in the field connected to.[35] Focusing on the representation of death in the caricatures of Honoré Daumier (1808–1879), the analysis in "Daumier und der Tod" connected to the central themes of "Terror und Traum" and "Kriegerdenkmale als Identitätsstiftungen der Überlebenden." In the beginning of the text, Koselleck thus introduced death in anthropological and epistemological terms, as "something that eludes human experience even though it is contained in the prospective knowledge of the fact that one has to die."[36] According to Koselleck, what is special about the representation of death in caricatures is that the caricaturists are "forced to make allegories or symbols, signs or signals of death—not death itself—into an object of exaggeration and omission . . . . Their image of death evokes laughter only to suffocate it. Thus in their work, death appears physically, so to speak."[37]

Koselleck then stated that death in modern times poses a special case. Suddenly, it is less comic strip sequences referring to the inescapability and the justification of death, than the manner of death and conveying the situation that is of interest: "The caricature wants to expose its causes and especially its reasons—the art and ruse of, the guile and technical perfection employed for murdering, annihilating, and obliterating."[38] As the events themselves overshadowed the pre-given symbolic meanings that had previously been used to depict the events, an art arose that dealt with death situationally and individually. Violent death, Koselleck specified, "gained historical uniqueness and was interpreted from situation to situation as new, able to be provoked and prevented. Constant, pre-given meanings gave way to historical reasons. But these, too, are surpassable. The actuality of violence leading to death detached itself from its premises, which were formally experienced as permanent."[39]

In Daumier's caricatures of death, Koselleck detected a comical exposure of the traditional symbols of death depicted alongside the specific situations and conditions of death. "In its difference from historical reality," he wrote of Daumier's style, "the caricature comes into its own—as quasi critique of ideology."[40] According to Koselleck, in modernity the "threat of unreality, the production of mass death from the absolute power of human beings themselves, ensconces itself everywhere,"[41] and Daumier's achievement was to document this process. In the very last lines of the article, Koselleck concluded: "If anyone succeeded in capturing the constantly changing but lasting and growing power of killing in a picture for the purpose of bearing witness to it, then it was Daumier."[42]

The cited sentence shows not only how, in his analysis of Daumier, Koselleck elaborated on the discursive features concerning war experience and violent death that he had outlined in earlier studies in the field. It also shows a new perspective on Koselleck's enduring concern with the ways in which political ideology and technology were putting the lives of an increasingly larger number of people put at risk in the age of modernity. This was a concern that Koselleck shared with Daumier, and, although he worked as a historian and not as a cartoonist, it is obvious that he understood his vocational obligation along the lines with which he described Daumier's: to document and criticize the cost of modern utopian thought. Similar to Dauimer, Koselleck saw in death the anti-picture and the limit to the modern historical-philosophical ideas of progression and eternity,[43] and in his eyes, experiences of violent death should lead us not to a search for political meaning or justification, but to commemorate the hopelessness of the experiences from a plurality of perspectives.

Koselleck's search for commemorative practices that draw attention to the loss of meaning, the hopelessness and the incommunicability involved in violent death also informed his introduction to the 1994 volume *Der politische Totenkult: Kriegerdenkmäler in der Moderne*. Here he stated that the medium of sculptural art perhaps offered a way out of what he called the "speechlessness" and "silence" of violent mass death.[44] In this respect, he referred to Rodin as an artist, who, with a sculpture of a defeated soldier after the wars in 1870/71, had managed to create a memorial that was de-militarized and de-nationalized and did not refer to any political party. However, according to Koselleck, due to thematizing defeat, Rodin's sculpture nevertheless communicated themes and symbols that are prone always to generate conflict. More concretely, by referring to the anthropological given constants of "winners" and "vanquished," Rodin had thematized what Koselleck at the end of the introduction depicted as perhaps insurmountable challenges involved in the search for practices of remembering that do not functionalize violent death for political purpose: "Only when 'winners' and 'vanquished' no more exist, would the prevailing age come to an end. But that is a utopian idea. What remain are those who have been killed. To commemorate them is the minimum, without which it is not possible to live on. Against the background of past experience, the question of whether memorials can rise to this challenge remains open."[45]

"Winners" and "vanquished" are a pair of counter-concepts that do not form part of the list of anthropological categories that Koselleck worked with from the 1950s onwards. However, from the way he used this pair of notions in *Der politische Totenkult* and in other texts such as "Erfahrungswandel und Methodenwechsel," he seemingly conceived of the pairing in a similar way and recognized it as part of the human condition.

Still, as the quoted passage reveals, he felt a certain longing to get rid of this particular pair of counter-concepts—a feeling toward which he took a characteristically skeptical attitude because he regarded it as utopian. Still, the normatively induced rejection of "winners" and "vanquished" sufficed to consistently exclude these notions from the list of categories that Koselleck recognized as truly anthropological. Here, there was a sense of utopian longing that was not easily dismissed—another way of departing from political realism in the image of Schmitt. The emphatic expression of the skeptical attitude in the quoted passage from *Der politische Totenkult* and the recurrence of the motive of overcoming the dichotomy of winners/vanquished indicate that this matter belonged to the deep structure of Koselleck's thought as it emerged in the post-war years. Arguably, this emergence was part of the anti-war sentiment of those years that fed in a rather direct way on something that one might label Germany's "culture of defeat" after 1945.[46] This was a discursive arrangement that was carried by utopian affect and skepticism toward the utopian affect, as well as by the very notions it sought to discard: The sense of defeat informed the hope to rid oneself of the notion of defeat. All this was part of a political common ground tacitly postulated by most participants of public debates in the Federal Republic. It seems plausible that Koselleck's 1994 reaffirmation of this discursive pattern was also a reaction to the mounting debates (from 1991 onwards) about future German military engagements abroad. If this course of argument is acceptable, this was another important, though subtle, dimension of political engagement in his writings on the commemoration of violent death, in which he wanted to retain the discursive arrangements of the "old" Federal Republic.

The Debates on the Neue Wache and the Holocaust Museum

During the 1990s Koselleck was to elaborate on his skepticism about the possibilities of finding appropriate ways to commemorate violent death that he had expressed in Der politische Totenkult. This took place in texts written in relation to the two German memorial debates that raged during this decade, in autobiographical texts, and in scholarly texts on experience and memory. The following sections take a closer look at these different types of texts and on the relation among them. We begin with Koselleck's interventions in the memorial debates. In many ways, these interventions represent a continuation of his scholarly work in the field, as they aimed to ensure that the memorials at issue represented the horrors and hopelessness of the past in appropriate ways. At the same time, they comprised a new discursive feature that is not found in Koselleck's earlier writings.

The first of the two debates concerned the plans proposed by Chancellor Helmut Kohl and his government in the early 1990s to renovate and turn the Neue Wache (New Guard House), a structure that was part of the surviving ensemble of classical Prussian buildings constituting the old representative center of Berlin, into united Germany's national memorial devoted to die Opfer von Krieg und Gewaltherrschaft (the victims of war and the rule of violence).[47] Already in 1964, there had been constructed a small central memorial with the same dedication, which referred not only to those who died in the two world wars and under the Nazi regime, but also to the victims of post-1945 Stalinism, and which with its equation of National Socialism and Stalinism served as a political tool in the Cold War.[48]

Kohl's proposal was also politically motivated.[49] It was thus closely related to a larger strategy of conservative identity politics, which Kohl launched in the early 1980s, and which, it has been said, was based on a language of patriotic pride and a strong rhetoric toward the East, and "pursued a symbolic rehabilitation of the German identity and history that demanded a gesture of forgiveness from Western powers for the Nazi past (indeed, of forgetting it)."[50]

The Neue Wache had been constructed between 1816 and 1818 and had already served the memorial politics of three German governments, when Kohl and his government launched their plan for the building in 1992. The proposal was to place a Pietà inside the Neue Wache. The piece had been sketched in 1937 by the socialist artist Käthe Kollwitz and portrays a mother grieving over her son's death in World War I. Kohl already had a smaller version of the Pietà placed on his office desk; it was an enlarged version of this that he wanted to use for the memorial.

In the months before the opening, there was an intense debate about this idea. Three aspects of the memorial were subject to extraordinary criticism.[51] Some argued that it was inappropriate to reuse a memorial that had served military and memorial purposes both before 1918 and after 1933. Others argued that the Pietà did not have sufficient expression to commemorate the victims of World War II, the Holocaust, and other dimensions of the terror committed in the name of National Socialism. Finally, several discussants were against the inscription on the Pietà, because in their eyes it obscured the distinction between victims and perpetrators in relation to twentieth-century wars and rules of violence.

The leveling of the victims was one of the issues that Koselleck commented upon, as he emerged as one of the staunchest critics of Kohl's plans for the Neue Wache in a series of newspaper articles and interviews.[52] All his principal objections to the memorial are found in his first contribution to the debate—the article "Bilderverbot," which was published in the *Frankfurter Allgemeine Zeitung* in April 1993.[53] In the article, he suggested that Kohl's decision had to be revised because, in his opinion, the two basic messages expressed by the Pietà, one concrete and the other symbolic, represented respectively inadequate and erroneous forms of remembrance for a German national memorial.

What Koselleck found inadequate in respect to the concrete message of the Pietà was the lack of reference to the extreme experiences of war and violence after 1918. That is, the experiences of World War II, National Socialism and the extermination camps, and the many different individuals and groups who were killed or in various ways died between 1933 and 1945. According to Koselleck, these experiences raised questions and demanded answers that were not referred to and reflected upon in the Pietà.

What Koselleck found erroneous in respect to the symbolic message of the Pietà was the way in which it also excluded some of the central experiences that a monument dedicated to *die Opfer von Krieg und Gewaltherrschaft* in the twentieth century should commemorate. More concretely, according to Koselleck, because of the Christian tradition portrayed by Maria with the dead Christ in her hands, the Pietà in fact excluded the millions of the Jews who were killed at the hands of National Socialist terror.

In addition, Koselleck argued that the Pietà should be given a different inscription. More specifically, he pointed to how the ambiguous meaning of the German world *Opfer* (meaning both victim and sacrifice) threatened to place the suffering of the victims of National Socialist ideology, conquest, and murder on a level with the active and voluntary *sacrificium* of the soldier in the *Wehrmacht*—a leveling that gravely misrepresented experiences of war. Against this background, Koselleck ended "Bilderverbot" by calling for time to discuss a more appropriate commemorative form.

However, although many other commentators criticized the memorial plan, the Kohl government neither postponed the date for the opening nor proposed any changes concerning the memorial's form. This provoked Koselleck to publish another article in the *Frankfurter Allgemeine Zeitung* titled "Stellen die Toten uns einen Termin?" in which he criticized the monumental form as well as the way in which Kohl and his government had attempted to steer and accelerate the political process in order to open the memorial at a certain date.[54]

In the beginning of the article, Koselleck wrote, "It is never too late for the Federal Republic to give a central memorial an appropriate form." To this, he ironically added: "The dead do not run away." He then launched a direct attack on the way in which the government had directed the memorial plans without consulting the parliament or the public. "Our society does not only feel patronized; it is patronized and knows it," he said. In addition, he insisted that, in line with the political traditions of the Federal Republic, the government should listen to the various interest groups and individuals and to scholarly experts instead of monopolizing and accelerating the decision-making from above. "The Federal Government seems to know, what it wants," he wrote in a tone of indignation. "Does it also know what it does? Obviously not. And does it know what it does not do? Evidently not either."

"Bilderverbot" and "Stellen die Toten uns einen Termin?" are typical of Koselleck's contributions to the memorial debates in the 1990s. In these contributions, he picked up on analytical themes from his scholarly work, such as the relations between inclusion and exclusion, and state and society, and he provided in the memorial debate a semantic check of the contemporary use of language, with the hope that historical clarification would lead to political clarity. In addition, his contributions to the debate all expressed a staunch defense of a democratic political culture, based on the belief that only an open, public discussion will lead to a proper way of dealing with the past. As a result, Koselleck became broadly known as a classic public intellectual, who voiced his opinion on societal matters unbound by party, political, or ideological ties. Indeed, Koselleck's only aim in the debate was to ensure that the experiences of war, violence, and terror were commemorated in an appropriate fashion.

It was with the same aim that, in "Stellen die Toten uns einen Termin?," Koselleck elaborated on his critique of the reference to the word *Opfer* in the Pietà's inscription and suggested an alternative inscription: "For the dead, fallen, killed, gassed, perished, missing." He preferred this inscription, because it commemorated not only those who died, but also how they died: "It is not only our moral and political obligation to remember the death, but also the agony of dying, the having-to-die under conditions that elude our imagination."[55]

This passage connected directly to the attempts to give voice to the suffering of those who died between 1933 and 1945 and to the reflections on how to communicate the incommunicable that Koselleck had first introduced in "Terror und Traum." However, in relation to the Neue Wache debate, he launched a discursive feature that is not found in any of his earlier texts on war experiences; this is an argument concerning a special German obligation to commemorate victims of twentieth-century terror and violence. This argument informed also "Stellen die Toten uns einen Termin?," at the opening of which Koselleck spoke of "the catastrophe that we Germans have caused and called upon us," and he later concluded: "The memorial should of course not be overburdened. It cannot, as it is customary to say, master the burden and the misery of our history. However, it can show for what we have to answer for. We owe that to the dead. Therefore, for us Germans, the situation demands a minimum of demonstration and a maximum of reticence."[56]

Koselleck repeated his argument about a special German responsibility to commemorate the crimes committed in the name of National Socialism in the debate of the Holocaust Memorial. The first initiative for this memorial was taken in 1989, when the citizen's initiative group Perspektive Berlin, led by the journalist Lea Rosh and the historian Eberhard Jäckel, collected more than 10,000 signatures, including those of Günter Grass and former Social Democratic Chancellor Willy Brandt, in support of the project. Later the same year, Perspektive Berlin and a newly formed circle for promoting the construction of a memorial for the murdered Jews of Europe were granted a location for the memorial on a property between Brandenburg Gate and Potsdamer Platz, close to the buried ruins of the Third Reich.

However, the process of deciding on a memorial form was problem-ridden and took almost ten years. Eventually, in November 1997, a commission recommended two designs, and soon after, Kohl opted for the proposal by the sculptor Richard Serra and the architect Peter Eisenmann, consisting of 4,000 upright concrete slabs in steel varying in height and length. Finally, in June 1999, the Bundestag voted to support the construction of the Holocaust Memorial along with a museum and information center.

Besides issues related to its memorial form, two dimensions of the Serra/Eisenmann proposal received much attention in the debate preceding the decision. The first concerned the question of whether a central monument was necessary at all. While those in favor of the monument argued that no other site in Germany included specific references to the extermination camps in Poland and the mass murder of the European Jews, others feared that another monument in Berlin would turn the city into what was spoken of as a capital city of remorse and promote a so-called negative nationalism instead of encouraging Germans to reflect on the Holocaust or to create a German identity based on positive achievements.

The second and most contested dimension of the memorial concerned whether it should be dedicated only to the memory of Jews or also to other victims of the Nazi regime. The discussion of this issue broke out in the beginning of the 1990s between Romani Rose, the chairman of the Roma and Sinti community in Germany, and Heinz Galinski and later Ignatz Bubis, who in 1992 succeeded Galinski as chairman of Germany's Jewish community. Rose argued that the omission of the Roma and Sinti people was an insult, because they belonged to the same category of Nazi victims as the Jews. Whereas Habermas defended the plans of the Holocaust memorial by stressing that Germans should not abstract away from the specific significance of the Jews and of anti-semitism for German history and self-understanding, the author Günter Grass also protested against the exclusion of Roma and Sinti, arguing that it would represent a continuation of Hitler's racial politics in terms of the hierarchy of victims.

This argument had already been launched by Reinhart Koselleck, who in a series of newspaper articles and interviews published between January 1997 and March 1999 emerged as the most persistent critic of a memorial devoted exclusively to the memory of the murdered Jews of Europe.[57] Koselleck was not against the plan of a new national memorial but hoped for a memorial that could make up for the mistakes that in his opinion had been committed in relation to the Neue Wache. Before the opening of the latter memorial, Ignatz Bubis and the State Minister Anton Pfeifer from the CDU came to an agreement that two plaques should be placed at the entrance: one with an overview of the history of the building, and one with a text along the lines of the famous speech delivered by the President of Germany, Richard von Weizsäcker given on 8 May 1985 on the occasion of the fortieth anniversary of the end of World War II.[58] Yet, when the memorial was opened on 14 November 1993, it was given an inscription that takes virtually no account of the criticism directed against the first proposal. To begin with, encouraging the spectator to view war almost like a natural disaster, it allowed for a broad definition of victims. Moreover, although it mentions the murdered Jews, Sinti and Roma, the inscription, it has been said, "is in the first instance a tribute to those Germans who died at the front, in bombing raids, or when fleeing the eastern territories before and after May 1945," while it "in good anti-communist tradition, fails to mention the Russians and Poles."[59]

This solution deeply disappointed Koselleck, who was against the idea of only commemorating one group of victims in the Holocaust Memorial.[60] Why, he asked in the article "Erschlichener Rollentausch" from April 1997, should the memorial not commemorate all the victims, including the Sinti and the Roma; the three and half million Russian prisoners of war; the millions of killed non-Jewish Poles; the hundreds of thousands murdered in the Balkans, in Greece, in Italy, in the Western and Nordic countries; the millions of dead in Ukraine, Belarus, and Russia; the homosexuals; the victims of euthanasia; and those killed for political and religious reasons? In his eyes, the principle of uniqueness was applicable to several groups of victims of Nazi violence, and he saw therefore no moral or political reason to commemorate exclusively the Jews.[61]

According to Koselleck, there were only two responsible solutions to the memorial: either to give to all groups their own memorial or to construct a single memorial for all those who were murdered by the Nazis. Koselleck preferred the latter solution and justified it by means of reasserting his belief that the German nation had a special obligation to ensure the realization of a memorial for the totality of terror committed during the Nazi regime. In the article "Die Widmung" from March 1999, he wrote: "As a nation of perpetrators (*Täternation*) constructing a national memorial in Berlin, we have the duty to remember everybody. And as perpetrators, we should not take upon ourselves to define a hierarchy of victims. Neither many individual memorials nor an ensemble of different memorials for various groups can provide what is needed: to found a comprehensive memorial for the totality of crimes committed by the National Socialists."[62]

While Koselleck's interventions did not have any influence on the 1999 decision taken by the Bundestag concerning the Holocaust Memorial, they were generally positively received in the debate as well as in the later literature about the topic.[63] However, some of his suggestions were also met with critique. This was first of all the case with his plea that Germany and the Germans should take responsibility for the victims of World War II and National Socialism. The suggestion was criticized by a number of commentators, who pointed out that the majority of the Germans participating in erecting the memorial were too young to have been involved with National Socialism and thus could hardly be assigned political responsibility in a direct sense.[64] Still, Koselleck insisted on a special German commemorative duty. "Not an individual German," he said in an interview during the Neue Wache debate, "but the sum of Germans, who acted under Hitler, is after all the Germans, whose legacy we have to compensate for in the Federal Republic."[65]

With lines such as these, Koselleck not only argued against those who wanted to distinguish the Germans of the past from the Germans of the present, but diverged also from trends that re-emerged after 2000 of dealing with the Nazi period from the perspective of the German victims, such as those who died in the Allied bombings or while fleeing the Red Army in the east. To be sure, Koselleck did not disagree with the fact that there had been many German victims between 1933 and 1945, but he continued to argue that the victims of the Nazi extermination should not be leveled with the German victims.

Primary Experience vs. Secondary Memory

It is tempting to read Koselleck's contributions to the memorial debates not only as scholarly contributions to public discussions, but also as a series of direct personal attempts to cope with and rework his own experiences of war. It is in this respect worth noting that his insistence on a special German responsibility to commemorate twentieth-century war and violence is better illuminated with reference to the autobiographical texts that he published in the 1990s than with reference to his scholarly texts that emerged before the debate. In fact, neither his interventions in the memorial debates nor the theoretical-methodological texts on memory and identity that he published in the 1990s can be understood without taking into account these autobiographical texts. "Even when he spoke on the highest level of abstraction about forms of experience and remembrance, also in relation to historiography," Willibald Steinmetz has written regarding this relation in Koselleck's writings, "his own experience was the touchstone upon which all theory had to stand its test."[66]

Nowhere is this relation more obvious than in the autobiographical text "Glühende Lava, zur Erinnerung geronnen" that Koselleck published in the *Frankfurter Allgemeine Zeitung* in the beginning of May 1995, in relation to the commemoration of the fiftieth anniversary of 8 May 1945.[67] This text not only connected different parts of his writings on war experiences; it also linked his identities as a scholar in the field and a survivor of war. "Glühende Lava, zur Erinnerung geronnen" begins with a description of how Koselleck's experience of the first days of May 1945 differed from the experiences of many other Germans. Hence, when the bells signaling peace rang on 9 May 1945, the war did not end for Koselleck, as he was in Russian captivity and soon began a long walk toward Auschwitz together with his fellow German prisoners of war. According to Koselleck, before he arrived at the camp its name and existence were unknown to him, and he was told by the Russians that millions had been gassed and killed in Birkenau. While initially, and like most of his fellow captives, Koselleck believed this information to be Soviet propaganda, he soon became spontaneously convinced that it was correct.

What convinced him was an incident in the camp with a former Polish inmate, who was taking care of the surveillance of the German prisoners of war and urging them to work faster in the kitchen. Suddenly, he took a stool and raised it into the air, to hit Koselleck in the head, but he then stopped and said: "Why should I smash your head? You gassed millions," and, full of anger, he instead threw the stool on the ground. Koselleck described his reaction to the incident in the following way: "It struck me—literally—that he spoke the truth. Gassed? Millions? That could not have taken place."[68]

These lines deserve attention for two reasons. First, they connect to Koselleck's interventions in the memorial debates, as they seemingly describe how the issue of a special German responsibility for the crimes committed during World War II was one that he had been confronted with and convinced about on a very personal level. If linked to his interventions in the memorial debates, his plea to the Germans to take upon themselves the responsibility and, in a moral way, also the guilt for crimes committed in the name of National Socialism, appears as a generationally and individually conditioned and motivated attempt to master the heritage of National Socialism and reconcile Germany with the past.

Secondly, the cited lines are interesting because they serve to introduce an epistemological argument about the conditions of human experience and memory that came to occupy center stage in Koselleck's theoretical writings on these issues in the 1990s. Most importantly, he wrote: "There are experiences that flow into the body like red-hot lava and petrify there. Irremovable, they can be retrieved at any time without changing. Few such experiences can be transformed into authentic memories; but when it happens, they are grounded in their sensorial [*sinnliche*] presence. The smell, the taste, the sound, the feeling and the visible surrounding, in short, all senses, in pleasure or pain, are awakened and need no effort of the memory."[69]

Koselleck then distinguished this kind of bodily experience from so-called linguistically communicated memory: "Indeed, there are numerous memories that I have often mentioned and repeated, but who's true sensorial presence [*sinnliche Wahrheitspräsenz*] has vanished long ago. Even for me, they are merely literary stories: when I listen to myself, all I can do is to believe in them, but I can no longer vouch for their sensory-based [*sinnlichen*] certainty. However, many things belong to the unchangeable primary experience, the petrified lava."

Summed up, what Koselleck introduced in "Glühende Lava, zur Erinnerung geronnen" was an argument concerning a fundamental difference between a primary, bodily experience and a secondary, linguistic memory.[70] The difference can be summarized as follows: According to Koselleck, primary experience that is made via body impression maintains its truth-presence and absoluteness, and it cannot be replaced or communicated. Linguistic memory, on the other hand, has to be maintained by means of being retold, but is bound to change and to lose its original meaning over time. As an elaboration of these differences, Koselleck again referred to Auschwitz. For him, what was experienced by the prisoners in Auschwitz in the early 1940s is only accessible via communicated memory, because he was not there. His primary experiences of war were made elsewhere, first of all in Russian captivity, where his body suffered the unforgettable impressions of what he described as "only hunger and constantly hunger, work and more work."[71]

In his theoretical writings on experience, memory and identity in the 1990s, Koselleck elaborated on this distinction between primary experience and secondary memory. This habitually took place in polemics against the notion of collective memory, which occupied a special place in the field of historical memory in the 1980 and 1990s. The growth of this field in the mentioned period had first of all to do with the French historian Pierre Nora's huge research project *Les Lieux de Mémoire* (1984–1993), in which he outlined a theory concerning how collective memory is created and maintained within so-called realms of memory (*lieux de mémoire*).[72] In the wake of the work of Nora and of scholars such as David Lowenthal, Raphael Samuel, and Simon Schama, the number of publications addressing historical memory virtually exploded. In the year

2000, the American expert in the field Jay Winter consequently spoke of a "memory boom."[73]

While Koselleck obviously found the study of experience and memory of great importance, he held deep reservations about the notion of collective memory. These reasons were first stated in the article "Erinnerungsschleusen und Erfahrungsgeschichten" from 1992—a text which was also informed by autobiographical experiences and concerns, even if these were not thematized directly.[74] Koselleck began the text by stating that everyone is "familiar with breaking points in their biography, which seem to mark a transition to another chapter in life."[75] According to Koselleck, these breaks are related to the making of radically new experiences. He explained: "When such experiences are reworked, both the ways of acting and attitudes as well as the consciousness of these attitudes can change."[76]

Koselleck then presented the two world wars as events that for many resulted in ruptures of experience that were until then unthinkable, and he outlined a number of theoretical and methodological issues that he argued must be considered when studying the influence of the two world wars on the social consciousness in Europe. Most importantly, according to Koselleck, it is simply impossible to speak of a collective mentality or of experiences in a general sense. Instead, it is necessary to clarify the different ways in which people make their experiences and the different ways in which these experiences are subsequently reworked. In other words, to clarify to what extent experiences and memories can be shared, one must study the conditions in which they are made, structured, and restructured.

For this analytical purpose, Koselleck made a distinction between so-called synchronic factors, which during a war determine the ways in which events can be experienced, and so-called diachronic factors that concern the subsequent reworking of the primary experience. With respect to the synchronic factors, he argued that historians must always pay attention both to the different ways in which human beings experience events during a war and to the different ways in which every human consciousness that afterwards reworks the experiences of war has been pre-conditioned beforehand. More concretely, he argued that human experiences of war depend on various pre-conditions such as linguistic traditions, religious and ideological beliefs, political relations, generational belonging, and societal background and class relation, all of which dispose the consciousness to different possibilities of experiencing the world. To these synchronic factors, Koselleck added the diachronic factors that concern the ways in which the experienced events are filtrated and reworked once the war is over. Here Koselleck pointed to the question of whether a person belonged to the winners or the vanquished as the most important factor, but he also listed other factors by means of which experiences of war can be forgotten, reinterpreted, and distorted, as new societal-political constellations are established.

"Erinnerungsschleusen und Erfahrungsgeschichten" is typical of Koselleck's attempts in the 1990s to deconstruct the notion of collective memory. These attempts represent a continuation of the mode of theorizing that Koselleck had pursued since the early 1950s. It was by emphasizing the anthropological and social conditions characterizing human life that he wanted to substitute the monolithic notion of collective memory with a definition of history as unfolding in the interaction among pluralities of non-convergent histories.

What was new in Koselleck's writings on memory and experience in the 1990s was that his deconstruction of history in the singular, in this case the notion of collective memory, went hand in hand with and was made possible by a vigorous defense of the personal experience against overarching notions of collective memory. This was for example the case with the article "Gebrochene Erinnerung? Deutsche und polnische Vergangenheiten" that Koselleck published in *Das Jahrbuch der Deutschen Akademie für Sprache und Dichtung* in 2001.[77] Elaborating on the argumentative lines from his earlier articles in the field, Koselleck stated in the text that memory encompasses a double meaning. On the one hand, memory exists as a primary individually-made experience, which is impregnated in the body and therefore is incommunicable and irreplaceable. On the other hand, memory is often conceived as collective memory. As for the latter form of memory, Koselleck agreed that there are certain common conditions of possible experience that people cannot escape, regardless of age, gender, confession, party membership, or nationality. However, he also argued that these experiences are always perceived and interpreted in different ways according to the backgrounds and dispositions of those making the experiences. In other words, according to Koselleck, in the same moment experiences are made, a plurality of memories is made, and there are consequently as many memories as there are people.

In line with his enduring critique of history in the singular, Koselleck placed this perspective against the core problem that he saw in the notion of collective memory: that it requires a *Handlungssubjekt*, which must be remembered collectively, such as the idea of the people, the class, or the party, which serves to mobilize people for a certain cause. He wrote: "There is therefore a veto-right of the personal experience that blocks for any incorporation in a collective memory. And it is a part of the often (and often vainly) claimed human dignity, that every human being has a right to an individual memory. Such an entirely personal right to a memory offers protection against ideological indoctrination, against mental control and subjection."

During the 1990s, as Koselleck frequently repeated his argument about the "veto-right of the personal experience," it became increasingly clear that it was closely related to his personal past. A direct example of this is found an interview conducted in 2005 in relation to the commemoration of the sixtieth anniversary of 8 May 1945. Here, with reference to his personal experiences of war, Koselleck unconditionally stated: "Every man has the right to have his own memory—that I will not allow to be collectivized."[78]

What is interesting in Koselleck's argument about the "veto-right of the personal experience" is that it can be read as both a continuation of and a break with his earlier work. On the one hand, it reiterated the claim to a plurality of histories that he had pursued since the 1950s, and it corresponded to earlier theoretical assumptions that went in similar direction. An important issue is his insistence on the social as opposed to the linguistic, which is, at the end of the day, still an insistence on the social and not the individual, but has the same tendency to postulate a sort of authenticity and reality that is opposed to a view of the world shaped by language and linguistically induced errors. In some sense, what Koselleck expressed in all of his writings and accentuated in his texts on war experience was a deep distrust in language and discourse—a distrust that speaks to an famous tradition of modern thought (distrust in language, the insistence on the inexplicability of things, breakdown of communication) that is found in many different strands of scientific and fictional literature.

Yet because of its much more radical claim to pluralism, Koselleck's argument about the "veto-right of the personal experience" can be read as a crucial break with his earlier work. This claim is first of all witnessed in his autobiographical texts such as "Glühende Lava, zur Erinnerung geronnen." There Koselleck expressed a wish to maintain his primary experience intact in its original form and for himself, and he also portrayed primary experience as more authentic, true, and superior to other forms of experience. He wrote: "Today, I know more than I could know back then, and I know things that I could not have known back then. And so it goes for later generations. But the incommunicability of knowledge made via primary experience cannot be overcome. To know is better than to know better."[79]

In short, when this epistemological and normative defense of the individual experience threatened to break with Koselleck's earlier work, it was because it placed stronger, if not insurmountable constraints on the possibilities of writing a mode of history that is based on grand narratives and generalized interpretations. While he continued to portray history as created in the social interaction between human beings, he described experience and memory as something that cannot be shared between human beings. That is, he described experiences and memories as histories that cannot become history, and thus came close to a relativistic standpoint according to which every experience can only be considered and understood on its own terms.

However, while it is possible to decipher from Koselleck's autobiographical writings a radical, relativist position, this is undermined or at least blurred by a different position that he conveyed in his autobiographical writings and pursued in theoretical texts. Hence, in "Glühende Lava, zur Erinnerung geronnen," Koselleck's categorical distinction between primary and secondary memory was, as we have seen, accompanied by a set of reflections on the way in which some of his primary experiences of World War II had lost their exactness and authenticity, as they had been communicated and thus transformed into literary stories. Here, as pointed out by Willibald Steinmetz, Koselleck described language as a medium by means of which primary experience will always be transformed: "Language itself, as a repertoire of pre-given concepts, metaphors, narrative patterns and ways of speaking, does not allow an entirely individual articulation of experience: by means of the linguistic communication of experience, in the linguistic communication of experience, the individual to some extent gives up the sovereignty of the personal memory."[80]

In his theoretical writings, Koselleck elaborated on this unavoidable merging of different modes of experiences and memories taking place through the human *Miteinandersein* and *Miteinandersprechen*. This is, for example, the place in "Gebrochene Erinnerung?" where he thematized the notion of secondary memory and its foundations in communicative practices. According to Koselleck, going in time and space beyond the primary experience, secondary memory is generated in schools, in families, and by historians who can rationally check the facts of the given memory, but who are always in ongoing competition with other producers of memory, such as churches, parties, and artists. On the other hand, this way of theorizing is also compatible with Koselleck's earlier work. Hence his assumption of the interaction between primary experience and secondary memory might even be interpreted as a new way of thematizing the interaction between different temporal layers in history.

However, in contrast to his previous attempts to theorize the existence of *Zeitschichten*, Koselleck expressed discontent with the merging of primary experience and secondary memory. This was especially the case in his autobiographical writings and is nowhere as evident as in the earlier mentioned article "Die Diskontinuität der Erinnerung."[81] What is special

about "Die Diskontinuität der Erinnerung" is not only the somewhat chaotic fashion in which it merged all the key points raised in his previous
writings in the field and hence directly connected his autobiographical
experiences to his scholarly theory; it is also the strong opinions that he
voiced on the memories of World War II in post-war German society and
the pessimism that he expressed about the possibilities of communicating
and representing what happened between 1933 and 1945.

Koselleck began the article by using his personal experiences of war to
argue that every secondary memory represents a discontinuity of primary
experience. With reference to this argument, he explained the conflict
between the 68ers and their parents, but he also lamented the moral critique that the 68ers had launched. According to Koselleck, this critique
was off the mark because the 68ers did not understand the complex nature of the primary experience made between 1933 and 1945. Here he re-
capitulated his defense of primary experience using phrases that were also
informed by a moral judgment: "To know is better than to know better. It
is easy to know better. It is hard to know."[82]

As he then ventured into a discussion of what was known of the Nazi
crimes in the period of National Socialism, he suggested that most Germans had only a fragmentary knowledge of these crimes and stated that
he himself knew nothing and felt betrayed when he learned of them after
the war, just as he felt discontent with the ways in which primary experiences of National Socialism and war had been reinterpreted in erroneous ways in the period after 1945. Among the examples that Koselleck
mentioned in this respect was the fact that the experience of the German
"capitulation" had been reinterpreted into a secondary memory of a German "liberation" that portrayed the Germans as victims.

It was against this background that he introduced three modes of memory through which the Nazi crimes are addressed: the scientific, the moral,
and the religious. While Koselleck recognized the need for all the three
forms of memory, he argued, as mentioned, that the crimes defy all efforts
to grasp them scientifically or morally, or atone for them through religion.
More concretely, according to Koselleck, the scientific explanation would
be subject to permanent overexertion in order to explain the unexplain-
able; the moral judgment would not gain in strength through repetition;
and the religious would make no sense for the non-Christians. Hence,
all three explanatory modes lead to "the aporia" and the obligation of
remembering the crimes by bypassing narratives that aim to explain or
make sense of them.

Finally, at the end of the article, Koselleck related his discussion of
the relation between experience and memory to the contemporary Holocaust Memorial debate and argued once again for a memorial form that

included all victims of the Nazi crimes but also portrayed the Germans as perpetrators—a so-called *Tätermal*. He wrote: "A *Tätermal*, that reminds us, who has to carry the responsibility for the killings, the annihilations and the gassings. We have to learn to live with this memory."[83]

Evidently, these lines testify to Koselleck's commitment with respect to finding an appropriate way to commemorate the crimes of National Socialism. More generally, "Die Diskontinuität der Erinnerung" points to the many epistemological, moral, and emotional issues that were involved in his writings on experience, memory, and identity and to how the arguments of the scholar and those of the survivor of war were inseparable and characterized by tensions.[84]

More generally, for Koselleck, to deal with National Socialism was to deal with "negative memories,"[85] and even if reflecting on the autobiographical helped him to rework personal traumas, there can be no doubt that, in his writings on experience and memory he encountered a number of epistemological and moral issues that he found difficult and painful to deal with. Hence, his writings in this field remained characterized by a degree of ambiguity, hesitance, and incompleteness that is not found in his work in other fields.

It should in addition be stressed that Koselleck's interest in memory matters was selective. Most of his respective writings were focused on World War II and seem to concern his own experiences and traumas. It was also in this context that his insistency of authenticity became a frequent and central motive of his writings and his diffidence regarding linguistic representations was expressed in the most uncompromising terms. It is in this respect noteworthy that he never aimed at what one might call an extensive and detailed representation, neither in the form of an academic analysis nor in the form of a comprehensive account of his personal experiences. After all, when Koselleck spoke of his war experience, he always structured his narratives around the same few, selected key events that all took place in 1945 and 1946, thus roughly leaving out detailed perspectives on his various experiences in the years between 1941 and 1945. While it is difficult to say whether this was because of un-reworked traumas or because all his most imposing primary experiences took place after 8 May 1945, it is obvious that his war narrative was deeply embedded in his thought as a totality and in his personality as a scholar and a public intellectual.

Accordingly, it is also worth stressing that the field of memory politics is virtually the only one in which Koselleck seriously attempted to become a public intellectual and to influence the present and the future, which he had defined as a key ambition of his work earlier in the 1950s. On the one hand, the strong rhetoric concerning these issues in his early writings contrasts with the after-all limited attempts he made at influencing social-political conditions by means of partaking directly in the public debate outside the realms of academia. On the other, Koselleck's choice not to link science directly to politics was certainly in accordance with the scholarly program for which he had laid the foundations in the 1950s.

Notes

1. Reinhart Koselleck, "Terror und Traum: Methodologische Anmerkungen zu Zeiterfahrungen im Dritten Reich," *Vergangene Zukunft: Zur Semantik geschichtlicher Zeiten* (Frankfurt am Main, 1979), 278–99.
2. Ibid., 292, 289 (CFOT).
3. Ibid., 283, 284.
4. Ibid., 293.
5. Ibid., 288.
6. See Meier, "Gedenkrede auf Reinhart Koselleck," 27; and Gumbrecht, "Pyramiden des Geistes," 29–31. For a critique of Gumbrecht's explanation of this silence (that *Begriffsgeschichte* was informed by the "latent" wish of the generation of German scholars, who had participated in World War II, to reconcile themselves with German history by leaving out those dimensions of history, especially issues related to National Socialism, which cannot be dealt with through language), see Stephan Schlak, "Der Sound der Sentimentalität," *Süddeutsche Zeitung* 2/1 (2007).
7. For the main trends in the research of National Socialism and the Holocaust from the 1940s until 2000, see Berg, *Der Holocaust*; and Ulrich Herbert, "Vernichtungspolitik: Neue Antworten und Fragen zur Geschichte des Holocaust," *Nationalsozialistische Vernichtungspolitik: Neue Forschungen und Kontroversen* (Frankfurt am Main, 1998), 9–66. For the silence in respect to the Nazi past among intellectuals who had been involved in Nazism, see Maurice Olender, *Race and Erudition* (Cambridge, 2009), 131–58.
8. For the mid 1980s debate between Broszat, who called for a historicization of the Nazi regime by writing it into the *Alltagsgeschichte* of the period, and Saul Friedländer, who contended that aspects of normality and criminality overlapped in the everyday life of Nazi Germany and that Broszat's proposal was in danger of creating a historical distortion by ignoring the extraordinary character of Nazism that lay in its criminality, see Peter Baldwin, *Reworking the Past: Hitler, the Holocaust, and the Historians' Debate* (Boston, 1990).
9. Koselleck, "Terror und Traum," 297 (CFOT).
10. Quoted from Saul Friedländer, *Memory, History and the Extermination of Jews of Europe* (Bloomington, 1993), 57. Friedländer brings up the letter in relation to a set of reflections on the difficulties of writing the history of the Nazi regime and the Holocaust. Although Friedländer has since provided a massive account of the history of the Nazi persecution (*Nazi Germany and the Jews, 1933–1939* (New York, 1997) and *The Years of Extermination: Nazi Germany and the Jews, 1939–1945* (New York, 2007), his position on the theme resembles Koselleck s in that he believes the Holocaust to pose tremendous difficulties that stand in the way of understanding it.

Therefore, Friedländer wants to avoid a closure of arguments presented on the issue. See Yehuda Bauer, *Rethinking the Holocaust* (New York, 2001), 7–8.

11. Koselleck, "Die Diskontinuität der Erinnerung," 219.

12. Ibid..

13. See also Gumbrecht, "Pyramiden des Geistes," 30–31.

14. With the exception of writing an introduction to a new edition of the published protocol of dreams that he had analyzed in "Terror und Traum." See Charlotte Beradt, *Das Dritte Reich des Traums: Mit einem Nachwort von Reinhart Koselleck* (Frankfurt am Main, 1981).

15. Steinmetz, "Nachruf auf Reinhart Koselleck," 429.

16. Reinhart Koselleck and Reiner Metzger, "Bundesrepublikanische Kompromisse: Die deutschen und ihr Denkmalskult. Rainer Metzger sprach mit Reinhart Koselleck," *Kunstforum* 136 (1996): 467–68.

17. Reinhart Koselleck, "Kriegerdenkmale als Identitätsstiftungen der Überlebenden," *Poetik und Hermeneutik. VIII. Identität*, ed. Odo Marquard and Karlheinz Stierle, 255–76 (München, 1979).

18. Thomas Nipperdey, "Nationalidee und Nationaldenkmal in Deutschland im 19. Jahrhundert," *Historische Zeitschrift*, Bd. 206 (1968): 529–85.

19. Born in 1918 into a prominent and wealthy Jewish family who were the owners of the Ullstein publishing company, Mosse went to school in Berlin before immigrating with his family to Britain in 1933. In 1936 they moved on to the United States. After a period as an early modern scholar, from the early 1960s onwards, Mosse devoted his career to studying the cultural and intellectual roots and characteristics of Nazism, fascism, anti-semitism, Jewish history, and later the history of sexuality. See George Mosse, *Confronting History: A Memoir* (Madison, 2000); Jeffrey Herf, "The Historian as Provocateur: Georg Mosse's Accomplishment and Legacy," *Vad Vashem Studies* XXIX (2001): 7–26; and Steven E. Ascheim, "Georg Mosse at 80: A Critical Laudatio," *Journal of Contemporary History* 32, no. 2 (1999): 290–312.

20. Mosse, *The Nationalization of the Masses*, 2.

21. Ibid.

22. However, he referred twice to Nipperdey: Koselleck, "Kriegerdenkmale," 259 n. 10, 262 n. 13.

23. The expression is taken from Stefan Goebel, *The Great War and Medieval Memory: War, Remembrance and Medievalism in Britain and Germany 1914–1940* (Cambridge, 2007), 3.

24. Koselleck, "Kriegerdenkmale," 258 (CFOT).

25. Ibid., 260.

26. Goebel, *The Great War*, 3–4.

27. Thus, Goebel, *The Great War*, 4. Koselleck was acquainted with Mosse's work, because, according to Koselleck, he attended Mosse's seminars (presumably in Bielefeld). See Reinhart Koselleck, "Conceptual History, Memory, and Identity," 118.

28. Goebel, *The Great War*, 2, 3.

29. Koselleck, "Kriegerdenkmale," 256 (CFOT).

30. Ibid., 257.

31. Ibid.

32. Ibid., 273.

33. Ibid.

34. Ibid., 274.

35. Reinhart Koselleck, "Daumier und der Tod," *Modernität und Tradition: Festschrift für Max Imdahl zum 60. Geburtstag*, ed. Gottfried Boehm, Karlheinz Stierle, and Gun-

dolf Winter, 163–78 (München, 1985). See the excellent account of Imdahl's and Koselleck's approaches to political iconography in Hubert Locher, "Denken in Bildern: Reinhart Koselleck's Programm *Zur politischen Ikonologie*," *Zeitschrift für Ideengeschichte*, Hf. III/4 (2009): 81–96. Koselleck and Imdahl first met each other at the Poetik und Hermeneutik conference in Gießen in 1963.

36. Koselleck, "Daumier und der Tod," 163 (CFOT).

37. Ibid.

38. Ibid., 164.

39. Ibid., 165.

40. Ibid., 175.

41. Ibid.

42. Ibid., 176.

43. See Palonen, *Die Entzauberung der Begriffe*, 289–90.

44. Reinhart Koselleck, "Einleitung," *Der politische Totenkult. Kriegerdenkmäler in der Moderne*, ed. Reinhart Koselleck and Michael Jeismann (München, 1994), 20.

45. Koselleck, "Einleitung," 20.

46. For the "culture of defeat," see Wolfgang Schivelbusch, *Die Kultur der Niederlage: der amerikanische Süden 1865, Frankreich 1871, Deutschland 1918* (Berlin, 2001).

47. For the history of the Neue Wache, see Bill Niven, *Facing the Nazi Past: United Germany and the Legacy of the Third Reich* (London, 2002), 197–202; Siobhan Kattago, *The Nazi Past and the German National Identity* (London, 2001), 136–41; and Peter Reichel, *Politik mit der Erinnerung: Gedächtnisorte im Streit um die nationalsozialistische Vergangenheit* (München, 1995), 231–46.

48. However, the inscription also leveled the Germans who had fallen in World War II and during the allied bombings with those who had been persecuted and murdered by the National Socialist perpetrators. After 1980, when the memorial was moved to Bonn's north cemetery, the leveling of victims even came to include the National Socialist perpetrators, as the cemetery housed the civilian dead of both wars, Soviet forced laborers, and members of the Waffen-SS. See Niven, *Facing the Nazi Past*, 197.

49. About fifteen years after the inauguration of the first national memorial, in 1981, the Social Democratic Chancellor Helmut Schmidt met political demands for a commemorative site by asking for "a memorial for those who lost their lives as a result of the failings and the crimes of the Third Reich, be this in the prisons or concentration camps, in the homeland during the bombing war, or at the front of the Second World War." Helmut Kohl, who in 1982 succeeded Helmut Schmidt as Chancellor, supported this call. While Kohl also wanted to include a reference to "racial madness," his proposal first of all reinforced the leveling of victims and the reference to totalitarianism expressed in the first memorial and in Schmidt's proposal. The idea was dropped again in 1986, but after the unification and without parliamentary consultation, in 1992 Kohl declared his plan to make the Neue Wache into a memorial for *die Opfer von Krieg und Gewaltherrschaft*.

50. Jeffrey K. Olick, "Genre Memories and Memory Genres: A Dialogical Analysis of May 8, 1945 Commemorations in the Federal Republic of Germany," *American Sociological Review* 64 (1999): 393.

51. Reichel, *Politik mit der Erinnerung*, 243.

52. Reinhart Koselleck, "Bilderverbot," *Frankfurter Allgemeine Zeitung*, 8/4 (1993); "Stellen uns die Toten einen Termin?," *Frankfurter Allgemeine Zeitung*, 23/8 (1993); Reinhart Koselleck, Ulrich Schmidt, "Als Denkmal unangemessen. Ein Gespräch mit Reinhart Koselleck über den Streit um die Neue Wache," *Süddeutsche Zeitung*, 30/10

(1993); Reinhart Koselleck, Andreas Seibel, Sigfried Weichlein, "'Mies, medioker und provinziell': Der Historiker Reinhart Koselleck kritisiert die Gestaltung der 'Neuen Wache' als nationale Gedenkstätte der Deutschen," *die tageszeitung*, 13/11 (1993).

53. Koselleck, "Bilderverbot."
54. Koselleck, "Stellen uns die Toten einen Termin?"
55. Ibid.
56. Ibid.
57. Reinhart Koselleck, "Vier Minuten für die Ewigkeit," *Frankfurter Allgemeine Zeitung*, 9/1 (1997); "Erschlichener Rollentausch," *Frankfurter Allgemeine Zeitung*, 9/4 (1997); "Die falsche Ungeduld," *Die Zeit*, 19/3 (1998); "Die Widmung", *Frankfurter Allgemeine Zeitung*, 3/3 (1999); Reinhart Koselleck, "'Denkmäler sind Stolpersteine': Der Historiker Reinhart Koselleck zur neu entbrannten Debatte um das geplante Berliner Holocaust-Mahnmal," *Der Spiegel*, no. 6 (1997): 190–92.
58. In the speech, attempting to dispense with sentimentalism and manipulative public relations, Weizsäcker called 8 May a day of both defeat and liberation. This contradictory statement was meant to honor the memory of all victims of war and tyranny and also to emphasize the singularity of the Holocaust.
59. Niven, *Facing the Nazi Past*, 200.
60. See Koselleck, "Mies, medioker und provinziell," in which he complained that, in comparison with other countries, the practice of commemorating the dead in Germany was provincial and sentimental in such a way that it oppresses the historical "truth."
61. Koselleck, "Erschlichener Rollentausch."
62. Koselleck, "Die Widmung."
63. However, Ignatz Bubis was deeply dissatisfied with the way in which Koselleck had portrayed his role and the role of the Jewish community in the debate. See Ignatz Bubis, "Holocaust-Mahnmal: Eine Replik auf Reinhart Koselleck," *Die Zeit*, 2/4 (1998), in which Bubis objected to how, in the article "Die falsche Ungeduld," Koselleck had referred to a rumor that Chancellor Kohl had promised Ignatz Bubis the construction of a Holocaust memorial for the Jews in return for Bubis's presence at the opening of the Neue Wache.
64. See, for example, Ruprecht Kampe, "Befremdliches bei Koselleck," *Frankfurter Allgemeine Zeitung*, 12/3 (1999); and Eduard Huber, "Koselleck macht es sich mit den Deutschen zu einfach," *Frankfurter Allgemeine Zeitung*, 13/3 (1999). This point of critique was also raised by the historian Ernst Nolte. See "Es war die Schuld die Ideologiestaaten," *Frankfurter Allgemeine Zeitung*, 2/9 (1993), in which Nolte further argued that the origins of the "final solution" lay not with anti-Semitism, but with an ideology that was supra-nationally conditioned and was taken to the extreme by Hitler, who came to function as the single ruler of Germany. Nolte moreover argued that the terror and the violent death of the twentieth century cannot be explained with reference to categories such as Germans or Russians, but only with reference to ideology and ideological states. He therefore pleaded for an inscription that would refer first of all to ideological states, and which would spare the Pietà from what he spoke of as Koselleck's one-dimensionally negative national concept of Germany.
65. Koselleck, "Als Denkmal unangemessen."
66. Steinmetz, "Nachruf auf Reinhart Koselleck," 427.
67. Koselleck, "Glühende Lava, zur Erinnerung geronnen."
68. Ibid.
69. Ibid.

70. See the excellent account of these issues in Aleida Assmann, *Der lange Schatten der Vergangenheit. Erinnerungskultur und Geschichtspolitik* (München, 2006), 127–28.
71. Koselleck, "Glühende Lava, zur Erinnerung geronnen."
72. Pierre Nora, ed., *Les Lieux de Mémoire*, vol. 3 (Paris, 1984–1992).
73. Jay Winter, "The Generation of Memory: Reflections on the Memory Boom in Contemporary Historical Studies," *Bulletin of the German Historical Institute* 27 (2000): 69–92.
74. Reinhart Koselleck, "Der Einfluß der beiden Weltkriege auf das Soziale Bewußtsein," in *Der Krieg des kleinen Mannes: Eine Militärgeschichte von unten*, ed. Wolfram Wette (München, 1992), 324–43 (reprinted as "Erinnerungsschleusen und Erfahrungsschichten: Der Einfluß der beiden Weltkriege auf das soziale Bewußtsein," *Zeitschichten: Studien zur Historik* (Frankfurt am Main, 2000), 265–86).
75. Koselleck, "Der Einfluß der beiden Weltkriege."
76. Ibid.
77. Reinhart Koselleck, "Gebrochene Erinnerung? Deutsche und polnische Vergangenheiten," *Das Jahrbuch der Deutschen Akademie für Sprache und Dichtung* (2001): 19–32. A slightly different version of the text is found in *Neue Zürcher Zeitung*, 22-23/9 (2001).
78. Koselleck, "Ich war weder Opfer noch befreit."
79. Koselleck, "Glühende Lava, zur Erinnerung geronnen."
80. Steinmetz, "Nachruf auf Reinhart Koselleck," 429.
81. Koselleck, "Die Diskontinuität der Erinnerung," 213–22. The article is based on a speech that he gave at a conference about the National Socialist dictatorship, which took place at the University of Heidelberg on 27 January 1999, in relation to the National Memorial Day for the victims of National Socialism.
82. Koselleck, "Die Diskontinuität der Erinnerung," 214.
83. Ibid., 222.
84. For a detailed discussion and critique of these tensions, see Gabriel Motzkin, "Moralische Antwort und Diskontinuität der Erinnerung," *Deutsche Zeitschrift für Philosophie* [47, no. 6 (1999): 1023–31. Motzkin's article was related to the philosopher Schlomo Avineri's decision to resign from board of the *Deutsche Zeitschrift für Philosophie* due its publication of Koselleck's article. Due to Avineri's decision, the editorial board found it appropriate to find an author (Motzkin) to critically evaluate Koselleck's article. What Motzkin first of all criticized, and what triggered Avineri's reaction, was an emotional stance, which, according to Motzkin and Avineri, informs the entire text without being explicitly thematized, and which in their opinion leads to a questionable moral stance toward the experiences of Nazism.
85. Reinhart Koselleck, "Formen und Traditionen des negativen Gedächtnis," in *Verbrechen Erinnern: Die Auseinandersetzung mit Holocaust und Völkermord*, ed. Volkhard Knigge and Norbert Frei, 21–32 (München, 2002).

7

THE FOUNDATIONS AND THE FUTURE OF KOSELLECK'S SCHOLARLY PROGRAM

It has been the main assumption of this study that Koselleck's program was structured around the aim of deconstructing all utopian and relativist notions of history in the singular with a view to a notion of history in the plural. This aim and the related analytical features were portrayed as a unifying pattern and a common objective in his varied body of work.

If, during more than half a century, Koselleck sought to deconstruct all utopian and relativist notions of history in the singular and subject these to epistemological and ideological critique, it was because he was convinced that both notions drew on theoretically-methodologically naïve and politically dangerous assumptions about history and politics that were based on erroneous understandings of the basic conditions of the humanly possible.

In his lifelong attempt to establish approaches to science and politics that went beyond utopianism and relativism, Koselleck insisted that history must be plural, and that it must be written from viewpoints that are also plural. This involved delineating (non-relativistic) stable, common viewpoints from which historical change could be described and (non-utopian) parameters of judgment on the basis of which the past and the present could be discussed. In this manner, Koselleck's program comprised at the same time a scientific and a political dimension.

Analytically, Koselleck wanted to integrate a plurality of histories into narrative forms of writing history that included generalizing interpretations, while bypassing notions of unity, progress, and meaning in history. In the course of his career, Koselleck pursued this ambition with shifting degrees of clarity, consistency, and success. The analytical framework he used was constantly in flux and somewhat unsystematic. This lack of a systematic approach can be partly explained with reference to his intellectual temperament and partly with reference to his belief in the necessity of plurality in historical writing.

Against the background of this overall interpretation, the book suggests a clear trajectory of Koselleck's career: Over the course of the 1950s, he worked on a set of problems raised by the experiences and the politics of the day as well as by the theoretical debates and preoccupations of his Heidelberg teachers. In the 1960s, he moved away from those problems under the influence of Conze and the concerns of disciplinary history, retaining but downplaying large parts of the conceptual foundations that had been established previously. After the activities of the 1960s had assumed a rigid, nearly institutional character in the form of *Geschichtliche Grundbegriffe*, Koselleck returned first to the theoretical concerns of his earlier projects, for which the concrete historical work he had by then conducted proved highly useful. Finally, with the distance of many decades, in a careful and often still implicit fashion, he turned toward the once burning, now "frozen lava" of his personal experiences.

Still, this apparent biographical plot line must be treated with caution. Primarily, it is the outcome of a feature of Koselleck's intellectual projects, which were so far-reaching and complex that they never quite reached a state of conclusion, remaining open for returns and revisions. Arguably, it was even characteristic of his ambitions that he worked in such a manner as to create a unified (though not properly systematic) intellectual biography for himself. Since the present study was predominantly based on published works and sources that related nearly exclusively to this intellectual biography, it mirrored those properties of Koselleck's intellectual activity. However, this could not be, and was not, a biographical perspective proper. Such a perspective, in his case, remains unexplored. Still, it would be likely to reveal more rupture, discontinuity, and fragmentation than the present study seems to imply.

While Koselleck's program, *habitus*, and career as a scholar was in many ways unique, the main objective of his program evidently transcends his life and work. To explain (historically) and contain (politically) the latent prospects of violent conflict in human societies is a challenge that continues to occupy human beings. We might add that since Koselleck began to emphasize pluralism, the majority of historians have meanwhile moved beyond utopianism and relativism. However, his work stands apart from mainstream historical writing by means of his specific attempt to make theoretical sense of the plurality of human history and to explore this plurality through empirical research. Indeed, there is no doubt that Koselleck has offered us an extraordinarily comprehensive and applicable set of tools to meet the challenge of historical plurality by means of analyzing where we come from, what our current situation is, and what the future holds for us. The temporal, spatial, and linguistic dimensions of the sweeping crisis-consciousness informing the global economy, the deep-seated and radical friend-enemy constellations in the Middle East, and the increasing antagonism between the *ungleichzeitige* phenomena of increasing globalization and nationalism are just three out of many examples of burning contemporary issues that theories and methods from Koselleck's vast oeuvre might help us understand. Indeed, the occasion for a broader and more comprehensive reception and discussion of his work has far from passed; it might even be expected in the future.

BIBLIOGRAPHY

Unpublished sources

Hauptstaatsarchiv Düsseldorf, Nachlass Carl Schmitt, RW265, Letters from Reinhart Koselleck to Carl Schmitt.

Monographs and articles

Albert, Claudia. Review of *Vergangene Zukunft*, by Reinhart Koselleck, *Das Argument*, 127
(1981): 423–24.

Algazi, Gadi. "Otto Brunner—'Konkrete Ordnung' und Sprache der Zeit." In *Geschichtsschreibung als Legitimationswissenschaft 1918–45*, ed. Peter Schöttler, 166–204. Frankfurt
am Main, 1999.

Altemos, Brigitte. "Lehrende und Lehrprogramm. Kontinuität und Wandel der Heidelberger Historie unter personellen Geschichtspunkten." In *Eine Studie zum Alltagsleben
der Historie. Zeitgeschichte des Faches Geschichte an der Heidelberger Universität 1945-
1978*, ed. Robert Deutsch, Heilwig Schomerus, and Christian Peters, 36–85. Heidelberg, 1978.

Arendt, Hannah. *The Origins of Totalitarianism*. New York, 1951.

Ascheim, Steven E. "Georg Mosse at 80: A Critical Laudatio." *Journal of Contemporary
History* 32, no. 2 (1999): 290–312.

Assmann, Aleida. *Der lange Schatten der Vergangenheit. Erinnerungskultur und Geschichtspolitik*. München, 2006.

Balakrishnan, Gopal. *The Enemy: An Intellectual Portrait of Carl Schmitt.* New York, 2000.

Baldwin, Peter. *Reworking the Past: Hitler, the Holocaust, and the Historians' Debate.* Boston, 1990.

Bambach, Charles R. *Heidegger, Dilthey and the Crisis of Historicism.* Ithaca, 1995.

Barsch, Jeffrey Andrew. "The Sense of History: On the Political Implications of Karl Löwith's Concept of Secularization." *History and Theory* 37, no. 1 (1998): 69–82.

Bauer, Yehuda. *Rethinking the Holocaust.* New York, 2001.

Becker, Frank. "Mit dem Fahrstuhl in die Sattelzeit? Koselleck und Wehler in Bielefeld." In *Was war Bielefeld? Eine ideengeschichtliche Nachfrage,* ed. Sonja Asal and Stephan Schlak, 89–110. Göttingen, 2009.

Beradt, Charlotte. *Das Dritte Reich des Traums: mit einem Nachwort von Reinhart Koselleck.* Frankfurt am Main, 1981.

Berding, Helmut. "Begriffsgeschichte und Sozialgeschichte." *Historische Zeitschrift,* Bd. 223 (1976): 98–110.

———. Review of *Vergangene Zukunft,* by Reinhart Koselleck, *Zeitschrift für Philosophische Forschung,* Bd. 34, Hf. 3 (1980): 461–64.

Berg, Nicolas. *Der Holocaust und die westdeutschen Historikern. Erforschung und Erinnerung.* Göttingen, 2002.

Bergeron, Louis, François Furet, and Reinhart Koselleck: "Das Zeitalter der europäischen Revolution 1780-1848." *Fischer Weltgeschichte.* Frankfurt am Main, 1969.

Bernstein, Richard. *Beyond Objectivism and Relativism: Science, Hermeneutics and Praxis,* 109–70. Oxford, 1984.

Biggemann, Wilhelm Schmidt. "Säkularisierung und Theodizee: Anmerkungen zu geschichtstheologischen Interpretationen der Neuzeit in den fünfziger und sechziger Jahre." In *Religion und Vernunft: Philosophischen Analysen,* ed. Helmut Holzhey and Jean-Pierre Leyvraz, 51-67. Stuttgart, 1986.

Blackbourn, David, and Geoff Eley. *The Peculiarities of German History: Bourgeois Society and Politics in Nineteenth-Century Germany.* Oxford, 1984.

Blanchard, Philippe, Reinhart Koselleck, and Ludwig Streit, eds. *Taktische Kernwaffen: Die fragmentierte Abschreckung.* Frankfurt am Main, 1987.

Blanke, Horst Walter. *Historiographiegeschichte als Historik.* Stuttgart-Cannstatt, 1991.

Blänkner, Reinhard. "Von der 'Staatsbildung' zur 'Volkwerdung': Otto Brunners Perspektivenwechsel der Verfassungshistorie im Spannungsfeld zwischen völkischem und alteuropäischem Geschichtsdenken." In *Alteuropa oder Frühe Moderne. Deutungsmuster für das 16. bis 18. Jahrhundert aus dem Krisenbewußtsein der Weimarer Republik in Theologie, Rechts- und Geschichtswissenschaft,* ed. Luise Schorn-Schütte, 87–135. Berlin, 1999.

Blanning, T.C.W. Review of *Critique and Crisis,* by Reinhart Koselleck. *German History* 7 (1989): 265–66.

Blaschke, Olaf, and Lutz Raphael. "Im Kampf um Positionen. Änderungen im Feld der französischen und deutschen Geschichtswissenschaft nach 1945." In *Neue Zugänge zur Geschichte der Geschichtswissenschaft,* ed. Jan Eckel, Thomas Etzemüller, 104–06. Göttingen, 2007.

Bleiber, Helmut. Review of *Preußen zwischen Reform und Revolution,* by Reinhart Koselleck. *Zeitschrift für Geschichtswissenschaft,* XIX Jg., Hf. 1 (1971): 112–15.

Blumenberg, Hans. *Die Legitimität der Neuzeit.* Frankfurt am Main, 1966.

Bock, Gisela. "Meinecke, Machiavelli und der Nationalsozialismus." In *Friedrich Meinecke in seiner Zeit: Studien zu Leben und Werk,* ed. Gisela Bock and Daniel Schönpflug, 145–75. Stuttgart, 2006.

Bock, Gisela, and Daniel Schönpflug, eds. *Friedrich Meinecke in seiner Zeit: Studien zu Leben und Werk.* Stuttgart, 2006.

Borst, Arno. *Meine Geschichte.* Lengwil, 2009.

Boyle, Nicholas. "Geschichte und Autobiographik bei Goethe (1810-1817)." *Goethe-Jahrbuch* 110 (1993): 163–72.

Braudel, Fernand. *La Méditerranée et le Monde Méditerranéen a l'époque de Philippe II.* Paris, 1949.

Brunner, Otto. *Land und Herrschaft: Grundfragen der territorialen Verfassungsgeschichte Südostdeutschlands im Mittelalter.* Baden bei Wien, 1939.

Brunner, Otto, Werner Conze, and Reinhart Koselleck, eds. *Geschichtliche Grundbegriffe: Historisches Lexikon zur politisch-sozialen Sprache in Deutschland, Bd. I-VIII.* Stuttgart, 1972–1997.

Bubis, Ignatz. "Holocaust-Mahnmal: Eine Replik auf Reinhart Koselleck." *Die Zeit,* 2/4 (1998).

Bulst, Neithart. "Koselleck in *Reinhart Koselleck 1923–2006: Reden zur Gedenkfeier am 24. Mai 2006, Bielefelder Universitätsgespräche und Vorträge,* vol. 9, ed. Neithart Bulst and Willibald Steinmetz, 45–50. Bielefeld, 2007.

Burke, Peter. Review of *Vergangene Zukunft,* by Reinhart Koselleck. *History of European Ideas* 8 (1987): 744–45.

Busck, Jens Gunni. *Koselleck og Luhmann. En teorisammenligning.* Unpublished MA thesis, Roskilde University Center, 2008.

Buselmeier, Karin, Dietrich Harth, and Christian Jansen, eds. *Auch eine Geschichte der Universität Heidelberg.* Mannheim, 1985.

Busse, Dietrich. *Historische Semantik. Analyse eines Programms.* Stuttgart, 1987.

Caldwell, Peter. "Ernst Forsthoff and the Legacy of Radical Conservative State Theory in the Federal Republic of Germany," *History of Political Thought,* vol. XV (1994): 615–40.

Carr, David. *Time, Narrative and History.* Bloomington, 1986.

———. Review of *Vergangene Zukunft,* by Reinhart Koselleck, *History and Theory* 26, no. 2 (1987): 197–204.

Christ, Heiner. Review of *Preußen zwischen Reform und Revolution,* by Reinhart Koselleck. *Das Argument,* no. 2 (1970): 141–42.

Chun, Jin-Sung. *Das Bild der Moderne in der Nachkriegszeit. Die westdeutsche 'Strukturgeschichte' im Spannungsfeld von Modernitätskritik und wissenschaftlicher Innovation 1948-1962.* München, 2000.

Conrad, Christoph. "Social History." In *International Encyclopaedia of the Social and Behavioural Sciences,* vol. 21, ed. N. J. Smelser and P. B. Baltes, 14299–306. Oxford, 2001.

Conze, Eckart. *Die Suche nach Sicherheit: Eine Geschichte der Bundesrepublik Deutschland von 1949 bis in die Gegenwart.* München, 2009.

Conze, Werner. "Die Stellung der Sozialgeschichte in Forschung und Unterricht." *Geschichte in Wissenschaft und Unterricht,* Jg. 3 (1952): 648–57.

———. "Vom 'Pöbel' zum 'Proletariat': Sozialgeschichtliche Voraussetzungen für den Sozialismus on Deutschland." *Vierteljahrschrift für Sozial- und Wirtschaftsgeschichte* 41 (1954): 333–68.

———. "Die Strukturgeschichte des technisch-industriellen Zeitalter als Aufgabe für Forschung und Unterricht," 1957. *Werner Conze: Gesellschaft—Staat—Nation.* Stuttgart, 1992. 66–85.

———. "Sozialgeschichte," 1966. *Werner Conze, Gesellschaft—Staat—Nation.* Stuttgart, 1992. 86–95.

———. "Das Spannungsfeld von Staat von Gesellschaft im Vormärz." In *Staat und Gesellschaft im deutschen Vormärz 1815-1848*, ed. Werner Conze, 207–70. Stuttgart, 1962.

———, ed. *Staat und Gesellschaft im deutschen Vormärz 1815-1848*. Stuttgart, 1962.

Conze, Werner, and Dorothee Mussnug. "Das historische Seminar," *Heidelberger Jahrbücher*, Bd. 57 (1979): 133–52.

Conze, Werner, et al., eds. *Bildungsbürgertum im 19: Jahrhundert, 4 Bd.*. Stuttgart, 1985–1992.

Cornelissen, Christoph. *Gerhard Ritter: Geschichtswissenschaft und Politik im 20. Jahrhundert*. Düsseldorf, 2001.

Daniel, Ute. "Reinhart Koselleck." In *Klassiker der Geschichtswissenschaft, Bd. 2: Von Fernand Braudel to Natalie Z. Davis*, ed. Lutz Raphael, 166–94. München, 2006.

Dehli, Martin. *Leben als Konflikt. Zur Biographie Alexanders Mitscherlichs*. Göttingen, 2007.

Demm, Eberhard. "Alfred Weber und die Nationalsozialisten." *Zeitschrift für Geschichtswissenschaft*, Nr. 47 (1999): 211–36.

———. "'Student Prince' der Nachkriegszeit: Nicolaus Sombarts dritter Memoirenband über seine Studienzeit in Heidelberg." *Rhein-Neckar-Zeitung*, 7/11 (2000).

Deutsch, Robert, Heilwig Schomerus, and Christian Peters, eds. *Eine Studie zum Alltagsleben der Historie. Zeitgeschichte des Faches Geschichte an der Heidelberger Universität 1945-1978*. Heidelberg, 1978.

Dietze, Carola. *Nachgeholtes Leben: Helmut Plessner: 1892–1985*. Göttingen, 2006.

Dipper, Christof. "Die Geschichtliche Grundbegriffe: Von der Begriffsgeschichte zur Theorie der historischen Zeiten." *Historische Zeitschrift*, Bd. 279, Hf. 2 (2000): 281–309.

Doering-Manteuffel, Anselm. *Wie westlich sind eigentlich die Deutschen? Amerikaniesierung und Westernizierung im 20. Jahrhundert*. Göttingen, 1999.

Dowe, Dieter. Review of *Geschichtliche Grundbegriffe: Historisches Lexikon zur politisch-sozialen Sprache in Deutschland, Bd. I*, ed. by Otto Brunner, Werner Conze, Reinhart Koselleck. *Archiv für Sozialgeschichte*, Bd. XIV (1974): 720–22.

Dunkhase, Jan Eike. *Werner Conze: Ein deutscher Historiker in 20. Jahrhundert*, Göttingen, 2010.

Dutt, Carsten. "Geschichte(n) und Historik. Reinhart Koselleck im Gespräch mit Carsten Dutt." *Internationale Zeitschrift für Philosophie* 2 (2001): 257–71.

Dutt, Carsten, and Reinhard Laube, eds. *Reinhart Koselleck: Sprache und Geschichte*. Göttingen, 2013.

Eckel, Jan. *Hans Rothfels: Eine intellektuelle Biographie im 20. Jahrhundert*. Göttingen, 2005.

Edwards Jason. "*Critique and Crisis* Today: Koselleck, Enlightenment and the Concept of Politics." *Contemporary Political Theory* 5 (2006): 428–46.

———. "The Ideological Interpellation of Individuals as Combatants: An Encounter between Reinhart Koselleck and Michel Foucault." *Journal of Political Ideologies* 12 (2007): 49–66.

Emmerich, W. "Heilsgeschehen und Geschichte." *Sinn und Form*, Bd. 46 (1994): 894–915.

Etzemüller, Thomas. *Sozialgeschichte als politische Geschichte. Werner Conze und die Neuorientierung der westdeutschen Geschichtswissenschaft nach 1945*. München, 2001.

———. "How to Make a Historian: Problems in Writing Biographies of Historians." *Storia della Storiografia* 53 (2008): 46–57.

Faber, Karl-Georg. Review of *Preußen zwischen Reform und Revolution*, by Reinhart Koselleck. *Neue politische Literatur*, Nr. 3 (1968): 396–400.

———. *Theorie der Geschichtswissenschaft. Dritte erweiterte Auflage*. München, 1974.

———. Review of Vergangene Zukunft, by Reinhart Koselleck, *Neue politische Literatur*, 2 (1980): 618–21.

Faber, Karl-Georg, and Christian Meier, eds. *Historische Prozesse: Theorie der Geschichte. Beiträge zur Historik*, Bd. 2. München, 1978.

Fahrenbach, Helmut. "Karl Löwith in der Weimarer Zeit (1928-1933): Philosophie—nach dem 'revolutionären Bruch im Denken des 19. Jahrhunderts.'" *Deutsche Zeitschrift für Philosophie*, 53 (2005): 851–69.

Faulenbach, Bernd. *Ideologie des deutschen Weges. Die deutsche Geschichte in der Historiographie zwischen Kaiserreich und Nationalsozialismus*. München, 1980.

Faÿ, Bernard. *L'esprit révolutionnaire en France du XVIIIe siècle*. Paris, 1925.

———. *La Franc-Maconnerie et la Révolution intellectuelle du XVIIIe siècle*. Paris, 1925.

———. *Benjamin Franklin*. Paris, 1929.

Fellner, Fritz. "Nationales und europäisch-atlantisches Geschichtsbild in der Bundesrepublik und im Westen in den Jahren nach Ende des Zweiten Weltkrieges." In *Deutsche Geschichtswissenschaft nach dem Zweiten Weltkrieg (1945-1965)*, ed. Ernst Schulin, 213–26. München, 1989.

Fillafer, Franz Leander. "The Enlightenment on Trial: Reinhart Koselleck's Interpretation of *Aufklärung*." In *The Many Faces of Clio: Cross-Cultural Approaches to Historiography*, ed. Franz Leander Fillafer and Edward Q. Wang, 322–45. Oxford, 2007.

Fisch, Jörg. "Die Suggestivkraft der Begriffe." *Tagesanzeiger*, 6/2 (2006).

Fischer, Fritz. *Griff nach der Weltmacht: Die Kriegszielpolitik des kaiserlichen Deutschland 1914-18*. Düsseldorf, 1961.

Fischer, Joachim. "Philosophischer Anthropologie. Ein wirkungsvoller Denkansatz in der deutschen Soziologie nach 1945." *Zeitschrift für Soziologie*, Jg. 35, Bd. 5 (2006): 322–447.

Flasch, Kurt. *Die geistige Mobilmachung: Die deutschen Intellektuellen und der Erste Weltkrieg*. Berlin, 2000.

Fletcher, Roger. "Recent Developments in West German Historiography: The Bielefeld School and Its Critics." *German Studies Review* 7, no. 3 (1984): 451–80.

Franke, Leo. "Review", *Philosophische Literaturanzeiger*, Nr. 14 (1961): 275–77.

Franz, Peter. "Gott mit uns." In *Kleines Lexikon historisches Schlagwörter*, ed. Kurt Pätzold and Manfred Weißbecker, 136–38. Köln, 2005.

Frei, Norbert. *1968: Jugendrevolte und globaler Protest*. München, 2008.

Frevert, Ute. *"Mann und Weib, und Weib und Mann": Geschlechter-Differenzen in der Moderne*. München, 1995.

Freyer, Hans. "Soziologie und Geschichtswissenschaft." *Geschichte in Wissenschaft und Unterricht*, 3 Jg. (1952): 15–20.

———. *Weltgeschichte Europas*. 2 Bd. Wiesbaden, 1948.

———. *Theorie des Gegenwärtigen Zeitalters*. Stuttgart, 1955.

Friedländer, Saul. *Memory, History and the Extermination of Jews of Europe*. Bloomington, 1993.

———. *Nazi Germany and the Jews, 1933-1939*. New York, 1997.

———. *The Years of Extermination: Nazi Germany and the Jews, 1939-1945*. New York, 2007.

Führ, Christopf, and Carl-Ludwig Furck, eds. *Handbuch der deutschen Bildungsgeschichte*, Bd. VI. *1945 bis zur Gegenwart. Erster Teilband. Bundesrepublik Deutschland*. München, 1988.

Gadamer, Hans-Georg. *Wahrheit und Methode: Grundzüge einer philosophischen Hermeneutik*. Tübingen, 1960.

Zentrum for Interdisziplinäre Forschung. "Gesamtliste ZIF Veranstaltungen zwischen 1968 und 1996." *http://www.uni-bielefeld.de/ZIF/Forschung/Gesamtliste-Veranstaltungen. pdf*, accessed 23/7 (2011).

Giesen, Bernard. "Nachruf auf Reinhart Koselleck (1923-2006)." *Berliner Journal für Soziologie*, Bd. 17 (2007): 264–65.

Goebel, Stefan. *The Great War and Medieval Memory: War, Remembrance and Medievalism in Britain and Germany 1914-1940*. Cambridge, 2007.

Gollwitzer, Heinz. Review of *Kritik und Krise*, by Reinhart Koselleck. *Geschichte in Wissenschaft und Unterricht*, 11. Jg. (1960): 303–04.

Görtemaker, Manfred. *Geschichte der Bundesrepublik Deutschland. Von der Gründung bis zur Gegenwart*. Frankfurt am Main, 2004.

Graf, Friedrich Wilhelm. "Die Macht des Schicksals entschuldigt gar nichts." *Frankfurter Allgemeine Zeitung*, 1/11 (1999).

———. "Ein Theoretiker unaufhebbarer Differenzerfahrungen. Laudatio auf Reinhart Koselleck." In *Das Jahrbuch der deutschen Akademie für Sprache und Dichtung* (2000), 139–45.

Green, Abigail. "The Federal Alternative: A New View on German History." *The Historical Journal* 46, no. 1 (2002): 187–202.

Grondin, Jean. "Heidegger und Hans-Georg Gadamer: Zur Phänomenologie des Verstehens-Geschehens." In *Heidegger-Handbuch. Leben-Werk-Wirkung*, ed. Diether Thomä, 384–90. Stuttgart, 2003.

———. *Hans-Georg Gadamer: A Biography*. New Haven, 2004.

Gumbrecht, Hans Ulrich. Review of *Vergangene Zukunft*, by Reinhart Koselleck. *Poetica*, Bd. 13 (1981): 345–59.

———. "Stichwort: Tod im Kontext. Heideggers Umgang mit einer Faszination der 1920er Jahre." In *Heidegger-Handbuch. Leben-Werk-Wirkung*, ed. Dieter Thomä, 98–103. Stuttgart, 2003.

———. "Pyramiden des Geistes. Über den schnellen Aufstieg, die unsichtbaren Dimensionen und das Abebben der begriffsgeschichtlichen Bewegung." In *Dimensionen und Grenzen der Begriffsgeschichte*, 7–36. München, 2006.

Günther, Frieder. *Denken vom Staat her. Die Bundesdeutsche Staatsrechtslehre zwischen Dezision und Integration 1949-1970*. München, 2004.

Haar, Ingo. *Historiker im Nationalsozialismus: deutsche Geschichtswissenschaft und der 'Volkstumkampf' im Osten*. Gottingen, 2000.

Habermas, Jürgen. "Verrufener Fortschritt—Verkanntes Jahrhundert. Zur Kritik an der Geschichtsphilosophie." *Merkur*, Jg. XIV (1960): 468–77.

———. *Strukturwandel der Öffentlichkeit*. Berlin, 1962.

———. "Einleitung" in *Stichwörter zur geistigen Situation der Zeit*. Bd. 1, ed. Jürgen Habermas, 7–35. Frankfurt am Main, 1979.

———. "Karl Löwiths stoischer Rückzug vom historischen Bewußtsein." In *Philosophisch-politische Profile*, 195–216. Frankfurt am Main, 1987.

Hacke, Jens. *Philosophie der Bürgerlichkeit. Die liberalkonservative Begründung der Bundesrepublik*. Göttingen, 2006.

Hagen, William W. "Descent of the Sonderweg. Hans Rosenberg's History of Old-Regime Prussia." *Central European History* 24, no. 1 (1991): 24–50.

Hahn, Silke. "Zwischen Re-education und Zweiter Bildungsreform: Die Sprache der Bildungspolitik in der Öffentlichen Diskussion." In *Kontroverse Begriffe: Geschichte des öffentlichen Sprachgebrauchs in der Bundesrepublik Deutschland*, ed. Georg Stötzel and Martin Wengeler, 165–210. Berlin, 1995.

Haikala, Sisko. "Criticism in the Enlightenment: Perspectives on Koselleck's Kritik und Krise Study." *Finnish Yearbook of Political Thought* 1 (1997): 70–86.

Hampsher-Monk, Ian, Karin Tilmans, and Frank Van Vree, eds. *History of Concepts: Comparative Perspectives.* Amsterdam, 1998.

Hardtwig, Wolfgang. "Jacob Burckhardt und Max Weber. Zur Genese und Pathologie der modernen Welt." *Geschichtskultur und Wissenschaft,* 189–223. München, 1990.

———. "Die Krise des Geschichtsbewusstseins in Kaiserreich und Weimarer Republik und der Aufstieg der Nationalsozialismus." *Hochkultur des bürgerlichen Zeitalters,* 77–102. Göttingen, 2005.

Heidegger, Martin. "Der Zeitbegriff in der Geschichtswissenschaft." *Zeitschrift für Philosophie und philosophische Kritik,* no. 160 (1916): 173–88.

———. *Sein und Zeit.* Halle, 1927.

Heinrich, Dieter, and Wolfgang Iser, eds. *Poetik und Hermeneutik X. Funktionen des Fiktiven.* München, 1983.

Helde, Thomas T. Review of *Staat und Gesellschaft im deutschen Vormärz 1815–1848,* ed. Werner Conze. *Journal of Economic History* 23, no. 3 (1963): 351–52.

Herbert, Ulrich. "Liberalisierung als Lernprozess. Die Bundesrepublik in der deutschen Geschichte—eine Skizze." In *Wandlungsprozesse in Deutschland. Belastung, Integration, Liberalisierung 1948-1980,* ed. Ulrich Herbert, 7–47. Göttingen, 2002.

———. "Vernichtungspolitik: Neue Antworten und Fragen zur Geschichte des Holocaust." *Nationalsozialistische Vernichtungspolitik: Neue Forschungen und Kontroversen,* 9–66. Frankfurt am Main, 1998.

Herf, Jeffrey. *Reactionary Modernism: Technology, Culture, and Politics in Weimar and the Third Reich.* New York, 1986.

———. "The Historian as Provocateur: Georg Mosse's Accomplishment and Legacy." *Vad Vashem Studies* XXIX (2001): 7–26.

Hersch, Jeanne, ed. *Karl Jaspers. Philosoph, Arzt, politischer Denker. Symposium zum 100. Geburtstag in Basel und Heidelberg.* München, 1986.

Herzfeld, Hans. Review of *Preußen zwischen Reform und Revolution,* by Reinhart Koselleck. *Jahrbuch für die Geschichte Mittel- und Ostdeutschlands,* 18 (1969): 377.

Hettling, Manfred. "Bürgerlichkeit in Nachkriegsdeutschland." In *Bürgertum nach 1945,* ed. Manfred Hettling and Bernd Ulrich, 7–37. Hamburg, 2005.

Hettling, Manfred, and Bernd Ulrich, eds. *Bürgertum nach 1945.* Hamburg, 2005.

Heydemann, Günter. *Geschichtswissenschaft im geteilten Deutschland. Entwicklungsgeschichte, Organisationsstruktur, Funktionen, Theorie- und Methodenprobleme in der Bundesrepublik Deutschland und in der DDR.* Frankfurt am Main, 1980.

Hilger, Andreas. *Deutsche Kriegsgefangene in der Sowjetunionen, 1941-1956. Kriegsgefangenenpolitik, Lageralltag und Erinnerung.* Essen, 2000.

Hobsbawm, Eric. *Interesting Times: A Twentieth-Century Life.* London, 2002.

Hoffmann, Stefan-Ludwig. "Reinhart Koselleck (1923-2006): The Conceptual Historian." *German History,* 24 (2006): 475–78.

———. "Was die Zukunft Birgt: Über Reinhart Kosellecks Historik." *Merkur: Deutsche Zeitschrift für europäisches Denken,* Jg. 63 (2009): 546–50.

———. "Zur Anthropologie geschichtlicher Erfahrungen bei Reinhart Koselleck und Hannah Arendt." In *Begriffene Geschichte: Beiträge zum Werk Reinhart Kosellecks,* ed. Hans Joas, Peter Vogt, 171-204. Frankfurt am Main, 2010.

Hoffmann, Sven Olaf. "Viktor von Weizsäcker: Art und Denker gegen den Strom." *Deutsches Ärzteblatt,* PP 5 (April 2006): 161.

Hohendahl, Peter Uwe. "Recasting the Public Sphere." *October* 73 (1995): 27–54.

Hohendahl, Peter Uwe, ed. *Öffentlichkeit: Geschichte eines kritischen Begriffs.* Stuttgart, 2000.

Hohls, Rüdiger, and Konrad H. Jarausch, eds. *Versäumte Fragen: Deutsche Historiker im Schatten des Nationalsozialismus.* Stuttgart, 2000.

Hölscher, Lucian. "Öffentlichkeit." In *Geschichtliche Grundbegriffe. Historisches Lexikon zur politisch-sozialen Sprache in Deutschland,* Bd. 4, ed. Otto Brunner, Werner Conze, and Reinhart Koselleck, 413–67. Stuttgart, 1978.

———. "Abschied von Koselleck." In *Begriffene Geschichte: Beiträge zum Werk Reinhart Kosellecks,* ed. Hans Joas and Peter Vogt, 84-93. Frankfurt am Main, 2010.

Hoppe, Jürgen. "Heidelberg Sommer." In *Deutsche Universitäten: Berichte und Analysen,* ed. Ernst Nolte. Marburg, 1969.

Horkheimer, Max, and Theodor W. Adorno. *Dialektik der Aufklärung: Philosophische Fragmente.* Amsterdam, 1947.

Huber, Eduard. "Koselleck macht es sich mit den Deutschen zu einfach." *Frankfurter Allgemeine Zeitung,* 13/3 (1999).

Ifversen, Jan. "Om den tyske begrebshistorie." *Politologiske studier* 6, no. 1 (2003): 18–34.

———. "Begrebshistorien efter Reinhart Koselleck." *Slagmark,* no. 48 (2007): 81–103.

Iggers, Georg G. *The German Conception of History: The National Tradition of Historical Thought from Herder to the Present.* Middletown, 1968.

———. *Historiography in the Twentieth Century: From Scientific Objectivity to the Postmodern Challenge.* Middletown, 1997.

Iggers, Georg G., ed. *Neue Geschichtswissenschaft: vom Historismus zur historischen Sozialwissenschaft.* München, 1978.

Jarausch, Konrad. *After Hitler: Recivilizing Germans, 1945-1995.* New York, 2006.

Jaspers, Karl. *Die Schuldfrage: ein Beitrag zur deutsche Frage.* Zürich, 1946.

———. *Vom Ursprung und Ziel der Geschichte.* Zürich, 1959.

———. "Von Heidelberg nach Basel." In *1945: Befreiung und Zusammenbruch. Erinnerungen aus sechs Jahrzehnten,* ed. Peter Süss. München, 2005.

Jauss, Hans Robert. "Antrittsrede vor der Heidelberger Akademie der Wissenschaften." *Jahrbuch der Heidelberger Akademie der Wissenschaften.* 1982.

———. *Toward an Aesthetic of Reception.* Minneapolis, 1982.

Jauss, Hans Robert, ed. *Poetik und Hermeneutik III: Die nicht mehr schönen Künste. Grenzphänomene des Ästhetischen.* München, 1968.

Jay, Martin. *The Dialectical Imagination: A History of the Frankfurt School and the Institute for Social Research 1923-1950.* Berkeley, 1996.

Jeismann, Michael. "Geschichte und Eigensinn. Zum siebzigsten Geburtstag des Historikers Reinhart Koselleck." *Frankfurter Allgemeine Zeitung,* 23/4 (1994).

———. "Wer bleibt, der schreibt. Reinhart Koselleck, das Überleben und die Ethik der Historikers." *Zeitschrift für Ideengeschichte,* Hf. III/4 (2009): 69–81.

Joas, Hans, and Peter Vogt, eds. *Begriffene Geschichte: Beiträge zum Werk Reinhart Kosellecks.* Frankfurt am Main, 2010.

Johnson, Eric A., and Reinhart Koselleck. "Recollections of the Third Reich." *NIAS Newsletter,* 22 (1999): 9–14.

Jordheim, Helge. "Thinking in Convergences—Koselleck on Language, History and Time." *Ideas in History* 2, no. 3 (2007): 65–90.

Junker, Detlef. "Theorie der Geschichtswissenschaft am Historischen Seminar der Universität Heidelberg im 19. und 20 Jahrhundert." In *Geschichte im Heidelberg. 100 Jahre Historisches Seminar, 50 Jahre Institut für Fränkisch-Pfälzische Geschichte und Landeskunde,* ed. Jürgen Miethke, 159–74. Berlin 1992.

Jureit, Ulrike. *Generationenforschung.* Göttingen, 2006.

Jureit, Ulrike, and Michael Wildt, ed. *Generationen: Zur Relevanz eines wissenschaftlichen Grundbegriffs*. Hamburg, 2005.

Kampe, Ruprecht. "Befremdliches bei Koselleck." *Frankfurter Allgemeine Zeitung*, 12/3 (1999).

Kant, Immanuel. "Über das Mißlingen aller philosophischen Versuche in der Theodicee." *Kants Werke, Akademie-Ausgabe*, vol. VIII, 253–71. Berlin, 1902.

Karner, Stefan. *Im Archipel GUPVI. Kriegsgefangenschaft und Internierung in der Sowjetunion 1941-1956*. München, 1995.

Kattago, Siobhan. *The Nazi Past and the German National Identity*. London, 2001.

Kaube, Jürgen. "Zentrum der intellektuellen Nachkriegsgeschichte." *Frankfurter Allgemeine Zeitung*, 18/6 (2003).

Kennedy, Ellen. "Carl Schmitt und die 'Frankfurter Schule': Deutsche Liberalismuskritik im 20. Jahrhundert." *Geschichte und Gesellschaft*, 12. Jg. (1986): 380–419.

Kersting, Franz-Werner. "Helmut Schelskys 'Skeptische Generation' von 1957. Zur Publikations- und Wirkungsgeschichte eines Standardwerkes." *Vierteljahresheft für Zeitgeschichte*, Jg. 50 (2002): 465–95.

Kesting, Hanno. *Geschichtsphilosophie und Weltbürgerkrieg. Deutungen der Geschichte von der Französischen Revolution bis zum Ost-West-Konflikt*. Heidelberg, 1959.

Klein, Ernst. Review of *Preußen zwischen Reform und Revolution*, by Reinhart Koselleck. *Das Historisch-Politische Buch*, XVI (1968): 298–99.

Kocka, Jürgen. Review of *Preußen zwischen Reform und Revolution*, by Reinhart Koselleck. , *Vierteljahrschrift für Sozial und Wirtschaftsgeschichte*, Bd. 75 (1970): 121–25.

———. "Theorien in der Sozial- und Wirtschaftsgeschichte." *Geschichte und Gesellschaft*, 1. Jg. (1975): 9–2.

———. "Geschichte—wozu?" Jürgen Kocka: *Sozialgeschichte. Begriff—Entwicklung—Probleme*, 112–31. Göttingen 1977.

———. "Werner Conze und die Sozialgeschichte in der Bundesrepublik Deutschland." *Geschichte in Wissenschaft und Unterricht*, Jg. 10 (1986): 595–602.

———. "Wir sind ein Fach, das nicht nur für sich selber schreibt und forscht, sondern zur Aufklärung und zum Selbstverständnis der eigenen Gesellschaft und Kultur beitragen sollte." In *Versäumte Fragen. Deutsche Historiker im Schatten des Nationalsozialismus*, ed. Rüdiger Hohls and Konrad H. Jarausch, 383–403. Stuttgart, 2000.

———. "Die Zukunft der Vergangenheit." *Der Tagesspiegel*, 6/2 (2006).

Kühn, Johannes. *Toleranz und Offenbarung*. Leipzig, 1923.

Koselleck, Reinhart. "Kritik und Krise: Eine Untersuchung der politischen Funktion des dualistischen Weltbildes im 18. Jahrhundert." Unpublished dissertation, University of Heidelberg, 1954.

———. Review of *Christianity, Diplomacy and War*, by Herbert Butterfield. In *Archiv für Rechts- und Sozialphilosophie*, Nr. 41 (1954/1955): 591–95.

———. Review of *Political Thought in England: Tyndal to Hooker*, by Christopher Morris. In *Archiv für Rechts- und Sozialphilosophie*, Bd. XLI (1954/1955): 136–37.

———. "Bristol, die 'zweite Stadt' Englands: Eine sozialgeschichtliche Skizze." *Soziale Welt*, 6 (1955): 360–72.

———. "Die Wiederentdeckung von John Adams." *Neue politische Literatur*, 1. Jg. (1956): 93–104.

———. "Zwei Denker der puritanischen Revolution [Harrington and Hobbes]." *Neue politische Literatur*, 2 Jg. (1957): 288–93.

———. Review of *The Political Writings of James Harrington and of Richard Peters*. *Neue Politische Literatur*, 2 Jg. (1957): 288–93.

———. *Kritik und Krise Eine Studie zur Pathogenese der bürgerlichen Welt*. Freiburg, 1959.

————. "Review of *Raynal et sa machine de guerre*, by Hans Wolpe. *Archiv für Rechts- und Sozial-Philosophie*, nr. 45 (1959): 126–28.

————. Review of *Staat und Gesellschaft im Wandel unserer Zeit*, by Theodor Schieder. *The Economic History Review* 12, no. 2 (1959): 325–26.

————. "Im Vorfeld einer neuen Historik." *Neue Politische Literatur*, Hf. 7 (1961): 577–87.

————. Review of *Staatsbildende Kräfte der Neuzeit*, by Fritz Hartung. *Das historisch-politische Buch*, Jg. IX (1961): 301.

————. Review of *Der neue Gebhardt*. *Das historisch-politische Buch*, Jg. IX (1961): 225–27.

————. Review of *Die Geschichte der Lage der Arbeiter unter dem Kapitalismus* (vol. 8+9, Berlin, 1960), by Jürgen Kuczynski. *The Economic History Review* 14, no. 2 (1961): 378–79.

————. Review of *Die Struktur der europäischen Wirklichkeit*, by Walter Felix Müller. *Das historisch-politische Buch*, Jg. IX (1961): 311.

————. Review of *Freiherr vom Stein im Zeitalter der Restauration*, by Werner Gembruch. *Das historisch-politische Buch*, Jg. IX (1961): 212.

————. Review of *Die deutsche verfassungsgeschichtliche*, by Ernst-Wolfgang Böckenförde. *Forschung im 19. Jahrhundert*, *Das historisch-politische Buch*, Jg. X (1962): 10-11.

————. Review of *Die letzten hundert Jahre. Gestalten, Ideen, Ereignisse*, by Kurt Seeberger. *Das historisch-politische Buch*, Jg. X (1962): 111.

————. Review of *Studien zur deutschen Geschichte des 19. und 20. Jahrhunderts*, by Siegfried A. Kaehler. *Das historisch-politische Buch*, Jg. X (1962): 111.

————. Review of *Die Rolle des Staates in den Frühstadien der Industrialisierung*, by Ulrich Peter Ritter. *Das historisch-politische Buch*, Jg. X (1962): 207.

————. "Staat und Gesellschaft in Preußen 1815-1848" in *Staat und Gesellschaft im deutschen Vormärz 1815-1848*, ed. Werner Conze, Stuttgart, 1962, 79-112.

————.Review of *Ursprünge des modernen Krisenbewußtseins*, by Ehrenfried Muthesius and *Die Ursprünge der totalitären Demokratie*, by J. L. Talmon, *Neue politische Literatur*, Hf. 11/12 (1963): 863-866.

————. Review of *Begegnungen mit der Geschichte*, by Theodor Schieder. *Das historisch-politische Buch*, Jg. XI (1963): 295.

————.Review of *Das deutsche Kaiserreich von 1871 als Nationalstaat*, by Theodor Schieder. *Das historisch-politische Buch*, Jg. XI (1963): 306.

————. Review of *Wilhelm von Humboldt und der Staat*, by Sigfried A. Kaehler. *Das historisch-politische Buch*, Jg. XIII (1965): 141.

————. "Geschichtliche Prognose in Lorenz v. Steins Schrift zur preußischen Verfassung." *Der Staat*, Bd. 4 (1965): 469–81.

————. "Historia Magistra Vitae. Über die Auflösung des Topos im Horizont neuzeitlich bewegter Geschichte." In *Natur und Geschichte: Karl Löwith zum 70. Geburtstag*, ed. Hermann Braun and Manfried Riedel, 196–219. Stuttgart, 1967.

————. *Preußen zwischen Reform und Revolution. Allgemeines Landrecht, Verwaltung und soziale Bewegung von 1791 bis 1848*. Stuttgart, 1967.

————. "Richtlinien für das Lexikon politisch-sozialer Begriffe der Neuzeit." *Archiv für Begriffsgeschichte*, Bd. XI (1967): 81–97.

————. "Vergangene Zukunft der frühen Neuzeit." In *Epirrhosis, Festgabe für Carl Schmitt*, Bd. 2, ed. Hans Barion et al., 549–66. Berlin, 1968.

————. "Der neuzeitliche Revolutionsbegriff als geschichtliche Kategorie." *Studium Generale*, 22 (1969): 825–38.

————. "Wozu noch Historie?" *Historische Zeitschrift* 212 (1971): 1–18.

———. "Begriffsgeschichte und Sozialgeschichte." In *Soziologie und Sozialgeschichte. Aspekte und Probleme*, ed. Peter Christian Ludz, 116–31. Köln, 1972.

———. "Über die Theoriebedürftigkeit der Geschichtswissenschaft." In *Theorie der Geschichtswissenschaft und Praxis des Geschichtsunterrichts*, ed. Werner Conze, 10–28. Stuttgart, 1972.

———. "Geschichte, Geschichten und formale Zeitstrukturen." In *Poetik und Hermeneutik V. Geschichte—Ereignis und Erzählung*, ed. Reinhart Koselleck and Wolf-Dieter Stempel, 211–22. München, 1973.

———. "Ereignis und Struktur." In *Poetik und Hermeneutik V. Geschichte—Ereignis und Erzählung*, ed. Reinhart Koselleck and Wolf-Dieter Stempel, 560–71. München, 1973.

———. "Zum Tode von Johannes Kühn." *Ruperto Carola*, Bd. 51 (1973): 143–44.

———. "Erläuterungen zum Bielefeld Modell für das Geschichtsstudium." *Geschichte und Sozialwissenschaften*, Sonderheft 6 der *Neuen Sammlung* (1974): 36–40.

———. "Zur historisch-politischen Semantik asymmetrischer Gegenbegriffe." In *Positionen der Negativität: Poetik und Hermeneutik VI*, ed. Harald Weinrich, , 65–105. München, 1975.

———. "'Erfahrungsraum' und 'Erwartungshorizont': Zwei historische Kategorien." In *Soziale Bewegung und politische Verfassung. Beiträge zur Geschichte der modernen Welt. Werner Conze zum 65. Geburtstag*, ed. Ulrich Engelhardt, Volker Sellin, and Horst Stuke, 13–33. Stuttgart, 1976.

———. "Standortbindung und Zeitlichkeit: Ein Beitrag zur historiographischen Erschließung der geschichtlichen Welt." In *Objektivität und Parteilichkeit in der Geschichtswissenschaft. Beiträge zur Historik. Bd. 1*, ed. Reinhart Koselleck, Wolfgang J. Mommsen, and Jörn Rüsen, 17–46. München, 1977.

———. "'Neuzeit': Zur Semantik moderner Bewegungsbegriffe." *Vergangene Zukunft. Zur Semantik geschichtlicher Zeiten*, 260–77. Frankfurt am Main, 1979. (first published in Koselleck, Reinhart, ed. *Studien zum Beginn der modernen Welt*. Bd. 20, 264–99. Stuttgart, 1977).

———. "Kriegerdenkmale als Identitätsstiftungen der Überlebenden." *Poetik und Hermeneutik. VIII. Identität*, ed. Odo Marquard and Karlheinz Stierle, 255–76. München, 1979.

———. "Terror und Traum: Methodologische Anmerkungen zu Zeiterfahrungen im Dritten Reich." *Vergangene Zukunft. Zur Semantik geschichtlicher Zeiten*, 278–99. Frankfurt am Main, 1979.

———. *Vergangene Zukunft. Zur Semantik geschichtlicher Zeiten*. Frankfurt am Main, 1979.

———. "Geschichtswissenschaft in Bielefeld. Die neue Orientierung eines alten Faches." In *Zwischenstation. Bielefeld, 1979*, ed. Karl Peter Grotemeyer, 70–78. Bielefeld, 1979.

———. "Die Verzeitlichung der Utopie." In *Utopieforschung*, ed. Wilhelm Vosskamp, 1–14. Stuttgart, 1982.

———. "Fragen an den Formen der Geschichtsschreibung." In *Formen der Geschichtsschreibung*, ed, Reinhart Koselleck, Heinrich Lutz, and Jörn Rüsen, 9–13. München, 1982.

———. "Begriffsgeschichtliche Probleme der Verfassungsgeschichtsschreibung." *Der Staat. Beiheft 6. Gegenstand und Begriffe der Verfassungsgeschichtsschreibung* (1983): 7–46.

———. *Vorbilder—Bilder, gezeichnet von Reinhart Koselleck. Eingeleitet von Max Imdahl*. Bielefeld, 1983.

———. "Daumier und der Tod." *Modernität und Tradition: Festschrift für Max Imdahl zum 60. Geburtstag*, ed. Gottfried Boehm, Karlheinz Stierle, and Gundolf Winter, 163–78. München, 1985.

———. "Jaspers die Geschichte und die Überpolitische." In *Karl Jaspers. Philosoph, Arzt, politischer Denker. Symposium zum 100. Geburtstag in Basel und Heidelberg*, ed. Jeanne Hersch, 291–302. München, 1986.

———. "Vorwort." to *Auch Klio dichtet oder die Fiktion des Faktischen: Studien zur Tropologie des historischen Diskurses*. by Hayden White, Stuttgart, 1986.

———. "Historik und Hermeneutik." In *Sitzungsberichte der Heidelberger Akademie der Wissenschaften* 1 (1987): 9–28.

———. "Werner Conze: Tradition und Innovation." *Historische Zeitschrift*, Bd. 245 (1987): 529–43.

———. *Critique and Crisis: Enlightenment and the Pathogenesis of Modern Society*. Oxford, 1988.

———. "Erfahrungswandel und Methodenwechsel: Eine historisch-anthropologische Skizze." In *Historische Methode*, ed. Christian Meier and Jörn Rüsen, 27–57. München, 1988.

———. "Sprachwandel und Ereignisgeschichte." *Merkur*, Nr. 8 (1989): 657–73.

———. "Einleitung." *Bildungsbürgertum im 19. Jahrhundert, Teil 2, Bildungsgüter und Bildungswissen*, 1–46. Stuttgart, 1990.

———. "Der Einfluß der beiden Weltkriege auf das Soziale Bewußtsein." In *Der Krieg des kleinen Mannes. Eine Militärgeschichte von unten*, ed. Wolfram Wette, 324–43. München, 1992 (later reprinted as "Erinnerungsschleusen und Erfahrungsschichten. Der Einfluß der beiden Weltkriege auf das soziale Bewußtsein." *Zeitschichten. Studien zur Historik*, 265–86. Frankfurt am Main, 2000).

———. "Vorwort." In *Geschichtliche Grundbegriffe. Historisches Lexikon zur politisch-sozialen Sprache in Deutschland*, Bd. VII, ed. Otto Brunner, Werner Conze, and Reinhart Koselleck, V–VIII. Stuttgart, 1992.

———. "Bilderverbot." *Frankfurter Allgemeine Zeitung*, 8/4 (1993).

———. "Goethes unzeitgemäße Geschichte." *Goethe-Jahrbuch*, Bd. 100 (1993): 27–39.

———. "Stellen uns die Toten einen Termin?" *Frankfurter Allgemeine Zeitung*, 23/8 (1993).

———. "Diesseits des Nationalstaates: Föderale Strukturen der deutschen Geschichte." *Transit. Europäische Revue*, Nr. 7 (1994): 63–76.

———. "Einleitung." In *Der politische Totenkult. Kriegerdenkmäler in der Moderne*, ed. Reinhart Koselleck and Michael Jeismann, 9–20. München, 1994.

———. "Some reflections on the temporal structure of conceptual change." In *Main Trends in Cultural History: Ten Essays*, ed. Willem Melching and Wyger Welema, 7–16. Amsterdam, 1994.

———. "Glühende Lava, zur Erinnerung geronnen." *Frankfurter Allgemeine Zeitung*, 6/5 (1995).

———. "Vielerlei Abschied vom Krieg." In *Vom Vergessen vom Gedenken. Erinnerungen und Erwartungen in Europa zum 8. Mai 1945*, ed. Birgitte Sausay, Heinz Ludwig Arnold, and Rudolf von Thadden, 19–25. Göttingen, 1995.

———. "Denkmäler sind Stolpersteine'. Der Historiker Reinhart Koselleck zur neu entbrannten Debatte um das geplante Berliner Holocaust-Mahnmal." *Der Spiegel*, Nr. 6. (1997): 190–92.

———. "Erschlichener Rollentausch." *Frankfurter Allgemeine Zeitung*, 9/4 (1997).

———. "Laudatio auf François Furet." *Sinn und Form*, Hf. 2 (1997): 297–300.

———. "Vier Minuten für die Ewigkeit." *Frankfurter Allgemeine Zeitung*, 9/1 (1997).

———. "Die falsche Ungeduld." *Die Zeit*, 19/3 (1998).

———. "Die Diskontinuität der Erinnerung." *Deutsche Zeitschrift für Philosophie* 47, no. 2 (1999): 213–14.

————. "Die Widmung." *Frankfurter Allgemeine Zeitung*, 3/3 (1999).

————. "Deutschland—eine verspätete Nation?" *Zeitschichten: Studien zur Historik*, 359–80. Frankfurt am Main, 2000 (first published in Dutch and was later included in Reinhart Koselleck. *Europäische Umrisse deutscher Geschichte. Zwei Essays*, 37–78. Heidelberg, 1999).

————. "Raum und Geschichte." *Zeitschichten: Studien zur Historik*, 78–96. Frankfurt am Main, 2000.

————. "Wie neu ist die Neuzeit." *Zeitschichten. Studien zur Historik*, 225–39. Frankfurt am Main 2000 (first published in a longer version in *Schriften des Historischen Kollegs* (1989): 37–52).

————. "Zeitschichten." *Zeitschichten: Studien zur Historik*, , 19–26. Frankfurt am Main, 2000 (first published in *Zeit und Wahrheit*, ed. Heinrich Pfusterschmid-Hardtenstein, 95–100. Wien, 1994).

————. *Zeitschichten. Studien zur Historik*. Frankfurt am Main, 2000.

————. "Gebrochene Erinnerung? Deutsche und polnische Vergangenheiten." *Das Jahrbuch der Deutschen Akademie für Sprache und Dichtung* (2001): 19–32 (a slightly different version of the text is found in *Neue Zürcher Zeitung*, 22-23/9 (2001).

————. *Goethes unzeitgemäße Geschichte*. Heidelberg, 2001.

————. "Formen und Traditionen des negativen Gedächtnis." In *Verbrechen Erinnern: Die Auseinandersetzung mit Holocaust und Völkermord*, ed. Volkhard Knigge and Norbert Frei, 21–32. München, 2002.

————. "Er konnte sich verschenken—Hans-Georg Gadamer gedenkend, des Lehrers und Freundes, der vor einem Jahr Starb." *Süddeutsche Zeitung*, 14/3 (2003).

————. "Formen der Bürgerlichkeit: Reinhart Koselleck im Gespräch mit Manfred Hettling und Bernd Ulrich." *Mittelweg 36, Zeitschrift des Hamburger Instituts für Sozialforschung*, 12 Jg (2003): 63–82.

————. "Ich war weder Opfer noch befreit. Der Historiker Reinhart Koselleck über die Erinnerung an den Krieg, sein Ende und seine Toten." *Berliner Zeitung*, 7/5 (2005).

————. *Begriffsgeschichten. Studien zur Semantik und Pragmatik der politischen und sozialen Sprache*. Frankfurt am Main, 2006.

————. "Dankrede am 23 November 2004." In *Reinhart Koselleck (1923-2006). Reden zum 50. Jahrestag seiner Promotion in Heidelberg*, ed. Stefan Weinfurter, 33–60. Heidelberg, 2006.

————. "Zur Begriffsgeschichte der Zeitutopie." *Begriffgeschichten: Studien zur Semantik und Pragmatik der politische und soziale Sprache*, , 267–68. Frankfurt am Main, 2006.

————. *Vom Sinn und Unsinn der Geschichte. Aufsätze und Vorträge aus vier Jahrzehnten*. Frankfurt am Main, 2010.

Koselleck, Reinhart, ed. *Historische Semantik und Begriffsgeschichte*. Stuttgart, 1979.

————. *Bildungsbürgertum im 19. Jahrhundert, Bd.2, Bildungsgüter und Bildungswissen*. Stuttgart, 1990.

Koselleck, Reinhart, Wolfgang J. Mommsen, and Jörn Rüsen. "Einführung." In *Objektivität und Parteilichkeit in der Geschichtswissenschaft. Beiträge zur Historik. Bd. 1*, ed. Reinhart Koselleck, Wolfgang J. Mommsen, Jörn Rüsen, 11–14. München, 1977.

Koselleck, Reinhart, and Ulrich Schmidt. "Als Denkmal unangemessen. Ein Gespräch mit Reinhart Koselleck über den Streit um die Neue Wache." *Süddeutsche Zeitung*, 30/10 (1993).

Koselleck, Reinhart, Andreas Seibel, and Sigfried Weichlein. "'Mies, medioker und provinziell': Der Historiker Reinhart Koselleck kritisiert die Gestaltung der 'Neuen Wache' als nationale Gedenkstätte der Deutschen." *die tageszeitung*, 13/11(1993).

Koselleck, Reinhart, and Reiner Metzger. "Bundesrepublikanische Kompromisse: Die deutschen und ihr Denkmalskult. Rainer Metzger sprach mit Reinhart Koselleck." *Kunstforum* 136 (1996): 467–68.

Koselleck, Reinhart, and Christof Dipper. "Begriffsgeschichte, Sozialgeschichte, Begriffene Geschichte. Reinhart Koselleck im Gespräch mit Christof Dipper." *Neue politische Literatur*, Nr. 2 (1998): 187.

Koselleck, Reinhart, Jussi Kurunmäki, and Kari Palonen. "Zeit, Zeitlichkeit und Geschichte—Sperrige Reflexionen: Reinhart Koselleck im Gespräch mit Wolf-Dieter Narr und Kari Palonen." In *Zeit, Geschichte und Politik: zum achtzigsten Geburtstag von Reinhart Koselleck*, ed. Jussi Kurunmäki, Kari Palonen, 9–33. Jyväskylä, 2003.

Koselleck, Reinhart, Javier Fernández Sebastián, and Juan Francisco Fuentes. "Conceptual History, Memory, and Identity: An Interview with Reinhart Koselleck." *Contributions* 2 (2006): 99–128.

Koselleck, Reinhart, and Wolf-Dieter Stempel, eds. *Poetik und Hermeneutik V. Geschichte—Ereignis und Erzählung*. München, 1973.

Koselleck, Reinhart, and Rolf Reichardt, eds. *Die Französischen Revolution als Bruch der gesellschaftlichen Bewußtseins*. München, 1988.

Koselleck, Reinhart, and Klaus Schreiner, eds. *Bürgerschaft: Rezeption und Innovation der Begrifflichkeit vom Hohen Mittelalter bis ins 19. Jahrhundert*. Stuttgart, 1994.

Kracht, Klaus Große. *Die Zankende Zunft: historische Kontroverse in Deutschland nach 1945*. Göttingen, 2005.

Kraus, Hans-Christoph. "Soldatenstaat oder Verfassungsstaat. Zur Kontroverse zwischen Carl Schmitt und Fritz Hartung über den preußisch-deutschen Konstitutionalismus (1934-1935)." *Jahrbuch für die Geschichte Mittel- und Ostdeutschlands*, Bd. 45 (1999): 275–310.

Kraus, Hans-Christoph, "Verfassungslehre und Verfassungsgeschichte. Otto Hintze und Fritz Hartung als Kritiker Carl Schmitts." *Staat—Souveränität—Verfassung. Festschrift für Helmut Quaritsch zum 70. Geburtstag*, ed. Dietrich Murswiek, 637–61. Berlin, 2000.

Krockow, Christian Graf von. "Staatsideologie oder demokratisches Bewusstsein. Die deutsche Alternative." *Politische Vierteljahresschrift*, Jg. VI. (1965): 118–31.

Krönig, Waldemar, and Klaus Dieter Müller. *Nachkriegs-Semester: Studierende und Studienbedingungen nach Kriegsende*. Stuttgart, 1990.

Krumreich, Gerd. "'Gott mit uns'? Der Erste Weltkrieg als Religionskrieg." In *'Gott mit uns': Nation, Religion und Gewalt im 19. und frühen 20. Jahrhundert*, ed. Gerd Krumreich and Hartmut Lehmann, 273–83. Göttingen, 2000.

Kuhn, Helmut. Review of *Der Begriff des Politischen*, by Carl Schmitt. *Kant-Studien*, Bd. XXXVIII, Hf. 1/2 (1933): 191–96.

———. Review of *Kritik und Krise*, by Reinhart Koselleck. *Historische Zeitschrift*, Bd. 192 (1961): 666–68.

Kurunmäki, Jussi, and Kari Palonen, eds. *Zeit, Geschichte und Politik: zum achtzigsten Geburtstag von Reinhart Koselleck*. Jyväskylä, 2003.

Küttler, Wolfgang, Jörn Rüsen, and Ernst Schulin, eds. *Geschichtsdiskurs 4. Krisenbewusstsein, Katastrophenerfahrungen und Innovationen 1880-1945*. Frankfurt am Main, 2001.

Laak, Dirk van. *Gespräche in der Sicherheit des Schweigens: Carl Schmitt in der politischen Geschichte der frühen Bundesrepublik*. Berlin, 1993.

———. "'Nach dem Sturm schlägt man auf die Barometer ein...' Rechtsintellektuelle Reaktionen auf das Ende des 'Dritten 'Reiches.'" *Werkstatt Geschichte*, Bd. 17 (1997): 25–44.

————. "Trotz und Nachurteil. Rechtsintellektuelle im Anschluß an das 'Dritte Reich.'" In *Verwandlungspolitik. NS-Eliten in der Westdeutschen Nachkriegsgesellschaft*, ed. Wilfried Loth and Bernd-A. Rusenik, 55–77. Frankfurt am Main, 1998.

Laube, Reinhard. "Zur Bibliotek Reinhart Koselleck." *Zeitschrift für Ideengeschichte*, Hf. III/4 (2009): 97–112.

Lausecker, Werner. "Werner Conze." In *Handbuch der völkischen Wissenschaften: Personen, Institutionen, Forschungsprogramme, Stiftungen*, ed. Ingo Haar and Michael Fahlbusch, 93–103. München, 2008.

Lehmann, Hartmut, and Otto Gerhard Oexle, eds. *Nationalsozialismus in den Kulturwissenschaften. Bd. 1. Fächer—Milieus—Karrieren*. Göttingen, 2004.

Lepsius, M. Rainer. "Bürgertum und Bildungsbürgertum." In *Demokratie in Deutschland*, 289–334. Göttingen, 1993.Liebsch, Burckhard. *Verzeitlichte Welt. Variationen über die Philosophie Karl Löwiths*. Würzburg, 1995.

Lindenberger, Thomas. "'Alltagsgeschichte' oder: Als um die zünftigen Grenzen des Faches noch gestritten wurde." In *Zeitgeschichte als Streitgeschichte*, ed. Martin Sabrow, Ralph Jessen, and Klaus Große Kracht, 74–91. München, 2003.

Lipsius, M. Rainer. "Bemerkungen zum Verhältnis von Geschichtswissenschaft und Soziologie." In *Theorie der Geschichtswissenschaft und Praxis des Geschichtsunterrichts*, ed. Werner Conze, 59–60. Stuttgart, 1972.

Locher, Hubert. "Denken in Bildern. Reinhart Koselleck's Programm *Zur politischen Ikonologie*." *Zeitschrift für Ideengeschichte*, Hf. III/4 (2009): 81–96.

Loewenstein, Bedrich. "Review", *Journal of Modern History* 48, no. 1 (1976): 122–24.

Lorenz, Chris. "'Won't You Tell Me, Where Have All The Good Times Gone?': On the Advantages and the Disadvantages of Modernization Theory for Historical Study." In *The Many Faces of Clio: Cross-Cultural Approaches to Historiography*, ed. Franz Leander Fillafer and Edward Q. Wang, 104–27. Oxford, 2007.

Löwith, Karl. *Das Individuum in der Rolle des Mitmenschen. Ein Beitrag zur anthropologischen Grundlegung der ethischen Probleme*. München, 1928.

————. *Meaning in History: the Theological Implications of the Philosophy of History*. Chicago, 1949.

————. *Mein Leben in Deutschland vor und nach 1933, Ein Bericht mit einem Vorwort von Reinhart Koselleck und einer Nachbemerkung von Ada Löwith*. Stuttgart, 1986.

Lüdtke, Alf. "Alltagsgeschichte." In *Lexikon Geschichtswissenschaft. Hundert Grundbegriffe*, ed. Stefan Jordan, 21–24. Stuttgart, 2002.

Lüdtke, Alf, ed. *Alltagsgeschichte. Zur Rekonstruktion historischer Erfahrungen und Lebensweisen*. Frankfurt am Main, 1989.

Luhmann, Niklas. "Weltzeit und Systemgeschichte. Über Beziehungen zwischen Zeithorizonten und sozialen Strukturen gesellschaftlicher Systeme." In *Soziologie und Sozialgeschichte: Aspekte und Probleme*, ed. Peter Christian Ludz, 81–115. Köln, 1972.

Lundgreen, Peter, ed. *Reformuniversität Bielefeld: 19169-1994: zwischen Defensive und Innovation*. Bielefeld, 1994.

Lüthe, Rudolf. Review of *Vergangene Zukunft*, by Reinhart Koselleck. *Philosophischer Literaturanzeiger*, 34/1 (1981): 27–31.

Mackrell, John. Review of *Critique and Crisis*, by Reinhart Koselleck. *History* 74 (1989): 93–94.

Makkreel, Rudolf A. "The Confluence of Aesthetics and Hermeneutics on Baumgarten, Meier, and Kant," *The Journal of Aesthetics and Art Criticism* 54, no. 1 (1996): 65–75.

Mandelkow, Karl Robert. *Goethe in Deutschland: Rezeptionsgeschichte eines Klassikers*, Bd. 1, 2. München, 1980/1989.

Marquard, Odo. "Anthropologie." In *Historisches Wörterbuch der Philosophie*, Bd. 1, ed. Joachim Ritter, 362–74. Basel, 1971.

Marquard, Odo, and Karlheinz Stierle, eds. *Poetik und Hermeneutik VIII. Identität.* München, 1979.

Mehring, Reinhard. "Zu Schmitts Dämonologie—nach seinem Glossarium." *Rechtstheorie. Zeitschrift für Logik, Methodenlehre, Kybernetik und Soziologie des Rechts*, 23 Bd., Hf. 1 (1992): 258–71.

———. "Carl Schmitt and His influence on Historians." *Cardozo Law Review* 21 (2000): 1653–64.

———. "Karl Löwith, Carl Schmitt, Jacob Taubes und das 'Ende der Geschichte.'" *Zeitschrift für Religions- und Geistesgeschichte* 48, no. 3 (1996): 234–38.

———. *Carl Schmitt zur Einführung.* Hamburg, 2001.

———. "Heidegger und Karl Löwith: Destruktion einer Überlieferungskritik." In *Heidegger-Handbuch. Leben-Werk-Wirkung*, ed. Dieter Thomä, 373–75. Stuttgart, 2003.

———. "Begriffssoziologie, Begriffsgeschichte, Begriffspolitik. Zur Form der Ideengeschichtsschreibung nach Carl Schmitt und Reinhart Koselleck." In *Politische Ideengeschichte im 20. Jahrhundert. Konzepte und Kritik*, ed. Harald Bluhm and Jürgen Gebhardt, 31–50. Baden-Baden, 2006.

———. *Carl Schmitt: Aufstieg und Fall.* München, 2009.

———. "Begriffsgeschichte mit Carl Schmitt." In *Begriffene Geschichte: Beiträge zum Werk Reinhart Kosellecks*, ed. Hans Joas and Peter Vogt, 138-168. Frankfurt am Main, 2010.

———. "In den Schichten der Zeit." *Die Zeit*, 10/2 (2006).

———. "Gedenkrede auf Reinhart Koselleck." In *Reinhart Koselleck 1923-2006: Reden zur Gedenkfeier am 24. Mai 2006, Bielefelder Universitätsgespräche und Vorträge, 9*, ed. Neithart Bulst and Willibald Steinmetz, 7–34. Bielefeld, 2007.

Meier, Christian. "Review of "Kritik und Krise", by Reinhart Koselleck". Ruperto Carola, Nr. 29 (1961): 258–64.

Meier, Christian, and Jörn Rüsen, ed. *Historische Methode.* München, 1988.

Meier, H. G. "Begriffsgeschichte." In *Historische Wörterbuch der Philosophie*. Bd. 1, ed. Joachim Ritter, 788–808. Stuttgart, 1971.

Meinecke, Friedrich. *Weltbürgertum und Nationalstaat. Studie zur Genesis des Deutschen Nationalstaats.* München, 1907.

———. *Die Idee der Staatsräson in der neueren Geschichte.* München, 1924.

———. "Ernst Troeltsch und das Problem des Historismus" [1923], *Friedrich Meinecke: Zur Theorie und Philosophie der Geschichte*, 369-378. Stuttgart 1959

———. *Die Entstehung des Historismus.* München, 1936.

———. *Die deutsche Katastrophe: Betrachtungen und Erinnerungen.* Zürich, 1946.

Meinel, Florian. "Review, essay— Ernst Forsthoff and the Intellectual History of the German Administrative Law". *German Law Journal* 8 (2007): 786–800.

Miethke, Jürgen, ed. *Geschichte im Heidelberg. 100 Jahre Historisches Seminar, 50 Jahre Institut für Fränkisch-Pfälzische Geschichte und Landeskunde.* Berlin, 1992.

Missfelder, Jan-Friedrich. "Die Gegenkraft und ihre Geschichte. Carl Schmitt, Reinhart Koselleck und der Bürgerkrieg." *Zeitschrift für Religions- und Geistesgeschichte* 58, no. 4 (2006): 310–36.

Mommsen, Hans. "Historical Scholarship in Transition: The Situation in the Federal Republic of Germany." *Daedalus*, no. 100 (1971): 458–508.

———. "Daraus erklärt sich, daß es niemals zuvor eine derartige Vorherrschaft alter Männer gegeben hat wie in der Zeit von 1945 bis in die 60er Jahre." *Versäumte Fragen. Deutsche Historiker im Schatten des Nationalsozialismus*, ed. Rüdiger Hohls and Konrad H. Jarausch, 163–90. Stuttgart, 2000.

Mommsen, Wolfgang J. *Die Geschichtswissenschaft jenseits des Historismus.* Düsseldorf, 1971.

———. *Kultur und Krieg: Die Rolle der Intellektuellen, Künstler und Schriftsteller im Ersten Weltkrieg.* München, 1996.

Moses, A. D. *German Intellectuals and the Nazi Past.* Cambridge, 2007.

Mosse, Georg. *The Nationalization of the Masses: Political Symbolism and Mass Movement in Germany from the Napoleonic Wars of Liberation through the Third Reich.* New York, 1975.

———. *Confronting History: A Memoir.* Madison, 2000.

Motzkin, Gabriel. "Moralische Antwort und Diskontinuität der Erinnerung", *Deutsche Zeitschrift für Philosophie* 47, no. 6 (1999): 1023–31.

Müller, Jan-Werner. *German Intellectuals, Unification and National Identity.* London, 2000.

———. *A Dangerous Mind: Carl Schmitt in Postwar European Thought.* New Haven, 2003.

Muller, Jerry Z. *The Other God that Failed: Hans Freyer and the Deradicalization of German Conservatism.* Princeton, 1987.

———. "'Historical Social Science' and Political Myth: Hans Freyer (1887-1969) and the Genealogy of Social History in West Germany." In *Paths of Continuity: Central European Historiography from the 1930s to the 1950s,* ed. Hartmut Lehmann and James Van Horn Melton, 197–229. Cambridge, 1994.

Müller, Oliver. "Subtile Stile: Hans Blumenberg und die Forschungsgruppe 'Poetik und Hermeneutik', *Kontroverse in der Literaturtheorie/Literaturtheorie in der Kontroverse,* ed. Ralf Klausnitzer and Carlos Spoerhase, , 249–64. Bern, 2007.

Nagel, Ivan. "Der Kritiker der Krise." In *Reinhart Koselleck (1923-2006): Reden zum 50. Jahrestag seiner Promotion in Heidelberg,* ed. Stefan Weinfurter, 23–30. Heidelberg, 2006.

Nevers, Jeppe. "Nyere bidrag til begrebshistorien." *Nyt fra historien,* Nr. 1 (2007): 1–12.

———. "Spørgsmålets politik: Kari Palonen og den nyere begrebshistorie." *Slagmark,* Nr. 48 (2007): 123–37.

Niethammer, Lutz, ed. *Bürgerliche Gesellschaft in Deutschland: historische Einblicke, Fragen, Perspektive.* Frankfurt am Main, 1990.

Nietzsche, Friedrich. "Vom Nützen und Nachteil der Historie für das Leben." *Werke,* Bd. 1. Berlin 1972–1997.

Nipperdey, Thomas. "Nationalidee und Nationaldenkmal in Deutschland im 19. Jahrhundert." *Historische Zeitschrift,* Bd. 206 (1968): 529–85.

———. "Wehlers 'Kaiserreich': Eine kritische Auseinandersetzung." *Geschichte und Gesellschaft,* Jg. 1, Hf. 1 (1975): 539–60.

———. "Wozu noch Geschichte?" In *Die Zukunft der Vergangenheit,* ed. G. D. Kaltenbrunner, 34–57. München, 1975.

———. *Gesellschaft, Kultur, Theorie. Gesammelte Aufsätze zur neueren Geschichte.* Göttingen, 1975.

———. *Deutsche Geschichte 1860-1866: Bürgerwelt und starker Staat.* München, 1985.

———. *Religion im Umbruch: Deutschland 1870-1918.* München, 1988.

Niven, Bill. *Facing the Nazi Past: United Germany and the Legacy of the Third Reich.* London, 2002.

Nolte, Ernst. "Es war die Schuld die Ideologiestaaten." *Frankfurter Allgemeine Zeitung,* 2/9 (1993).

Nolte, Paul. "Der Historiker der Bundesrepublik. Rückblick auf eine 'lange Generation.'" *Merkur,* Nr. 53 (1999): 413–32.

———. *Die Ordnung der deutschen Gesellschaft. Selbstentwurf und Selbstbeschreibung im 20. Jahrhundert.* München, 2000.

———. "Gleichzeitigkeit des Ungleichzeitigen." In *Lexikon Geschichtswissenschaft: Hundert Grundbegriffe,* ed. Stefan Jordan, 134–36. Stuttgart, 2002.

Nora, Pierre, ed. *Les Lieux de Mémoire*, vol. 3. Paris, 1984–1992.

O'Boyle, Leonora. Review of *Staat und Gesellschaft im deutschen Vormärz 1815–1848*, ed. Werner Conze. *Journal of Modern History* 35, no. 3 (1963): 299.

Obenaus, Herbert. Review of *Preußen zwischen Reform und Revolution*, by Reinhart Koselleck. *Göttingschen Gelehrte Anzeiger*, 222 Jg., 1970: 155–67.

Oberkrome, Willi. *Volksgeschichte. Methodische Innovation und völkische Ideologisierung in der deutschen Geschichtswissenschaft 1918-1945*. Göttingen, 1993.

Odysseos Louiza. "Violence after the State? A Preliminary Examination of the Concept of 'Global Civil War.'" http://www.louizaodysseos.org.uk/resources/OdysseosSGIR2007.pdf (2007), accessed 24/7 (2011).

Oelmüller, Willi, ed. *Wozu noch Geschichte?* München, 1977.

Oexle, Otto Gerhard. "Sozialgeschichte—Begriffsgeschichte—Wissenschaftsgeschichte. Anmerkungen zum Werk Otto Brunners." *Vierteljahrschrift für Sozial- und Wirtschaftsgeschichte*, Nr. 71 (1984): 305–41.

———. *Geschichtswissenschaft im Zeichen des Historismus*. Göttingen, 1996.

Olender, Maurice. "'The Radical Strangeness of Nazi Barbarism Has Paralyzed a Generation of Intellectuals': Dialogue with H. R. Jauss" [1996]. In *Race and Erudition*, ed. Maurice Olender, 139–45. Cambridge, 2009.

Olender, Mauric, ed. *Race and Erudition*. Cambridge, 2009.

Olick, Jeffrey K. "Genre Memories and Memory Genres: A Dialogical Analysis of May 8, 1945 Commemorations in the Federal Republic of Germany." *American Sociological Review* 64 (1999): 381–402.

Osterhammel, Jürgen. "Gesellschaftsgeschichte und Historische Soziologie." In *Wege der Gesellschaftsgeschichte*, ed. Jürgen Osterhammel, Dieter Langewiesche, and Paul Nolte, 81–102. Göttingen, 2006.

Palonen, Kari. "An Application of Conceptual History to Itself: From Method to Theory in Reinhart Koselleck's Begriffsgeschichte." *Finnish Yearbook of Political Thought* 1, no. 1 (1997): 39–69.

———. "The History of Concepts as a Style of Political Theorizing: Quentin Skinner's and Reinhart Koselleck's Subversion of Normative Political Theory." *European Journal of Political Theory* 1, no. 1 (2000): 91–106.

———. *Die Entzauberung der Begriffe: Das Umschreiben der politischen Begriffe bei Quentin Skinner und Reinhart Koselleck*. Münster, 2004.

Pankakoski, Timo. "Conflict, Context, Concreteness: Koselleck and Schmitt on Concepts." *Political Theory*, no. XX (2010): 1–31.

Pannenberg, Wolfhart. "Erfordert die Einheit der Geschichte ein Subjekt?" In *Poetik und Hermeneutik V. Geschichte—Ereignis und Erzählung*, ed. Reinhart Koselleck and Wolf-Dieter Stempel, 478–90. München, 1973.

Peters, Christian. "Lehrangebot und Geschichtsbild. Ein Beitrag zu einer Sozialgeschichte des Faches Geschichte an der Heidelberger Universität." In *Eine Studie zum Alltagsleben der Historie. Zeitgeschichte des Faches Geschichte an der Heidelberger Universität 1945-1978*, ed. Robert Deutsch, Heilwig Schomerus, and Christian Peters, 1–38. Heidelberg, 1978.

Plessner, Helmut. *Das Schicksal des deutschen Geistes: im Ausgang seiner bürgerlichen Epoche*. Zürich, 1935.

———. *Die verspätete Nation: Über die politische Verführbarkeit bürgerlichen Geistes*. Stuttgart, 1959.

Polenz, Peter von. Review of *Geschichtliche Grundbegriffe: Historisches Lexikon zur politisch-sozialen Sprache in Deutschland*, Bd. I, ed. by Otto Brunner, Werner Conze, Reinhart Koselleck. *Zeitschrift für germanistische Linguistik*, Bd. 1 (1973): 235–41.

Pompkin, Jeremy. "The Concept of Public Opinion in the Historiography of the French Revolution." *Storia della Storiografia*, 20 (1991): 77–92.

Popper, Karl. *The Open Society and Its Enemies*. London, 1945.

Preisendanz, Wolfgang, and Rainer Warning, eds. *Poetik und Hermeneutik VII. Das Komische*. München, 1976.

Price, Arnold H. Review of *Preußen zwischen Reform und Revolution*, by Reinhart Koselleck. The American Historical Review 73, no. 4 (1968): 1178–79.

Puhle, Hans-Jürgen, ed. *Bürger in der Gesellschaft der Neuzeit: Wirtschaft, Politik, Kultur*. Göttingen, 1991.

Quaritsch, Helmut, ed. *Complexio Oppositorum*. Berlin, 1988.

Raphael, Lutz. *Geschichtswissenschaft im Zeitalter der Extreme: Theorien, Methoden, Tendenzen von 1900 bis zur Gegenwart*. München, 2003.

———. "Nationalzentrierte Sozialgeschichte im programmatischer Absicht: Die Zeitschrift 'Geschichte und Gesellschaft. Zeitschrift für Historische Sozialwissenschaft' in den ersten 25 Jahren ihren Bestehens." *Geschichte und Gesellschaft* 25 (1999): 5–37.

———. "Trotzige Ablehnung, Produktive Missverständnisse und verborgene Affinitäten. Westdeutsche Antworten auf die Herausforderungen der 'Annales'-Historiographie (1945-1960)." In *Geschichtswissenschaft um 1950*, ed. Heinz Duchhardt and Gerhard May, 75–80. Mainz, 2002.

Reichardt, Sven, and Malte Zierenberg. *Damals nach dem Krieg: Eine Geschichte Deutschlands 1945 bis 1949*. München, 2008.

Reichel, Peter. *Politik mit der Erinnerung: Gedächtnisorte im Streit um die nationalsozialistische Vergangenheit*. München, 1995.

Reintal Angela, and Reinhard Mußnug, eds., *Briefwechsel Ernst Forsthoff—Carl Schmitt (1926-1974)*. Berlin, 2007.

Remy, Steven P. *The Heidelberg Myth: The Nazification and Denazification of a German University*. Cambridge, 2002.

Rentsch, Thomas. *Das Sein und der Tod. Eine kritische Einführung*. München, 1989.

Richter, Melvin. *The History of Political and Social Concepts: A Critical Introduction*. Oxford, 1995.

Riedel, Manfred. "Karl Löwiths philosophischer Weg." *Heidelberger Jahrbücher*, Nr. 14 (1970): 120–33.

Ries, Wiebrecht. *Karl Löwith*. Stuttgart, 1992.

Ringer, Fritz K. *The Decline of the German Mandarins: the German Academic Community, 1890–1933*. Cambridge, 1969.

Ritter, Gerhard A. "Hans Rosenberg 1904-1988." *Geschichte und Gesellschaft*, Bd. 15 (1989): 282–302.

———. *Machtstaat und Utopie: Vom Streit um die Dämonie der Macht seit Machiavelli and Morus*. München, 1940.

———. *Europa und die deutsche Frage. Betrachtungen über die geschichtliche Eigenart des deutschen Staatsdenkens*. München, 1948.

Ritter, Joachim. "Zur Neufassung der 'Eisler'—Leitgedanken und Grundsätze eines Historischen Wörterbuch der Philosophie." *Zeitschrift für philosophische Forschung* 18, no. 4 (1964): 704–08.

———. "Leitgedanken und Grundsätze eines Historischen Wörterbuch der Philosophie." *Archiv für Begriffsgeschichte*, Bd. XI (1967): 75–80.

Rohlfes, Joachim. "Das Lexikon 'Geschichtliche Grundbegriffe.'" *Geschichte in Wissenschaft und Unterricht*, Bd. 21 (1980): 525–30.

Rohr, Donald G. Review of *Preußen zwischen Reform und Revolution*, by Reinhart Koselleck and also of *Staat und Gesellschaft im deutschen Vormärz, 1815–1848*, ed. Werner Conze. *Central European History* 1, no. 3 (1968): 285–88

Rorty, Richard, ed. *The Linguistic Turn: Essays in Philosophical Method*. Chicago, 1967.

Rosenberg, Hans. *Bureaucracy, Aristocracy and Autocracy: The Prussian Experience 1660-1815*. Cambridge, 1958.

Scheibe, Moritz. "Auf der Suche nach der demokratischen Gesellschaft." In *Wandlungsprozesse in Deutschland. Belastung, Integration, Liberalisierung 1948-1980*. ed. Ulrich Herbert, 245–77. Göttingen, 2002.

Schelsky, Helmut. *Die skeptische Generation: Eine Soziologie der deutschen Jugend*. Düsseldorf-Köln, 1957.

Scheuerman, William E. "Unsolved Paradoxes: Conservative Political Thought in Adenauer's Germany." In *Confronting Mass Democracy and Industrial Technology: Political and Social Theory from Nietzsche to Habermas*, ed. John P. McCormick, 221–42. Durham, 2002.

Schieder, Theodor. "Zum Gegenwärtiges Verhältnis von Geschichte und Soziologe." *Geschichte in Wissenschaft und Unterricht*, 3 Jg. (1952): 27–32.

Schieder, Wolfgang. "Soziologie zwischen Soziologie und Geschichte. Das wissenschaftliche Lebenswerk Werner Conzes," *Geschichte und Gesellschaft*, Jg. 13 (1987): 244–66.

———. "Wir können keine Kommentare erzwingen, denn schließlich waren wir nicht das hohe Gericht," in *Versäumte Fragen: Deutsche Historiker im Schatten des Nationalsozialismus*, ed. Rüdiger Hohls and Konrad H. Jarausch, 281–99. München, 2000.

Schildt, Axel. *Moderne Zeiten. Freizeit, Massenmedien und 'Zeitgeist' in der Bundesrepublik der 50er Jahre*. Hamburg, 1995.

———. "Ende der Ideologien. Politisch-ideologische Strömungen in der 50er Jahren." In *Modernisierung im Wiederaufbau: die Westdeutsche Gesellschaft in der 50er Jahre*, ed. Axel Schildt and Arnold Sywottek, 627–35. Bonn, 1993.

———. "Materieller Wohlstand—pragmatische Politik—kulturelle Umbrüche: Die 60er Jahre in der Bundesrepublik." In *Dynamische Zeiten: Die 60er Jahre in den beiden deutschen Gesellschaften*, ed. Detlef Siegfried and Karl Christian Lammers, 21–53. Hamburg, 2000.

Schildt, Axel, Detlef Siegfried, and Karl Christian Lammers, eds. *Dynamische Zeiten: Die 60er Jahre in den beiden deutschen Gesellschaften*. Hamburg, 2000.

Schilling, Kurt. Review of *Kritik und Krise*, by Reinhart Koselleck. *Archiv für Rechts- und Sozialphilosophie*, Bd. XLVI (1960): 147–53.

Schivelbusch, Wolfgang. *Die Kultur der Niederlage: der amerikanische Süden 1865, Frankreich 1871, Deutschland 1918*. Berlin, 2001.

Schlak, Stephan. "Der Sound der Sentimentalität." *Süddeutsche Zeitung*, 2/1 (2007).

———. *Wilhelm Hennis: Szenen einer Ideengeschichte der Bundesrepublik*. München, 2008.

Schmeider, Eberhard, Review of *Preußen zwischen Reform und Revolution*, by Reinhart Koselleck. *Schmollers Jahrbuch für Wirtschafts- und Sozialwissenschaften*, Bd. 90, Hf. 3 (1970): 357–58.

Schmidt, Alfred. "Zum Problem einer marxistischen Historik." In *Wozu noch Geschichte?*, ed. Willi Oelmüller, 154–59. München, 1977.

Schmitt, Carl. *Politische Theologie. Vier Kapitel zur Lehre von der Souveränität*. Berlin, 1922.

———. "Zu Friedrich Meineckes 'Idee der Staatsräson.'" *Archiv für Sozialwissenschaften und Sozialpolitik*, Bd. 56 (1926): 226–34.

———. *Die Diktatur*. 2 Aufl. München, 1928.

————. *Hugo Preuss. Sein Staatsbegriff und seine Stellung in der Deutschen Rechtslehre.* Tübingen, 1930.

————. "Das Zeitalter der Neutralisierungen" [1929]. *Der Begriff des Politischen*, 79–95. München, 1932.

————. *Der Begriff des Politischen.* München, 1932.

————. *Legalität und Legitimität.* Berlin, 1932.

————. *Staatsgefüge und Zusammenbruch des Zweiten Reiches: Der Sieg des Bürgers über den Soldaten.* Hamburg, 1934.

————. *Über Drei Arten des rechtswissenschaftlichen Denken.* Hamburg, 1934.

————. "Der Staat als Mechanismus bei Hobbes and Descartes." *Archiv für Rechtsphilosophie und Staatsphilosophie*, Bd. XXX, Hf. 4 (1937): 622–32.

————. *Der Leviathan in der Staatslehre des Thomas Hobbes: Sinn und Fehlschlag eines politischen Symbols.* Hamburg, 1938.

————. *Positionen und Begriffe im Kampf mit Weimar-Genf-Versailles 1923-1939.* Berlin, 1940.

————. "Die letzte Globale Linie" [1943]. *Carl Schmitt: Staat, Grossraum, Nomos: Arbeiten aus den Jahren 1916-1969*, 441–52. Berlin, 1995.

————. "Drei Stufen historischer Sinngebung." *Universitas*, 5 (1950): 927–31.

————. *Der Nomos der Erde.* Köln, 1950.

————. *Ex Captivitate Salus.* Köln, 1950.

————. *Gespräch über die Macht und den Zugang zum Machthaber.* Pfullingen, 1954.

————. Review of *Kritik und Krise*, by Reinhart Koselleck. *Das Historisch-Politische Buch*, Jg. VII (1959): 301–02.

————. *Glossarium: Aufzeichnungen der Jahre 1947-1951.* Berlin, 1991.

Schoeps, Hans Joachim. Review of *Preußen zwischen Reform und Revolution*, by Reinhart Koselleck. *Zeitschrift für Religions- und Geistesgeschichte* 20 (1968): 88–91.

Scholz, Günther. "Zum Historismusstreit in der Hermeneutik." In *Historismus am Ende des 20. Jahrhunderts: eine Internationale Diskussion*, ed. Günther Scholz, 198–202. Berlin, 1997.

Schöttler, Peter, ed. *Geschichtsschreibung als Legitimationswissenschaft. 1918-1945.* Frankfurt am Main, 1997.

Schulin, Ernst. "Friedrich Meinecke und seine Stellung in der deutschen Geschichtswissenschaft." In *Friedrich Meinecke Heute: Bericht über ein Gedenk-Colloquium zu seinem 25. Todestag am 5. und 6. April 1979*, ed. Michael Erbe, 50-75. Berlin, 1981.

————. "Friedrich Meinecke." In *Deutsche Historiker*, ed. Hans-Ulrich Wehler, 39–57. Göttingen, 1973.

Schulin, Ernst, ed. *Deutsche Geschichtswissenschaft nach dem Zweiten Weltkrieg: 1945-1965.* München, 1989.

Schulze, Winfried. *Soziologie und Geschichtswissenschaft. Einführung in die Probleme der Kooperation beider Wissenschaften.* München, 1974.

————. *Deutsche Geschichtswissenschaft nach 1945.* München, 1989.

Schulze, Winfried, and Otto Gerhard Oexle, eds. *Deutsche Historiker im Nationalsozialismus.* Frankfurt, 2000.

Schüssler, Werner. *Jaspers zur Einführung.* Hamburg, 1995.

Schütte, Christian. *Progressive Verwaltungsrechtswissenschaft auf konservativer Grundlage: Zur Verwaltungsrechtslehre Ernst Forsthoffs.* Berlin, 2006.

Schwartz, Michael. "Leviathan oder Lucifer. Reinhart Kosellecks 'Kritik und Krise' revisited." *Zeitschrift für Religions- und Geistesgeschichte*, Jg. 45 (1993): 33–57.

Schweitzer, Arthur. Review of *Preußen zwischen Reform und Revolution*, by Reinhart Koselleck., *Political Science Quarterly* 85, no. 1 (1970): 158–59.

Seifert, Arno. Review of *Vergangene Zukunft*, by Reinhart Koselleck. *Historischen Jahrbuch*, Jg. 101 (1981): 276–77.

Sharpe, Kevin. *Reading Revolutions: The Politics of Reading in Early Modern England*. London, 2001.

Sheehan, James. Review of *Gesellschaft, Parlament und Regierung. Zur Geschichte des Parlamentarismus in Deutschland*, ed. Gerhard A. Ritter, and *Regierung und Reichstag im Bismarckstaat, 1871-1880: Cäsarismus oder Parlamentarismus*, by Michael Stürmer. *Journal of Modern History* 48, no. 3 (1976): 567–72.

Simon, W. H. Review of *Preußen zwischen Reform und Revolution*, by Reinhart Koselleck. *The English Historical Review* 84, no. 330 (1969): 194–95.

Skinner, Quentin. "Meaning and Understanding in the History of Ideas." *History and Theory* 8 (1969): 3–53.

Smid, Stefan. Review of *Vergangene Zukunft*, by Reinhart Koselleck. *Archiv für Rechts-und Sozialphilosophie*, Bd. LXXI (1985): 564–67.

Solchany, Jean. "Vom Antimodernismus zum Antitotalitarismus. Konservative Interpretationen des Nationalsozialismus in Deutschland 1945-1949." *Vierteljahreshefte für Zeitgeschichte*, Jg. 44, Hf. 3 (1996): 373–94.

Sombart, Nicolaus. *"Rendezvous mit dem Weltgeist": Heidelberger Reminiszenzen 1945–1951*. Frankfurt am Main, 2000.

Sperber, Jonathan, "State and Civil Society in Prussia: Thoughts of a New Edition of Reinhart Koselleck's 'Preußen zwischen Reform und Revolution.'" *Journal of Modern History* 57, no. 2 (1985): 278–96.

———. "Master Narratives of Nineteenth-Century German History." *Central European History* 24 (1991): 69–91.

Steber, Martina. "Herbert Butterfield, der Nationalsozialismus und die deutsche Geschichtswissenschaft." *Vierteljahrsheft für Zeitgeschichte* 55 (2007): 269–307.

Steger, Hugo. "Sprache im Wandel." In *Die Geschichte der Bundesrepublik Deutschland. Band 4: Kultur*, ed. Wolfgang Benz, 14–52. Frankfurt am Main, 1989.

Steinmetz, Willibald. "Nachruf auf Reinhart Koselleck (1923-2006)." *Geschichte und Gesellschaft*, Bd. 32 (2006): 412–32.

Stråth, Bo. Review of *Die Entzauberung der Begriffe*, by Kari Palonen. *European Journal of Social Theory* 8 (2005): 530–32.

———. Review of *Futures Past*, by Reinhart Koselleck. *European Journal of Social Theory* 8, no. 4 (2005): 527–32.

———. Review of *Zeitschichten*, by Reinhart Koselleck. *European Journal of Social Theory* 4, (2001): 531–35.

Stürmer, Michael. "Begriffsgeschichte oder der Abschied von der schönen neuen Welt." *Der Staat*, 17 (1978): 270–72.

Sywottek, Arnold. *Geschichtswissenschaft in der Legitimationskrise: Ein Überblick über die Diskussion um Theorie und Didaktik der Geschichte in der Bundesrepublik Deutschland 1969-1973*. Bonn-Bad Godesberg, 1974.

Talmon, J. L. *The Origins of Totalitarian Democracy*. New York, 1960.

Taubes, Jacob. *Abendländische Eschatologie*. Bern, 1947.

———. "Geschichtsphilosophie und Historik: Bemerkungen zu Kosellecks Programm einer neuen Historik." In *Poetik und Hermeneutik V. Geschichte—Ereignis und Erzählung*, ed. Reinhart Koselleck and Wolf-Dieter Stempel, 490–99. München, 1973.

Thies, Christian. *Arnold Gehlen zur Einführung*. Hamburg, 2000.

Tribe, Keith. Introduction to *Futures Past: on the Semantics of Historical Time*, by Reinhart Koselleck, vii–xx. New York, 2004.

Troeltsch, Ernst. *Der Historismus und seine Probleme* [1922], *Gesammelte Schriften*, Bd. 3. Tübingen, 1961.

Vann, Richard T. "Historians' Words and Things." *Journal of Interdisciplinary Studies* 18, no. 3 (1988): 465–70.

Vengeler, Martin. "'1968' als sprachgeschichtliche Zäsur." In *Kontroverse Begriffe: Geschichte des öffentlichen Sprachgebrauchs in der Bundesrepublik Deutschland*, ed. Georg Stötzel and Martin Vengeler, 383–404. Berlin, 1995.

Vierhaus, Rudolf. "Laudatio auf Reinhart Koselleck." *Historische Zeitschrift*, Bd. 251 (1989): 529–38.

Vopa, Anthony J. La, "Conceiving a Public: Ideas and Society in Eighteenth-Century Europe." *The Journal of Modern History* 64, no. 1 (1992): 79–116.

Walker, Mack. Review of *Preußen zwischen Reform und Revolution*, by Reinhart Koselleck. *Journal of Social History* 2/3 (1969–70): 183–87.

———. *German Home Towns: Community, State and General Estate, 1648-1871*. Ithaca, 1971.

Wehler, Hans-Ulrich. *Krisenherde des Kaiserreichs 1871-1918*. Göttingen, 1970.

———. "Soziologie und Geschichte aus der Sicht des Sozialhistorikers." In *Soziologie und Sozialgeschichte: Aspekte und Probleme*, ed. Peter Christian Ludz, 60–80. Köln, 1972.

———. "Absoluter und Totaler Krieg. Von Clausewitz zu Ludendorff." *Politische Vierteljahrschrift*, Jg. X (1969): 220–48.

———. "Geschichtswissenschaft Heute." In *Stichwörter zur Geistigen Situation der Zeit*, Bd. 2, ed. Jürgen Habermas, 714–26. Frankfurt Am Main, 1979.

———. *Deutsche Gesellschaftsgeschichte*, vol. 1 (1700–1815) and vol. 2 (1815–1845/1849). Stuttgart, 1987.

———. "Historiker sollten auch politisch zu den Positionen stehen, die sie in der Wissenschaft vertreten." *Versäumte Fragen. Deutsche Historiker im Schatten des Nationalsozialismus*, ed. Rüdiger Hohls and Konrad H. Jarausch, 252–53. Stuttgart, 2000.

———. *Eine lebhafte Kampfsituation. Ein Gespräch mit Manfred Hettling und Cornelius Torp*. München, 2006.

Weinfurter, Stefan, ed. *Reden zum 50. Jahrestag seiner Promotion in Heidelberg*. Heidelberg, 2006.

Welskopp, Thomas. "Westbindung auf dem 'Sonderweg': Die deutsche Sozialgeschichte vom Appendix der Wirtschaftsgeschichte." In *Geschichtsdiskurs. Bd 5. Globale Konflikte, Erinnerungsarbeit und Neuorientierungen seit 1945*, ed. Wolfgang Küttler, Jörn Rüsen, and Ernst Schulin, 191–237. Frankfurt am Main, 1997.

White, Hayden. *Metahistory: The Historical Imagination in Nineteenth Century Europe*. Baltimore, 1973.

———. Review of *Vergangene Zukunft*, by Reinhart Koselleck. *American Historical Review* 95, no. 5 (1987): 1175–76.

———. Foreword to *The Practice of Conceptual History: Timing History, Spacing Concepts*, by Reinhart Koselleck. Stanford, 2002.

Wiggershaus, Rolf. *The Frankfurt School: Its History, Theories and Political Significance*. Cambridge, 1995.

Winkler, Hans August. "Ein Erneuerer der Geschichtswissenschaft: Hans Rosenberg: 1904-1988." *Historische Zeitschrift*, Bd. 248 (1989): 259–52.

Winter, Jay. "The Generation of Memory: Reflections on the Memory Boom in Contemporary Historical Studies." *Bulletin of the German Historical Institute*, 27 (2000): 69–92.

Wittkau, Annette. *Historismus: zur Geschichte des Begriffs und des Problems*. Göttingen, 1992.

Wolfrum, Edgar. *Die Bundesrepublik Deutschland 1949–1990*. Stuttgart, 2005.

———. *Die geglückte Demokratie: Geschichte der Bundesrepublik Deutschland von ihren Anfängen bis zur Gegenwart*. Stuttgart, 2006.

Wolgast, Eike. *Die Universität Heidelberg 1386-1986*. Berlin, 1986.

———. "Die neuzeitliche Geschichte im 20. Jahrhundert." In *Geschichte im Heidelberg. 100 Jahre Historisches Seminar, 50 Jahre Institut für Fränkisch-Pfälzische Geschichte und Landeskunde*, ed. Jürgen Miethke, 127–57. Berlin, 1992.

Wolin, Richard. "Karl Löwith: The Stoic Response to Modern Nihilism." In Richard Wolin, *Heidegger's Children: Hannah Arendt, Karl Löwith, Hans Jonas, and Herbert Marcuse*, 71–100. Oxford, 2001.

Wüttenberger, Thomas. Review of *Geschichtliche Grundbegriffe: Historisches Lexikon zur politisch-sozialen Sprache in Deutschland*, Bd. I, ed. by Otto Brunner, Werner Conze, Reinhart Koselleck. *Archiv für Rechts- und Sozialphilosophie*, Bd. LXI/4 (1975): 589–91.

Zorn, Wolfgang. Review of *Geschichtliche Grundbegriffe: Historisches Lexikon zur politisch-sozialen Sprache in Deutschland*, Bd. I, ed. by Otto Brunner, Werner Conze, Reinhart Koselleck. *Archiv für Kulturgeschichte*, Bd. 59 (1977): 243–47.

INDEX

"Bristol, die 'zweite Stadt' Englands. Eine Sozialgeschichtliche Skizze," 104
"Daumier und der Tod," 279–280
"Die Diskontinuität der Erinnerung," 273–274, 294–295
Die Verzeitlichung der Utopie, 61
"Die Widmung," 287
"Erinnerungsschleusen und Erfahrungsgeschichten," 291–292
"Erschlichener Rollentausch," 287
Festschrift, 173–174, 279–280
"Gebrochene Erinnerung? Duetsche und polnische Vergangenheiten," 292, 294
Geschichtliche Grundbegriffe, 2, 57, 119, 167–196, 243–256
"Glühende Lava, zur Erinnerung geronnen," 289
Habilitation, Preußen zwischen Reform and Revolution, 102–155 *passim*
"Historik und Hermeneutik," 66, 73
"Kriegerdenkmale als Identitätsstiftungen der Überlebenden," 276–278, 279
Kritik und Krise, 1, 7, 22, 25, 31, 42–87 *passim* 99n135
Preußen zwischen Reform und Revolution, 1, 6, 119, 132–144, 249
review articles, 111
"Staat und Gesellschaft in Preußen 1815-1848," 125–126
"Standortbindung und Zeitlichkeit," 235
"Terror und Traum," 271–274, 279
"Über die Theoriebedürftigkeit," 231
Vergangene Zukunft, 2, 221–223, 253, 271
Vom Sinn und Unsinn der Geschichte, 2
"Wozu noch Historie?", 218, 231
Zeitschichten, 2, 226–231 *passim* 269
"Kriegerdenkmale als Identitätsstiftungen der Überlebenden" (Koselleck), 276–278, 279

Kritik und Krise (Koselleck), 1, 7, 22, 25, 31, 42–87 *passim* 99n135
Kuhn, Helmut, 83–84, 86, 98–99n133
Kühn, Johannes, 6–7, 19, 20–21, 36n56, 101–102, 115, 117, 156n5, 179
Toleranz und Offenbarung, 21, 49, 241

L
League of Nations, 156–157n18
left-liberal scholars, 30, 212
legitimacy, 117–118
lexicon. *See* semantics
liberal conservatives, 16
liberal democracy, 44
liberalism, 26, 71, 107, 156–157n18
critique of, 23–26
linguistics, 152. *See also* semantics
conceptual analysis, 56–57, 136–141, 278, 281
counter concepts, 188–189
experience beyond language, 184
language and time, 184–185
language as *energeia*, 181
langue, 180–181
lexicon project, 167–196
parole, 180–181
religious language, 179
social history and, 178–186
sound *versus* referent, 180
Iluminati, 50–52
Locke, John, 49, 55
Löwith, Karl, 19, 21–23, 52–57 *passim* 75, 94n80, 101, 155n3, 173
historical consciousness, 46
Meaning in History, 23, 51, 84, 127, 184
Lübbe, Hermann, 209–210, 213, 257n20

M
making of the historian, 4, 7, 103
Marcks, Erich, 137
Marxism, 175, 215, 216–217
Mehring, Franz, 100n147
Mehring, Reinhard, 187, 189
Meier, Christian, 216, 241, 250
Meinecke, Friedrich, 29, 30–31, 43, 44, 59–60, 61–63, 68, 75, 79, 93n71, 144, 187